Possessing the Pacific

Possessing the Pacific

*Land, Settlers, and Indigenous People
from Australia to Alaska*

Stuart Banner

Harvard University Press
Cambridge, Massachusetts
and London, England
2007

Map by Philip Schwartzberg, Meridian Mapping

Library of Congress Cataloging-in-Publication Data

Banner, Stuart, 1963–
Possessing the Pacific : land, settlers, and indigenous people
from Australia to Alaska / Stuart Banner.
p.   cm.
Includes bibliographical references and index.
ISBN-13: 978-0-674-02612-4 (hardcover : alk. paper)
ISBN-10: 0-674-02612-8 (hardcover : alk. paper)
1. Oceania—Colonization—History.
2. Northwest, Pacific—Colonization—History.
3. Land settlement—Oceania—History.
4. Land settlement—Northwest, Pacific—History.
5. Indigenous peoples—Land tenure—Oceania—History.
6. Indigenous peoples—Land tenure—Northwest, Pacific—History.
7. Indigenous peoples—Legal status, laws, etc.—Oceania—History.
8. Indigenous peoples—Legal status, laws, etc.—Northwest, Pacific—History.
9. Oceania—Race relations.
10. Northwest, Pacific—Race relations.
I. Title

DU29.B24   2007
325′.3091823—dc22   2007011902

Acknowledgments

The research for this book required travel to some very nice places. I received an enormous amount of help from librarians and archivists at the Mitchell Library in Sydney, State Records New South Wales in Sydney, the Alexander Turnbull Library in Wellington, Archives New Zealand in Wellington, the University of Auckland Library, the Hawaii State Archives in Honolulu, the Hawaiian Historical Society in Honolulu, the Huntington Library in San Marino, the British Columbia Archives in Victoria, the Oregon Historical Society in Portland, the Knight Library at the University of Oregon in Eugene, the Beinecke Rare Book and Manuscript Library at Yale University in New Haven, the Alaska State Library in Juneau, the Alaska State Archives in Juneau, the British Library in London, the U.K. National Archives (formerly called the Public Record Office) in Kew, Washington University in St. Louis, the UCLA law library, and the Department of Special Collections at UCLA's Young Research Library. For financial support I am grateful to Dan Ellis, Dan Keating, and Joel Seligman at Washington University; Jon Varat, Norm Abrams, and Mike Schill at UCLA; the University of California Pacific Rim Research Program; the UCLA Academic Senate; and the John Simon Guggenheim Memorial Foundation.

Many friends have offered helpful suggestions on one chapter or another over the years. No doubt I am forgetting people, but I'd like to thank Cliff Ando, John Bowen, Andrew Buck, Ariela Gross, Bruce Kercher, Dan Klerman, Russell Korobkin, Bert Kritzer, Henry Reynolds, Carol Rose, Hilary Schor, Clyde Spillenger, Nomi Stolzenberg, Chris Tomlins, Adam Winkler, and Steve Yeazell; participants at meetings of the American Law and Economics Association, the American Society for Legal History, the Australia and New Zealand Law and History Society, and the British Legal History Conference; and participants in workshops at the Alexander Turnbull Library, Arizona State University, Cornell University, the University of Chicago, Washington University, UCLA, and Yale University. Earlier versions of parts of this book have been published as "Two Properties, One Land: Law and Space in Nineteenth-Century New Zealand," *Law and Social Inquiry* 24 (1999): 807–852; "Conquest by Contract: Wealth Transfer and Land Market Structure in Colonial New Zealand," *Law and Society Review* 34 (2000): 47–96; "Why *Terra Nullius?* Anthropology and Property Law in Early Australia," *Law and History Review* 23 (2005): 95–131; and "Preparing to be Colonized: Land Tenure and Legal Strategy in Nineteenth-Century Hawaii," *Law and Society Review* 39 (2005): 273–314. I am grateful to these journals' anonymous referees for their helpful comments and to the editors of the journals for permission to reproduce this material. And thanks again to Joyce Seltzer and Wendy Nelson for their usual good advice.

Contents

Illustrations

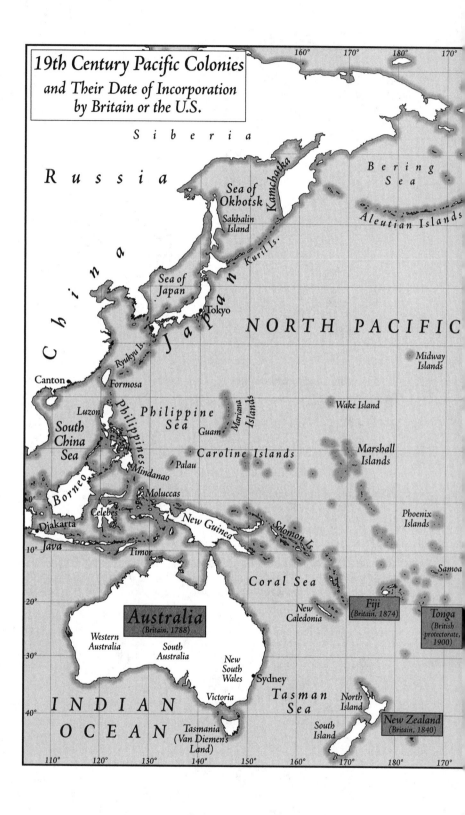

19th Century Pacific Colonies
and Their Date of Incorporation
by Britain or the U.S.

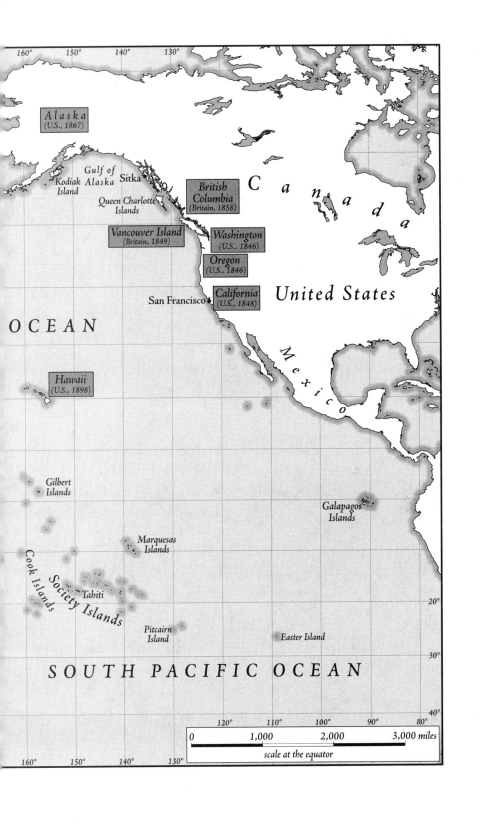

160°   150°   140°   130°

Alaska
(U.S., 1867)

Gulf of
Alaska Sitka
Kodiak
Island
Queen Charlotte
Islands

British
Columbia
(Britain, 1858)

C a n a d a

Vancouver Island
(Britain, 1849)

Washington
(U.S., 1846)

Oregon
(U.S., 1846)

San Francisco **California**
(U.S., 1848)

United States

OCEAN

M e x i c o

Hawaii
(U.S., 1898)

Gilbert
Islands

Galapagos
Islands

Marquesas
Islands

Cook Islands

Society Islands

Tahiti

Pitcairn
Island

Easter Island

20°

30°

SOUTH PACIFIC OCEAN

40°

160°   150°   140°   130°   120°   110°   100°   90°   80°

0   1,000   2,000   3,000 miles

scale at the equator

Introduction

The Pacific World and Its Atlantic Antecedents

OVER THE COURSE of the nineteenth century, English-speaking whites settled throughout the Pacific. From Australia to Alaska, areas with scarcely any white inhabitants in 1800—areas that were almost completely unknown to whites in 1760—were established settler colonies by 1900. Some, like Australia, New Zealand, British Columbia, Fiji, and to some extent Tonga, became part of the British Empire. Others, like California, Oregon, Washington, Alaska, and eventually Hawaii, were governed by the United States. Despite the great distances between some of these places, people and ideas regularly circulated among them, to a degree that justifies thinking of the entire region in the nineteenth century as a single Anglophone Pacific world. Indeed, because present-day national boundaries were not yet fully drawn, in some respects the peoples of the region had more in common in the nineteenth century than they do now. As David Igler has observed, the Pacific was "international before it became national."[1]

In each of these colonies, white settlers hoped to acquire land, but in each they also met indigenous people living on the land. Colonial settlement thus gave rise to some basic legal questions. Did indigenous people *own* their land? If whites wanted to obtain it, could they simply occupy it, or would it have to be purchased from the indigenous inhabitants? What human activities gave rise to property rights in land? If land was to be purchased, who would be the sellers, and who the buyers? By what procedure should indigenous owners be identified? Could land be purchased by individual settlers, or did it need to be purchased by a government? Such issues were fundamental to the development of the nineteenth-century Pacific world. They have remained fundamental ever since. To this day, nearly all of these places are scenes of litigation and political struggle over land claims that stem directly from decisions made in the nineteenth century about indigenous people and their land.

These were not new questions in the nineteenth century. All had been vigorously debated with respect to the colonization of North America from the late sixteenth century on. By the nineteenth century, both Britain and the United States were committed to a formal policy of recognizing American Indians as the possessors of some form of property rights in their land. Both normally acquired Indian land in transactions structured as consensual treaties. In practice, there was considerable trespassing on Indian land in the United States and Canada, and many of the treaties were characterized more by compulsion than by consent, but neither Britain nor the United States had an official policy of disregarding the property rights of indigenous people.

Despite this uniform background, the methods of land acquisition that developed in the Anglophone settler colonies of the Pacific world were astonishingly diverse. The British treated Australia and British Columbia as *terra nullius*—as land owned by no one, and therefore available for the taking. In New Zealand and Fiji, by contrast, the British recognized the indigenous people as owners of their land and established intricate administrative procedures for converting indigenous land tenure arrangements into the familiar English system and for adjudicating the validity of past purchases. The United States treated California as terra nullius, but entered into a series of treaties with Indian tribes for the purchase of Oregon and Washington, and accorded Alaska natives a weak form of property right midway between those accorded the Indians of California and the Indians of Oregon and Washington. In Hawaii, the indigenous people themselves, assisted by white advisors, engineered a massive transformation of their land tenure system, which facilitated the sale of most of Hawaii to whites. The indigenous government of Tonga, also assisted by white advisors, successfully managed to prevent any land from being sold to whites.

This catalog of land acquisition methods understates the diversity among the Anglophone Pacific colonies, because even when two colonies ended up with identical methods of land acquisition, those outcomes were reached by differing paths. Australia, for example, was treated as terra nullius from the start, by design. California and British Columbia were not. California ended up as terra nullius only after the Senate refused to ratify a series of treaties with the state's tribes, by which time their land had largely been taken, while the British began purchasing land in British Columbia and only later switched to terra nullius, for reasons that at the time were perceived by many whites to be genuinely humanitarian. In all these places, save Tonga, a great deal of land was transferred from indigenous people to settlers, but in no two colonies was it transferred in the same way.

These differences are all the more remarkable when one recalls that these events took place within a relatively short period of time, within legal and cultural frameworks that were otherwise quite similar. All these colonies were either governed or heavily influenced by the Anglo-American legal system. The white settlers and government officials were similar from one colony to the next—in fact, they were often the very same people, either serial migrants or colonial officials with multiple postings over their careers. There were cultural affinities between the indigenous inhabitants of New Zealand, Fiji, Tonga, and Hawaii, as well as the natives of California, Oregon, Washington, British Columbia, and southern Alaska. Yet land policy differed dramatically in each colony.

These differences loom large today, because their effects continue to influence indigenous–white relations throughout the Pacific. Today, for example, Tongans own all the land in Tonga, Fijians own much of Fiji, and the Maori own significant parts of New Zealand, but Hawaiians own little of Hawaii, aboriginal Australians own very little of Australia, and aboriginal Oregonians own scarcely any of Oregon. Land claims are front-page news in some of these places but not others. Indigenous people enjoy treaty rights in Washington but not California. They have been beneficiaries of massive compensation in Alaska but not British Columbia. Such present-day variations are largely traceable to decisions made in the nineteenth century about whether indigenous people were the owners of their land and, if so, how that land was to be acquired.

Though a great deal has been written about nineteenth-century contacts between whites and indigenous people in most of these places, there has been very little scholarship addressing the precise question I consider here.[2] This is in part because histories of indigenous people tend to be written on a thick ethnographic basis, as the history of this or that tribe, or as the history of the indigenous people living in this or that present-day country. For most purposes, that is a virtue. There are some wonderfully detailed studies of individual tribes, small areas, and short periods of time. I am well aware of how difficult such work is, and much of it has been extraordinarily valuable to me, so I am the last person who would complain that a work of history has too narrow a subject. But the tight focus of most of the literature means that little attention has been given to a comparative perspective on the process of land transfer between indigenous people and whites.

The issue of comparative land acquisition policy did not receive much explicit attention in the nineteenth century, either. Of course, many people argued about what land policy ought to look like. Some of those normative arguments had a comparative dimension. In Australia and British Columbia, for example, opponents of terra nullius sometimes cited British policy in eastern North America as a model. But neither British nor American government officials ever laid out any scheme for distinguishing between colonies in which indigenous property rights would be recognized and colonies in which they would not. Nor was any such scheme elaborated by academic commentators, in an era that ended just before the emergence of international law as an academic discipline.[3] These were ad hoc colony-specific decisions that no one, whether inside or outside of government, tried to organize within any kind of comparative theoretical framework. Historians, accustomed to seeing events through the eyes of those who lived through them, tend to emphasize issues that were frequently discussed in the past. This one was not.

Meanwhile, much of the research on this topic, especially in New Zealand and British Columbia, has been undertaken in connection with litigation, either directly or indirectly. To prove a land claim, one needs a fine-grained knowledge of exactly who did what, and where, and when. In court, a comparative overview of the Pacific colonies is far less useful.

The final reason for the lack of previous efforts to explain these differences across colonies has to do with what I think is an implicit assumption often made by historians. Accounts of the relationship between colonies and imperial capitals often seem to assume that policy decisions, including those regarding land policy, emanated from the center out to the periphery—that decisions in London or in Washington dictated what would happen in the colonies. After spending some time trying to figure out why events transpired so differently in otherwise similar places, I'm persuaded that, if anything, the opposite was the case—that is, that conditions on the periphery, especially the actions and characteristics of indigenous people, and the ways they were perceived by early white settlers, generated local policies that were later incorporated into decisions made in London or Washington.

To be sure, settlers and government officials arrived in each colony with intellectual baggage that predisposed them toward particular policies. The nature of that baggage changed over time, moreover, in response to intellectual trends in Britain and the United States, so part of the divergence among colonies can be attributed to the simple fact that some were colonized before others. A variety of interrelated local factors, however, played a greater role. Was there indigenous agriculture before whites arrived? How did whites perceive the level of civilization and technological capacity of the local indigenous people? Did local indigenous people pose a substantial military opposition? Did white settlers arrive before their government formally exercised sovereignty, or did the formal exercise of sovereignty come first? Were the indigenous people politically unified under a single leader, or were they divided into multiple tribes? The answers to questions like these were what drove actual practice in the earliest years of white settlement in any given place, and once that practice lasted long enough it was extraordinarily difficult to dislodge, because a growing number of colonists had a vested interest in perpetuating it. Customs developed in the early years thus tended to harden as formal colonial land policy in later years.

THE PACIFIC WORLD

The Europeans who first explored the Pacific in the early sixteenth century were only the most recent arrivals in the region. Archaeological evidence suggests that the Aborigines came to Australia, probably from Southeast Asia, at least fifty thousand years ago. (It is of course an anachronism to call the place they lived "Australia," but the possible alternative names will be less clear to present-day readers. The same will be true of some of the other names throughout the book.) Alaska natives arrived from Siberia ten to forty thousand years ago. There is evidence of human activity in British Columbia and Washington beginning around 10,000 to 8000 B.C., and in California not long after that. Polynesian navigators are thought to have reached Tonga around 4000 B.C., Fiji around 1500 B.C., Hawaii around A.D. 500, and New Zealand only around A.D. 1200, not long before the first Europeans arrived.

These migration patterns, supplemented by ongoing contact in some cases, produced cultural similarities across great distances. Early white settlers noticed affinities between natives of the northwest coast of North America, ranging from the Oregon-California border all the way up to southern Alaska. They saw that the Maori of New Zealand looked and sounded a bit like Hawaiians, despite being separated by thousands of miles of ocean. The most important of these groupings, for our purposes, involved the ways different peoples obtained their food. Aboriginal Australians, isolated for tens of thousands of years, had not developed agriculture when whites arrived. Neither had the people of the west coast of North America. The Polynesians had; farming was ubiquitous in New Zealand, Fiji, Tonga, and Hawaii. These differences would prove very important when Anglo-Americans began to think about acquiring land.

The first two and a half centuries of European involvement in the Pacific saw only scattered contacts and no permanent settlement. The English privateer Francis Drake landed on the west coast of North America in the 1570s, for example, and the Dutch explorer Abel Tasman reached New Zealand, Australia, and Tonga in the 1640s, but neither of these voyages was followed by any sustained effort to learn more about either region. Europeans were already engaging in trade in Indonesia, which is only a few hundred miles from the north coast of Australia, so occasional European ships landed in Australia, including Dutch expeditions at the start of the seventeenth century and at least one English pirate ship at the end, but again these were not part of any organized plan of colonization. By the middle of the eighteenth century, Europeans knew little more about the Pacific than they had known two hundred years before.

The three expeditions led by James Cook between 1768 and 1779 inaugurated the era of sustained contact between Europe and the Pacific. On the first trip Cook and his crew spent several months in New Zealand and Australia, on the second they returned to New Zealand and visited Tonga and several other of the island chains in the South Pacific, and on the third they reached Hawaii, Alaska, and British Columbia. The reports of Cook and his colleagues opened the Pacific to European exploitation. Within a couple of decades, European voyages to all these areas became routine. Spain, France, and England sent explorers throughout the southern and northern Pacific, Russia sent ships across to the northwest coast of America, and commercial vessels from all these countries plus the United States crisscrossed the Pacific in search of fish, whales, furs, sandalwood, and all sorts of trading opportunities with indigenous people. Not far behind the traders were the missionaries, pursuing thousands of fresh souls. And not far behind the missionaries were white settlers.

The first significant Anglophone settlement in the Pacific was a result of the American Revolution, which deprived Britain of its accustomed place to send convicts and led to the selection of New South Wales as a replacement. In 1788 just over a thousand people, about three-quarters of them prisoners, landed at what is now Sydney. The other regions of the Pacific were first settled by smaller private groups rather than a large official expedition. English-speaking settlers began trickling into New Zealand and Hawaii in the first few decades of the nineteenth century. Emigrants from the eastern United States began moving to Oregon in the 1820s and 1830s. A relatively small number of Spanish-speaking whites had lived in California since the eighteenth century, but they were overwhelmed by English speakers from the United States with the close of the Mexican War and the discovery of gold in the late 1840s. Fiji and British Columbia saw their first significant white settlement in the middle decades of the nineteenth century, Alaska toward the end of the century. By 1900 there were 3.7 million whites living in Australia, 1.4 million in California, three-quarters of a million in New Zealand, half a million in Washington, four hundred thousand in Oregon, nearly two hundred thousand in British Columbia, thirty thousand in Alaska, and a few thousand in Fiji. In all but Alaska and Fiji, whites formed a large majority of the population; they would become a majority in Alaska by the next census ten years later. Barely more than a century after Cook, much of the Pacific had been effectively taken over by whites.

In some colonies, the formal exercise of sovereignty preceded significant white settlement. Britain began governing in Australia as soon as the first Britons arrived. There was a negligible white population in British Columbia before Britain assumed sovereignty over Vancouver Island in 1849 and the mainland in 1858. The United States purchased Alaska in 1867 before there was much white settlement there, even by Russians. Elsewhere, however, substantial settlement preceded formal colonization. New Zealand became a British colony in 1840 and Fiji in 1874, and both already had large white populations. The same was true of Oregon (which originally included what is now Washington) when it became an American colony in 1846, California in 1848, and Hawaii in 1898. Settlement and colonization each promoted the other. The assumption of sovereignty was often a direct result of settlement, as governments felt compelled to intervene in disputes between settlers and indigenous people. And settlement could be a result of sovereignty, as emigrants felt more comfortable moving to a place under the control, nominally at least, of their home government.

White migration patterns produced similarities among these colonies mirroring the similarities produced in an earlier era by nonwhite migration. Most obviously, the large majority of the white residents of the British colonies in Australia, New Zealand, Fiji, and British Columbia were emigrants, or the descendants of emigrants, from Britain. The large majority of the white population of the American colonies of California, Oregon, Washington, Alaska, and Hawaii came from elsewhere in the United States. There was also significant movement between Pacific colonies. Many of the Britons entering New Zealand and Fiji had resided most recently in Australia. California attracted many emigrants from Oregon (especially during the gold rush); Alaska and Hawaii attracted many from California. Many of these emigrants eventually returned home, giving rise to a crisscrossing exchange of white inhabitants among the colonies of the British South Pacific and the American Northwest.

Cultural similarities across Pacific colonies were strengthened by the fact that all were more or less governed by Britain and the United States. The great distances between Atlantic capitals and Pacific colonies meant that supervision by the British or American governments was not nearly as strong in practice as in theory, but the British Colonial Office and the American Departments of War and the Interior were able to exert some control over their agents in the field, even if it was not as much as they wished. Those agents, meanwhile, were often even more well-traveled than the settlers they governed. All had some sort of experience in Britain or the United States, and many held posts in more than one colony. Peter Burnett was a judge in Oregon and then the governor of California, Arthur Hamilton Gordon was governor of Fiji and then New Zealand (and then Ceylon, all after postings in New Brunswick, Trinidad, and Mauritius), and there were many more like them. As a result, Britons in British Columbia were, in a cultural sense, much like Britons in New Zealand or indeed in Britain, and Americans in Hawaii were not all that different from Americans in California or New York.

These colonies were divided between two empires, the British and the American, but of course the two empires were far more alike than different, because they had split from a single empire not long before. (As James Cook lay dying in Kealakakua Bay, revolutionary and loyalist militias were fighting in Georgia.) Most Americans were descendants of Britons. They, and their government officials, were mostly English-speaking Protestants who shared a broad set of beliefs, not least about the value of land and the capacities of nonwhites.

Despite the great distances separating the Anglophone Pacific colonies, then, the colonies were alike in many respects. Some had similar nonwhite inhabitants; all had similar white inhabitants. They were settled by whites at approximately the same time and formally colonized by Britain or the United States at approximately the same time. And one of the most important similarities across colonies involved whites' experience concerning how land was to be acquired from indigenous people. In London and Washington, in Auckland and San Francisco, whites were aware that the subject had a long history. In North America, English-speaking whites had been obtaining land from indigenous people since the early seventeenth century. By the time the First Fleet sailed into Sydney, Britain and the new United States both had well-developed rules and well-known practices governing the acquisition of land.

ATLANTIC ANTECEDENTS

In the seventeenth century, as Britons began settling in North America, they had little doubt of their right to establish governments. *Sovereignty*, they agreed, was theirs by virtue of the English discovery and settlement of North America. There was a lively debate, however, over *property*—that is, over whether land had to be purchased from the Indians or whether it could simply be seized.[4] There were several theories in circulation justifying seizure. Some argued that Christians had a right to take land from non-Christians. Others claimed that the Indians themselves were nomads who lacked any conception of property rights in land, and that the land was accordingly unowned. Some asserted a broader right of conquest, according to which any powerful society might plant colonies on the land of a weaker people. This combination of arguments underlay the early colonial charters, documents in which the English government granted property rights to land in North America without regard to whether the land was already inhabited.

By the early eighteenth century, however, these arguments for conquest had largely died out. Notions that the powerful had a right to take land from the weak, or that Christians were justified in evicting non-Christians, were hardly taken seriously. Meanwhile, the recognition that the Indians of eastern North America practiced agriculture and respected the boundaries of others' farms made it impossible to think of them as lacking a property system of their own. Europeans had a long intellectual tradition of associating farming with property rights in land, a tradition reaching back to ancient Greece and Rome and amplified by early modern writers like Locke and Grotius. By the eighteenth century, the early assertions of a right of conquest had been abandoned in favor of recognizing the Indians as owners of their land.

Settlers and their colonial governments had been purchasing land from Indians almost from the beginning. Land was plentiful and inexpensive, so it could be acquired far more cheaply by purchase than by force. Almost every colony enacted statutes governing the purchasing process, statutes that typically required the consent of the colonial government before buying Indian land. The surviving records of land purchases suggest that purchasing was very common, and that the land sold ranged in size from small parcels bought by individuals up to enormous tracts purchased by colonial governments. Instructions from England consistently reminded colonial Americans not to take land from the Indians without their consent. By 1763, when the Earl of Egremont, the British secretary of state, emphasized the importance of "guarding against any Invasion or Occupation of their Hunting Lands, the possession of which is to be acquired by fair Purchase only," his words only summarized a century or more of colonial practice. It was a "well judg'd Policy," remarked William Johnson, the colonial superintendent of Indian affairs in the 1750s and 1760s, that the English government "have always made an Indian Purchase the Basis or Foundation of all Grants."[5]

If the recognition of Indian property rights and the purchasing of Indian land were common at the official level, practice was far more mixed on the ground. There was always considerable trespassing by settlers on land still owned by the Indians, and the problem seems only to have grown worse as the settler population increased. Land purchasing was frequently infected by fraud. Sometimes colonial officials tried to prevent trespassing and fraud, but often they did nothing, and sometimes they were active participants themselves. To make matters worse, there was often great disagreement within tribes over whether to sell land and no clear rules as to who exactly had the authority to sell a tribe's land. Purchasers were able to exploit this ambiguity by identifying willing sellers and buying from them, even if their authority was disputed by other members of the tribe. Even when purchasing was conducted honestly, the combined pressures of settler trespassing and environmental change (brought on by the proximity of settler communities and their domestic animals) no doubt pushed Indians into selling land. In the end, the fact that the English formally recognized Indian property rights seems to have done the Indians little practical good in the seventeenth and eighteenth centuries. This pattern would be repeated in the nineteenth-century Pacific.

The formal recognition of indigenous property rights would, however, remain a staple of British and American policy for some time. Britain continued to acquire land in North America by purchase. After the American Revolution, so did the United States. As whites grew more powerful with respect to Indians, these treaties tended to become formal devices thinly veiling the exercise of force, but the transactional form never disappeared, even in dealings with nonfarming Indians farther west. In North America, neither Britain nor the United States ever adopted a formal policy of ignoring the property rights of indigenous people.

Such was the background for the Anglo-American colonization of the Pacific. The North American experience had produced two assumptions that were part of the basic intellectual makeup of a late eighteenth-century English speaker. First, property rights in land did not depend upon Christianity or whiteness. Nonwhites were not perceived to be as civilized as whites, but they were nevertheless the owners of their land. Second, land could be lawfully acquired from indigenous people only by purchase. Neither English nor American law recognized any right of settlers to obtain indigenous peoples' land by force.

These assumptions were incorporated in the instructions James Cook received before his first voyage in 1768. They would not survive his return.

chapter one

———◁∞∞▷———

Australia

Terra Nullius by Design

T HE BRITISH TREATED Australia as terra nullius—as unowned land. Under British colonial law, Aboriginal Australians had no property rights in the land, and colonization accordingly vested ownership of the entire continent in the British government.

The doctrine of terra nullius remained the law in Australia throughout the colonial period. In the first half of the nineteenth century it survived the rise of an active British humanitarian movement seeking to improve the conditions of indigenous people throughout the empire. The movement achieved many successes, such as the abolition of slavery in the colonies. In Britain and Australia there were vocal, powerful people, both inside and outside the government, who urged that terra nullius had been a terrible injustice to the Aborigines.[1] Yet at the end of this period terra nullius was as firmly a part of the law as ever. Decades of agitation—not just by fringe groups but also by well-placed insiders—had not changed a thing.

Why was British land policy in Australia so different from what it had been in North America? And why were the opponents of terra nullius unable to end it?

THE CONSENT OF THE NATIVES

In 1768 the Royal Society hired James Cook to take a ship to the South Pacific to observe the transit of Venus across the sun, the measurement of which, from several parts of the world simultaneously, would help astronomers determine the distance between the sun and the earth. James Douglas was the president of the Royal Society. He knew that Cook's expedition was likely to encounter "natives of the several Lands where the Ship may touch." He instructed Cook to "exercise the utmost patience and forbearance" when he met them. In particular, he warned Cook not to attempt the conquest of their land, because any such attempt would be unlawful. "They are the natural, and in the strictest sense of the word, the legal possessors of the several Regions they inhabit," Douglas reasoned. "No European Nation has a right to occupy any part of their country, or settle among them without their voluntary consent. Conquest over such people can give no just title."[2]

These were not Cook's only instructions. The government was putting up the money for the trip, and the government had a motive of its own. Once Cook was finished with Venus he was to head south, to look for the southern continent that had long been suspected to exist. If Cook found such a place, the government's secret instructions read, and if there were any people living there, he was to "endeavour by all proper means to cultivate a friendship and alliance with them." Cook was *not* to seize the land if it was inhabited. He was told instead: "You are also *with the consent of the natives* to take possession of convenient situations in the country in the name of the king of Great Britain, or, if you find the country uninhabited take possession for His Majesty."[3]

Cook served two masters, but so far as indigenous people and their land were concerned, the Royal Society and the government gave him the same instruction. If he arrived in any populated places, known or unknown, the residents of those places were to be treated as owners of the land.

Cook could hardly have been surprised, because such had long been British policy in North America, where settlers had been accustomed to purchasing land from the Indians since the early seventeenth century. Whether to treat North America as terra nullius had been a topic of lively debate in the seventeenth century, but by Cook's lifetime the debate had long been over. In 1763, only five years before Cook set sail, the imperial government had proclaimed that whatever land in North America had not yet been sold to the British still belonged to the Indians and could be acquired only by Crown purchase. Members of the Royal Society and the government anticipated that if there really was an inhabited continent in the South Pacific, and if it turned out to be suitable for colonizing, Britain would buy it from the natives, just like it was buying North America. Terra nullius was not a standard feature of colonial land policy.[4]

Indeed, in the 1780s, when the British government initially chose western Africa over Australia as the place it would transport its convicts, its first step was to try to purchase land. Richard Bradley was sent to negotiate. He managed to secure the consent of a local chief to sell the island of Lemane, four hundred miles up the Gambia River, for an annuity of seven pounds ten shillings a year. But "in conducting this business," Bradley explained upon his return to England, "I experienced Difficulties which I had no Idea of when I engaged with Your Lordship to undertake it. The Principal Men of the Country disputed the right of the Chief to dispose of the Island, and to obtain their Consent the expence of the Purchase was increased." The government had to reimburse Bradley for £375 worth of goods he distributed to satisfy these other claims. The government eventually rejected Lemane because of concerns about disease. The next choice was Das Voltas Bay, on the southwestern coast of Africa, in present-day Namibia. One of the advantages of this site, explained the government committee responsible for choosing the location of the penal colony, was that it was "highly probable that the Natives would without resistance acquiesce in ceding as much land as may be necessary for a stipulated rent."[5] In the end, Das Voltas Bay was rejected too, and the government turned to Australia. But the episode demonstrates a working assumption of the people responsible for managing Britain's colonies: if a new colony was to be established in an inhabited area, the land would be purchased from the inhabitants.

This assumption did not survive Cook's trips to Australia. As Cook and his crew described the newly discovered southern continent, it was different in some critical respects from other places the British had colonized.

Australia, Cook reported, was very sparsely populated. "The Natives do not appear to be numberous," Cook noted a week after landing at Botany Bay in 1770; "neither do they seem to live in large bodies but dispers'd in small parties along by the water side." Joseph Banks, the naturalist who traveled on Cook's first voyage, was more emphatic. "This immense tract of land," he marveled, "considerably larger than all of Europe, is thinly inhabited even to admiration." Banks admitted that he had seen only a small part of the coast and none of the interior. "We may have liberty to conjecture however," he concluded, that the interior of the continent was "totally uninhabited," because without a supply of fish "the wild produce of the Land seems scarce able to support them." Tobias Furneaux, commander of one of the ships taking part in Cook's second voyage, reported that on Van Diemen's Land (present-day Tasmania) "we never found more than three or four huts in a place, capable of containing three or four persons each only." From these accounts, Britons learned that Australia was mostly empty. As Arthur Phillip noted to himself in 1787, while preparing for the long trip to become the first governor of New South Wales, "the general opinion" was that "there are very few Inhabitants in this Country."[6]

If a newly discovered area was scarcely populated, did the discoverers have the right to appropriate some of the land? This was not a new question. It had been debated in Europe ever since the discovery of North America, without ever really being resolved. Lawyers in England and throughout Europe agreed that settlers had a legal right to occupy uninhabited land. But what about land that was inhabited very sparsely?

Many agreed that there had to be some limit to the amount of land a small group might claim, or else a single person could claim an entire continent. "Should one family, or one thousand, hold possession of all the southern undiscovered continent, because they had seated themselves in Nova Guiana, or about the straits of Magellan?" asked Walter Raleigh in the late sixteenth century. "Why might not then the like be done in Afric, in Europe, and in Asia?" The idea was absurd, and it meant that a people could not legitimately claim property rights in too big an area. By the time the British reached Australia, the best-known exponent of this view was the Swiss philosopher Emerich de Vattel, whose *Law of Nations* was published in French in 1758 and first translated into English in 1760. There was not enough space in the world for a small society to claim too large an area, Vattel reasoned. Such a society would "usurp more extensive territories than, with a reasonable share of labour, they would have occasion for, and have, therefore, no reason to complain, if other nations, more industrious and too closely confined, come to take possession of a part of those lands."[7] In an enormous continent with a tiny population, there would be plenty of unowned land available for the taking.

There was another side to the argument that took place during the colonization of North America. Parts of Britain were also thinly populated, and yet no one thought it lawful for strangers simply to move in. The sparser the indigenous population, moreover, the cheaper it would be to buy land, which made purchase a more attractive alternative to conquest. In North America, for these reasons, there had been many purchases of tracts so enormous that they must have included large regions that were thinly populated. But Australia, from Cook's and Banks's reports, seemed to present sparseness of an entirely different magnitude. North America had some empty places, but Australia sounded like an empty continent.

The Aborigines were not just few in number, Cook and his colleagues explained. They were also less technologically advanced than other indigenous people the British had encountered. They had no clothing. They built only the most rudimentary kind of shelter, "small hovels not much bigger than an oven, made of pieces of Sticks, Bark, Grass &c., and even these are seldom used but in the wet seasons." And most important of all, Cook explained, "the Natives know nothing of Cultivation." Unlike the Indians of eastern North America, and unlike the Polynesians Cook met on the way to Australia, the Aborigines were not farmers. They were hunter-gatherers, who, as Furneaux described them, "wander about in small parties from place to place in search of Food."[8]

The absence of Aboriginal farms was crucial, because the British were heirs to a long tradition of thought associating the development of property rights with a society's passage through specific stages of civilization. The most familiar statement of this view in the late eighteenth century was again from Vattel, who held that nonagricultural peoples' "unsettled habitation in these immense regions cannot be accounted a true and legal possession," and that European farmers accordingly might lawfully settle on their land.[9] Vattel was writing with reference to North America—like many eighteenth-century European intellectuals he erroneously believed that American Indians were not farmers—but his words obviously applied to Australia as well.

Under different circumstances the British might nevertheless have purchased the land. American Indians were not just farmers; they were also formidable military opponents, whose land could have been conquered only at an enormous cost in money and in British lives. This calculation played a part in the British decision to purchase land rather than seizing it, and, after the American Revolution, in the American government's decision to continue doing so. As Henry Knox, the first U.S. secretary of war, advised Congress, "it may be wise to extinguish with a small sum of money, a claim which otherwise may cost much blood and infinitely more money." The British government was accordingly interested to hear whether the Aborigines would put up much resistance to the occupation of Australia. On this point, Cook and Banks had a firm opinion. "I do not look upon them to be a warlike People," Cook explained. "On the Contrary I think them a timorous and inoffensive race, no ways inclinable to Cruelty." The government committee responsible for choosing a location for the new penal colony asked Banks directly: "Do you think that 500 Men being put on shore there would meet with that Obstruction from the Natives which might prevent their settling there?" Banks replied: "Certainly not." He predicted that "they would speedily abandon the Country to the New Comers."[10] Not long after this colloquy, the government of the United States would begin purchasing land from nomadic, nonagricultural tribes on the North American plains, in part because of the long American tradition of obtaining Indian land by purchase, but also in part because of the calculation described by Henry Knox. Regardless of who owned what, it was cheaper to buy the plains than to conquer them. In

Australia, the same calculation suggested the opposite policy. The Aborigines were not thought capable of fighting back.

The Cook voyages brought back one final piece of information about the Aborigines that also played a role in setting land policy. Members of the expeditions tried to engage the Aborigines in trade, but reported no success. Unlike other peoples the British had encountered, the Aborigines seemed to show no interest in British manufactures. "We never were able to form any connections with them," Cook admitted, because "they had not so much as touch'd the things we had left in their hutts on purpose for them to take away." Despite the crew's best efforts, the Aborigines "set no Value upon any thing we gave them, nor would they ever part with any thing of their own for any one article we could offer them." Banks concluded that there would be no way to purchase land from them, because "there was nothing we could offer that they would take" in return.[11]

Such was the picture Britons had of Australia at the end of Cook's expeditions. It was enormous and populated by only a handful of hunter-gatherers, people so primitive that they did not farm or show any interest in trade, people who could offer no meaningful military resistance. These were attractive characteristics for a potential colony—so attractive, and in some respects so misleading, that one may suspect some wishful thinking on the part of Cook, Banks, and the various audiences for their reports. James Matra, who proposed placing a colony there in 1783, argued that among Australia's advantages was that it was "peopled by only a few black inhabitants, who, in the rudest state of society, knew no other arts than such as were necessary to their mere animal existence." A pamphlet of the mid-1780s urging colonization emphasized that the continent was "the solitary haunt of a few miserable Savages, destitute of clothing."[12] Unlike most parts of the world, Britons could believe, Australia really was terra nullius.

By 1787, when Arthur Phillip was getting ready to travel to New South Wales as the colony's first governor, nineteen years had passed since James Cook had been told not to take land without the consent of the natives. Phillip's instructions were very different. He was *supposed* to seize the land by force. "Immediately upon your landing," Phillip was ordered, "after taking measures for securing yourself and the people who accompany you as much as possible from any attacks or interruptions of the natives . . . proceed to the cultivation of the land." Cook's voyages had persuaded the British government that there was no need to buy Australia.[13]

THE MISERABLEST PEOPLE IN THE WORLD

The early British residents of Australia exhibited a far greater contempt for the Aborigines than British colonists showed toward indigenous peoples in other places. Settlers in North America made their share of disparaging remarks about Indians, but they also had many good things to say about Indian technology, Indian social life, Indian political organization, and so on. Comments on the Aborigines, by contrast, were mainly variations on a single theme. The tone was set by William Dampier, who washed up on the north coast of Australia in 1688. "The Inhabitants of this Country are the miserablest People in the World," Dampier reported when he got back to England. "Setting aside their Humane Shape, they differ but little from Brutes." The men who sailed with the First Fleet had the same opinion. One marine called them "the most wretched of the human race"; another "the most miserable of God's creatures"; a carpenter found them "the most miserable of the human form under heaven." William Anderson, the surgeon on Cook's last voyage, opined that "with respect to personal activity or genius we can say but little of either." Anderson was hardly alone. The marine George Thompson thought the Aborigines "a lazy, indolent people, and of no ingenuity." One of the soldiers found them "a very dirty and lazy set of people." Even some of the missionaries thought so. "The Aborigines daily present more astounding proofs of their desperately low state," reported the Methodist missionary William Walker. By 1809 the naturalist George Caley, sent to New South Wales by Joseph Banks to gather botanical specimens, could sum up two decades of British observations. "I believe it is universally said," Caley told Banks, "that the natives of New South Wales are the most idle, wretched and miserable beings in the world."[14]

What exactly was wrong with the Aborigines? What was it about them that the British perceived as so wretched and miserable?

To begin with, many Britons found the Aborigines unbearably ugly. "The features of these people are by no means pleasing," noted Daniel Southwell, one of the marines with the First Fleet. Other observers made the same point less politely. "The Native Blacks are I think the ugliest race I ever beheld," Ann Gore informed a friend back in England. George Worgan, a surgeon with the First Fleet, found it difficult "to touch one of them, for they are Ugly to Disgust." "The aborigines of New South Wales are the ugliest race of beings conceivable," proclaimed the merchant Edward Lucett; "some monkies I have seen might feel injured by a comparison." Compounding Britons' disgust was what seemed a repulsive lack of hygiene. The Aborigines are "not very prepossessing," explained John Hunter, a naval captain with the First Fleet, "and what makes them still less so, is, that they are abominably filthy; they never clean their skin, but it is generally smeared with the fat of such animals as they kill, and afterwards covered with every sort of dirt." British sailors were not known for being overly choosy about their sexual partners, but James Campbell found Aboriginal women so repulsive as to be, "in my opinion, an antidote to all desire." Robert Mudie had never been to Australia, but by 1829 he could confidently assert, based on his survey of firsthand accounts, that "the native Australians have certainly but slender claims to what we are accustomed to term personal beauty."[15]

Disgust was more than skin deep. Britons perceived the Aborigines to be astonishingly primitive. They "seemed to be amazing stupid," declared the missionary William Pascoe Crook, who arrived in 1803. "They knew not how to put a cup to their mouth but when presented with anything to drink would put their chin in the vessel." And their unfamiliarity with cups was nothing compared with their utter lack of clothing or adequate shelter. "They go quite Naked," the naval lieutenant Newton Fowell was startled to discover, "and I believe have no proper place of abode." William Bradley was a lieutenant on the same ship as Fowell, and he was likewise taken aback by how the Aborigines "appear to live chiefly in the caves & hollows of the rocks." Some blamed the Aborigines' lack of clothing or shelter on their stupidity. "The people have not the most distant idea of building any kind of place which may be capable of sheltering them from the bad weather," John Hunter reasoned; "if they had, probably it would first appear in their endeavours to cover their naked bodies with some kind of cloathing, as they certainly suffer very much from the cold in winter." Others more charitably found the absence of clothing or houses among the Aborigines proof that in mild climates such things were unneeded. Arthur Phillip noted that even though the Aborigines were "in so rude and uncivilized a state as not even to have made an attempt towards clothing themselves," they nevertheless spent time carving stone statues. "Had these men been exposed to a colder atmosphere," Phillip concluded, "they would doubtless have had clothes and houses, before they attempted to become sculptors."[16] But whatever the reason for it, the Aborigines' lack of clothing or proper houses was taken as proof of their primitiveness.

Most important of all from the perspective of property rights, British settlers confirmed that Cook and Banks were right in observing that the Aborigines lacked agriculture. "To the cultivation of the ground they are utter strangers," reported the marine Watkin Tench. Because they grew no crops, affirmed another account, the Aborigines were forced to subsist on the most unappetizing animals: "they scruple not to eat lizards and grubs, as well as a very large worm found in the gum-trees."[17] The absence of agriculture implied the absence of any property rights the British were bound to respect, and more broadly reinforced the prevailing belief in the Aborigines' backwardness. No farms, no houses, no clothes—could a people be any more savage?

As a result, it quickly became conventional British opinion that the Aborigines were the most primitive people in the world. A report from 1791 characterized them as "certainly the Lowest Class of Human beings." The shipwright Daniel Paine, who lived in New South Wales in the 1790s, agreed that "the Native Inhabitants are the most irrational and ill formed Human beings on the Face of the Earth." When they were compared with other indigenous people the British had met, the Aborigines were always found wanting. In the contest for last place in the scale of civilization, "they may perhaps dispute the right of precedency with the Hottentots, or the shivering tribes who inhabit the shores of Magellan," Watkin Tench observed. "But how inferior they show when compared with the subtle African; the patient watchful American; or the elegant timid islander of the South Seas." British observers consistently ranked the Aborigines last in the hierarchy. They were "far behind other savages," "the lowest link in the connection of the human races," "the lowest of the nations in the order of civilization." They were compared unfavorably with the Maori, who were agriculturalists and were capable of being usefully employed by settlers, and with the Burmese and Malayans, who, unlike the Aborigines, were "susceptible of civilization." John Russell, the secretary for the colonies, contrasted the "half-civilized" Indians of Canada with the Aborigines, who were "little raised above the brutes."[18]

If the Aborigines of continental Australia were not "the *last* link in the long chain of humanity," that was only because there was one group that was even worse—"the aborigines of Van Diemen's Land," who "have less ingenuity, and are more destitute of comforts and conveniences, than even the inhabitants of New South Wales." As one learned article in the new *Tasmanian Journal of Natural Science* put it, "the Aborigines of Tasmania have been usually regarded as exhibiting the human character in its lowest form." But the Aborigines of Tasmania and the continent were usually lumped together, into a single group occupying the bottom rung of the ladder of humanity. The Reverend Joseph Orton, a Methodist missionary in Australia in the 1830s, summed up the prevailing view. "It is the universal opinion of all who have seen them," he affirmed, "that it is impossible to find men and women sunk lower in the scale of human society. With regard to their manners and customs, they are little better than the beasts."[19]

Indeed, British writers often compared the Aborigines with monkeys. Sometimes the comparison was meant to be a metaphor. The marine Robert Scott, for example, told his mother: "I never saw such ugly people they seem to be only one degree above a beast they sit exactly like a monkey." But some writers, decades before Darwin, wondered whether there might be more to the resemblance. Might the Aborigines be "the connecting link between man and the monkey tribe?" asked the naval surgeon Peter Cunningham. "Really some of the old women only seem to require a tail to complete the identity: while the manner in which I have seen these aged beldames scratch themselves, bore such a direct analogy to the same operation among the long-tailed fraternity, that I could not, for the life of me, distinguish the difference." Another writer likewise suggested that the

Aborigines of Van Diemen's Land "may almost be said to form the connecting link between man and the monkey tribes." The idea was commonplace at least as early as the 1830s, when Charles Napier found it necessary to refute "all those who have called the natives of Australia 'a race which forms the link between men and monkeys.'" By the 1840s the point had been made so many times that James Dredge was becoming exasperated. Dredge, one of the growing number of Britons critical of terra nullius, recognized that he was battling against the popular British image of the Aborigines as occupying a "position at the very lowest point in the scale of rationality." Too many Britons, he complained, declare "the native inhabitants of Australia to be neither brutes nor men, but an intermediate species of formation compounded of both."[20]

But whether the Aborigines were considered half human or fully human, there was something close to a consensus among the early British residents of Australia that the Aborigines were the least civilized human beings they had ever seen—as Cunningham put it, they were "at the very zero of civilization." James Grant, a naval lieutenant who arrived in New South Wales in 1800, made the same point in language that drew upon the discourse of late eighteenth-century anthropology. "The native of New Holland," he concluded, "is found in the genuine state of nature." David Collins, the first judge in New South Wales, used the same phrase. "The natives about Botany Bay, Port Jackson, and Broken Bay," he recalled, "were found living in that state of nature which must have been common to all men previous to their uniting in society."[21]

The "state of nature," as Europeans understood it, was a state in which humans had not yet appropriated land as property. Property in land required a minimum degree of social organization, of civilization, of law—property in land required a society to take the first steps to remove itself from the state of nature. All human societies had begun in the state of nature, but most of them had progressed since then, and one of the ways they had progressed was by assigning property rights in land. If the Aborigines were still in the state of nature, then by definition they did not own their land. The land was terra nullius.

When the British got to Australia, therefore, they did exactly what Phillip was told: they simply took whatever land they wished to use, and

1. Thomas Medland, *View of a Hut in New South Wales* (1789). Their earliest contacts with Australia persuaded Britons that Aboriginal Australians were more primitive than the peoples they had encountered elsewhere in the world. As this late eighteenth-century engraving suggests, Aborigines were found to lack markers of civilization such as clothing, adequate shelter, and agriculture. This perception contributed to Britain's failure to recognize Aboriginal property rights in land. Nla.pic-an9000393, National Library of Australia.

defended it by force from the Aborigines. At the start this task turned out to be nearly as easy as Joseph Banks had predicted. The "settlers have little to apprehend from the natives, against whom I have never thought any defense necessary," Phillip reported back to England in 1790. Lieutenant Governor Philip Gidley King agreed that the Aborigines "shew no signs of resistance." In some places in later years, Aborigines were able to fight back successfully for a time, but in the end they were defeated. Other indigenous peoples in British colonies, like American Indians earlier and the Maori later, were military opponents strong enough to fight the British to a standstill for long periods, but Aboriginal groups were too small, and at too much of a technological disadvantage relative to the British, to be as effective. "There is no reason to presume that the black natives are numerous," one British official said of Van Diemen's Land in the 1820s, "or that they will oppose any serious resistance to the extension of the future settlements."[22] He could have been speaking about any part of Australia.

The establishment of terra nullius was aided by the fact that the earliest British contacts with Australia were large, well-armed expeditions controlled by the imperial government. The North American colonies and New Zealand, by contrast, were settled first by small, weak groups operating largely outside the reach of the government. When the first settlers arrived, they were in no position to take land by force and there were no government representatives on site to tell them not to buy it. So in North America and New Zealand, the earliest British settlers purchased much of their land from the Indians and the Maori. Had Australia not been a penal colony, the first British settlers might have been scattered missionaries and whalers, who would have been less able than the government to seize Aboriginal land by force. In Australia, however, the government got there first.

Terra nullius was put into practice for many years before it received formal expression as legal doctrine. From the beginning, Britons interpreted disputes about land between themselves and the Aborigines as evidence that the *Aborigines,* not the settlers, lacked sufficient understanding of ownership. When Aborigines ate the corn growing on settler farms, for instance, the settlers understood the cause as "their ignorance of our laws relative to the right of property" rather than the reverse.[23] Terra nullius was virtually uncontested in the early years of colonization, and the Aborigines had no legal standing to contest it, so there was no occasion for any declaration that it was part of the law.

The earliest formal statements of terra nullius arose in legal contexts that on the surface had little to do with the acquisition of land. The first such statement appears to have been made in 1819, when a dispute arose between Lachlan Macquarie, the governor of New South Wales, and Barron Field, judge of the New South Wales Supreme Court, over whether the Crown, acting through Macquarie, had the power to impose taxes on the residents of New South Wales, or whether that power was reserved to Parliament, as was the case with taxes imposed on residents of Britain. Earl Bathurst, the secretary for the colonies, referred the question to Attorney General Samuel Shepherd and Solicitor General Robert Gifford, who concluded that Field was right. Parliament, not the Crown, had the authority to tax New South Wales. Conquered provinces, Shepherd and Gifford explained, fell within the king's prerogative power, and could thus be taxed by the Crown, but New South Wales was not a conquered province. Instead, "the part of New South Wales possessed by His Majesty, not having been acquired by conquest or cession, but taken possession of by him as desert and uninhabited," fell within the exclusive power of Parliament.[24] This was a question of constitutional law that did not concern the Aborigines directly, but it nevertheless provided an occasion for what seems to have been the government's first formal declaration of their legal status. Or rather their lack of status, as their land was deemed "desert and uninhabited" before the British arrived. Under English property law, the Aborigines did not exist.

A similar occasion arose three years later, when it became necessary to determine whether Macquarie's successor as governor, Thomas Brisbane, had the authority to make law in New South Wales by proclamation. The question landed on the desk of James Stephen, who would later play a big role in colonial policy as undersecretary for the colonies in the 1830s and 1840s, but who in 1822 was still a law clerk in the Colonial Office. Stephen based his opinion on the same reasoning Shepherd had used to resolve the question of taxation. The power of a colonial governor was delegated from the Crown, Stephen explained, and the Crown had no power to make laws without Parliament's consent, except in two situations. The first was in settlements that had been conquered by force, where the king could exercise power as conqueror; the second was in settlements that had been ceded to the Crown, in which the king would succeed to the legislative power of the former sovereign. New South Wales did not fall within either exception, however, because the colony "was acquired neither by conquest nor cession, but by the mere occupation of a desert or uninhabited land."[25] Again, in a dispute not involving the Aborigines, they were officially declared to have no property rights in land.

These legal opinions ratified a state of affairs that had existed ever since the First Fleet arrived in 1788. Three decades of contact with the Aborigines had reinforced the assumption with which British colonization began—that the Aborigines were the most primitive people on the face of the earth, scarcely more civilized than animals. They had not managed to farm, or build proper houses, or do any of the tasks that established ownership of land. As a result, British lawyers and colonial officials concluded, Britons were no more bound to respect the property rights of Aborigines than they were to respect the property rights of kangaroos.

THE REAL PROPRIETORS OF THE SOIL

From the onset of British colonization, however, there were colonists who disagreed with this picture of the Aborigines and their lack of property rights. Terra nullius rested on some empirical assertions about Aboriginal life—that the Aborigines were few in number, that they roamed throughout the land without a sense of boundaries, that they claimed no particular territories as their own. In the earliest years of colonization, each of these assumptions came into question, and as they did, so did the doctrine of terra nullius.

The very first British residents of Australia realized immediately that James Cook and his colleagues had seriously underestimated the Aboriginal population. "The natives are far more numerous than they were supposed to be," Arthur Phillip reported back to England. Not only were there more on the coast than Cook had stated, but Joseph Banks's speculation that the interior was uninhabited turned out to be utterly wrong. As members of the First Fleet explored their new colony, they found, as naval officer William Bradley noted in his journal, "an astonishing number of the Natives all around." Australia was still much more sparsely populated than England—on current estimates of the precontact Aboriginal population, 1 to 1.5 million people were spread over the entire continent—but Australia was not nearly as empty as Cook and Banks thought it would be.[26]

Nor, as the early settlers quickly learned, did the Aborigines lack property. Within a few months of landing, naval captain John Hunter recognized that "they have one fixed residence, and the tribe takes its name from the place of their general residence." This fact was not evident to the casual observer, Hunter explained. "You may often visit the place where the tribe resides, without finding the whole society there," but that was only because "their time is so much occupied in search of food, that the different families take different routes." But in times of crisis, "in case of any dispute with a neighbouring tribe, they can soon be assembled." It was not long before other British writers pointed out the same thing—that tribes were nomadic, but each within its own boundaries.[27]

The Aborigines were even discovered to divide land up among individuals, and to pass such property rights down from one generation to the next. "Strange as it may seem," marveled the judge David Collins, "they have also their real estates. Ben-nil-long gave repeated assurances, that the island Me-mel . . . close by Sydney Cove, was his own property; that it had been his father's, and that he should give it to By-gone, his particular friend and companion." Collins recognized that this understanding of the relationship between people and land was similar to the British conception. "To this little spot he appeared much attached," Collins remarked. "He likewise spoke of other persons who possessed this kind of hereditary property, which they retained undisturbed." A few decades later, the Irish lawyer George Fletcher Moore, one of the first settlers in Western Australia, provided a similar observation. "It appears that among themselves the ground is parcelled out to individuals, and passes by inheritance," he explained. "The country formerly of Midgegoroo, then of his son Yagein, belongs now of right to two young lads (brothers), and a son of Yagein." George Augustus Robinson, the colonial government's protector of Aborigines in Port Phillip, was struck that "when Tung.bor.roong spoke of Borembeep and the other localities of his own nativity he always added, 'that's my country belonging to me!! That's my country belonging to me!!'" When Robinson realized that the people under his protection evidenced a tie to their land little different from that experienced by residents of Britain, he was prompted to some pointed criticism of terra nullius. "Some people have observed," Robinson remarked, "in reference to the natives occupying their country, what could they do with it? The answer is plain—they could live upon it and enjoy the pleasures of the chase as do the rich of our own nation."[28]

If there was any doubt that the Aborigines understood themselves to own their land, it was dispelled by the obvious fact that they did not acquiesce when the British occupied it. In 1804, when Governor Philip Gidley King asked a group of Aborigines about "the cause of their disagreement with the new settlers they very ingenuously answered that they did not like to be driven from the few places that were left on the banks of the river, where alone they could procure food." By the 1820s, George Augustus Robinson learned, the Aborigines of Tasmania "have a tradition amongst them that white men have usurped their territory."[29] As time went on, it became more and more apparent that terra nullius rested, in part, on a shaky empirical foundation. It was true that the Aborigines were not farmers, but they were more numerous and more property-conscious than had been expected.

As a result, early colonial officials sometimes wrote things that betrayed some uncertainty about terra nullius. William Bentinck, the Duke of Portland, would in a few years be the prime minister, but in 1800, while still home secretary, he sent instructions to New South Wales concerning an upcoming survey of portions of the Australian coast not yet visited by the British. After describing where the ship was supposed to go and what its captain and crew were supposed to do, Portland included a curious sentence. If the captain found any "places which appear to him of importance to Great Britain, either on account of the convenience of the shelter for shipping or the probable utility of the produce of the soil," Portland instructed, "he is to take possession in His Majesty's name, with the consent of the inhabitants, if any."[30] At this point terra nullius had been in effect for twelve years, and yet here was an important official in Whitehall telling the governor of New South Wales not to take land without the Aborigines' permission. Maybe this was simply a slip; maybe Portland was unaware that land policy in Australia was different from land policy in North America. Or maybe Portland doubted the right of the colonists to appropriate the Aborigines' land.

The French explorer Nicholas Baudin was in New South Wales two years later, and he took the opportunity to give Governor Philip Gidley King a piece of his mind about terra nullius. "To my way of thinking," Baudin declared, "I have never been able to conceive that there was justice and equity on the part of Europeans in seizing, in the name of the Governments, a land seen for the first time, when it is inhabited by men who have not always deserved the title of savages or cannibals which has been given them, whilst they were but the children of nature and just as little civilised as are actually your Scotch Highlanders or our peasants in Brittany, who, if they do not eat their fellow men, are nevertheless just as objectionable." Baudin reproached King for "seizing the soil which they own and which has given them birth."[31]

A British colonial governor might not have been expected to pay much attention to the hectoring of a French explorer, but whether or not Baudin was responsible, King evidently had some misgivings about terra nullius in the years following. In 1807, while turning over the office to his successor, William Bligh, King gave Bligh some advice about the Aborigines. The colonists always urged him to punish the Aborigines severely when they stole crops, King related, but he could never bring himself to do it. "As I have ever considered them the real Proprietors of the Soil," he explained, "I have never . . . suffered any injury to be done to their persons or property."[32] Unlike Portland's instruction, King's could not have been a mistake. As governor, King was the man ultimately responsible for implementing the policy of terra nullius, by granting parcels of Crown land and coordinating the colony's defense against the Aborigines. That King would call the Aborigines "the real Proprietors of the Soil" suggests he felt some discomfort in that role.

Bligh's successor as governor, Lachlan Macquarie, seems to have felt a similar unease. In 1814 he set aside some land for a school for Aboriginal children, and some more land to be occupied and farmed by Aboriginal adults. In the proclamation announcing these acts, Macquarie explained that appropriations of land were something "to which they are in some degree entitled when it is considered that the British Settlement in this Country" had been effected by "necessarily excluding the Natives from many of the natural advantages they have previously derived from the animal and other productions of this part of the Territory."[33] His language was carefully chosen, but Macquarie's point seems clear: the Aborigines were entitled to land in compensation for the land that had been taken from them, an entitlement that presumed they had some kind of property right in the land the British now occupied. Macquarie had no need to say that. He had already justified setting aside land by citing the need to improve "the very wretched state of the Aborigines." He could have stopped short of adding compensatory justice as a second reason. Like King, Macquarie may have felt some qualms about terra nullius.

Beginning in the 1820s these doubts began to ripen into an apparently widespread belief, in both Britain and Australia, that terra nullius was an injustice toward the Aborigines. In 1827, for example, after some high-profile murders of settlers by Aborigines, the *Sydney Gazette* raised the question whether the murders were a "perfectly natural and justifiable" response to the British occupation of land belonging to the Aborigines. "Does the mere effecting a settlement by no other right but that of the strongest," the paper asked, "and retaining possession owing to the physical weakness of the owners of the soil, for a period of forty years, does that divest them of their natural right to resist and expel the invaders, whenever they were in a situation to do so? We think not." When Aborigines killed settlers, another writer pointed out, they were merely "following the example we have set them, and acting on the principle that *might* is *right.*" As time went on, more and more colonists came to believe, as one magazine put it in the late 1820s, that "our claim to the country was not exclusive, as the blacks had prior possession."[34]

Some of the early opposition to terra nullius came from the missionaries who worked among the Aborigines and the church organizations that supported them. "Their country has been taken from them," George Augustus Robinson declared in 1830. "Can we wonder then at the hatred they bear to the white inhabitants?" Robinson believed that "we should make some atonement for the misery we have entailed upon the original proprietors of this land." After twenty years as a missionary in New South Wales, Lancelot Threlkeld concluded that Britain owed the Aborigines "the price of the Land of their Birth." A Quaker committee in London pointedly asked why the British purchased land from nomadic tribes in other colonies but seized land from the Aborigines, who "consider themselves the real owners of the soil."[35] Religious groups like these were at the peak of their influence on British colonial policy. In an era thick with religiously motivated reform movements of all kinds, the churches were helping to abolish slavery throughout the empire, and in general focusing attention on the welfare of indigenous people in the growing number of

British colonies. Their attack on terra nullius was just one aspect of this broader goal.

But the missionaries were hardly alone in opposing terra nullius. "It may be doubted," a correspondent to the *Sydney Herald* asserted in 1835, "that a people can be justified in forcibly possessing themselves of the territories of another people, who until then were its inoffensive, its undoubted, and ancient possessors." As one correspondent to the *Southern Australian* newspaper complained in 1839, "it is now in vain to talk about the *injustice* of dispossessing the natives," because it had become so clear that colonial land policy was based not on justice but "upon the principle of expediency and self-interest." The complaint was repeated many times through the 1840s and 1850s. Terra nullius was "sophistry of law," declared the scientist P. E. de Strzelecki, after four years exploring Australia and discovering that the Aborigines were "as strongly attached to . . . property, and to the rights which it involves, as any European political body." James Dredge resigned in protest as assistant protector of Aborigines, in part, he explained, because "they have been treated *unjustly;* their country has been taken from them, and with it their *means of subsistence*—whilst *no equivalent has been substituted.*" Again and again, commentators asked: "Has the Government a right to take possession of the country, and, without any consent from the original proprietors, sell the land" to settlers?[36]

Australian judges encountered attacks on terra nullius in a series of cases beginning in the late 1820s. The first of these appears to have been the 1827 prosecution of the soldier Nathaniel Lowe for killing an Aborigine the settlers called Jackey Jackey. Lowe's lawyer must have been aware of the growing controversy surrounding terra nullius. He used the arguments against it to mount a roundabout challenge to the jurisdiction of the court. Lowe could not be prosecuted, his lawyer contended, because Lowe was only punishing Jackey Jackey for a murder Jackey Jackey had committed. Such privately inflicted punishments were necessary, the lawyer continued, because Aborigines could not be tried in colonial courts. And the reason Aborigines could not be tried in colonial courts, finally, was that the British occupation of Australia was contrary to natural law. "It seems to me almost doubtful," Lowe's lawyer argued, "whether taking possession of a country under these circumstances we have a right to establish empire among ourselves, and that our civil polity is for this reason repugnant to the law of nations." By that logic, the lawyer conceded, the court lacked the jurisdiction to try *anyone*, not just Lowe, but at the very least, he claimed, the Aborigines, being "the free occupants of the demesne or soil," could not be tried in colonial courts.[37]

The argument was unsuccessful in Lowe's case, but it was quickly picked up by lawyers representing Aboriginal defendants in criminal cases, who could put it to a much more straightforward use in arguing that the court lacked jurisdiction over their clients. "The aboriginal natives were the primary tenants of the soil," insisted one defense lawyer; "they subsisted in the woods by fishing and hunting, and it was illegal for any one to disturb them in the possession of these natural rights." His client's killing of a white man, he argued, should accordingly be classified as a defensive act of war rather than a civil homicide. When an Aboriginal man named Lego'me was prosecuted for robbing the settler Patrick Sheridan, Lego'me's lawyer turned his cross-examination of Sheridan into a brief lecture on the justice of terra nullius. Wasn't Sheridan aware, the lawyer inquired, "that he had been a squatter for some time on Lego'me's ground, and had frequently committed great depredations on his kangaroos[?]" Sheridan's response—"he believed the ground belonged to Government"—suggests he understood the point the lawyer was trying to make. Australia had neither been conquered by Britain nor ceded to Britain by the Aborigines, contended defense counsel in a third case. "We had come to reside among them," he reasoned, "therefore in point of strictness and analogy to our law, we were bound to obey their laws, not they to obey ours." These arguments did not prevail. In one 1836 case they had the opposite effect—they elicited an extended judicial defense of terra nullius, resting on the standard justification that the Aborigines had not attained a sufficient level of civilization and social organization to possess any property rights the British were bound to respect.[38] But the fact that such arguments could be made at all in this context is evidence of their growing respectability among Australian lawyers.

Indeed, criticism of terra nullius came from the highest reaches of government, in both the Colonial Office and Parliament. The men who ran the Colonial Office in the 1830s and 1840s were sympathetic to arguments that the indigenous people inhabiting British colonies ought generally to be better treated. In 1837 a select committee of the House of Commons found it unconscionable that land had been allocated to settlers "without any reference to the possessors and actual occupants. . . . It might be presumed that the native inhabitants of any land have an incontrovertible right to their own soil: a plain and sacred right, however, which seems not to have been understood." The Aborigines' "undisputed property" had been taken from them, the committee declared, "without the assertion of any other title than that of superior force."[39]

In the mid-1830s, when Britain began setting up the new colony of South Australia, these attacks on terra nullius appeared to be on the verge of changing colonial land policy. In 1835, the Colonial Office instructed the South Australian Colonization Commission that it could not sell unexplored land to settlers, because the new colony "might embrace in its range numerous Tribes of People, whose Proprietary Title to the Soil, we have not the slightest ground for disputing. Before His Majesty can be advised to transfer to His Subjects, the property in any part of the Land of Australia," the Colonial Office warned, "He must have at least, some reasonable assurance that He is not about to sanction any act of injustice towards the Aboriginal Natives." This letter marked a revolution in the colonization of Australia. For the first time, the imperial government recognized the Aborigines as owners of their land.[40] The advocates for Aboriginal land rights might well have believed they had accomplished a substantial victory.

The change was not lost on members of the South Australian Colonization Commission. "In the Colonization of Australia," they protested, "it has invariably been assumed as an established fact, that the unlocated tribes have not yet arrived at that stage of social improvement, in which a proprietary right to the soil exists." The Commission pointed out that the land in the other Australian colonies had simply been allocated to settlers, regardless of whether it was inhabited by Aborigines. Thenceforth the Commission became very careful in wording its correspondence, to give the appearance of respecting Aboriginal property rights without actually committing itself to doing so. In its first annual report to the Colonial Office, sent in 1836, the Commission promised to protect the Aborigines "in the undisturbed enjoyment of their proprietary right to the soil," but immediately added: "wherever such right may be found to exist." The Commission likewise declared that "the location of the colonists will be conducted on the principle of securing to the natives their proprietary right to the soil, wherever such right may be found to exist." One can almost see the commissioners smiling, secure in the knowledge that they, at least, would be quite unlikely to find an Aboriginal tribe with a property right in land. The Commission instructed its agents in South Australia to "see that no lands, which the natives may possess in occupation or enjoyment, be offered for sale until previously ceded by the natives to yourself," and to "take care that the aborigines are not disturbed in the enjoyment of the lands over which they may possess proprietary rights, and of which they are not disposed to make a voluntary transfer."[41] Again, whether the Aborigines would actually be found to *possess* any of the land they occupied was a decision largely within the Commission's own control.

In the end, the government of South Australia "complied" with the Colonial Office's instructions, not by purchasing land from the Aborigines, nor even by recognizing that the Aborigines had the right to refuse to cede it, but by authorizing the protector of Aborigines, a colonial official, to participate in the process by which settlers selected plots of land. The protector, explained Governor George Gawler in 1840, would have "the privilege of selecting before all other claimants small portions of land," which he would hold for the "use & benefit" of the Aborigines. Gawler proudly cited this procedure as evidence of his awareness "that these people possess well defined & very ancient rights of proprietary & hereditary possession of the available lands."[42] The Colonial Office gave its approval. Setting aside small parcels for Aborigines was nothing new; by 1840 the government of New South Wales had been doing so for some time. Despite the apparent change in land policy in the mid-1830s, the colonization of South Australia looked just the same as in the older Australian colonies. Terra nullius survived.

The doctrine survived another challenge in the mid-1830s as well. The possibility that the Aborigines might be deemed to own their land provided an incentive for speculators to purchase parts of it from them and then claim title to what they had acquired. It did not take long. In 1835 a consortium led by John Batman bought more than half a million acres from a group of tribes near Port Phillip Bay, in exchange for annual payments of blankets, knives, clothing, and other goods. The would-be purchasers conceded that the purchase required confirmation by the Crown, but they argued that the Aborigines, not the Crown, were the ones with the right to sell the land. To make their case before the Colonial Office, they retained the well-known barrister and MP (and future judge) Stephen Lushington, who opined that he did "not think that the right to this Territory is at present vested in the Crown." But the government countered with lawyers of its own, who pointed out that private land purchasing from indigenous people had long been prohibited in the British colonies, so the Batman purchase was void regardless of whether the land was owned by the Aborigines or the Crown. And even that was too moderate for the Colonial Office, which, just when it was defending the property rights of Aborigines in South Australia, insisted that no such property rights could exist in the older Australian colonies. In response to Lushington's opinion, Lord Glenelg maintained that he "is not aware of any fact or principle which can be alleged in support of such a conclusion," and suggested that Lushington was laboring "under a misapprehension of some of the most material parts of the case."[43] Again, terra nullius remained in force.

   Indeed, despite all the controversy surrounding Aboriginal land rights in the middle decades of the nineteenth century, whenever the question of land ownership came up the government always resolved it in favor of terra nullius. In 1834, for example, when a dispute arose as to whether the governor of New South Wales was obliged to provide the colonial legislature with an accounting of the revenues from the sale and rent of Crown lands, Chief Justice Francis Forbes concluded that the governor was under no such obligation, because the revenues belonged to the Crown, not to the colony. That was true, Forbes explained, because New South Wales had been "acquired by the act of His Majesty's subjects settling an uninhabited country." The same year, in litigation over the ownership of a parcel of land in Sydney, Forbes held that "the right of the soil, and of all lands in the colony, became vested immediately upon its settlement, in his Majesty." In 1839, when some doubted the authority of the colonial government to charge a fee for pasturing on Crown land, Lord Normanby, the secretary of state for the colonies, instructed Governor George Gipps that ownership of the "Waste Lands in the Colony"—that is, the lands not yet granted to settlers—was "clearly in the Crown" and not anyone else, including the Aborigines. The Supreme Court of New South Wales registered its agreement in 1847. In denying a new trial for a defendant convicted of stealing coal from land to which the Crown had reserved the mineral rights, the court affirmed that all the ungranted land in Australia belonged to the Crown.[44] No matter the context, terra nullius proved impossible to dislodge.

NO TITLE TO THEIR LAND

Some of the doctrine's staying power can be attributed to the simple fact that there was another side to the debate. Every bit of land not in the possession of Aborigines was one more bit available for settlement. The standard arguments in favor of terra nullius thus still had their appeal.

Decades after the British arrived, the Aborigines were still not farming nearly as much as the British would have liked. "I am not aware that they have shown any disposition to till the ground," the physician Alexander McShane informed a parliamentary committee in 1841. Among the settlers, this lack of progress tended to be ascribed to the Aborigines' "invincible aversion to labour and to abiding in one place more than a few days together." This view was not unanimous. Some could see the Aborigines' side of things. "What great inducement does the monotonous and toilsome existence of the labouring classes in civilized communities offer," wondered the government surveyor Clement Hodgkinson, "to make the savage abandon his independent and careless life, diversified by the exciting occupations of hunting, fishing, fighting, and dancing?" But most British Australians seem to have perceived the Aborigines to possess not a genuine preference for traditional ways but rather an incapacity for improvement. "They are frequently set down as too stupid to be taught, and barely raised above brutes," remarked the Reverend Henry William Haygarth. Although Haygarth thought that verdict a bit harsh, he was nevertheless certain that "their idleness is unquestionable, and their dislike to all restraint seems bred in the bone."[45]

If the Aborigines were nonfarming nomads, then by conventional European standards they had still not acquired property rights in land. For every colonial writer who doubted the justice of terra nullius, there was another ready to defend it on the familiar ground that the Aborigines "were the *inhabitants,* but not the *proprietors* of the land." They had no property, declared the barrister Richard Windeyer, because "they have never tilled the soil, or enclosed it, or cleared any portion of it, or planted a single tree or grain or root." When the British arrived, Australia was still in its primordial, unowned state, open to the claims of whoever cultivated it first. "In our opinion, we have exactly the same right to be here, that the older inhabitants have," explained the *Southern Australian* in 1839. "We found the country in the state in which ages before the black people had found it—its resources undeveloped, unappropriated! In landing here, we exercised a right which we possessed in common with them." The point was made again and again: the British, not the Aborigines, had been the first people to perform the acts necessary to convert the occupation of land into ownership. Britons "cannot but feel ourselves delighted at the sight of smiling harvests taking place of naked wastes," applauded one observer, "since man's business, as an inhabitant of this world, is to improve and cultivate the face of the earth."[46]

Even if terra nullius had been unjust, others argued, there was no point worrying about it, because the Aborigines were dying out, so the land would belong to the British soon enough anyway. Belief in the eventual extinction of the Aborigines has of course proven false, but in the first half of the nineteenth century the Aboriginal population was declining. It was not unreasonable to conclude that the decline would continue.[47]

In any event, some reasoned, the spread of an advanced, Christian civilization over the face of the earth was an end that might justify some otherwise distasteful means. William Pridden was an Essex minister who was no supporter of terra nullius. "In most instances in which a country is taken possession of, and its original inhabitants are removed, enslaved, or exterminated," he noted, in a tone heavy with sarcasm, "the party thus violently seizing upon the rights of others is considered the superior and more civilized nation of the two." But that did not mean the British ought to leave Australia. "It is a gain to the cause of truth and virtue for Christian England to possess those wilds, which lately were occupied by miserable natives," Pridden reasoned; "and, while we own that it is wrong to do evil that good may come, yet may we, likewise, confess with thankfulness the Divine mercy and wisdom which have so often brought good out of the evil committed by our countrymen in these distant lands." To say that terra nullius was wrong was only to raise, not to answer, a difficult ethical question. For virtually all Britons of the period, colonization was an unalloyed good, the humanitarian thing to do, a way of bringing to others the benefits of European civilization. As an editorial from a contemporary South African colonial newspaper put it, "civilization is a toilsome, a laborious, and a *progressive* work." It was "the sacred duty of government to put forth all its energy and influence so that the movement may be productive of the greatest amount of good." But how could the British lift up the Aborigines if the British couldn't come to Australia? Would the British be helping or hurting the Aborigines by allowing them to deny colonists access to land? Would the Aborigines be better off, in this life and the next, as primitive pagan nomads or civilized Christian farmers? There were probably many who, considering themselves hardheaded pragmatists, took Pridden's point of view and concluded that terra nullius was unjust but necessary. Lachlan Macquarie accordingly had no doubt of "the justice, good policy, and expediency of civilizing the aborigines, or black natives of the country and settling them in townships," where they could stay in one place and be taught agriculture, freeing up the rest of the continent for Britons.[48]

Terra nullius thus had its supporters as well as its critics. But there was another reason the doctrine had so much staying power, a reason that may have been even more important. Even the critics of terra nullius tended not to argue in favor of recognizing Aboriginal property rights. They proposed two remedies for the injustice of terra nullius: compensating the Aborigines, and setting aside parcels of unallocated land as permanent Aboriginal reserves.[49] But the one thing they generally did *not* advocate was treating the Aborigines as the true owners of their land.

Saxe Bannister, for example, the former attorney general of New South Wales, found it unconscionable that Britain had taken the Aborigines' land. "The unjust seizure of it," he argued, was contrary to "the natural sense of right, and the feelings of independence" possessed by the Aborigines. But his solution was not to give the land back or to change the law so as to prohibit future seizures. He proposed instead to compensate the Aborigines, with part of the increment by which British occupation had increased the value of the Aborigines' former land. "The soil, daily increasing in value, is a most important fund," Bannister concluded. "Where we gain possession, the value of the land should at least be set apart for establishments to enable the native people to enjoy beneficially what is left." Others had the same idea. When "we deprive them of their lands and means of subsistence, in justice we ought to remunerate them," declared a witness before a committee of the New South Wales Legislative Council in 1838; "the land being their property until usurped by us." Colonization increased the value of the land so much, reasoned the penal reformer Alexander Maconochie, that even if part of the increase was paid to the Aborigines, "there will always be found in judicious colonization a large balance for ourselves." Proponents of compensation conceived of the plan along the lines of the government's power of eminent domain. The Aborigines might not have the right to oppose having their land taken, but they would have a right to be reimbursed for the land's value afterward. As John Bede Polding, the Roman Catholic archbishop of Sydney, urged in 1845, "If it is necessary for the purposes of civilized life, to occupy his land," the government should see that "it is not taken away without remuneration."[50]

The idea of remuneration was certainly not foreign to the Colonial Office, which was long accustomed to administering colonies in which indigenous people were compensated for their land. Earl Grey, the secretary of state for the colonies in the late 1840s, believed that "in assuming their Territory the settlers in Australia have incurred a moral obligation of the most sacred kind" to compensate the Aborigines, if not in cash, at least by making "all necessary provision for the[ir] instruction and improvement." In New South Wales, Governor Thomas Brisbane, at least, was amenable to paying the Aborigines as well. At a meeting with the Wesleyan missionary William Walker in 1821, Brisbane seemed positively enthusiastic. "Great things ought to be done," Brisbane told Walker. "The Mother Country is transmitting annually from 30 to 40,000 £ of goods to the American Indians, as compensation for their country: we have taken the land from the Aborigines of this country, and a remuneration ought to be made." Walker was so pleased with Brisbane that he told his employer, "I cannot forbear loving him."[51] But compensation would never be awarded.

The other oft-proposed remedy for the injustice of terra nullius was to allocate reserves for the Aborigines. The merchant George Fife Angas was one of the founders of South Australia, but he believed that "positive injustice has been done to the natives" by the founding of the colony, because the Aborigines' land had been taken from them. Questioned by a House of Commons committee in 1841, Angas made his view clear.

> Were they not migratory tribes? —No, they had distinct limits; every family had a location.
>
> Had they such a fixed residence previously to the settlement of any Europeans in the country? —Yes, it was accurately defined; not only was the district of the tribe defined, but the districts of the families of the tribe were so also.
>
> Defined in relation to each other? —Defined in relation to each other.
>
> Then did they recognise the rights of property in land? —In that sense they did.
>
> They respected each other's portions of land? —Clearly so. Those who trespassed upon others were put to death if they could be taken hold of.
>
> Have they been dispossessed of those portions? —Certainly; in every instance where the whites have settled down, they have dispossessed the natives of the portion of land which they formerly occupied.
>
> Has land been sold under the authority of the commissioners which was actually in the occupation of the aborigines? —Most unquestionably.
>
> Have the aborigines been dispossessed in consequence? —I believe that to be the fact.

Angas could hardly have made the point more clearly or forcefully. The settlers of South Australia had robbed the Aborigines of their land. But after all his testimony, when the committee finally asked him what he proposed as a solution, all Angas could suggest was that 10 percent of the colony's land not yet sold to settlers should be set aside for the use of the Aborigines. And even that 10 percent would not actually be owned by Aborigines on Angas's plan. The land would be owned instead by a board of trustees, made up of settlers, which would establish villages where Aborigines would live with missionaries "and a few families of Christian people." The colony's land commissioner would have the authority to allocate land within these villages among Aboriginal individuals and families.[52]

Unlike compensation, the allocation of Aboriginal reserves was a policy that the colonial government actually implemented. The remarks of colonial governors suggest that it was motivated by precisely the feeling Angas expressed—the sense that Aborigines deserved some land because Britons had taken the land on which they formerly lived. When Macquarie set aside ten thousand acres in 1820, for example, he explained that it was because "the rapid increase of British population, and the consequent occupancy of the lands formerly dwelt on by the Natives, [had] driven these harmless creatures to more remote situations." Two years later, Macquarie again reported that the Aborigines were "entitled to the peculiar protection of the British government, on account of their being driven from the sea-coast by our settling thereon, and subsequently occupying their best hunting grounds in the interior." Governor George Gipps acknowledged the Aborigines as "the original possessors of the soil from which the wealth of the Colony has been principally derived."[53] But when land was set aside, it was done in the manner Angas described, analogous to a trust with the Aborigines as beneficiaries and settlers as trustees, with the power to make the important decisions.

From the distance of more than a century and a half, the early critics of terra nullius are liable to be accused of lacking the courage of their convictions, or perhaps even of dishonestly assuming a posture of humanitarianism. Why, if they thought the doctrine unjust, did they refrain from seeking to have it abolished? Why did they limit themselves to arguing for compensation, whether in the form of money or land? Why didn't they simply try to persuade the government to treat the Aborigines as owners of their land?

The answer will be obvious to anyone familiar with present-day litigation over indigenous people's land claims in former British colonies. Reversing terra nullius would have posed a terrible administrative problem for settlers and their government. The land titles of every single landowner in Australia were based on a purchase from the Crown. Every landowner had either obtained his land from the government or occupied the final link in a chain of conveyances that had originated with a grant from the government. And the Crown's title to the land rested on the legal fiction that the Crown had instantly become the owner of all the continent in 1788. In short, every landowner in Australia had a vested interest in terra nullius. To overturn the doctrine would have been to upset every white person's title to his or her land. The result would have been chaos— no one would be sure of who owned what.

Everyone from the Colonial Office to the bush knew this was true. In London, Lord Glenelg had little difficulty recognizing that John Batman's ostensible purchase from the Aborigines could not be approved. "It is indeed enough to observe," he pointed out, "that such a concession would subvert the foundation on which all Proprietary rights in New South Wales at present rest." George Grey made the same point: to admit that the Aborigines owned any part of Australia was to admit that they owned all of it. And as a correspondent to the *South Australian Register* calling himself "An Old Settler" noted, even to suggest that the Aborigines owned their land was politically impossible. "If the land is indeed their own," he realized, "the Colonists of South Australia have no title to their land, for a 'voluntary surrender' of it has never been made." If terra nullius were abandoned, he wondered, and if the Aborigines were to try to reclaim their land, "would not the Colonists, as a matter of course, be at once called upon to rise *en masse* and resist so diabolical an attempt, and would not your newspaper be filled with glowing accounts of the bravery and skill displayed by the Colonists in repelling this atrocious native *aggression*?"[54] The number of landowners in Australia was steadily increasing, and all of them—every single one—depended on terra nullius for the security of their titles.

The administrative problems involved in abandoning terra nullius were not insuperable as a logical matter, but each of the conceivable devices for solving those problems was politically infeasible. The government might have discarded the doctrine only prospectively, so that only Crown land would be returned to the Aborigines and settlers would retain title to land the Crown had already granted to them. Something like this would become law in the 1990s. In the nineteenth century, however, such a plan would have deprived the government of what was anticipated to be a major source of revenue, the sale and lease of Crown land. It would have hindered the government's efforts to attract more emigrants to Australia. It would not have benefited the tribes that most needed help, the ones unlucky enough to have had the British reach their land first. These tribes might have been compensated for the land not returned to them, but of course some of the Britons most sympathetic to the Aborigines were already arguing for compensation, without any success. Many, in any event, believed that the land reserves being set aside were compensation enough. An alternative plan might have been to recognize Aboriginal ownership only of certain parts of the continent, thus freeing up the rest for British settlement and not interfering with the land titles of any existing owners. Again, however, many of the humanitarians among the British would have contended that such a policy was already being carried out, in the form of setting aside reserves, and that the Aborigines' interests would be better served if the land allocated for them were managed by Britons.

The brute fact was that terra nullius, once under way, was extraordinarily difficult to reverse, because every British landowner in Australia depended on it. Indeed, for the same reason, *any* colonial land policy would have been difficult to reverse. The exact opposite situation had arisen more than a century before in North America, where the Indians had been recognized as owners of their land. Many of the seventeenth-century settlers of North America purchased land from the Indians. By the later part of the century, the land titles of a great many colonists rested on an initial purchase from the Indians. To deny the capacity of the Indians to sell land would have been to upset the settled expectations of a substantial number of settlers. In the 1680s, when the imperial government briefly reorganized the administration of the New England colonies, the government announced its intention to invalidate all land titles based on "pretended Purchases from Indians," on the theory that "from the Indians noe title cann be Derived." The result was an uproar, led by some of the most prominent people in New England. If a purchase from the Indians could not serve as the root of a valid land title, declared a group of Boston merchants, then *"no Man was owner of a Foot of Land in all the Colony."*[55] The imperial government had to back down.

Any colonial land policy, whether terra nullius or its opposite, produced a powerful political force to keep that policy in place. Once the government went down one path or the other, it could not change. In Australia, terra nullius began with an on-the-ground anthropology. Some of the early British perceptions of Aborigines were wrong—that the Aborigines were very few in number, and that they lacked a conception of property. Some were right—that they were not farmers, and that they would not offer as much military resistance as other indigenous peoples the British had encountered. Had the British known more about the Aborigines from the start, they might have recognized Aboriginal property rights. But once terra nullius had been implemented, it could not be stopped, even when British opinion about the Aborigines began to change.

chapter two

New Zealand

Conquest by Contract

I N NEW ZEALAND, unlike in Australia, the British encountered an agricultural people, the Maori, with conspicuous rights to particular areas of land. And unlike in Australia, which was first settled by a well-armed government expedition, the earliest Britons in New Zealand were scattered individuals and private groups, who lacked the strength to seize land by force. By the time the British exercised sovereignty in 1840, white settlers had been purchasing land from the Maori for years. Practice turned into law upon colonization, as Britain formally recognized the Maori as owners of all the land in New Zealand, and the new colonial government began acquiring land through purchase. Over the next twenty years, much of New Zealand passed from Maori to British ownership, until by the late 1850s and early 1860s the Maori of the North Island succeeded in putting a near stop to land sales. At that point, the British were forced to change tactics.

CURIOUS PEOPLE

The earliest Europeans to reach New Zealand were astonished to discover that the Maori were farmers. "In a country that has been described as being peopled by a race of cannibals," marveled John Savage after returning to England in 1805, "you are agreeably surprised by . . . the patches of cultivated ground in the neighbourhood of the bay; on each of which is seen a well-thatched hut, and a shed at a little distance." James Cook, whose 1769 visit was the second European encounter with New Zealand and the first since that of Abel Tasman over a century before, observed "a great deal of Cultivated land." Cook managed to purchase "of the natives about 10 or 15 pounds of sweet Potatous," a stroke of luck possible because "they have pretty large Plantations of these." Joseph Banks was more effusive. "So well was ground tilld," he noted (using the word "curious" in its eighteenth-century sense of "careful"), "that I have seldom seen even in the gardens of curious people land better broke down." Banks saw sweet potatoes "rangd in rows . . . all laid by a line most regularly," and a vegetable resembling the cucumber "set in small hollows or dishes much as we do in England." Nearly two hundred acres were in cultivation, "tho we did not see 100 people in all." The Maori did not just farm as in England; they also appeared to divide their farms much like the English. "These plantations were from 1 or 2 to 8 or 10 acres each," Banks found, and "each distinct patch was fencd in generaly with reeds placd close by another so that scarce a mouse could creep through."[1]

These initial reports were confirmed by the early nineteenth-century missionaries, who were eager consumers and observers of Maori agriculture. "Throughout the island they have their potato cultivations," explained William Wade, "and in many parts grow the kumara, or sweet potato, taro, maize, pumpkins, water-melons, and the kind of gourd which forms their calabashes." Samuel Marsden rejoiced at the "incredible labour and patience" of Maori farmers, who "suffer no weeds to grow, but . . . root up everything likely to injure the growing crop." The Maori even seemed to share the British view of how best to use the land and its resources. "A great work is going on here," John King approved in 1819, "in cutting down a large Forrest and burning it off in order to plant it . . . this is pleasing & promising." That a reputedly savage people like the Maori could be so hard working, so skilled—so nearly civilized—in this respect was miraculous. "When the badness of their tools is considered, together with their limited knowledge of agriculture," considered the painter Augustus Earle, "their persevering industry I look upon as truly astonishing."[2]

Such observations had strong implications for the colonizing venture the British assumed lay ahead. The Maori were evidently farther along the path to civilization than some of the other peoples the British had encountered elsewhere. "He possesses hardly anything in common with the savage aborigines of the greater part of the new world, and of Australia," concluded the *New Zealand Journal*. This meant, on the one hand, that the Maori could be more easily assimilated to the British way of life. "The art of cultivating the ground does not require to be taught; the natives already possess it in a high degree," exulted one colonial propagandist. To become industrious farmers, the Maori "merely require direction, with the stimulus of a proper reward, to induce them to extend their cultivation to an indefinite extent." Colonization promised to proceed more smoothly in New Zealand than it had in places with less advanced aboriginal populations. As James Radcliffe proudly reported to the Aborigines Protection Society, the avowedly humanitarian organization in London taking the greatest interest in the Maori, "they are in the strictest sense of the word an agricultural people dwelling in villages and every way capable of being civilised." But this same advancement simultaneously meant, on the other hand, that the process of acquiring land would not be as simple as it had been in Australia, where the absence of agriculture had implied the absence of any basis for recognizing aboriginal property rights to land. Radcliffe was aware of the looming problem. "In the division of their lands their Boundary lines are well defined," he began, "and they have, as just notions upon the rights of private property, as any European nation. . . . But before New Zealand can become a thriving British colony, the natives must be dispossessed of these fertile tracts."[3] The question of how to reconcile this tension would bedevil policymakers in New Zealand for the rest of the century.

As both peoples would soon learn, the physical similarity of British and Maori agricultural methods masked some fundamental differences between British and Maori conceptions of property. The British tended to allocate property rights in land on a geographic basis. Land was divided into pieces, each piece was assigned to an owner, and the owner was ordinarily understood to command all the resources within that geographic space. He could harvest the plants that grew spontaneously, or plant crops, or place animals on the land, or catch fish in the water, or do virtually anything else he liked as much or as little as he pleased. An owner of land was likewise understood to control the access of others. If he wished, he could allow others to enter the geographic space within his control, on whatever terms he chose, but he could also exclude others entirely. These powers were understood to be unbounded in time. A landowner would not live forever, but his powers over the land would; he merely had to assign them to someone else, either while he was still alive or upon his death, and the new owner would assume all the rights of the old. If he failed to do so, the state would do it for him, through the rules of intestate succession.

The reality of British landholding was often more complex than this ideal. A piece of land might be owned by several people at once. Others might own a future interest in the land, the right to assume possession upon the death of another person or the occurrence of a future event. Still others might have rights to use the land for certain limited purposes, rights the law classified as easements, licenses, and profits. Traces of old common rights had survived centuries of enclosure. The state had an ambiguous power to limit the owner's discretion as to the use to which he would put his land. But these intrusions into the ideal of command over a geographic space were understood as just that—as exceptions to a rule, as overlays on a fundamental norm. Equally important, they were with rare exception products of a landowner's free choice, whether the current owner or one of his predecessors. Future interests, easements, and so on normally existed because they had been voluntarily created by a landowner, who presumably had chosen to give up some of his power over space in exchange for something he valued more highly. Governmental powers over nominally private land had also been consented to in a less direct sense, as part of the social contract creating the state, and in the ongoing process of government, in which landowners at least had a voice.

The Maori, by contrast, tended to allocate property rights among individuals and families on a functional rather than a geographical basis. That is, a person would not own a zone of space; one would instead own the right to use a particular resource in a particular way. One might possess the right to trap birds in a certain tree, or the right to fish in a certain spot in the water, or the right to cultivate a certain plot of ground. Possession of such a right did not imply the possession of other rights in the same geographic space. The same tree, for instance, could be used for fowling by one family, for berry-gathering by another, and so on. Nor did possession of a use-right in one place preclude possession of use-rights in other places as well. A family might be understood to have the right to one place for sleeping, another for cultivating, another for catching eels, and others for various other activities. These rights were typically handed down from generation to generation within the family, so long as each new generation continued to use the right in question.[4] The Maori, like the British, possessed multiple rights over resources, but whereas the British ordinarily bundled these rights into a single geographic space, the Maori did not.

Another fundamental difference between British and Maori conceptions of property involved the means used to remember the property rights already in existence. Any property system requires some way of knowing what rights have already been allocated, to forestall disputes from arising and to resolve them when they do. The British had for centuries divided their land by written surveys and memorialized their land transactions in written agreements. The Maori, lacking writing, had developed a different method. Because property rights derived largely from one's ancestry, individuals trained themselves to remember their genealogy and the history of their kin group. The strategic use of landmarks, such as stones and marks in trees, served to aid the memory. "In going through a large forest," recalled the missionary Richard Taylor,

> a Chief who was my companion, said it belonged to him. I asked how he knew his boundaries, he said he would point them out when we reached them; at last he stopped at the foot of a very large tree, whose root ran across the road; he pointed out to a hollow in it, and asked me what it was. I said, it was like a man's foot. He replied, I was right; it was the impression cut by one of his forefathers, and put his foot into it to show it fitted. This, said he, is one of my boundaries, and now we are entering on the land of another.
>
> In a similar way when travelling over the central plains, where apparently human beings had never resided, one of my natives suddenly stopped by a stream, and said, that land belonged to his family. I expressed my doubts,

and asked him how he could tell. He went into some long grass, and kept feeling about with his feet for some time, then calling me to him, he pointed out four hearth-stones, and triumphantly said, here stood my father's house, and going thence to the stream, he pointed out a little hollow in the rocky side, over which an old gnarled branch sprung, and said, in this hollow of the stream, we used to suspend our eel baskets from the branch. In fact, they have many marks which, though they might pass unnoticed by Europeans, clearly indicate to them their respective rights.

These techniques could be as baffling to the British as the British method initially was to the Maori. "The manner of making known the boundaries of land amongst the Maories is very good amongst the Maori people," one British tenant complained to his Maori landlord, "because every man has been told by his father or relations where the boundaries of his land are. Now amongst the Europeans it is not so. I cannot understand your boundaries." He pleaded with his landlord to "let the boundaries of the runs be surveyed. Then the boundaries will be plain."[5]

The Maori system of property existed within political and economic contexts quite different from those to be found in Britain at the time, and these contexts had profound effects on the organization of property rights, effects that caused further divergence from British property arrangements.

The Maori were politically divided into *iwi*, or tribes, sets of interlocking kin groups with common genealogy and leadership. The *iwi* were composed of *hapu*, or subtribes, which were in turn made up of *whanau*, or extended families. The division into *hapu* and *whanau* was not clearcut; because of intermarriage, the same individual might have ancestors from, and thus membership in, more than one. As of 1845, the thirty *iwi* on the North Island averaged around two thousand members each, but there was wide variation in size among them. Although individuals did not exert control over geographic spaces, *iwi* did, and *hapu* sometimes did as well, within the larger territory controlled by the *iwi*. Individual use-rights were located within this physical space. The tribal unit's relationship with its land accordingly corresponded more closely to the European conception of sovereignty than that of property ownership. It was the *iwi*, like the European state, that enforced the use-rights of individuals and families against encroachment from other tribe members, and that defended those use-rights against attack from other *iwi*.[6]

The chiefs of tribal units, like European government officials, did not command more property than the ordinary people within their jurisdiction, but they had a greater than ordinary power to allocate property to others. These opportunities arose frequently. Property rights had to be maintained by use; if abandoned for long enough, sometimes only a few years, a right would revert back to the tribe and could then be allocated to someone else. Land and natural resources were so plentiful in comparison to the number of people that it made sense for tribes to move from one block of land to another periodically, rather than continue to exploit the same block persistently. These shifts would again have afforded the opportunity to allocate some property rights, although this opportunity would have been limited by the practice of returning periodically to each block of land and resuming the old pattern of use. Such cycling was necessary because of the requirement that rights be used in order to be maintained. As one very old man recalled in the late nineteenth century, his tribe followed "our custom of living for some time on each of our blocks of land, to keep our claim to each, and that our fire might be kept alight on each block, so that it might not be taken from us by some other tribe." Finally, land could be acquired by one tribe by conquest from another, in the intermittent warfare that occurred among tribes. In this circumstance, property rights would need to be allocated from scratch. The authority of a chief thus normally included the creation of property rights, when the situation arose, but not the destruction of existing property rights. Chiefs enjoyed property rights of their own, but these were defined in the same way as those enjoyed by anyone else, in that they were by and large inherited from ancestors, and it was up to the chief himself to exploit them or have them revert to the tribe. In this regard the chiefs were quite different from the monarchs of Europe, who held vast amounts of land, none of which they worked themselves. The contrast was not lost on the Maori. "We are not like the King of England," one chief noted in the 1830s. "We are going to work to get food."[7]

The precontact Maori economy provided very little occasion for the accumulation of personal wealth. There was no money, and few other durable goods, capable of being saved. The resources naturally present on the land exceeded the ability of the relatively small population to consume them. Land was accordingly not understood as something that one might wish to sell. There existed little with which it could have been purchased, and had there been more to exchange for it, the price at which land might have sold would have been extremely low. Any sale, moreover, would have had to have been within the tribal group that exercised control over the land. An individual could no more alienate land outside the tribe than an English landowner could transfer his land to the sovereignty of France. Intertribal gifts of territory did occur from time to time, but, like international transfers of sovereignty over territory in Europe, they were extraordinary events. One tribe might transfer land to another as compensation for a murder, for instance, or as a gift in recognition of assistance during a war. Because such transfers would necessarily terminate the property rights of each of the tribe members who used the resources located on the land, they could not have been undertaken without at least a rough consensus as to their appropriateness.[8] But there were no transactions among the Maori comparable to the sale of land in Britain.

This was yet another basic difference between British and Maori notions of property in land. By the nineteenth century, land had been bought and sold in Britain for hundreds of years, long enough for specialized methods of entering into and documenting land transactions to be familiar to anyone with the means to participate in them. The difference ought not to be overstated—the English ordinarily could not sell land outside the "tribe" either, in the sense that for centuries aliens had been generally prohibited from owning land in England.[9] But the difference was still important. It would prove to be a fertile source of misunderstanding between the two cultures in the early years. Under pressure from settlers wishing to acquire land, this is the aspect of Maori property-related thought that would change the most rapidly.

The presence of a real estate market in Britain and its absence in precontact New Zealand created a broad divergence in the two cultures' understanding of the relationship between people and land, but the contrast has sometimes been overdrawn. The colonists were, to be sure, on occasion prone to declaring that "land is but a durable commodity, like any other which is bought or sold in the market," and to assuming that "land, from which no profit can possibly be derived, is of course worthless." The Maori, on the other hand, experienced what has been called a "close, spiritual relationship with the land," one tied up with personal and tribal history and with myths of the origin of mankind. "One did not own land," a recent prominent student of Maori thought has concluded. "One belonged *to* the land."[10]

Historians have sometimes been too quick to conclude, however, that the British possessed a "mechanistic view of land as a simple commodity able to be exploited by individuals pursuing material wealth," in contrast to the Maori "transcendental bond with their land which was treated as a dearly loved person." To the British, land was much more than a commodity, a truth that can be perceived most directly by considering all the connotations of the English word *home.* Colonists were, of course, a disproportionately mobile group, simply by virtue of their willingness to give up their homes and begin a new life halfway around the globe. But they had not lost their sense of attachment to a place, their nonmonetary preference for one geographic space over all others. "Everything that you can see is your very own," exclaimed Maria Atkinson shortly after moving to Taranaki, "the absolute possession of land gives a sort of certainty that with common industry and care, you are in what may be your *home* till death . . . the feeling of coming home as it were to a country *wanting* you . . . is enough to make the most sluggish nature 'feel spirited.'" When war threatened, she reflected, "We (or most of us do) love the place with a sort of family affection which will make us cling on to the last." British people sometimes moved from one piece of land to another, but so did the Maori; neither group had a self-evident claim to a greater attachment to the land. And for the British, no less than the Maori, land was intertwined with collective history. The concept of "England"—a place where one's ancestors had lived, a community whose history extended back farther than anyone could know without the aid of myths of origin—was one worth dying to defend. Some colonists recognized that the Maori felt the same way. "The pride of each tribe centers in its power to maintain its own possession against aggression," observed two early leaders of the settler community. "This spirit in the native people is closely akin to one which, if we were speaking of ourselves, we should describe as patriotism."[11]

For the British, as for the Maori, land was also an important source of status within the community. A Briton earning his fortune in business would normally purchase land for the social benefits it would bring, often when he could scarcely expect the land to turn a profit. Land was, for the British, the basic source of political rights. Voting in Britain and its colonies, including New Zealand, was contingent on the ownership of land. Indeed, in New Zealand local elections, until near the end of the nineteenth century, the more land one owned, the more votes one could cast. Meanwhile, undeveloped land in nineteenth-century Britain and its colonies was increasingly coming to be revered precisely as a refuge from the corrupting values of the marketplace, a contrast celebrated especially in poetry and painting. There would be serious misunderstandings between Maori and British conceptions of property, but they were not caused by any failure on the part of the British to perceive the nonmonetary virtues of land. As Tom Brooking suggests, "One of the great misfortunes of New Zealand is that it has been settled by two peoples who are romantic and even sentimental about land."[12]

The British struggled for several decades to understand the Maori system of property rights. Looking back on the process in the 1870s, the lawyer and government official Henry Sewell recalled: "It was as difficult for us to enter into and comprehend the tribal and communistic rights of the Natives, as it was for the Natives to enter into and comprehend our system of individual titles." The British were heirs to a long tradition of thought, as old as ancient Rome and elaborated by writers like Hobbes and Locke, associating communal ownership with primitive peoples and individual property rights with civilization. Some of the difficulty can be attributed to simple prejudice, an unwillingness to accept the practices of savages as worthy of consideration. The early settler Frederick Maning, for instance, clearly doubted the possibility of a property system based on inherited use-rights. These rights, he claimed to recall,

> had lain dormant until it was known the pakeha [European] had his eye on the land. Some of them seemed to me at the time odd enough. One man required payment because his ancestors, as he affirmed, had exercised the right of catching rats on it, but which he (the claimant) had never done, for the best of reasons, i.e., there were no rats to catch. . . . Another claimed because his grandfather had been murdered on the land, and—as I am a vera-

cious pakeha—another claimed payment because *his* grandfather had committed the murder! Then half the country claimed payments of various value, from one fig of tobacco to a musket, on account of a certain *wahi tapu,* or ancient burying-ground, which was on the land, and in which every one almost had had relations, or rather ancestors, buried, as they could clearly make out in old times, though no one had been deposited in it for about two hundred years, and the bones of the others had been (as they said) removed long ago.

The surveyor Frederick Carrington, unwilling to believe some Maori claims of ownership, reported that "sometimes a man has told me that he possessed a district for 30 miles, or right up to such a mountain; sometimes they have the most minute boundaries."[13] This sort of attitude was doubtless to be found among many of the settlers, particularly those without much Maori contact.

Much of the difficulty, however, stemmed from two circumstances for which the British cannot be as easily faulted. First, coming from a culture in which property rights were organized by geographic space, and observing many Maori exercising use-rights within the same zone of land, many colonists erroneously concluded that the land was held by all in common, and that property rights were therefore unknown. "The right of individual property has never existed in New Zealand," affirmed Edward Gibbon Wakefield before a committee of the House of Commons. Such a view lasted a long time. As late as 1879, the legislator William Rees recalled that before contact "a system of Communism prevailed, and speaking generally, no native held absolutely to himself any portion in particular, of the surrounding territory of the vicinity in which he lived."[14]

This view persisted in part because of its appeal to writers eager to contrast the equality associated with this supposed Maori communism with the sharp wealth disparities to be found in nineteenth-century Britain. Because of the absence of individual property rights, reported Charles Hursthouse, "there is neither great individual wealth nor poverty among them." "From the community of property among the New Zealanders," agreed the physician Arthur Thomson, "no man could become rich, and no man poor. Schemers and speculators never reduced families to starvation . . . and a dread of the hard fare of the workhouse never crossed the minds of men." Placed in a warm light, the Maori's supposed lack of property rights evoked a time before the fall, when the fruits of the earth were equally available to all. But the view also persisted, ironically enough, because of the opposite sentiment. A world without property rights could also be understood as one in which "'might was right,' to all intents and purposes. . . . No right to land existed but in the pleasure of the most in-fluential chief in the neighbourhood." When H. T. Kemp tried to argue to Native Minister Donald McLean that Maori property before coloniza-tion had been governed by rules, someone noted in the margin of Kemp's memo: "The simple plan that he should take who hath power & he should keep who can." This darker picture also had its appeal, as a means of emphasizing how much better things had become with British rule. "This state of things some writers call a reign of absolute liberty," huffed the Wesleyan minister Thomas Buddle; "it is the absolute liberty of the strong to tyrannize over the weak. What a boon is conferred upon such a people in the establishment of British law!"[15]

The second obstacle to British understanding of Maori property was that the British, because they were primarily interested in learning how they might purchase Maori land, were focusing their inquiry at precisely the point on which Maori thought had not been developed. Without sales of land, there had been no reason to elaborate any principles as to how or when land might be sold. Suddenly confronted with offers to purchase land, the Maori had to improvise such principles quickly. The uncertainty of the early years likely caused practice to develop differently in different places, a diversity not always recognized by early British authorities on Maori life, who sometimes assumed local practices to be uniform. Partici-pants in early transactions reported wildly disparate rules governing the sale of land. The trader Joseph Montefiore explained to the House of Lords in 1838 that chiefs had the power to sell their tribes' land without consulting tribe members. At the same hearing, a member of the Kawia tribe named Nayti explained precisely the opposite, that he could sell any of his land without consulting the chief. The British naval officer Thomas McDonnell believed that the chief could sell some land without consult-ing the tribe but not other land. The settler John Blackett and the sur-veyor Charles Kettle opined that all tribe members had to unite in the sale. One witness affirmed that actual use was necessary to secure a property right; another believed one could purchase land, return to England without using it, and then come back years later as the land's undisputed owner. "The laws of property," William Wakefield complained, "are very undefined."[16] The Maori law of land sales was in the process of forming, and the British, viewing all Maori property arrangements from a perspective that placed sales front and center, accordingly had a difficult time comprehending the subject.

By the middle decades of the nineteenth century, however, as purchasing practices stabilized, colonists with a genuine interest in Maori practices seemed to have no trouble understanding Maori property in land. It was understood that although tribes controlled geographic spaces, individual property rights within those spaces were organized functionally rather than geographically. The British had seen the Maori enforce these rights, which gave further evidence of their reality. Most important of all, the British realized that even though at any given moment the Maori were occupying only a small fraction of the country, the Maori nevertheless understood that they owned it all. "Every inch of land in New Zealand has its proprietor," Ernst Dieffenbach reported in 1843. The following year, a dismayed member of the House of Commons pressed an early purchaser on this point—"You mean that some native or other claims all the land?"—and received the answer he hoped not to hear. "Every bit of it," testified Walter Brodie; "if I settled myself on an uninhabited spot, 20 miles from a native, he would soon come and turn me out, and I should find out that he had a right to the land." British writers more sympathetic to the Maori were awestruck that land could be so intimately known. "There is no part of it, however lonely, of which they do not know the owners," marveled the lawyer William Swainson. "Forests in the wildest part of the country have their claimants. Land, apparently waste, is highly valued by them. Forests are preserved for birds; swamps and streams for eel-weirs and fisheries. Trees, rocks, and stones are used to define the well-known boundaries."[17]

Some of the more historically minded colonists recognized that Maori property rights resembled the system that had once existed in England, in which multiple people had possessed use-rights within the same geographic space. "Among our Anglo Saxon Fathers," explained William Martin, New Zealand's first chief justice, some land "was the property of the community. It might be occupied in common." Such land "could not be alienated in perpetuity; and therefore on the expiration of the term for which it had been granted, it reverted to the Community, and was again distributed by the same authority." This ancient method of owning English land, Martin concluded, "corresponded to the Native Tenure" in New Zealand. William Rees realized that the Maori had "a system of land tenure that had been unknown in Europe for centuries," one which once "England possessed, but which has long since passed away." Even farther back, suggested the lawyer Singleton Rochfort, Britain's political structure had resembled that of New Zealand. "When Julius Caesar first landed in Britain he found the inhabitants divided into upwards of forty distinct nations, each enjoying a state of independence." These reflections fit well into a larger framework of thought in which the British were farther along than the Maori in the course of civilization. The Maori were not biologically inferior (as many would come to believe later in the century); they were simply at an earlier point in their progress.[18] It made sense, on this view, that Maori property arrangements should closely resemble those upon which the British had long ago improved, and that the humanitarian thing for the British to do would be to help the Maori improve as well.

British perceptions of Maori property in land became crucial in the 1840s, when Britain assumed colonial authority over New Zealand and it became necessary to decide whether and to what extent the Crown should recognize Maori property rights. Three choices were in theory possible. Britain could, as in Australia, refuse to recognize any aboriginal property rights. It could, as in North America, recognize Maori rights in the whole of New Zealand. And third, between these two poles, it could recognize Maori ownership of the land the Maori were physically occupying when the British assumed sovereignty, but declare the rest of the land to be unowned.

The first possibility was precluded by prevailing British legal thought, which associated land ownership with cultivation. The Maori "are not mere wanderers over an extended surface in search of a precarious subsistence," Secretary of State for the Colonies John Russell reminded William

Hobson, the first colonial governor of New Zealand. They were rather "a people among whom the arts of Government have made some progress; who have established by their own customs a division and appropriation of the soil." New Zealand thus could not be treated like Australia, as terra nullius. As the Colonial Office prepared for the assumption of sovereignty over New Zealand, James Stephen re-read *Johnson v. M'Intosh,* the 1823 case in which the United States Supreme Court held that American Indians merely had a right to occupy their land, the ownership of which was vested in the government. "Such is American law," Stephen noted. "British law in Canada is far more humane, as there, the Crown purchases of the Indians, before it grants to its own subjects." In any event, he reasoned, "the New Zealanders are not wandering tribes, but bodies of men, till lately, very populous, who have a settled form of Government, and who have divided and appropriated the whole Territory amongst them. They are not huntsmen, but after their fashion, agriculturalists." *Johnson v. M'Intosh,* "though it may be good American law, is not the law we recognize."[19]

The real choice accordingly lay between recognizing the Maori as owners of all of New Zealand or as owners only of the parts they were physically occupying at the time. On this question there was much division of opinion, both within the government and outside. The English text of the 1840 Treaty of Waitangi, the document formally ceding sovereignty over New Zealand to Britain, was ambiguous on this point.[20] Article 2 confirmed to the Maori "the full exclusive and undisturbed possession of their Lands and Estates Forests Fisheries and other properties which they may collectively or individually possess." But what exactly did it mean to "possess" property? Did the Maori possess all of New Zealand, or only the land they were currently using?

Both before and after the signing of the treaty, a vocal British humanitarian lobby pressed for the former. "What right have we to sit and coolly dispose of distant countries, inhabited by Aboriginal people," asked John Beecham, "who have as valid a claim to the lands which they occupy, as we have to our native soil?" Dandeson Coates, speaking for the Church Missionary Society, used the law of England and all other civilized nations on behalf of the Maori. "In all countries," he argued, "a proprietary right in land is enjoyed where in many cases the land is not actually occupied for agricultural, mining, or other purpose." The humanitarians were supported by those who had already purchased Maori land, whose titles depended on the government's recognition that their vendors actually owned the land they had sold. Recognizing Maori ownership over land not currently in use was not just legally right, suggested Edward Gibbon Wakefield, but it would also amount to scarcely any sacrifice of British interests. The very fact that so much land was unoccupied at any given time meant that the Maori would be eager to sell it for next to nothing.[21]

Many settlers, meanwhile, seeing what appeared to be vast areas of unutilized land, favored recognizing Maori rights only in the land actually being cultivated. "Whether a nation barely reclaimed, if reclaimed, from cannibalism," editorialized the *New Zealand Gazette* in 1843, "could be said either according to the law of nations or of common sense to possess rights of property in land on which they never trod except to indulge in their pastime of war, or in travelling from one of their unsettled homes to another, may very reasonably be doubted." This view clearly had its element of self-interest, but it also fit well with a strand of thought current in Britain at least since the time of Locke—that property rights in land were acquired by mixing one's labor with the land, and that land not labored upon was accordingly unowned. Such was the position taken in 1846 by Earl Grey, the new secretary of state for the colonies. Grey was willing to concede that the Maori "practised to a certain extent a rude sort of agriculture," and therefore that "to that portion of the soil, whatever it might be, which they really occupied, the aboriginal inhabitants, barbarous as they were, had a clear and undoubted claim." But Maori property rights could extend no farther. "The savage inhabitants of New Zealand," Grey instructed the colonial government, "had themselves no right of property in land which they did not occupy." To this argument the humanitarians had a standard rejoinder: it was simply not true that English law required one to labor upon land before a property right would be recognized. "This is the case with many moors and wastes in England and Scotland," they pointed out, which were quite clearly owned although "used for sporting only," if at all.[22]

In the end, the government chose to recognize Maori property rights in the entirety of New Zealand, in part because of the North American precedent emphasized by James Stephen, and in part because of the fear that any other course would involve Britain in a costly war against the Maori. Maori ownership would remain a source of persistent resentment among many colonists for the rest of the century. It hardly seemed just that a settler should be denied access to land lying unused, and which the Maori appeared to have no intention ever to use, simply because someone alleged that his ancestor had once been there. The quantity of land in New Zealand was manifestly far in excess of that which the Maori could ever hope to bring under cultivation. Why should they be allowed to prevent settlers from doing so? In fairness, was there no limit to the amount of land a people could claim? "Suppose a fertile country of fifty millions of acres is occupied only by half-a-dozen savages, who claim it all because they happened to be born there." Would such a claim have to be recognized? Many colonists perceived the equities to lie on their side, as refugees from "a small island containing many millions of inhabitants who have not sufficient land to raise the necessaries of life, and the people are perishing for want."[23] When so few Maori had so much, and so many British immigrants had so little, in whose favor did true humanitarianism lie?

VERY ANXIOUS TO SELL

The recognition of Maori property rights meant that in the absence of war the British could acquire land only by purchase. Until 1865, land was purchased from tribes rather than from the Maori as individuals. The British were interested in acquiring geographic spaces, not individual rights to use particular resources, so they necessarily had to deal with the tribe as a whole, the only political unit with the authority to take action with respect to an entire zone of land. Before the British assumption of sovereignty in 1840 (and briefly in 1844–1846), the purchasers were individuals and private companies; afterward, the sole legal purchaser was the Crown.

The earliest colonists, mostly traders and missionaries, typically bought plots of land from the tribe that controlled the area in which they lived, in exchange for commodities like guns, ammunition, tobacco, blankets, clothing, and tools. As the early trader J. S. Polack explained, a prospective purchaser needed to deal with the chiefs of the relevant tribes and subtribes, and ask each "to speak with his friends and the claimants of the extent and situation of the allotment you may require, stating the amount you propose giving." Each chief "will acquaint his tribe of your proposals, and after discussing the matter, if all the parties, who are interested, feel agreeable to dispose of it, the chief will send for you." Payment was then to be "delivered to the principal chief, who distributes to each claimant what he imagines he may be entitled to." This general sort of procedure appears to have eventually developed wherever settlers offered to purchase land. Although the concept of selling land was a new one, chiefs had traditionally possessed the authority to represent the tribe in its interactions with other tribes and to distribute unallocated resources. Chiefs seem to have been able to slip naturally, whenever a land sale was proposed, into the roles of negotiator, coordinator of tribal discussion, and distributor of the proceeds. All three roles required an intimate knowledge of the relative property holdings and social standing of tribe members, knowledge not easily available to outsiders. When asked in 1838 by the House of Lords how he figured out whom to pay for the land he purchased, the missionary John Flatt expressed his relief to have discovered that "they settled that Difficulty among themselves." As Flatt conceded, "I do not know the exact Rule."[24] A prospective purchaser did, however, need to know something about the tribe's political organization, in order to be sure that the people with whom he was dealing were in fact authorized to represent everyone holding use-rights in the area he sought to purchase. Such local knowledge could be acquired only after a period of residence among the Maori.

Expectations in 1839 and early 1840 that New Zealand would soon become an British colony produced a flood of purported land purchases on the part of speculators, who hoped that the prospect of increased British immigration would cause land values to rise. "Tracts of eligible land, of sufficient extent to constitute whole earldoms in England, have already been acquired in New Zealand, by the merest adventurers," exclaimed the Sydney minister John Dunmore Lang. Some of these purchases were so large that acres or square miles were inadequate measurements; the deeds could be worded only in degrees of latitude. When William Wakefield, for instance, ostensibly bought on behalf of the New Zealand Company the northern part of the South Island and the southern part of the North Island, the southern boundary was at 43 degrees, while the northern boundary was a line running from 32 degrees on the east coast to 41 degrees on the west. William Wentworth and John Jones, two Sydney speculators, went even farther; they purported to buy the entire South Island. These purchases were also for commodities, often in astonishingly small quantity. John Ward, the secretary of the New Zealand Company, sheepishly informed the House of Commons that Wakefield's purchase was estimated to include twenty million acres of land, and had been purchased for goods worth approximately £45,000. Having acquired the land for less than a halfpenny per acre, Ward admitted, the Company was busily selling it to settlers at a pound per acre.[25]

Most of these nonresident speculative purchasers knew virtually nothing about Maori property ownership or political organization. When these transactions were investigated by the new colonial government in the early 1840s, the supposed Maori sellers were typically found not to have possessed the authority to speak for all the rights-holders within the enormous zones purchased. When, for example, the New Zealand Company's claim to the area that is now Wellington was examined, William Wakefield could produce only one Maori witness to the transaction, who promptly confessed that he had no right to sell the land.[26] The sum of all these early individual purchases is often said to have exceeded the total land area of New Zealand.

"Was there ever such a mess?" asked one newspaper. The new colonial government took two steps to sort it out. As to past transactions, it established a land claims commission, with the authority to validate or reject all private land purchases from the Maori. Land purchased from people lacking the authority to sell, or purchased by means of fraud, or purchased at too low a price (determined not by abstract justice but by a stated scale of prices), was returned to the Maori. Purchases were capped at 2,560 acres; all validly purchased land in excess of this amount was retained by the Crown. Most of the purchases were so patently unsupportable that they

2. Donald McLean, seated under the tree at left, purchased on the colonial government's behalf the land for the town of Wairoa, New Zealand, at this 1865 meeting with the land's Maori owners. The Maori were farmers and formidable military opponents, and the first British settlers were scattered individuals and private groups with no capacity to take land by force, so land purchasing became common well before Britain assumed sovereignty over New Zealand. F-110517-1/2, Rhodes Album, Alexander Turnbull Library, Wellington, New Zealand.

were not even submitted to the commission. Of the 9.3 million acres submitted, only 468,000 were found to have been obtained validly, of which 142,000 were retained by the Crown as surplus. That left 326,000 acres in the hands of settlers, and 8.8 million returned to the Maori.[27]

As to future transactions, the new government prohibited private purchasing entirely. The English text of the Treaty of Waitangi had given the Crown "the exclusive right of Preemption over such lands as the proprietors thereof may be disposed to alienate." The principle of preemption—that only the Crown, not private individuals, can buy aboriginal land—was by 1840 one of long standing in the older British colonies in North America. It had been proclaimed by the British government in 1763 at the close of the Seven Years' War. It had been adopted by the United States after the American Revolution. It was familiar to officials in New Zealand and in the Colonial Office. A few years later, the Supreme Court of New Zealand, drawing heavily on past American practice, would reaffirm the principle, on the ground that because under British law the Crown is the source of all land titles, title obtained from elsewhere is no good as against the Crown. One of the new colony's very first statutes accordingly recited that "the sole and absolute right of preemption from the said aboriginal inhabitants vests in and can only be exercised by Her said Majesty," and that all other pretended purchases without the government's consent "shall be absolutely null and void."[28]

For most of the next twenty-five years, land purchasing was a function performed by the colonial government. The sellers were still tribes, and transactions were still arranged in much the same way. "The money would be laid down in a lump in the presence of all the people," Hone Peeti recalled years later, "and subsequently it would be disbursed amongst them" by the chiefs. Government land purchase agents, working year in and year out among the Maori, often attained fluency in the language and familiarity with Maori property arrangements and political organization, knowledge that smoothed the course of dealing. Their surviving journals suggest the degree of effort that could go into the project of purchasing land. James Grindell, an interpreter with the Land Purchase Department in the 1850s, noted that, while waiting for a tribe's response to a purchase offer, "[I] employed myself the remaining part of this week making out a genealogical list of the various tribes and families in the Manawatu, with a short notice of their claims to the lands which they occupy for my guidance in future negotiations with the natives." Between 1846 and 1853, these full-time, knowledgeable purchasers acquired on the government's behalf 32.6 million acres of land, or just under half the country, at an average purchase price of less than a halfpenny per acre. Government purchases were concentrated in the sparsely populated South Island, thirty million acres inhabited by fewer than three thousand people. By 1860 virtually the entire South Island had been sold "for an almost nominal sum," as Governor Thomas Gore Browne put it.[29] Although the government had managed to purchase several million acres on the North Island as well, most of the North Island remained in Maori hands.

In the early years, the Maori were "very anxious to sell" their land, John Flatt reported. "Yes, very anxious, even up to the time of my leaving," agreed the trader George Earp. "People frequently come from the interior, and they would come up to any one who would talk to them, and make them all sorts of offers." This willingness arose because the Maori had so "much more than they seem to require for themselves," one 1821 observer concluded. In 1844–45, when the government briefly waived its right of preemption and allowed private purchasing, people came streaming into Auckland "in great numbers to hawk their lands for sale up and down the streets."[30]

The Maori, all agreed, seemed to welcome British colonists. Samuel Stephens, a surveyor for the New Zealand Company, was gratified to discover in 1842–43 that the natives near Nelson were "anxious to have a settlement of white men amongst them." The Waikato chief Te Wherowhero, reported the painter George French Angas a few years later, was "anxious to have *pakehas* amongst his people," and had accordingly "offered certain lands for sale to the British Government for that purpose." The missionary Alfred Nesbit Brown, on a visit to the Waikato in 1834, found that the local people "had long been expecting Missionaries to live with them and had set apart a piece of ground for them to reside upon." They were so eager for missionaries, in fact, "that they informed us of their having six Wives for the Miss[ionarie]s besides the land." (A dismayed Brown noted: "so degraded are these poor heathen & so ignorant of the occupation of Missionaries.") As Nayti straightforwardly told the House of Lords, "I would sell; I like English people." Even as late as 1879, when the novelty of British settlement had to have long worn off after decades of scattered warfare, Resident Magistrate Spencer von Stürmer reported from Hokianga that "the Natives here are constantly impressing upon me" their desire "that Europeans would settle amongst them."[31]

British settlement was valued primarily as a means of engaging with the market economy the British brought; land sales earned European products or the means of acquiring them. Anglo-Maori trade had its darker side. The introduction of European weapons in the early nineteenth century created, in effect, an arms race, in which tribes hastened to acquire guns in order to defend themselves against other tribes who were making the same acquisitions. This would not be the last time that the fragmented and competitive nature of Maori political authority would produce insurmountable barriers to collective action. Even the more peaceful forms of trade could be viewed as an insidious fostering of dependence. "The natives are very anxious to have the white people settled among them," Jessie Campbell wrote to her mother from Wanganui in 1843, because "they cannot live now without tobacco, blankets, etc. all of which the Pakehas or White people provide them with."[32] The introduction of alcohol soon became widely recognized as an example of this phenomenon. In retrospect, so too was the introduction of tobacco.

But trade had its positive aspects as well. The early encounters between Maori and Europeans were an economist's dream: on one side was a group with an abundance of land and some agricultural products but few other assets, on the other was a group with surplus manufactured goods eager to obtain land. That there were enormous gains to be had from trade was evident to all. The Maori generally welcomed European products, technology, and agricultural methods. When the first European trader arrived among the Arawa in 1830, for instance, tribes came from all directions, eager to begin trade. By the 1860s, Maori all over the country owned horses, guns, European clothing, and European tools. Some of these goods could be acquired by selling food, and many tribes, upon encountering Europeans, began for the first time to produce crops for external sale rather than for their own consumption.[33] But the Maori's dominant asset was land.

Without selling land, participation in the new market economy would in most circumstances have been impossible.

Two aspects of the new colonial political order also had the effect of promoting land sales in the 1840s and 1850s. The colonial government conspicuously desired to purchase land, which may have made tribes, nervous that the government would favor sellers over nonsellers, quicker to offer land for sale.[34] Territorial relationships among tribes, meanwhile, took on a sharper edge. Before colonization, disputed zones of land between the acknowledged territories of two tribes could be left in dispute, either to remain unvisited or to be shared by members of both. The prospect of land sales suddenly made those zones more valuable, as they could now be converted into money. The result was a classic prisoners' dilemma, or rather a series of dilemmas all over the colony. Where land was claimed by two tribes, neither tribe could afford to decline to sell, for fear that the land would be sold by the other. Without consultation between the tribes, the land would be sold even if neither tribe individually wished to sell. The problem could be solved only by coordinating the activities of tribes. The Maori would manage to achieve such coordination only in the 1850s, after much of the land had already been sold.

Early willingness to sell land also stemmed in large part from cultural misunderstandings as to the import of the transaction. The earliest European traders were, of necessity, bicultural. Without the presence of many other Europeans, traders learned the Maori language, married Maori women, and were effectively accepted as members of a tribe. The "sale" of land, in this context, was a way of bringing an outsider into the community, with the same privileges and responsibilities as other members. Traders from Sydney were "settled among the natives," Richard Hodgskin observed in the late 1830s, "living in security under the protection of the chiefs, on whose territory they resided."[35] This sort of transaction was as new to the Maori as it was to the British, but the Maori seem to have understood it as creating the familiar relationship between the "purchaser" and the land's resources. A British person residing in their midst, like any tribe member, owned the right to use particular resources in particular ways (such as land for cultivation), but not the ability to convey those resources to others, and only so long as the right was maintained by actual use.[36] The Maori interpreted the transaction within the categories of their own property system.

As the pace of settlement increased in the 1840s, and the British began living in communities of their own rather than among the Maori, they began more and more to interpret transactions within their own categories instead. They often believed themselves to have acquired the right to use every resource within a geographic space. This divergence in understanding caused each side to look upon the other's conduct as at variance with the agreement. When the British used land for a purpose other than that for which the Maori intended it to be sold, the Maori saw overreaching. One purchaser in Whangarei, for instance, tried in 1844 to remove manganese from land he believed he owned outright, and was told that while he may have purchased the right to use the land, he had not purchased the right to remove the stones from the land. A similar incident happened a few years later in Rotorua. When the Maori, on the other hand, perceiving the British to be taking more than they had bargained for, demanded extra payment, the British saw an unreasonable seller asking to be paid twice for the same land. The result, complained one government official to Colonial Secretary Andrew Sinclair, was "a most injudicious system by which in fact the Natives obtained nearly double payment for their lands."[37] Maori disaggregation of use-rights could, at its worst from the British perspective, allow the "sale" of the same geographic space several times over, on the assumption that many people would simultaneously be using the same resources, or that different people would be using different resources in the same place. Here the British saw simple deviousness. The mixture of two inconsistent systems of property rights produced mistrust on both sides.

Some of the more perceptive early colonists recognized what was happening. Charles Terry, who was in New Zealand during the large speculative purchases of 1840, complained that "the natives were quite unconscious of what they had really conveyed by these ready-made deeds." Thomas Cholmondeley, writing in 1854, cut to the heart of the issue. "Until quite recently," he concluded, "when they sold land to the stranger, they thought they only sold the right to do that which they had themselves been used to do with it, which was to use it in common with another to dwell and build upon." But noticing this disparity did not necessarily mean that one would refrain from exploiting it. William Wakefield traveled to New Zealand in 1839 bearing instructions from his employer, the New Zealand Company, to explain as clearly as possible to the Maori just what the sale meant. "It may be doubted," he was told, "whether the native owners have ever been entirely aware of the consequences" of selling land. "Justice demands . . . that these consequences should be as far as possible explained to them." On board the *Tory* during the long trip, Wakefield reflected in his journal that "the insecurity of all the uncivilized Aborigines of European Colonies essentially depends on their weakness arising from comparative ignorance."[38] He then promptly bought up one-third of the country.

Such became the standard way even the purchasers most sympathetic to the Maori addressed this cultural gulf; rather than purchasing property according to the Maori sense of the transaction, they tried to explain to the Maori the meaning of a sale in Britain. The purchase of use-rights within the Maori property system would have required settlers to live among the Maori in mixed communities and to adopt many Maori methods of acquiring food, whereas the purchase of geographic spaces enabled the British to replicate the communities and the farms they had left. Had the British been successful early in accurately conveying the meaning of a sale, perhaps little harm would have been done. But in the early years of land purchasing, the practical obstacles to translation were insuperable. Because the European conception of a land sale did not exist in Maori culture, the Maori language lacked words to describe what the British believed they were doing. Deeds translated into Maori had to use existing Maori words, so translation was necessarily imprecise. Recent close analyses of the wording of early Maori deeds suggest that the Maori would have understood some as conveying only use-rights, and only the ability to exploit those rights as part of a Maori community, and others as conveying less than what the British thought they were receiving. Because the Maori lacked writing before European contact, and in the early nineteenth century still possessed a primarily oral culture, they would not have conceptualized a written deed as the sole means of putting an agreement into effect, and they would likely have been unaware that contemporaneous oral statements were not as important as what was written on paper. And, of course, not all purchasers were well-meaning or fluent in Maori. Because they were under pressure to acquire land as quickly as possible, it is not likely that all purchasers wished to ensure a congruence between English and Maori interpretations of each transaction.[39]

The date at which the Maori realized what the British meant by a sale most likely varied from place to place, as different tribes experienced purchases and their aftereffects at different times. By the 1860s at the latest, the British meaning of a land sale appears to have been understood throughout the colony. The Maori still owned a large majority of the North Island.

Colonists disagreed as to whether, once the Maori understood the British meaning of a sale, they were able to bargain with the British as equals. The question was important, because different answers generated different ideas as to the appropriateness of protective legislation. Many of the British humanitarians, who typically had never been to New Zealand themselves, were certain that the Maori lacked the intelligence to negotiate with the British. "Can thinking persons really believe that a barbarous, uncivilized people are in a condition to make a 'perfectly-understanding' bargain for the transfer of their lands?" asked an indignant John Beecham. "The child would 'freely' part with a diamond in the rough, of incalculable value, for a showy trinket of no worth; but would any one attempt to justify such a bargain with a child, on the ground that the child gave its 'perfectly-understanding consent'?" The Maori are "immeasurably inferior" to the British, affirmed the Reverend Montague Hawtrey, in the course of advocating "Exceptional Laws in Favour of the Natives of New Zealand."[40]

Settlers who had actually bargained with the Maori often disagreed. "They have like the Jews a great natural turn for traffic," observed the missionary Samuel Marsden, who accordingly suspected that the Maori had "sprung from some dispersed Jews, at some period or other." The surveyor Samuel Stephens less charitably decried "the usual jewishness and avarice of their tribes." Jewish or not, the Maori were often perceived as skilled negotiators, who drove a hard bargain in any circumstance. "They will exact payment for the most trifling service," William Brown complained. "If they saw a white man drowning, their first idea would be to bargain for the extent of the *utu* (payment) for saving him." This shrewdness was equally manifest in land negotiations. As settlement increased the demand for land, the Maori increased their prices accordingly. "Some 3 Years ago the Natives would have been satisfied with £300 for their Land here," wrote the missionary William Ronaldson from Wanganui in 1844, "but the other day they refused £1,000." One experienced land purchaser believed the Maori to be "a great deal sharper" than the Europeans with whom they had to negotiate. When the colonial government created the office of Protector of Aborigines, in part to prevent too much one-sidedness in land purchases, he scoffed: "Talk of a protector for the natives indeed; they want a protector for the whites, I think, more than for the natives; it is very seldom that you hear of a native being imposed upon."[41]

Yet many of the settlers believed the opposite, that the Maori were no match for the British when it came to negotiating a land purchase. "Large tracts of land are parted with by the natives for a camp-kettle, or a few trinkets," the *New Zealand Gazette* argued in 1839, "and even the missionaries . . . have shown themselves not less expert than the rest of the population in this species of cheating." The trader Joseph Montefiore believed that once the Maori had made "progress in Civilization" they would "be aware that they had made very bad Bargains." The Supreme Court of New Zealand relied heavily on this perception to justify the Crown's right of preemption. "To let in all purchasers, and to protect and enforce every private purchase," the court explained, "would be virtually to confiscate the lands of the Natives in a very short time."[42]

Neither view was uncolored by personal motives. Settlers who had already purchased land had every incentive to represent the Maori as shrewd sellers, in order to protect the validity of their own titles, which might be called into question otherwise. People who had not purchased land, or who hoped to obtain more, had an interest in upsetting the transactions that had already taken place.[43] Maori bargaining skill, like Maori understanding of the British property system, most likely varied from place to place. Tribes from which land had been bought earliest, and near which British towns first grew, were probably the quickest to develop the capacity to negotiate as equals. In the early transactions, the British had an enormous advantage over the Maori: they had the experience of previous colonial ventures in North America and Australia. They had a good sense of the prices at which land would sell ten or twenty years into the future. They knew that land prices would shoot up with the declaration that New Zealand was a British colony, and would rise again as more British emigrants arrived. The Maori, never having been colonized before, had no way of acquiring this information until the anticipated events actually happened. A single kettle was one more kettle than anyone had ever offered for the land before. The value of information has rarely been so high. As settlement began to raise the price of land, district by district, the Maori could see what was occurring and could adjust their future bargaining tactics accordingly. Eventually, after enough land purchasing, the British informational advantage would have dissipated.

Yet all these circumstances—misunderstandings as to the meaning of a sale, Maori inexperience in selling land, Maori inability to predict the future course of prices—would have been much less important had the colonial government not been the sole legal land purchaser for all but one of the years 1840 to 1865. In a perfect market, where would-be land purchasers competed with one another to buy land, Maori beliefs as to the meaning of a sale would not have affected the prices the Maori received for land. The purchasers would have bid up prices to the level at which they would have been had the Maori possessed complete information as to the intentions of the British. The same is true of Maori inability to predict future prices. If prospective purchasers had to compete with one another, the market price for land would have turned out the same. Inexperience in negotiating might have mattered, to the extent that it would have caused the Maori to accept an early offer rather than waiting for a better one, but that is a lesson that could have been easily learned.

No market is perfect, of course, and the high costs of transportation and communication probably made colonial land markets less perfect than most. Nevertheless, it seems likely that the government was able to exploit its informational advantage to a far greater extent than it could have in a competitive market. If an offer to buy land was misinterpreted as an offer to share use-rights, a low price might not seem as low as it really was, and there were no other purchasers legally entitled to offer a higher one. If the Maori wrongly believed that land prices would remain stable, they might accept an inadvisably low price, without the chance of being rescued by another prospective purchaser offering a better one. A competitive market is a powerful corrective for ignorance. One need not know the market value of what one owns in order to receive its market value upon sale. When there is only one lawful purchaser, on the other hand, a seller will pay very dearly for ignorance, as the purchaser can squeeze out the full disparity between what an asset is really worth and what the seller thinks it is worth. Between 1840 and 1865, that is in large measure what happened to the Maori.

The power of preemption made the colonial government simultaneously a monopsonist with respect to the Maori and a monopolist with respect to the British; it was the only lawful purchaser of Maori land and the only lawful seller of Maori land to settlers. The government unsurprisingly realized a tidy profit in these roles. "There being but a single buyer and no competition," admitted former attorney general William Swainson, "the price given is below the market value." By 1844 it had paid slightly over four thousand pounds for land, but had realized more than forty thousand pounds in land sales. Similar profits from land dealings continued through the 1850s. The result was a steady stream of revenue for the government, which was spent on government services.[44] Because the government was British, staffed entirely by British people and managed primarily for the benefit of the settler population, the net effect of preemption was to transfer wealth, from the Maori and from British purchasers of Maori land, to the British population generally. Most of the British residents of New Zealand were land purchasers at one time or another, so the net effect was very nearly a wealth transfer from the Maori to the British.

The Maori were not slow to figure this out. "The natives have heard of the Government buying at a cheap and selling at dear rate," explained a man named Paora. "They do not like it. The natives do not know what is done with the money."[45] The British humanitarians with an interest in the Maori complained as well. "From the *smallness of the price paid, and the largeness of the price demanded by the resale*," argued the *New Zealand Journal*, "the natives are taught to know and to believe that they are oppressed and unfairly dealt by." As a result, William Porter observed on the floor of the House of Representatives in 1855, "the Natives [are] anxious to sell to settlers, but averse to sell to Government—a difficulty which would increase as the Natives acquired more intelligence."[46]

Price comparisons between different periods are never perfect, because of the many factors that can influence prices and because of the variable quality of land offered for sale, but it is at least suggestive that after Hawke's Bay was opened to competitive private purchasing in 1865, private purchasers acquired 145,233 acres in the district between 1865 and 1873, for a total of £101,335, or an average price per acre of over thirteen and a half shillings. Before 1865, when the government had been the sole lawful purchaser, land in Hawke's Bay had sold for a bit over six pence per acre. Land prices obtained by the Maori from private purchasers were thus twenty-seven times higher than prices obtained from the government. After several years spent purchasing nearly the whole South Island on the government's behalf, Walter Mantell concluded that he had acquired over £2,000,000 worth of land for the payment of £5,000 and promises of schools and hospitals.[47] Schools and hospitals for a population of three thousand were worth nowhere near £1,995,000 in the first half of the nineteenth century. Much of the shortfall is attributable to the government's monopsony power.

Preemption was defended primarily on paternalistic grounds. Settlers and land speculators, it was often urged, would quickly swindle the Maori out of their land if unchecked by government. (The implicit assumption in the argument was that government land purchasers would use more honorable methods.) Looking back on the scramble of 1839 and 1840, the argument made some sense. No longer were speculators purporting to snap up huge territories from Maori lacking the authority to sell. The government purchasers of the 1840s were more careful in attempting to secure the consent of the proper tribes, and the proper individuals within those tribes. And if prices were not very high, they were at least a bit higher than they had been during many of the so-called purchases of 1839 and 1840. Preemption was an established part of British colonial policy, much older than the colonization of New Zealand, but it seemed a perfect fit for the new colony.

The argument contained a great deal of hypocrisy as well, as was frequently noted at the time. Government monopsony was not the only alternative to an unregulated private market. An obvious third path would have been to allow competitive private purchasing, and thus provide the Maori with a price more closely approximating the land's market price, while policing the market to prevent the reemergence of the dubious transactions of 1839 and 1840. But doing so would have required the colonial government to give up a major source of revenue in the spread between purchase and sale prices for Maori land, and that cost was too high. "The object of the preemptive right is less to protect native interests, than to prevent the Natives from coming into competition with the Crown in the disposal of waste lands," argued one of preemption's sharpest critics. Preemption's long life as part of British colonial law was doubtless due in large part to the advantage it gave to the government rather than to any benefits it provided for the native population. In New Zealand, preemption had been instituted ostensibly "to prevent third parties from taking undue advantage" of the Maori, but by forcing the Maori to accept a purchase price well below what it would have been in a competitive market, "the Government thus stands in the place of these very third parties, and whilst professing solicitude for the welfare of the Natives, literally renders them the victims of its own cupidity."[48]

Preemption was possible only because the British were politically organized into a single unit capable of enforcing its monopoly over land. Had the Maori been able, they could have fought back with the same weapon, by forming a single organization to control the sale of land, and then either setting the price of land higher than that offered by the government or refusing to sell at all. Before the 1850s the Maori were simply too divided to organize in this way. Ancient tribal divisions could not be erased in a few years. Preemption demonstrated the importance of political organization in structuring the marketplace. Two peoples converged, and the well organized was able to take wealth from the poorly organized.

MAKE FAST THE LAND

Maori political fragmentation often caused difficulties for the colonial purchasing program, by adding to the costs of completing transactions.

Government purchasers sometimes found themselves negotiating simultaneously with more than one tribe, each of which claimed the land the government sought to acquire. "Our lands we cannot divide," two tribes informed Donald McLean in 1844, "as it is joint property and . . . if we divide our lands it will cause disputes." When McLean responded that "the governor wishes me to find out the distinct portions belonging to each individual or Tribe," he discovered that the would-be sellers were unable even "to divide themselves into tribes." Government surveyor (and future Native Land Court judge) Theophilus Heale complained that the only way to learn which tribe possessed which land "was by separate interviews with the different claiming tribes, who had a constant tendency to exaggerate their claims in order to counteract the exaggerations which they knew the other parties would use." The effect of the prospect of selling land was that "all the old disputes and tribal feuds were renewed and exasperated."[49]

Even in peaceful conditions, where a purchase could be made from a single tribe, the cost of making the acquisition was often substantial, because of the sheer number of individuals possessing rights within the relevant geographic space. "From such complicated titles to land," future native secretary Edward Shortland noted, "it will be evident to any one, that to make an unexceptionable purchase of land from the aborigines of New Zealand requires both experience and caution." A purchaser had to learn who possessed what rights, and who was authorized to speak and receive payment on the tribe's behalf. The whole process, McLean explained, was "a matter of considerable difficulty," which required government officials "to acquire a knowledge of the Native tribes" and "to give their undivided energy and attention to the purchase of land." Even after an agreement had been reached, the question of who would receive the money for further distribution to tribe members could take much time to resolve. Given the task of paying two hundred pounds in silver to a group already assembled, government land purchaser J. W. Hamilton took an entire day simply to figure out who should get the money, a problem Hamilton could solve at the day's end only by proposing to make an initial division into three allotments and then letting the sellers subdivide it further after he had gone home. Late in the evening, when more disagreement arose as to exactly where Hamilton should leave one of the three allotments, he escaped only by pretending his knowledge of Maori was insufficient to understand what was being asked of him.[50] The difficulty in getting large numbers of people to agree on the terms of a sale was a factor present in each transaction, and one that added significant costs to each purchase.

The situation grew even more acute from the British perspective in the 1850s, when the Maori were able to exploit these transaction costs in an effort to prevent future land sales. Individual Maori who opposed particular land sales had long tried various ad hoc ways of disrupting them. Small groups sometimes sabotaged surveys, by pulling out pegs or using force to prevent surveyors from entering an area. William Bertram White recalled having to perform "a flying survey" in 1843, when "Rangiaiata had sworn he would eat the next man who went there." Walter Mantell, surveying in the South Island in 1848, recorded in his journal, "Metehau set fire to the men's hut attempted to pull the tent down and was about to attack me with a tomahawk but was prevented by the other Natives." Beginning in the late 1840s, however, these efforts grew larger and better organized, as more and more Maori came to perceive that land sales generally were contrary to their long-term collective interest. It was reported in 1847 that the Maori in Wellington had persuaded those near Taranaki to abandon a contemplated sale. The following year saw the first of several widely attended meetings devoted to the subject of land sales, at which representatives of several tribes discussed the possibility of organizing so as to bring sales to a halt. These efforts continued for several years. "There is another monster meeting to be held soon," future Native Land Court judge John Rogan reported from New Plymouth in 1855, "which I suspect has reference more to their confederation against the sale of land" than to any other issue of the day.[51]

By the mid-1850s, the tribes inhabiting much of the North Island had succeeded in organizing so as prevent further land sales. A Board of Inquiry examining land-purchasing practices reported in 1856 on the formation of "a league," the members of which "refuse to sell their lands. . . . This league . . . embraces nearly the whole of the interior of the island, and extends to the east coast and to the west coast." At "a grand council of nearly all the most influential chiefs of this island," the *Spectator* reported in 1856, "the first subject of discussion was the land: it was unanimously decided that no more should be sold by the natives to the Government." The King movement, as the organization soon became known, was formally headed by a king, but the king lacked much true governmental authority, which remained with the tribes. He was instead largely a formal device for mutually agreeing not to sell land; each tribe would place its land under the king's authority, which gave the king the right to forbid sales. "Our first object is to make fast the land," summarized Tomo Whakapo at one King movement meeting. "Men have heard in all parts of the island, and have brought their land and themselves too, and said [to the king] here is our land and our blood, hold them fast." Later in the century, when the King movement occupied a smaller and more concentrated territory, it would take on many of the characteristics of an independent state. But in its early stages it was primarily a confederation of tribes who agreed not to sell land to the government. "O man who persists in selling land," exhorted the movement's newspaper, *Te Hokioi,* "yours is not simply a sale, but a casting away of the sacred things of God. . . . Although the parcel of land may be yours, you will not be allowed to sell it." By 1860, entire districts were reported to be in sympathy with the movement, and land sales had nearly ground to a halt.[52]

Agreements not to sell are usually very difficult to enforce, because of the opportunities for profit available to defectors. Each participant faces a strong incentive to be the first to cheat, in order to become the only seller of a commodity the cartel has made scarce. For this reason most cartels do not last very long. The King movement succeeded in restricting sales in part because of the government's power of preemption. Unlike most sellers, Maori land sellers faced a single purchaser. A restriction on the supply of land would not cause the price of land to go up unless the government was willing to pay the higher price. Because the government would not pay a higher price, would-be defectors were not tempted by the prospect of land prices higher than normal. Without this incentive to cheat, there was little cheating.

The King movement also succeeded in restricting sales because the Maori were able to exploit the high transaction costs associated with purchasing land from tribes. A rough tribal consensus was required to sell land, which meant that any sizeable contingent opposing a sale, even one short of a majority, would be able to block it. Once a contingent of that size sympathized with the King movement, *all* future sales would effectively be blocked. High transaction costs had hindered the Maori in the early years, when sales were viewed as desirable; they helped the Maori in the 1850s, when sales were not.

Resistance to land sales succeeded just as increased emigration was causing the British to anticipate a large rise in the demand for land. Government officials felt strong public pressure to ensure an adequate supply of land. They were accordingly alarmed by Maori efforts to restrict sales. "Submission to Her Majesty's Sovereignty," Governor Gore Browne lectured a Maori assembly in 1861, requires that "men do not enter into combinations for the purpose of preventing other men from acting, or from dealing with their property, as they think fit. This is against the law." Looking back two decades later, the minister James Buller conceded that "they had the same right to make such a league as the British workmen have to form 'trades unions,'" but that didn't mean he had to like it. "In the one case as in the other," he concluded, "the tendency was mischievous, because of the coercive spirit." British sympathy for restricting land sales was considered nearly tantamount to treason. When two missionaries anonymously published a circular urging the Maori not to sell their land, the result was a government investigation and "much public indignation." Officials looked for signs that the movement "is likely to die out," as one reported hopefully, or that "there are few amongst the Natives who will not admit that the arguments we use to shew them that it would be for their good to sell the land are right and proper."[53] But such signs were few.

The pressure on the colonial government to ensure an adequate supply of land was placed squarely on government land purchasers, who increasingly felt the need to complete transactions quickly, a need intensified by the private purchases and leases being unlawfully conducted in areas where government purchasers had been unable to acquire land. In Hawke's Bay, for instance, officials found much of the land they sought to purchase already occupied by settlers leasing directly from local tribes. Under this pressure, government land purchasers cracked. In the 1850s they increasingly began to cut corners. The government began to receive more and more complaints that its land purchasers had not obtained the consent of an entire tribe or even a majority of the owners within a geographic space, but had negotiated quick, secret agreements with a minority faction willing to sell. "The former mode of buying land was that all the people should assemble," charged Renata Tamakihikurangi in 1861, "but afterwards it went wrong, and this was the cause—the sale by single individuals" rather than by all owners acting collectively.[54]

By the early 1860s, conflict over ostensible land purchases from a mere handful of owners had erupted into full-scale war against the King movement. "You saw what the cause of the whole war was," accused Teni te Kopara. "This is the cause and the evil—Land. There are many living on it, all claiming the land through common ancestors," who had not been consulted by government purchasers in the previous decade. Even many government officials agreed. "If proper care had been taken to inquire as to the owners," conceded James Mackay, who had himself been a land purchaser in the 1850s, "in that case the war would not have arisen."[55] At the war's end, the colonial government would accordingly devote considerable attention to transforming its method of purchasing Maori land. If purchases could no longer be made from tribes, perhaps they could be made from individuals.

chapter three

New Zealand

Conquest by Land Tenure Reform

L ONG BEFORE THE British encountered difficulty in purchasing land from tribes, the idea of reforming the Maori property system had been circulating among the settlers and the British humanitarians. Most perceived the British method of assigning property rights in land, in which rights were organized by geographic space and embodied in written records, to be a great advance over an unwritten system organized by use-rights. Some advocates of reform seem genuinely to have had the best interests of the Maori in mind. "Each plot should be assigned to one, or at most a few individuals," urged one British writer in 1847, and "all land should be held under title-deeds from the Crown." The alternative, he believed, would be the certain extinction of the Maori.[1] Other proponents of anglicizing Maori land ownership were more interested in protecting British land purchasers from the ambiguities of a property system with no written records or surveyed boundaries. So long as land could be easily purchased from tribes, however, the colonial government was able to avoid the labor, the expense, and the risk of angering the Maori that would have inevitably been associated with reform.

As the North Island tribes began refusing to sell in the 1850s, colonial officials, facing strong public pressure to acquire more land, started casting about for alternative methods of purchase. Settlers "lusting for 'fresh fields & pastures new' will soon begin to howl" if more land could not be obtained, worried Prime Minister Edward Stafford. "Under such a pressure . . . the existing system—were it the very wisest & best ever devised—cannot be maintained." The problem was "the necessity which it involves of obtaining the consent of a large number of the owners," argued the Anglican bishop George Selwyn. One obvious alternative was finally to substitute the British for the Maori system of property ownership. If individual Maori owned geographic spaces, and had the liberty to decide for themselves whether or not to sell, a vast amount of land would be available for purchase. Tribe members dissenting from the tribe's collective decision not to sell would no longer be bound to follow; they could simply sell their own parcels. "Much of the land held by individual natives under a Crown title, would speedily come into the market and become available for purposes of colonisation," the former attorney general William Swainson predicted.[2]

Inquiries among the Maori confirmed the likelihood that many would sell their land if given the opportunity. The Maori in Otaki looked so favorably upon the "individualisation of title," reported Archdeacon Octavius Hadfield in 1858, that they would even "be quite prepared to bear the whole expence of the necessary surveys." At a meeting between government officials and the chiefs of some of the tribes participating in the King movement, some of the chiefs declared that "if they got their Crown titles they should withdraw from the movement." A group of Auckland settlers, petitioning the government to convert Maori property rights into British, believed some Maori landowners so eager to sell that they were already carrying out the conversion on their own, by drawing "rude maps on which each allotment is marked with its owner's name."[3]

So the prospect of converting the Maori into the British system of property rights in land moved to the center of settler consciousness in the late 1850s and early 1860s, as a means of piercing Maori resistance to land sales. The project was often referred to as "individualizing title," a name that accurately enough conveyed the anticipated end result—individual Maori ownership of plots of land—but was misleading as applied to the process as a whole. The Maori already had, in a nontechnical sense, "individual titles," but they were titles to particular resources rather than geographic spaces. What the colonists anticipated was not so much individualizing Maori ownership as reorganizing it in spatial terms, to resemble British practice.

The perceived need to break down Maori refusal to sell land was the catalyst that caused the colonial government to consider seriously the possibility of transforming the Maori system of property rights, but once the issue was on the public agenda it provoked an outpouring of a host of other British attitudes toward land ownership. These attitudes further strengthened the support for converting Maori property rights into British ones. All were longer term in nature; that is, they did not spring from the immediate situation with respect to land sales.

CIVILIZATION AND BARBARISM

Many colonists had an insight that would come readily to many today—that the Maori system of property rights was less efficient than the British system, in the sense that land could be more productive if divided spatially, because of the incentives provided by the ownership of geographic space. "So long as their lands are held in common they have, properly speaking, no individual interest in improvements," argued Resident Magistrate Walter Buller, "and consequently there is little or no encouragement to industry or incentive to ambition." Legislative Councillor Henry Tancred contrasted British and Maori property ownership: "The one implies a busy, active, bustling life; the other, a life of indolence and inactivity."[4] As these examples suggest, the argument was sometimes expressed too bluntly, in terms suggesting the speaker believed the Maori to possess no individual property at all. Property owned as a true commons will, in the absence of compensating regulation, provide incentives toward inactivity, but a system of property ownership organized in terms of individual use-rights need not. The owner of a right to catch birds in a particular tree does not face the collective action problem associated with a true commons. No one else can free ride on his bird-catching efforts. The more birds he catches, the more he can eat, and, if there is a market for birds, the wealthier he will be. The most strongly worded condemnations of Maori property ownership on grounds of inefficiency were thus unjustified, if taken literally.

If these criticisms are understood more loosely, however, as using words like *commons* and *communal* to refer not to a nonexistent true commons but rather to the Maori system of property ownership as it actually was, and as referring not to productivity in the abstract but to productivity for certain commercial purposes, the criticisms were on target. For many land uses unknown before European contact, Maori property division probably *was* less efficient than British. Large-scale commercial farming, for instance, required coordinating the activities of many people occupying a large area of land. The British normally accomplished this by uniting ownership of all the land in a single person, who was then understood to have the power to direct the activities of everyone else present on the land. For the Maori to have organized a large commercial farm without abandoning their system of property rights would have required coordinating every individual with the right to use a resource in the relevant space. This would not have been impossible, particularly if the task of organization could have been undertaken within the preexisting tribal political system, but it would most likely have been more costly than the British way. These greater administrative costs would have made Maori commercial farming, all other things being equal, less profitable than British commercial farming. The comparison may be drawn even more sharply with a land use like constructing and operating a hotel. The administrative cost of assembling the necessary land area within the British system of property rights may not have been trivial, but it was probably much lower than it would have been within the Maori system, where it might have required the consent of hundreds of individuals possessing use-rights. The British, who had long inhabited a market economy, had developed a system of property ownership conducive to it. The Maori, who had not, had not. The market economy that arrived in New Zealand with the British favored the spatial division of land.

A second kind of productivity argument was also frequently made in support of transforming Maori land ownership. If any single proposition could have commanded near unanimity among the settlers, it was that, as the *Taranaki Herald* put it, "the want of land—open, available, accessible land—when hundreds of thousands of acres lie waste and unprofitable around, is the great misfortune under which we labor." Most Maori land was not currently being cultivated, and that, to many colonists, was an intolerable waste of the colony's most valuable asset. "They have too much land, and they do not use it," complained one minor government official. "Unless the land is in a state of production the Natives should be compelled to make it productive."[5] Land not under cultivation was, in the telling phrase used officially throughout the century, "waste land." (Land converted from its natural state to agricultural uses was, by contrast, "improved" land.) There was something intuitively wrong about letting perfectly good land sit uncultivated, especially when back in Britain there were millions of people with no land at all.

The Maori were not the only ones criticized for wasting land by letting it lie uncultivated. In the early years of colonization, the settler newspapers were unsparing in their criticism of absentee landowners, Europeans committing the same sin. The newspapers consistently urged the colonial government to impose a tax on unoccupied land, as a way of discouraging absentee ownership and putting more land into cultivation.[6] That the argument was applied equally to Europeans and Maori is strong evidence of the sincerity with which it was held. Criticism for not using land was not just a cover for racial prejudice. An antipathy to waste ran deep.

A third kind of efficiency argument was well summed up by Edward Shortland, the former native secretary. "What greater boon to both races," he asked, "than an inexpensive and safe means of exchanging surplus lands for cash, or other property, with mutual satisfaction?" A well-functioning land market would in principle enhance the wealth of all participants, by directing land ownership toward those who valued it most highly and allowing others to obtain something else instead. The advantage to thwarted land purchasers in opening up a land market was obvious, perhaps so obvious in retrospect that one can lose sight of the potential advantages to the Maori that were perceived at the time. But this was a point that was sometimes made by people who appear to have been genuinely interested in Maori welfare. In the market economy the Maori could not avoid entering, it was not necessarily in their interest to have all their eggs in one basket, even if that basket was land. "The greatest blessing next to the Gospel we could confer on the Aborigines would be to persuade them (if it were possible to do so) to sell three fourths of their waste lands," argued the missionary Jonathan Morgan in 1861. "If they would sell three fourths, and invest the money in sheep and cattle . . . they would in a very few years have an independent income, and be able to support and educate their children, provide endowments for their schools and churches, etc. etc."[7] The Maori had lived for centuries without investing capital in their land because there was no capital to invest, but continuing in that way after colonization would only ensure increasing poverty relative to the British. Capital could be obtained only by selling part of the land, the Maori's only significant asset. The sale of some Maori land, in short, would lead to greater productivity for the portion the Maori retained. If the traditional Maori property system was retarding sales, that was only harming the Maori in the long run. They would therefore gain as much as the British from a switch to the British property system.

But the Maori's failure to cultivate much of their land was, in the eyes of the British, much more than inefficient resource use. It was the violation of one of the most familiar—in fact, the very first—of the Lord's commands. As every settler knew well, just after creating Adam and Eve, God had instructed them in no uncertain terms to "replenish the earth and subdue it." Noah had received the same command, with the same priority, right after the end of the flood. Allowing fertile land to lie uncultivated was worse than a waste; it was a sin. "In fulfilling the work of colonization we are fulfilling one of our appointed tasks," Henry Sewell explained on the floor of the Legislative Council. "It is our duty to bring the waste places of the earth into cultivation, to improve and people them. It was the law laid upon our first parents—to be fruitful and multiply, and replenish the earth and subdue it—to restore the wilderness to its original gardenlike condition. In doing this work we are fulfilling our mission."[8] The Maori were not the only ones whose relationship with the land was suffused with myths of origin.

Any means of bringing more land into cultivation, whether by the Maori or the British, would help fulfill the biblical injunction. If the Maori system of property rights was deterring cultivation, by preventing sales to the British or by giving the Maori a diminished incentive to farm on their own, then reforming the system would be a form of missionary work. It would be a way of facilitating the salvation of the Maori, by turning them from a path that threatened to incur the Lord's anger. "As far as I can see," argued the Reverend James Buller, "without the co-operation of the sons of Japhet [the British], those descendants of Shem [the Maori] could not fulfill the Divine command to "'replenish the earth and subdue it.'" One judge suggested, without any hint of irony, that "substituting a freehold title for the existing one, by native custom," would be "in other words [to] evolve light from darkness, order from chaos."[9]

The close relationship the settlers perceived among farming, Maori property rights, and Christianity can be seen in a letter sent in 1859 from a well-meaning British farmer named Crompton to Thomas Williams, his Maori neighbor.[10] "You know me well," Crompton began. The two had been on good terms for eight years: they had often loaned each other equipment, and Crompton's wife had frequently given European medicine to Williams's children when they were sick. Crompton had always been careful to prevent his cattle and his sheep from disturbing Williams and the members of his tribe. "Let all these things be a proof to you of my kindly feelings towards you and your people," Crompton urged. "Listen then to my words of remonstrance and advice."

If Williams would consider English families, explained Crompton, he would "see that their children increase more rapidly than the Maories, and they do not die young nearly so often as the Maori children. Now why is this?" There was no biological difference between the English and the Maori. Both peoples were "the children of Adam. It is climate only which has made the difference in the colours of the skin," he suggested. "My blood is the same colour as yours. Cut my flesh & cut yours there will be seen no difference between them." The answer was that "the English obey Gods commands better than the Maories," by cultivating the earth more industriously, and were accordingly receiving God's blessing in the form of large healthy families. By contrast, Crompton reasoned, "your Nation is suffering a punishment" in the form of poor health and population decline. "Beware of insulting the Almighty in this manner," he warned. The only way for the Maori to gain God's favor would be "to obey the commands of God. Cultivate your soil and grow more wheat & potatoes. Breed more cattle and sheep." That goal, in turn, could be achieved only by modeling Maori property ownership on the English system. "Divide your lands into good sized farms," Crompton urged Williams, "and give to each Maori a farm for himself & his children for ever and let no man else have a claim to it." With dominion over geographic space, "by his own labour he will soon begin to have wheat and potatoes to sell . . . and cows bullocks carts & ploughs and all that he wants." By reforming the system of Maori property holding, Crompton concluded, "you will obey one of Gods commands and he will cause blessings to follow your obedience." Agriculture was much more than a way of producing food.

Property reform was also widely perceived to have important political implications. Converting to British titles, supporters argued, would simultaneously break down traditional Maori political structures and better integrate Maori individuals and the colonial government.

Maori tribes, to the dismay of many settlers, were effectively mini-states within the larger colonial state. In many parts of the colony, tribal authority was still more important than the authority of the colonial government. The power of the tribe as a political structure was derived in part from its control over land. To rid the colony of traditional Maori property ownership, therefore, would be to go a long way toward subverting the authority of the tribe over the individual. Property reform would have "a great political effect in breaking down tribal influences and tribal power," Sewell urged. "The breaking down of this tribal power is an object of the first importance." A board appointed by the government to assess the feasibility of land reform reached the same conclusion. "While they continue as communities to hold their land," the board reasoned, "they will always look to those communities for protection, rather than to the British laws and institutions."[11] Tribal authority would recede from land selling, as the tribes found their jurisdictions reduced, but it would diminish even in the areas the Maori retained if land ownership could be reconceptualized as a link between the individual and the state without the intermediation of the tribe.

The prospect of destroying tribal authority was unlikely to be viewed with favor by the chiefs who wielded that authority. Both the Maori and the British accordingly realized that the chiefs were likely to be the strongest opponents of property reform. The elderly chief Te Heuheu of the Ngati Tuwharetoa feared that accelerated land sales would make "the influence of the native chiefs pass away." Samuel Locke reported that "the leading men amongst the Natives seem to be in doubts." But as Locke recognized, the potential diminution of the chiefs' authority was likely to be favorably viewed by "the democratic parties" within the tribes, younger men resentful of the limitations imposed upon them by the traditional political structure. "The chiefs at present lay claim to some right over the whole of the land," explained a member of the Ngatipikiao in 1856, "but it is resisted by the young men." Such men might well find their own power within the community augmented by the removal of tribal author-ity. From the British perspective, these were potential allies, and were likely to be the earliest land sellers once given the opportunity. As Freder-ick Maning predicted, it was "the middle-aged and younger Natives," those less likely to share in tribal political authority, who would welcome "a means for extricating themselves from the Maori tenure."[12]

With the tribe no longer intervening between the state and the individ-ual, the colonial government would be able to exert more effective control over the Maori. Officials had long recognized this as one effect of land purchasing. Donald McLean explained in 1854 that "in the acquisition of every block of land, the Natives residing thereon . . . become amenable to English Law, and imperceptibly recognise the control of the Government in their various transactions." Property reform promised to have the same results even on land the Maori still retained. British-style titles would cause the Maori to form concentrated settlements in permanent locations, Francis Fenton hoped. "Amidst a fixed and large population . . . public opinion is formed, and can easily be moulded into a beneficial and pro-ductive form by the superintendence and care of the central power." When individuals could hold land free from the demands of the tribe, William Swainson predicted, "the Governor's power and influence over the natives would be materially increased."[13]

Property reform, it was hoped, would destroy traditional Maori collec-tive political institutions, but it would simultaneously empower Maori in-dividuals to exercise political rights in the colonial state, both directly and indirectly. In the most direct sense, voting required possessing freehold or leasehold land. The value of the necessary land was set so low that virtu-ally every owner or renter of land in the British sense was eligible to vote. Possession of use-rights, however, whether as easements under English law or within the traditional Maori framework, did not qualify one for the vote, regardless of their value. The distinction meant that most of the British, but barely any of the Maori, could vote. That seemed unfair to many, Maori and British alike, but the only solution perceived by most settlers was to change Maori property-owning practices rather than British electoral qualifications. "They can obtain the franchise just as any other man in N.Z. can, by having possession of land under Crown grants," the Taranaki settler Maria Atkinson pointed out. "Holding their own wide uncultivated wastes as they do in communistic style, it would be impossible to ground their right to vote on this sort of ownership."[14] Settlers who sincerely had the Maori's best interests at heart could, on this view, favor conversion to British-style ownership, as the only way the Maori would ever gain the right to vote and the political representation that went along with it.

In a more diffuse sense, the British were the heirs to the long tradition of thought associating freehold land ownership with civic responsibility, with the capacity for self-government and public-minded decision making. "Many of the rights of citizenship are inseparable from an individual tenure of property," Judge Henry Monro argued. "Conversion of the Native communal into an English proprietary tenure" would accordingly "confer upon its possessors of either race, not only the rights of owners of the soil, but those also of freeholders—in a word, of citizens." From New Plymouth, where an early experiment in anglicizing Maori land rights took place in 1863, Charles Brown proudly reported: "The Natives have given, in one of the Road Districts of this Province, where they hold individual titles, a proof of their capacity" for participation in government. They had voted for "a Road Rate of Sixpence an acre" and had demonstrated their good judgment by "electing two Europeans and one Native as Commissioners to expend the money," even though they outnumbered the Europeans.[15]

Productivity, Christianity, and sound government were independent reasons to reform Maori land tenure, but reform promised benefits that were even more fundamental. Over and over again, the colonists associated "civilization" with property organized by geographic space. "The difference between a people holding their country as commonage and holding it as individualized real property," Frederick Maning declared, "is, in effect, the difference between civilization and barbarism." Countless similar examples could be given. "All parts of the House were agreed," J. D. Ormond asserted in the House of Representatives, "that the individualization of title was one of the most direct and effectual steps they could take for the civilization of the Native people." Property reform, argued the legislator Charles Kettle, "would tend more to their elevation than anything else." In order to "raise these Natives out of their present low social condition, and bring civilizing agencies to operate successfully among them," Walter Buller explained, "we must commence by individualizing their lands." The failure to do so would mean "that the Maories of two generations hence will be essentially *Maori* in their manners and habits, and that they will have made little, if any, progress in the arts and comforts of civilization."[16] The feeling was so widely held that proponents of reform did not need to explain why British-style land ownership equated to civilization in order to be understood.

When they did explore the equation, their comments suggest that "civilization" was less a single concept than a broad category of desirable characteristics they found present in themselves but absent in the Maori. One subset of these characteristics encompassed all the traits conventionally subsumed under the heading of morality. Native Minister C. W. Richmond found it "indisputable that the communistic habits of the Aborigines are the chief bar to their advancement. Separate landed holdings are indispensable to the further progress of this people. Chastity, decency, and thrift cannot exist amidst the waste, filth, and moral contamination." From Wanganui, Resident Magistrate R. W. Woon reported that "their morals are not likely to improve as long as they adhere to their communistic habits, and live in the unsettled way they do." Edward Stafford castigated "that Maori communism which was the very ruin and destruction of the Maori character." But "civilization" was more than moral character. Sometimes it referred to simple neighborliness. "I have been a neighbour of Natives who held land over which Native title had not been extinguished, and I have had neighbours who held land under Crown grant," Attorney General Frederick Whitaker would later recall, "and I say that where the Natives held under Crown grant they were as pleasant and as easily dealt with as any neighbours I have ever had, while those Natives over whose land the Native title had not been extinguished were the most disagreeable neighbours." Sometimes "civilization" apparently meant a nuclear family on the British model. By "locating them on separate and individual holdings," suggested Josiah Flight in 1855, "the native woman would have a better chance of taking her proper place in the family, and be brought to exercise that humanizing influence without which our best plans for raising the social state of the Maori race will prove unavailing." Whatever civilization was, it was always something the British had but the Maori did not, and it was something that could be promoted by helping the Maori "abandon their communistic habits and ideas."[17]

The ambiguity of "civilization" as it was used in these various contexts, and its elusive connection to any particular system of property rights, suggest it was a shorthand way of describing a vague feeling that the Maori ought in general to be more like the British, a feeling that although vague was so widely shared among the British that listeners would instantly understand what one meant. Human history was understood as a progression toward civilization. In New Zealand, as in the other colonies, that meant progress from the native way of life to the British. The two ways of life differed in many respects, so progress could be achieved on any number of fronts, but some were much more difficult than others for the colonial government to influence. Property law was unusual among these respects, in that it was completely within the colonial government's control. Property law could literally be changed with the proverbial stroke of a pen, unlike, say, Maori religious beliefs or the Maori language. For this reason, it must have been particularly tempting to reform the Maori system of property.

It bears emphasizing, in view of the modern tendency to look back on European settlers worldwide as single-minded pursuers of aboriginal land, that mixed motives lay beneath all of the reasons for transforming the Maori property system that were in circulation in mid-nineteenth-century New Zealand. Many of the people advancing arguments in favor of "individualizing title" other than the naked desire to obtain land were doubtless primarily interested in the land and using a humanitarian rhetoric as a means of persuasion. Sometimes the cloak could wear quite thin. "There was no question that the vast bulk of the Native territory must pass eventually into the hands of the Europeans," John Sheehan argued on the floor of the House; "there was no use trying to disguise that fact, and talk philanthropic nonsense, because the colonization of the North Island would not, and could not, be accomplished unless we became masters of the greater portion of the territory."[18] But many of the strongest advocates for "individualizing" Maori land ownership appear to have been genuinely motivated by the desire to promote the welfare of the Maori. The question of which land policies would be in the best interests of the Maori was not as easily answered, either by the British or by the Maori themselves, in the middle decades of the nineteenth century as it might seem today. In the path of an onrushing market economy, were the Maori better off practicing traditional agriculture or British-style commercial farming? Were they better off exercising traditional tribal political rights or voting for members of Parliament? Were they better off with much land and no money or less land and some money? The answers were not clear at the time. All of these were variants of a single, fundamental question: Were the Maori better off separate from British institutions or as participants in them? The Maori were divided, and so were the genuine humanitarians among the British. The Maori who wished to engage with the market economy and the colonial government cannot all be dismissed as foolish, any more than the British who favored the same can all be dismissed as land-grabbers seeking rhetorical cover. *We* know how it would come out in the end—the Maori ended up with much less land and very little money—but no one could know that at the time.

A NATIVE LAND COURT

The goal—exchanging traditional Maori land tenure for individual spatial holdings evidenced by Crown grants—was easily enough stated, but figuring out how to achieve the goal was not a simple matter. Should the government try only to ascertain tribal boundaries, or should it partition tribal land into individual holdings? In either case, who should draw the boundaries, colonial officials or the Maori themselves? Ought the program to be compulsory for all Maori land, compulsory only for Maori land offered for sale, or optional? Was it even possible to draw lines between tribes and between individuals? If an individual tribe member possessed, say, the right to pick berries in one place, the right to till soil in another, and the right to catch eels in a third, what single area of land would be the correct size to constitute the equivalent? And where should it be located? To anyone who thought seriously about the issue, the obstacles looked formidable.

The next several years nevertheless saw a flurry of proposed methods of instituting British-style land ownership among the Maori, a process that culminated in the Native Lands Act of 1865. The act created a new court, the Native Land Court.[19] Upon receiving an application from Maori land-owners, the court was to consider the claims of the applicants and anyone else alleging an interest in the land, and, after the land had been surveyed, to issue a certificate of title stating "the names of the persons or of the tribe who according to Native custom own or are interested in the land." A group receiving land could further petition to have the land subdivided among the group's members. Maori land to which certificates of title had been issued could be leased or sold; land not yet passed through the court could not.

The Native Land Court opened its doors in 1866. After a year's work, the judges believed themselves to be succeeding in all the directions anticipated by proponents of reform. Land was moving to market. "Most of the blocks hitherto certified," reported Chief Judge Francis Fenton, "have been brought into Court for the purpose of enabling sales or leases to be made to Europeans." Land retained by the Maori was being used more productively, as British-style titles were spurring the Maori to work harder and to invest capital. "The Native Lands Act is a perfect success so far as this part of the country is concerned," explained Judge Frederick Maning from Hokianga. "The natives are getting crown grants and enclosing farms for themselves, laying down grass and going to very great expence." Even the civilization of the Maori, that most slippery of goals, was on the horizon. Maning saw the likelihood of "a completely new set of circumstances with regard to the Maori people—a revolution in fact—which must of necessity displace barbarism and bring civilization in its stead."

He concluded that the Native Lands Act of 1865 "holds out to the Maori people their last chance of temporal salvation."[20]

As for the first and most easily measured of these goals, the breaking down of Maori resistance to selling land, the Native Lands Act was in fact very successful, because of the way it transferred power from tribes acting collectively to individuals wishing to sell. Any single Maori person could start the machinery of the Native Land Court by filing an application to have title ascertained, even if every other tribe member wished to keep out of the court. Because rights to land were often the only significant asset a Maori person possessed, and because the steadily expanding market economy offered increasing opportunities for going into debt, the odds were good that at least one tribe member would need to sell. The 1873 commission appointed to examine land purchasing in Hawke's Bay reported, "Nearly all the sales which we investigated were made . . . in discharge of a previous debit balance."[21] A single individual's filing in the Native Land Court would necessarily draw the entire tribe into court, because the court would be determining the rights of everyone in the land, not just the initial applicant. If one stayed out of the proceeding, one risked losing one's interest in the land. Even if, as more and more Maori began to perceive, the collective tribal interest lay in keeping land out of the Native Land Court and off the real estate market, that sort of collective action was extraordinarily difficult, because it required keeping every single tribe member from taking on more debts than he could repay without alienating land, and persuading every single member to eschew what was by far his most accessible way of earning money.

The proceeding resulted in the issuance of a certificate of title to all the tribe's members collectively, evidencing their ownership of the land in question. A few hundred people would collectively be the registered owners of a large block of land. That was not, in itself, enough to cause the land to be sold if most of the owners did not wish to sell. Here, however, the standard rules of English property law created another collective action problem. To use a stylized example, if 500 tribe members together owned an unpartitioned block of land, each possessed the right to use the entire block. The law did not recognize particular rights of individual people, whether to geographic space or to the use of any one resource.

This was true of all land, not just Maori land, although of course little or no non-Maori land was owned collectively in this way by large numbers of people. Each of the 500 owners would also have the right to sell or lease his interest. A purchaser or lessee would acquire exactly what the seller or lessor had possessed—the right to use the entire block, shared with 499 other people.

All it took was a single Maori owner with debts to pay, and a single British settler willing to risk a small investment, for this scenario to occur. The settler leases the owner's share. He puts his cattle out to pasture on the entire block, without regard to the use-rights of anyone else on the land. The other 499 owners have no legal redress; under English law the settler has the right to use the entire block. They do too, of course, but unlike the settler, they may still feel constrained by the norms of Maori resource use, which prevent them from encroaching on the property rights of other tribe members. In any event, without capital to invest, the other 499 owners could not obtain the cattle and other items they would need to mimic the settler, and they could not get that capital without selling at least some of the land. Traditional law offers no redress to the owners, either, because the settler is highly unlikely to admit its authority, and the only way to enforce it would be physically to drive the settler off his land, an act that would be punishable in the colonial courts. The other 499 owners accordingly have to accept that their entire block will be occupied by someone else. Their only realistic choices are to either formalize the situation, and receive some money, by selling their interests to the settler, or continue to submit to what is from their perspective an unremunerated occupation with no end in sight. A sale could come to look pretty good. And so, owner by owner, a settler could acquire all 500 shares in the block of land, even if only one owner wishes to deal with the settler at the start of the process, and even if that owner only wishes to lease his interest. Individual Maori owners, when recognizing in advance that this pattern of incentives would be created, would have no reason to expect that all 499 of their co-owners would decline to sell, and so would be pushed toward selling in circumstances where they otherwise would not sell.

Later statutes addressed the issue with only slight success. The Native Lands Act of 1869 banned sales by less than a majority of the owners. The

Native Lands Act of 1873 mandated that sales or leases be consented to by *all* the owners. The same statute required Native Land Court judges, upon receiving an application to put land through the court, to make a preliminary inquiry to ascertain whether the application was "in accordance with the wishes of the ostensible owners thereof." Such provisions only pushed the collective action issue earlier in time. Settlers now needed to pasture cattle and secure the consent of the sellers before, rather than after, signing the contract and applying to the Native Land Court. In any event, the 1873 preliminary inquiry requirement, a task resented by the court's judges, was effectively repealed by an 1878 statute making it optional with the judges rather than compulsory.[22] The weakness of this legislative response unsurprisingly suggests that the British were more interested in purchasing land than in facilitating Maori resistance to selling.

The fraction of Maori owners wishing to sell their land was not so low as one in five hundred, which facilitated land sales all the more. "Opinion is much divided on the question," one resident magistrate reported in 1880. "Some are for shutting up and monopolizing their lands altogether; some are for selling portions thereof, so as to let in the European element; and others—the extravagant and reckless—would part with every acre they have."[23] The effect of the Native Lands Act of 1865 was to empower whatever fraction wished to sell to impose that view on the others. Before 1865, when selling had required a tribal consensus, a minority could prevent a sale. After 1865, a minority could force a sale.

The same set of incentives was at work with more specialized kinds of land as well. Gold mining required expensive machinery, so in the gold-mining district of Hauraki, Maori property owners leased their land to miners rather than mining the gold themselves. Whether or not it was in the local tribes' collective interest to enter into these leases—and it may not have been, as mining would cause ecological damage interfering with Maori agriculture—the difficulty of collective action pushed them into leasing. Any individual owner could enter into a lease for the use of an entire collectively owned block. No individual owner could afford to refrain from leasing his land, for fear that it would just be leased by someone else.[24]

3. A crowd gathers outside a session of the Native Land Court in Ahipara, New Zealand, in this undated photograph. The Court broke Maori resistance to land sales by, in effect, authorizing willing sellers to impose that preference on other tribe members. In the late nineteenth and early twentieth centuries, as a result, the Maori sold most of their remaining land. F-26780-1/2, Taafe Collection, Alexander Turnbull Library, Wellington, New Zealand.

The costs of collective action had once prevented land sales. Now the British had used their lawmaking power to flip the structure of incentives the other way; now the costs of collective action promoted land sales. Maori land flooded onto the market, causing the price to plummet by the early 1870s. Each year, more and more land passed through the Native Land Court and became available for sale. By the late 1860s the court was ordering certificates of title to roughly three-quarters of a million acres per year. The pace would slacken in some years, to just over half a million acres in 1872–73, and to slightly under half a million in 1876–77, but would generally hold steady at seven or eight hundred thousand acres per year until sales began to slow in the 1880s. From 1865 through 1899, approximately eleven million acres in the North Island would be permanently transferred by purchase from the Maori to the British through the medium of the Native Land Court. Several million more would be temporarily transferred by lease.[25]

Land purchasing was often intertwined with debt collection. Merchants who sold goods to the Maori on credit were able to take their property rights in land as security; when debtors were unable to repay, the land would serve as payment. Many Maori took advantage of this opportunity, and many lost their land. The government occasionally intervened weakly to limit the worst effects of the process, particularly the speed with which alcoholism could cause a person buying drinks on credit to lose his land. The Native Lands Frauds Prevention Act of 1870, for instance, declared that no alienation of Maori land would be valid if "contrary to equity and good conscience," or if part of the purchase price consisted of alcohol. The act created trust commissioners, who were to examine every transaction in Maori land for compliance with the statute. In practice, the trust commissioners could not (and often would not) exercise close control, and few if any sales were disallowed. An 1878 statute prohibited the mortgaging of Maori land that had already been passed through the Native Land Court, but that did little to prevent such transactions, which appear still to have been entered into in large numbers afterward, and it said nothing about loans made on the security of land that had not yet been through the court. Again, the weakness of the legislative response suggests that most members of the white community were not bothered by the frequency with which Maori property owners lost their land in payment of their debts. "The intemperance and waste so noticeable amongst the Maori landlords of Hawke's Bay are matters much to be regretted; but, in my judgment, it is not part of our duty to stop eminently good processes because certain bad and unpreventable results may collaterally flow from them," concluded Francis Fenton, "nor can it be averred that it is the duty of the Legislature to make people careful of their property by Act of Parliament, so long as their profligacy injures no one but themselves."[26]

The colonial government's willingness to allow the cycle of credit and foreclosure to continue was harshly criticized by some at the time. "It is quite clear, I think, that if Natives are allowed to sell their lands to an unlimited extent," one government official argued in 1871, "or on the strength of them to obtain credit from merchants to any amount, that their lands must soon all pass out of their hands and that those Natives who may survive a period of dissipation will become a disaffected lot of paupers." An angry writer to the *Otago Daily Times* complained:

> It is a matter of notoriety that in the North Island, owing to the absence of all regulations and restriction on the sales of Native Land, many valuable tracts are passing into the hands of rapacious and unscrupulous parties for very small consideration indeed.
>
> In some cases a considerable extent of rich agricultural land has been acquired for the (alleged) value of a grog score, with perhaps a few trifling articles of clothing in addition. It is quite an easy matter for a publican to procure the signature of a drunken Maori to a promissory note; and this being, as a matter of course, dishonoured at maturity, recourse is had to a mortgage, which in due time falls in, and the land becomes the property of the publican.
>
> . . . . .
>
> The result of this state of matters will be, that in the course of a few years, the Maoris having disposed of all their lands, will become a race of sturdy beggars.[27]

The Native Land Court was in this manner the conduit for the flow of a vast quantity of land from Maori to British owners over the rest of the century. This need not have been detrimental to the Maori, had they received a fair price for the land. In that case they would simply have been exchanging one asset for another of equal value. The opening up of Maori land to private purchasers in 1865 promised to create a competitive market that would give rise to prices much higher than those paid under the government monopsony in effect during the preceding decades. The Maori could have ended the century with less land but much more money. The actual operation of the court was extremely costly, however, and all those costs fell squarely on the Maori. In the end, the cost of selling land caused the Maori to receive much less than their land was actually worth.

THE LAND-TAKING COURT

By 1868, when it had been in operation for only two years, the Native Land Court was already so unpopular among the Maori that it had come to be called the "land-taking Court." The complaints came pouring in. "It has now become known that many grievances exist," summarized former chief justice William Martin in early 1871, "and that the Court itself has come to be regarded by many of the most intelligent Natives with strong suspicion and dislike." Things would only get worse. The more the court worked, the more hated it would become. "From my mixing with them I think they are all very much opposed to the Native Land Court," reported the surveyor John Gwynneth in 1891. "Nearly all the Natives I come into contact with speak against it."[28]

The court's judges sometimes accepted Maori public opinion with equanimity. "It is not to be expected that so complete a revolution as is implied in the exchange of a communal and often disputed tenure . . . for one definite," reasoned Henry Monro, "could be carried out over so large an area as that of the North Island of New Zealand without some occasional hardships being inflicted upon individuals in its progress." Fenton was even blunter. "Don't *let us deceive ourselves,*" he wrote to McLean; "it is beyond the power of man to transfer the entire land of a country from one race to another without suffering to the weaker race." When judges were not resigned to the unpopularity of their work, that tended to be because they did not perceive it. "There is no need to endeavour to make the court popular," assured Maning; "it is highly so." When asked whether litigants resented paying court fees, Edward Puckey answered: "Not so far as I know. They pay cheerfully."[29]

The reasons for Maori displeasure with the way the Native Land Court functioned were numerous, but they were all versions of the same complaint. The process of converting Maori to British property rights was proving very costly, and the Maori were bearing virtually all those costs.

That the process would be an expensive one was inevitable. In an undisputed case, conversion required at minimum a survey of the land and the time and attention of the claimants and court personnel. Even if all cases had been undisputed, converting the title to millions of acres of land possessed by tens of thousands of people would have been a costly process. Disputed cases could cause those costs to multiply very quickly. Some costs were, in this sense, inherent in the project. But many were not. The particular design and staffing of the Native Land Court imposed substantial costs as well. The inevitability of some costs, moreover, did not mean that the way those costs were allocated was also unavoidable. The way the court's proceedings were structured imposed nearly all the costs on the Maori rather than on the British.

Error

The Native Land Court, critics agreed, often resolved disputed cases by confirming title in the wrong people. Most of the cost of these errors fell on the true Maori owners of the land, who should have been awarded title. Some fell as well, in a more attenuated sense, on all Maori property owners in land not yet passed through the court, whose title was thereby rendered less secure. Some of the cost also fell on British purchasers who had arranged to buy land contingent on the Native Land Court's determination of ownership, who were likely to have financed the litigation. Repeat purchasers could compensate for these losses by offering lower prices; Maori sellers, as we will see, could not compensate by demanding higher ones.

Some of the error was attributable to corruption. Government officials, including Native Land Court judges, bought and sold Maori land on their own accounts. Private purchases by government officials were a recurring source of scandal. The court's Maori assessors were also sometimes accused of benefiting personally from their decisions. There were occasional accusations that a litigant had bribed one of the judges or assessors.[30] All told, however, the amount of error produced by corruption was likely dwarfed by the error attributable to a few other causes.

One problem was that the officials who managed the process were much more interested in facilitating land sales to the British than in ensuring that land was registered to its true Maori owner. Where these goals came into conflict, the former tended to prevail. The clearest example arose when the Native Land Court was called upon to interpret section 23 of the Native Lands Act of 1865, which stated that certificates of title could specify the names of persons or tribes, provided "that no certificate shall be ordered to more than ten persons." In conjunction with section 24, which authorized the court to order more than one certificate for a single piece of land, section 23 was almost certainly intended to mean that where there were more than ten owners, the court should either register the land in the tribal name or subdivide the land so that no part of it was owned by more than ten people. Instead, the court simply picked ten of the claimants and awarded the land to them, not as agents or trustees for the remaining owners, but as the sole owners. As Fenton suggested, this interpretation was "in furtherance of the great object of these laws . . . namely, the extinction of the Native communal ownership."[31] Limiting ownership to ten tribe members would facilitate sales, by giving purchasers fewer sellers with whom to deal.

It was also, as many protested, an enormous intra-Maori transfer of land. In each tribe putting land into the court, ten people acquired legal title to land that had formerly been the property of hundreds or thousands. In many tribes, one official recognized, the ten "appropriated to themselves the whole or the greater part of the purchase money or rents, or have mortgaged the lands so deeply that, when sold, there was no residue to be divided amongst the outsiders." A petition of 554 former landowners in Hawke's Bay despaired that "the grantees acted toward the others interested as if they were persons out of sight and living at a distance." The life's savings, so to speak, of thousands of people were wiped out. In Hawke's Bay alone, 569,000 acres belonging to nearly four thousand people were vested in only 250 grantees. Parliament responded quickly to the outcry with the Native Lands Act of 1867, which specified that for blocks with more than ten owners the certificate could bear the names of only ten, but should also note that there were additional owners, and the names of these other owners should be registered in court. The following year, however, in the first case in which the issue arose, Chief Judge Francis Fenton interpreted the 1867 act to provide the judges with the continued discretion to order certificates bearing the names of only ten people. Some of Fenton's colleagues on the court did register the additional names. By 1870, however, of the 1,769 certificates of title the court had ordered in its first five years of operation, most of which probably related to land owned by more than ten people, only 84 bore a notation that the land had more than ten owners. The issue was eventually put to rest prospectively by the Native Lands Act of 1873, which simply instructed the court to produce a document "declaring the names of all the persons who have been found to be the owners" without numerical limitation.[32] In the interim, a tremendous amount of land ended up in the hands of the wrong people, because Native Land Court judges were more interested in creating a land market than in distributive justice among the Maori.

A second problem resided in what might be called judicial values. The men appointed to the Native Land Court were generally lawyers, who had grown accustomed to practice in British and colonial courts. Colonial judges tended to bring British norms into all colonial courts, not just the Native Land Court. But the Native Land Court was unusual in that its litigants were all Maori, most of whom were encountering British judicial values for the first time, and it was unusual in that the disputes it was meant to resolve often involved not just a pair of inconsistent claims but several. The resulting confusion was a fertile source of error.

One fundamental norm of British court procedure, for instance, was the principle that a judge should consider only the evidence presented in court in reaching a decision. The judge was understood to be barred from pursuing his own extrajudicial inquiries into the facts, and from engaging in out-of-court communication with the litigants. In ordinary disputes among the British, where all relevant interests—typically only two—could be expected to present evidence in court, the norm made a great deal of sense, as it provided some assurance of equal treatment to both sides. Native Land Court judges brought this norm into their work. "I never allow any Native to say one word to me on the merits of any claim until it comes before me in court," Frederick Maning asserted with pride. "The result has been excellent . . . all parties have confidence in the impartiality of the court." Attorney General Frederick Whitaker agreed. A judge of the Native Land Court, he urged, "should stand entirely free from communication with any of the parties to a suit until the matter comes before him for judicial investigation."[33]

In many cases, however, some of the owners of land were not present in court, either because they had not received notice of the proceeding or because the cost of attending court was too high. Often the claimants present in court were only a subset of the true owners, and sometimes they were not even the true owners at all. In such cases, the judges' failure to consider evidence other than that presented in court could prove ruinous to the missing. This was perhaps unavoidable sometimes, but what made it so galling to many Maori was that often the judges could have learned of the true state of ownership simply by broadening their inquiry a bit, to include a visit to the land or interviews with people who had not been formally called as witnesses, many of whom were in the courtroom watching. "I have myself gone to the Native Land Court, and sat there during the progress of a case, just to see how it went on," explained the Maori teacher Mary Tautari, "and I have actually seen people who ought to have the land absolutely lose it." Whatever the value in other courts of the norm limiting consideration to in-court evidence, in the Native Land Court it looked like self-willed blindness, which advanced no goal besides awarding land to the wrong people. Wiremu te Wheoro, one of the court's Maori assessors, complained in 1870 that "with the present system of investigation, no matter where the land is, it is not inspected, and the land becomes the property of him who has made the most plausible statement; it goes, together with the houses and the cultivations which are upon it, to a stranger. In some cases, perhaps, the Judge of the Court has seen the cultivations and the houses, but he only pays attention to the statements made by the parties before him, and says that it would not be right for him to speak of what he has seen, but only to take what is stated in the Court."[34] Te Wheoro resigned in disgust two years later.

Colonial officials soon realized the frequency with which the norm was producing mistakes and began to urge the judges to abandon it. "The functions of the officer who presides in a Native Land Court and those of a Judge in a Court of Law are so unlike as to be almost opposite," Edward Stafford argued. Although a judge could afford to sit back and let the parties bring the facts to him, "the officer who presides in a Native Land Court has simply to find out the facts" without such severe procedural limitations. Native Minister Donald McLean argued in the House of Representatives that "some of the Judges of the Court entertained, in practice, what he conceived to be a most vicious principle, viz., that of knowing nothing of matters of fact relative to the inquiries they were prosecuting unless they were actually brought to their notice within the precincts of the Court." As a result, he admitted, "in some cases the wrong persons would have titles conferred upon them." In the Native Lands Act of 1873, McLean included a provision requiring the judges to make their own independent inquiries, before hearing the evidence, as to the ownership of the relevant land. The judges were not pleased with such a direct assault on a cherished value. "Under this section a judge would have the whole of his time taken up in travelling about the country making extra judicial and impertinent enquiries and collecting one sided and for the most part false evidence," fumed Maning, "which would only be calculated to warp his judgment when the case actually came into court." Whitaker reported a few years later that the provision "has created a great deal of difficulty" for the Native Land Court judges. The preliminary inquiries normally began with the people who had submitted the claims, ex parte contact that, the judges believed, "creates a great deal of jealousy. If one of the parties to a suit in the European Courts were permitted to go before the Judge and make an *ex parte* statement the practice would be most thoroughly condemned," he concluded, "and that appears to me to be a principle which should equally apply to the Native Courts." This resistance was enough to cause Parliament to amend the statute in 1878 to make the preliminary inquiry optional with the judges.[35] The procedure was rarely, if ever, used thereafter. The judges continued to limit themselves to in-court evidence, and the erroneous awards of land mounted up.

Mistakes might have been relatively few but for a related judicial norm, that of finality. In British and colonial courts, once a decision had been reached it was final. It could not be reopened by nonlitigants who had had the opportunity to participate in the case. Again, the norm made perfect sense in the traditional context of British litigation, where there were usually only two possible parties to any dispute and one could expect them to be present. And again the judges brought the norm into the Native Land Court, where the number of potential parties to any dispute was unknown and there was no assurance that all were present. Many cases were resolved quickly as default judgments, when only one set of claimants showed up. Once these decisions had been reached, they were beyond re-examination, even if later claimants could prove themselves to be the true owners. Again, the norm looked to many Maori like willful blindness. "If a person did not appear in Court on the day fixed, the Crown grant would be issued to the person who made his statement in Court, even though it should be false, the Court could not upset it, seeing that no person appeared to object," Wiremu te Wheoro complained. "The land is gone through a man's absence, and it is lost through lies."[36]

This combination of judicial values transplanted into the context of the Native Land Court produced a dismal set of incentives. Many Maori litigants quickly realized that if they testified unopposed at a hearing, their evidence was likely to be credited and they would be registered as the owners of the land. Some were encouraged to file claims to land in which they possessed either no property rights or fewer rights than they claimed. Some were encouraged to give false testimony in court. It did not take long before everyone involved, British and Maori alike, lamented what seemed to be an epidemic of lying in the Native Land Court. "At a recent sitting of a Native Lands Court," James Mackay recounted in 1877, "I heard a native misrepresenting a case which was within my personal knowledge; on his leaving the Court I expostulated with him on his conduct. He replied, 'I was not giving evidence to you who knew the question, but to the Court who do not know anything about it,' and doubtless there are numerous instances of the same class."[37]

"The Maoris are less affected by the administration of the oath than Europeans are," believed Native Land Court judge Robert Ward. Akapita te Tewe took a more pragmatic view. "The evidence given on oath in the Court might be of some account," he remarked, "if God were present to chastise the man who lied; as it is there is no deterrent." He recognized that "it is the system pursued by the Court that affords encouragement to this sort of thing."[38]

Lying most likely increased as time went on. Part of the increase, as the former native land agent William Moon pointed out, was due to the deaths of the older Maori men who had a better knowledge of tribal history and could rebut misstatements of fact. Much of the rise in lying, however, was attributable to a change in appointments to the Native Land

Court. The earliest judges were generally men with experience as land purchasers, who knew the Maori language and Maori property ownership practices. As John White urged in 1871, "the judges must be men who can enter into the witness's mode of thought, customs of life, and history, to arrive at a clear view of the case." Toward the end of the century, the court tended to be staffed with lawyers rather than former land purchasers. James Mackay charged in 1891 that "a great many of the appointments that have been made to it of late years have been of men who knew nothing at all about Native custom, and who could not speak Maori." The practice of law in ordinary courts was no preparation at all for the Native Land Court, where a knowledge of Maori life was the most important qualification. "The position of a man who presides in the Native Land Court without having a personal knowledge of the matters that are brought before him is extremely difficult," noted the solicitor Edwin Dufaur, who practiced in the Native Land Court in Auckland. "It is just like putting a civilian [that is, an expert on civil law, as opposed to common law] on the Supreme Court bench, and asking him to decide the case put before him."[39] As the judges became less and less informed about the subject of their cases, the chance of getting caught in false testimony doubtless decreased.

Lying was enough in itself to produce erroneous outcomes, but it may also have created error in a more diffuse way, by causing some of the Native Land Court judges to be extraordinarily hostile to the Maori litigants appearing before them. "I have just got back safe from Bedlam those Rawara I have always considered to be just as great savages as they were in Captn. Cook's time," complained Frederick Maning. But he was plotting his revenge: "I shall however give them a lesson they don't expect a sort of trick of my trade they have not taken into their speculations just yet." Whatever the trick was, it was probably not conducive to a careful consideration of the merits of the case. Other judges felt the same way. One 1876 hearing degenerated into angry squabbling between Judge John Rogan and Chief Henare Potae over who was drunk more often, after Rogan unaccountably refused to let Potae give evidence on behalf of his tribe's claim. Sitting in Ohaeawai, Judge Edward Puckey so feared being "at the mercy of the Natives" that when one litigant threatened to jump on a table Puckey abruptly adjourned the case to a nearby community.[40] Some of the judges developed a dislike for the litigants before them that could not have helped accurate decision making.

Judicial values permeated the court's decision making, repeatedly causing British judges and Maori litigants to take divergent views of how cases ought to be managed. Where litigants valued oral testimony and unwritten arrangements, judges prized the written word, so much so that in one case, when the Ngaitahu complained that the government land purchasers' oral promises of schools and hospitals had remained unfulfilled, Fenton believed himself bound by the common law's parol evidence rule and unable to consider promises "not contained or referred to in the Deed." Where litigants urged that cases could be decided more quickly and accurately if the judges rather than lawyers were to conduct the questioning, officials saw only the danger of the judge being placed "in the position of becoming a partisan."[41] When judicial norms clashed with the goal of ensuring that Maori land was registered to its true owners, it was often the norms that prevailed.

An additional cause of error was simple carelessness, an utter lack of concern on the part of many judges and other government officials as to which Maori claimants ended up owning land or receiving money. It could take many forms, any of which could be enough to wipe out someone's entire possessions. In 1875, Aria Hikurangi complained to the Napier newspaper *Te Wananga* that an apparent clerical error in the Native Land Court had caused a member of an entirely different tribe to be inserted in the grant to his tribe's land. An 1891 commission reported that "in some cases the Government has omitted names of owners from grants. . . . Lands belonging to one hapu were awarded to another; names which should have been inserted were omitted." One of the more spectacular examples of inattention to detail came to light in 1880, when it was discovered that government land purchase officer John Young had been seizing land as payment for debts without bothering to examine whether the land was owned by the same people who owed the debts. The auditor who examined Young's accounts was astonished at their "utterly random character" and the "flagrant disregard for accuracy displayed in these transactions." But what made Young's conduct even more remarkable, he concluded, was that "there seems to have been no attempt on the part of Mr. Young to turn the inaccuracies in these cases to his personal advantage." Young was careless, not corrupt. In fact, when Young was prosecuted for larceny, the court directed a verdict of acquittal, on the ground that although Young's accounts were no doubt fraudulent, there was no evidence that he had any idea of putting money in his own pocket. He simply did not care how land or money were distributed among the Maori.[42]

Carelessness was normally less sensational, but it could have even greater effects. In the Native Lands Act of 1865, Parliament neglected to address the intra-Maori distributional issues that would inevitably arise when land was divided. The default rules of ordinary English property law accordingly applied. Individuals were deemed to all own equal shares, when in fact property rights within a tribe were often not equally distributed. This oversight would be corrected prospectively in 1869, but in the interim a significant redistribution of property ownership had occurred, from Maori owning above-average amounts of property to those owning below-average amounts. The 1865 act had also failed to specify whether multiple owners would receive titles as joint tenants or tenants in common, the two main forms of concurrent ownership in English law. The difference was that at death the shares of tenants in common would pass to whomever they chose; the shares of joint tenants would pass to the surviving co-owners. In nineteenth-century English property law, the default rule was that co-owners would be deemed joint tenants. Children found themselves, to their surprise, unable to inherit the land of their parents. Joint tenancy exacerbated the effect of the ten-owner rule, because the death of one of the ten would cause his share to be distributed among the remaining nine, and so on with later deaths, until the number of registered owners was even smaller and even less representative of all the true owners. Again, the oversight was corrected in 1869, but not until a substantial amount of land had been taken from some Maori and given to others.[43]

Officials were sometimes so lax in publicizing Native Land Court hearings, when failure to attend would cause the forfeiture of an owner's rights, that they had to be reminded to distribute the notices they were given. After several erroneous default judgments caused by the failure of the true owners to receive adequate notice, in 1873 Parliament moved to correct the problem, but the ostensible solution was to require the applicants themselves to send a copy of their application "to each of the tribes hapus or persons named in the application, or believed by the applicants to be interested in any portion of the land comprised in the application." This was not a likely way of flushing out potential opposition to a claim. It also imposed substantial additional costs on the applicants. The following year, the House of Representatives received a petition, bearing 5,500 Maori signatures, asking for a repeal. In one case, the petition showed, applicants had been required to serve notice to more than 2,700 people, with each notice written out, enclosed in an envelope, and delivered, before the court could be allowed to sit. Such a burden would have been well beyond the means of most Maori landowners. Parliament quickly repealed the notice requirement. But that just left matters in the state they had been in before. Notice was published in the *Kahiti,* the Maori-language version of the official *New Zealand Gazette,* but actual notice depended on how aggressive public officials were in circulating the *Kahiti* in Maori communities, which were often located far from centers of British population. "How many European inhabitants were there who saw the *Gazette?*" asked Robert Hart on the floor of the House, implying that very few did. "And how could they feel assured, therefore, that Natives who might be living at a distance of fifty, sixty, or seventy miles from the place of publication ever saw the notices[?]" Wiremu Patene received a *Gazette* to learn that his land was at that very moment the subject of litigation in another town; he immediately set off in a canoe and arrived just in time to save the land from being awarded to someone else. "The *Gazettes* should be circulated more generally throughout the country," he concluded. "It often happens that men prefer claims to land in which they have no interest, and they deceive the Pakehas who are desirous of purchasing."[44] There was no way to be sure, before a claim was actually heard, exactly who needed to be notified. Notice was normally a matter of giving general publicity to a hearing rather than gaining the attention of any particular people. The attitudes of the individuals actually doing the notifying could thus matter a great deal.

Many colonial officials simply did not care very much whether one Maori individual or another received land. Of all the officials participating in allocating land titles, this was perhaps most true of Frederick Maning, who was appointed a judge of the Native Land Court at its creation in 1865 and served until 1876. Early in his judicial career he was already quite bitter about relationships between settlers and the Maori. "The law is a sham," he argued in 1869, "the Government is a sham, the Parliament is a sham, we are all talking nonsense to one another and making believe we believe each other, everything and everybody is all a sham, and we shall live in a dreamland until we fairly conquer the rebel natives (meaning all of them) and when we are absolute masters of the country it will be time enough to talk of technical law and civilized justice." As a judge, his contempt for the Maori grew stronger, as he came to resent the litigants before him. "The utter insolence and barbaric ignorant overweening conceit of these Maori brutes," he complained to future Native Land Court judge Spencer von Stürmer in 1872. "Untill you can make a tiger live on hay you can make nothing of the Maori, but a mean, treacherous, vain, lying and dangerous roudy, cunning as Satan and dangerous as the serpent." Land litigation, in his view, required him to "run about at the beck and call of Maori brute beasts." Sitting in Hawke's Bay in 1873 he reported "stolid ignorance, pampered, truculent, conceited barbarism, hungering and thirsting for our wealth, too lazy to labour to create wealth for themselves, envying us, hating us, but fortunately, to a certain degree, fearing us." "I have been in bedlam for a couple of weeks," he complained in 1867, "suffering the tortures of Maori litigation." He continually longed to "get rid of this Land Court trade as soon as I conveniently can," to escape "all the time wadeing through a mass of quarrelling, lying, cheating, and always liable to be deceived and do something wrong." But Maning lasted over a decade on the Native Land Court, miserable all the while. From Napier in March 1873: "the fact is it is killing me." From Waitangi in July 1873: "I am allmost at my wits end, and do not know how I shall ever pull through this court." In 1876, at the end of his career: "I am thoroughly sick of these Maori schemes having had enough of them the last ten years." Looking back on his service on the court, Maning concluded that the Maori were "d[amne]d Canibals who are scarcely done picking human flesh out of their teeth. . . . It is absolutely useless to even think of doing anything for them they are past all help."[45]

This was not the ideal state of mind in a man with the responsibility of determining which Maori tribes and individuals owned which land. It is hard to imagine that Maning could have put his disgust for the Maori aside and devoted careful attention to the merits of each claim. Maning may have been extreme in the vituperation of his private correspondence, but many officials most likely shared his indifference to issues of justice between Maori. For this reason, matters of the greatest importance to the Maori could be decided in the most casual, offhand way. Mistakes accordingly proliferated.

Most of these countless errors—caused by the desire to facilitate land sales, the importation of familiar judicial values into the unfamiliar context of the Native Land Court, and simple carelessness—were not the result of malice on the part of Native Land Court judges or other government officials. In most cases, the managers of the process were not profiting personally from the mistakes. Error in the Native Land Court did not normally benefit the British at the expense of the Maori; it typically caused some Maori to gain a windfall at the expense of others. Officials were not hostile to individual Maori so much as they were indifferent to the Maori in general. In this respect they were representative of the voters they served, most of whom had few interactions with the Maori.[46] If one Maori person rather than another ended up with a piece of land, few in power were likely to get upset.

In the short run, the loss to the true owner was offset by the gain to the person wrongly awarded the land. But over time, the accumulation of errors almost certainly reduced the income the Maori overall received for selling land. When the likelihood of error encouraged non-owners or partial owners to make arrangements to sell land, they had less of an incentive to hold out for a better price than a true owner secure in his rights would, because of their need to push the land through the Native Land Court before the truth was discovered. The likelihood of error would have caused a rational purchaser to offer less for land, to compensate for two risks: first, that after making preliminary expenditures the land would be awarded to someone else and he would be unable to buy it; and second, that after buying it he would discover that his vendors had not been the true owners, which would not necessarily disturb his own title but could cause him to suffer harassment from a competing group of Maori, who had no other means of redress. As security of ownership diminishes, so too does the value of what is owned. In this way, the mistakes of the Native Land Court imposed costs on the Maori generally.

Distance and Time

Error was an indirect cost, but the Native Land Court imposed direct costs on the Maori as well. Foremost among these were the costs of attending the court itself.

Native Land Courts were typically held in British population centers, which could be far from the Maori communities where the litigants and witnesses lived. "At the late sitting of the Land Court here" in Gisborne, Resident Magistrate James Booth informed the Native Department in 1884, "many applicants came from distances ranging up to a hundred miles." The Maori MP Wiremu Pere complained that the court sat in Cambridge, the nearest colonial town of any size, to consider land owned by people in "Taupo and Rotorua, and other distant places," requiring them "to come a long distance to attend sittings of the Court."[47]

Distance alone might not have been a serious problem had the court been able to resolve cases quickly. But sittings of the court often lasted several months. Cases could involve the testimony of scores of witnesses, each of whom had to provide a long account of tribal history and genealogy. When a case had multiple groups of claimants, each group would cross-examine each witness, which could cause delay to expand exponentially. "The Court has been sitting for the last five months," reported one spectator in 1883, "and has not yet settled a single question." The solicitor Edwin Dufaur blamed the government's method of paying the judges in part according to the number of days they spent in court. "While the judges are getting a guinea a day maintenance-money," he argued, "they will be content to let things go on in the fashion I speak of. . . . Look at the Court at Marton. It has been sitting since June last, and will continue to sit until the Natives are sucked dry." Equally serious from the perspective of Maori litigants and witnesses traveling to court sittings was the court's standard practice of accumulating many cases for a single sitting but not setting any schedule for their hearing, which required each participant to attend the entire sitting to be sure he would be present when his case was called. "The Natives congregated at the opening of the Court have to remain weeks or months even without a chance of their business being earlier reached," explained J. E. MacDonald, Fenton's successor as chief judge. At one sitting, "arrears of seven years I believe were gazetted at once."[48] Even a simple uncontested case that could be resolved in a day often required attendance at court, far from home, for several months.

Because court sittings were scheduled without reference to the agricultural calendar, attendance often required large numbers of people to be away from their land during critical seasons. An entire year's crop could be lost. Probably even more costly was the need for food and lodging for several months while attending court. One often heard of cases in which such "expenses were so great that the value of the land was absorbed in the outlay incurred attending the sittings of the court. A company that supplied the Natives with provisions charged for it, and the amount they had to pay equalled the value of the land." The land purchaser John Lundon recalled that "the first Court held at Hokianga lasted three months during which time the Natives were kept hanging about the place, and, although they were paid £13,000 for their land, they went away without their money." Because of the cost of food and lodging, "they lost the money and lost the land, and were worse off therefore than when the Court began." In Cambridge, which hosted at least several hundred visiting Maori litigants every year, "the meanest house or stable has let readily for £3 a week throughout the time that the Native Land Court has been sitting," MP Joseph Ivess reported. "Residents in that district look anxiously for the coming-round of the Native Land Court, because they regard it as their harvest."[49]

Waiting around British cities with nothing to do, living in boardinghouses and shanty towns, subsisting on advances at high rates of interest from the British purchasers of their land, Maori property owners watched the proceeds of their land gradually slip away. Many turned to alcohol, and it became a commonplace in the colonial press that the advances made by land purchasers "mostly went for rum of the very worst kind, and the whole time of the sitting of the Court was spent by the natives— men, women, and children—in drunkenness and debauchery." Unhealthy living conditions and, for many, initial exposure to European disease caused horrible health problems in the temporary Maori communities that sprang up for court sittings. "There has been a considerable amount of sickness in places where they have been temporarily crowded in tents," observed one government official in 1881. "Especially during the Land Court," another reported a few years later, "there have been an exceptional number of deaths." Where the court sat, the Maori population dropped the fastest.[50]

Occasional voices were raised within the government, and by those with the stature to influence the government, concerning the effects of distance and delay. As to distance, William Martin urged as early as 1865: "Instead of bringing the Natives to our Courts of Justice, we must carry our Courts to them." R. W. Woon, the resident magistrate in Wanganui, suggested that the local tribes would greatly prefer "the Court to sit in their midst, where they could more easily and more cheaply procure food, and obtain house accomodation." As to delay, officials sometimes complained that Native Land Court judges "have not shown that efficiency which they ought to display." In 1890, Chief Judge H. G. Seth-Smith proposed saving time in individual cases by requiring all claims and counter-claims to be made in writing. Judge Alexander Mackay thought time could be saved if the parties were compelled to confer before the hearing and narrow the issues to be tried. Fenton conceded that "it seems a great pity to summon every body to attend at a certain day, when their cases may not come on for a month." He considered some possible alternatives. One might schedule groups of cases for each week, numbers 1 to 20 the first week, 21 to 40 the next week, and so on, "but it may have objections: then claimants in No. 2 may be claimants or opponents in number 100." Or one might have everyone attend on the first day, and then work out the order in which the cases would be heard, "so that people may return to their homes and come again."[51] Nothing ever came of any of these speculations.

The absence of any reform was due in large part to the Native Land

Court judges, who were adamant in their defense of the court's practices. "It would be impossible for the Court to go and sit at every Native village," Edward Puckey asserted. Requiring the court to hear claims near the land under adjudication, Maning argued, "would be to go as far as possible to insure a one sided investigation and often a wrong decision." One might reasonably suspect that the judges preferred the comfort of European-style hotels and restaurants, a luxury that would have been lost by sitting in Maori rather than British population centers. If the court moved slowly, explained Chief Judge J. E. MacDonald, that was because "the investigation of Maori tribal titles to land, is of necessity a work of time and patience, owing not only to the vague origin and nature of such titles, but to the character of the evidence by which they are sought to be established, being assertion mostly legendary." Seth-Smith agreed; it simply took a long time to resolve claims "based on ancestral rights, known only by tradition," a problem exacerbated by the tendency of the witnesses to lie. There was no way to get around the need to schedule large numbers of cases for single sittings, Maning insisted. "Many claims must be heard at the same time and place or the business could not be got through at all."[52]

The lack of reform was also due to a lack of interest among most colonial officials and most colonists. "The working of the Native Lands Court has been a scandal to contemplate for many years past," the *New Zealand Herald* noted in 1883, "but as the chief sufferers were the Maoris, nobody troubled themselves very much."[53] As a result, the costs to the Maori simply of attending court drained away much of the value of their land.

Fees

Using the services of the Native Land Court also imposed significant costs. The court itself charged fees for everything it did, from ordering certificates of title to hearing witnesses, the most significant of which was the £1 it charged each litigant for each day his case was being heard. In this respect it was identical to the other courts in New Zealand and elsewhere in the British Empire, which charged comparable fees to litigants. The Native Land Court was unusual, however, in that all the litigants before it were Maori, and most had very little money. A pound per day was often enough to prevent a litigant from being heard, which could cause land to be erroneously awarded to his opponent. The fee was imposed on all parties, including those attending to court solely to oppose an application filed by someone else, for each day their case was before the court, whether or not they actually spoke that day. When a single case lasted weeks or months, the fee mounted. Many understandably resented the ability of a claimant, even one filing a claim lacking any merit, to impose substantial costs on the land's true owners. "They go according to the call of the *Gazette,* when the pound is thrown at them," lamented the Nga Puhi leader Hone Mohi Tawhai in 1871, "so the thoughts of the people get wearied by reason of the fear of that pound."[54]

Court fees were in any event very small compared to the other kinds of fees Maori litigants had to pay in order to make use of the Native Land Court. Title could not be obtained without first having the land surveyed. In forest or scrub, that meant cutting and clearing boundary lines four feet wide. The judges recognized right away that, as Fenton put it in 1867, the "great difficulty in the rapid conversion of the Maori titles and the individualization of holdings is the necessity and expense of surveys." Surveying costs were large enough, Judge W. B. White explained, to prevent many cases from being brought at all. The cost per acre rose the smaller the block surveyed, which made subdividing a tribal holding into individual plots proportionally much more expensive than delineating the outer boundaries of the tribal holding in the first place, and accordingly deterred applications for subdivision.[55]

Because Maori property owners typically could not pay surveyors until they had sold some of the land being surveyed, surveyors of Maori land faced delays and risks of nonpayment they did not normally face when surveying for British clients, and the prices charged to the Maori accordingly tended to be higher. Surveyors ran the risk that their clients would lose in the Native Land Court, in which case they would be unable to pay for the survey. When their clients won, surveyors obtained a lien on the land, but if they were not paid the ability to go after the land was not much of a substitute. As the surveyor-turned-politician Charles Heaphy explained, "few surveyors can afford to have undefined landed estates scattered about where they may have been working." The court's long delays had an adverse impact on the surveyors as well as Maori landowners. Surveyors themselves were forced to obtain advances at steep discounts from prospective land purchasers, the cost of which they then tried to recoup from their clients.[56] All these uncertainties raised the price of surveying. The result was a vicious circle: the inability of many Maori landowners to pay surveyors raised the price of surveying to all Maori landowners, which in turn caused even more to be unable to pay surveyors.

Another necessary fee, and one that could easily exceed those paid to the court and to the surveyor, was the fee paid to a lawyer. In disputed cases it quickly became the norm for each side to employ a lawyer, to counter the lawyer employed by the other. Maori litigants and court officials repeatedly asked the government to ban lawyers from appearing. "The lawyers know nothing whatever about the titles of Maoris to land," Wiremu te Wheoro argued; "it would be by far the best plan to let the Maoris prove their titles themselves. Large sums of money are needlessly spent upon lawyers." In 1873 Parliament accordingly required the court's judges to examine witnesses directly, "without the intervention of any counsel or other agent." Five years later, however, after protests from the judges, who felt ill at ease performing what they perceived to be an advocate's role, Parliament authorized the court to allow counsel to appear. Lawyers again became the norm. The same court delays that built up the costs of food, lodging, and court fees also built up the costs of lawyers, who typically charged by the hour or the day. Lawyers, many alleged, had the incentive and the ability to prolong cases in order to increase their fees. "The European purchaser from one section arranged to have a lawyer in Court," as a newspaper described one case, "and the contending section, who were also backed up by a European, had another lawyer. These learned gentlemen were paid by the day, and of course it was in their interest to make the case spin out as long as possible."[57] As with the other costs, lawyers' fees had to come out of the proceeds of the land when it was sold.

Virtually all these administrative costs fell in the first instance on the Maori owners of the land being passed through the Native Land Court. That need not necessarily have meant that the owners ultimately bore those costs. The administrative costs associated with the Native Land Court were analogous to a very high sales tax, imposed on the seller. Other sales taxes, and indeed many of the costs faced by a seller, are routinely passed on in large measure to the purchasers of whatever is being sold, in the form of higher prices. Contemporary observers of the Native Land Court, however, believed that the Maori bore all the cost of obtaining British-style titles. "Commercially speaking," explained Native Minister John Bryce, "I should say it would in all cases fall upon the owners of the soil." When it didn't, Bryce reasoned, it was because the buyers "are not working on sound commercial principles." "The Natives suffer in consequence of this excessive cost," agreed Resident Magistrate George Preece, "as they get a smaller price, or a smaller amount of rent, as the case may be, owing to this expense of obtaining a title."[58]

Why were the Maori unable to pass these costs on to British land purchasers? Between a buyer and a seller of an item, the incidence of a tax depends on their relative abilities to find a substitute for that item. The more easily a buyer can buy something else instead, the more he will be able to force the seller to bear the ultimate burden of the tax; the more easily the seller can sell something else instead, the greater the burden forced on to the buyer. The Maori had no substitute. All they owned was land. Whatever the administrative cost of selling it, they had to sell it if they wanted to sell anything. The British, on the other hand, had an excellent substitute. Between 1840 and 1865, the colonial government had purchased over thirty million acres of land. For the rest of the century and beyond, most of it was for sale or lease. Land purchased from the government was very close to a perfect substitute for land purchased from the Maori. In land sales, the government was the Maori's greatest competitor. The price charged by the government was typically low and the terms of payment generous, in order to encourage settlement. That price became an effective ceiling on the price the Maori could charge. It was competition from the government, the same government that was imposing all the administrative costs in the first place, that prevented the Maori from passing those costs on to British purchasers.[59]

The sum of the administrative costs associated with the Native Land Court often amounted to a significant fraction of the value of the land,

and sometimes to all of it. Maori landowners face "so many expenses, the money goes and so does the land," Wiremu te Wheoro wrote to Donald McLean. "Behold there is the survey one, the court two, the Lawyers three, the Native Interpreters four, the Crown Grant five and the giving of the land to the other side."[60] By the end of the process, the value received by Maori property owners was much less than the market value of their land.

In 1861 the Maori owned twenty-two million acres in the North Island; by 1911 they owned only seven million. A small portion, less than a sixth, had been confiscated by the government after the wars; the rest had been sold through the Native Land Court. By the end of the century, approximately half of all adult males in New Zealand owned land, a figure much higher than in Britain or Australia, the biggest sources of emigrants. Part of the disparity in value between the land and its proceeds thus enabled many settlers to gain a higher standard of living. More and more of the Maori meanwhile, without their former land but also without much to show for it, were becoming landless rural laborers.[61]

Many noticed the disparity between the price received by the Maori and the value of Maori land once it moved into the settler real estate market. In 1883 the MP James Parker Joyce was indignant that North Island property "passes from the Natives, in some cases, for less than they would get for a year's rental in the South for land of inferior quality." Maori MP Henare Tomoana put it more plainly: "Although the Natives have parted with a great deal of their land, they have nothing left of the proceeds at the present time." But value could be a malleable concept when applied to land for which there had been no market before the British arrived. "If the European race had never come into these seas, the value of these islands would still be only nominal," Fenton argued. "The immense value that now attaches to these territories is solely to be attributed to the capital and labour of the European." The fraction of land retained by the Maori, pointed out the Reverend James Buller, is "worth immeasurably more than the whole island was forty years ago."[62] In this light, British land purchasing had been a net gain to the Maori. They had no cause to complain.

POWER AND MARKETS

Between 1840 and 1865, the colonial government established a market in Maori land with a single purchaser, the government itself. Whatever the degree of misunderstanding between buyer and seller as to the meaning of transactions, whatever the disparity in the parties' skill at negotiating or ability to predict future land values, the government as sole purchaser could exploit them to the fullest. After 1865 the government established a different kind of market in Maori land, one that imposed enormous costs on Maori sellers, costs that could not be passed through to land purchasers because the government itself offered a low-priced substitute. In both types of market, the Maori received much less for their land than they would have in a market constructed differently, in which buyers competed with one another to offer the best price, and in which administrative costs were lower and borne more equally.

Many observers recognized what was happening. Many did not, no doubt due to a mixture of convenience and genuine misperception. The land had been bought, after all, not conquered by force as in Australia. If the Maori now found themselves poorer than before, or regretting sales they had made in the past, that was not the fault of the British. The Maori must have been imprudent.

Attorney General Robert Stout argued that Maori poverty at the end of the nineteenth century was due to the fact that "the Natives cannot equal the Europeans in buying, or selling, or in other things. They have not gone through that long process of evolution which the white race has gone through." The MP William Gisborne agreed. "They are like children," he urged, "who have shown themselves incompetent" to look after their own interests when selling land. But this was no less controversial a point than it had been earlier in the century. Many settlers believed precisely the opposite. "The natives are quite as sharp if not sharper in dealing with land than the whites," Cuthbert Peek wrote in 1883. "There is an impression abroad that the European, generally, has the best part of the bargain," concluded Native Land Court Judge W. E. Gudgeon, "but this is absolutely untrue; the Maori is a rogue from his birth."[63]

If the Maori were skilled bargainers, their poverty could be attributed to a second form of imprudence. They were simply frittering away the proceeds of the sales. "It is a sad thing to see these fine people exchanging their land for drink," editorialized the *Herald* during a Native Land Court sitting in Rotorua. "That is really what, in the end, the transaction amounts to." The money was all being spent by the chiefs, argued another newspaper, while "the great bulk of the native race has been made poor and dependent."[64] A market could be a powerful ideological screen, causing observers to assume that whatever went on behind it was value-enhancing to all sides. If the people on one side routinely came up short, the fault had to lie with those people rather than with the market itself.

Some Maori losses in these transactions were caused by outright fraud by the British. Some were caused by an inability to bargain as well as the British. Some sellers frittered away the proceeds. But much of what the Maori lost in the nineteenth century cannot be attributed to the actions of individuals, whether sharp practice by buyers or imprudence by sellers. Those losses were due instead to the structure of the market in which buyers and sellers operated. Even if the Maori had been perfectly informed, even if no fraud had been committed, even if sellers had wisely invested the proceeds, the Maori would still have been much poorer at the end of the century.

The British possessed two attributes the Maori did not, and those made all the difference. The first was the ability to organize themselves within the market as a single entity for the purpose of buying land at low prices. Had the British, like the Maori, been split into multiple political units, they would have been no more able to exercise monopsony power than multiple firms are able to cartelize for the same purpose. The second attribute possessed by the British but not the Maori is one that has implicitly lain beneath the entire discussion. The British had the power to set the rules of the game. The market looked the way it did because the British were powerful enough to design it and to rebuff Maori efforts to impose a different structure. That power rested on the military and technological superiority that allowed European states to colonize much of the world rather than vice versa. The British had the muscle to select exactly which property rights they would enforce and how they would be enforced. The transfer of land from the Maori to the British was thus a function of British power, as in Australia, but in New Zealand, more often than not, it was power exercised through the legal system rather than on the battlefield.

chapter four

Hawaii

Preparing To Be Colonized

IN THE LATE NINETEENTH and early twentieth centuries, throughout the Pacific Rim, European and American colonizers reorganized traditional indigenous systems of property rights in land, in order to make them look more like European property systems. In New Zealand, the British colonial government established the Native Land Court in the 1860s, to convert Maori usufructuary rights into English fee simple titles. Soon after, Britain set up a similar institution to reallocate property rights in Fiji. In the western United States, the Dawes Act of 1887 authorized the same kind of reorganization of tenure in much of the land still possessed by American Indians. Similar processes took place in the German colonies of New Guinea and Samoa, in French Polynesia, and in the joint British-French New Hebrides (present-day Vanuatu). Although these schemes varied in their details, they were all structurally similar to the enclosure of European common fields over the preceding several centuries. Government-appointed commissioners were to determine who owned the right to use the various resources present on the land, and to replace those customary use-rights with written documents evidencing the ownership of parcels of land itself. Indigenous oral property systems based on command over individual resources were converted into European written property systems based on command over zones of land.

These reforms were intended by their framers to serve two goals. Colonial governments expected that converting land tenure to the European style would facilitate the civilization of indigenous people, by providing them with greater incentives toward agricultural productivity. At the same time, colonial governments hoped that the eradication of complex indigenous property systems would bring indigenously owned land more efficiently onto the real estate market, where it could be purchased by settlers of European descent.

The consensus today among historians is that wherever these schemes were rigorously carried out they were disastrous for the indigenous people involved. In the United States, the allotment of Indian reservations smoothed the way for the Indians to lose tens of millions of acres of land, and, instead of encouraging Indian farming, reduced the amount of Indian land under cultivation. New Zealand's Native Land Court was the engine that drove a massive transfer of land from the Maori to British settlers and their government. Because of their results, these land tenure reforms are often viewed with considerable cynicism today, as thinly veiled colonial land grabs.

It comes as a bit of a jolt, then, to recall that the very first of these schemes took place in the independent Kingdom of Hawaii. The Māhele (or Division) of 1845–1855 dismantled much of the traditional Hawaiian system of property rights in land, and replaced it with the Anglo-American system of alienable fee-simple titles. The remarkable thing about the Māhele is that it was undertaken by the Hawaiians themselves. Land tenure reform elsewhere throughout the Pacific Rim was imposed on indigenous people by colonizers, often over bitter resistance from those whose property rights were being reformed. But Hawaii at the time of the Māhele was not a colony. To be sure, Hawaii was weak relative to the United States and the European powers. By the time of the Māhele there were many Europeans and Americans living in Hawaii, some of whom occupied significant positions in the government of Kamehameha III. Foreign residents had been urging land tenure reform on Kamehameha and other powerful Hawaiians for a long time before the Māhele, and non-Hawaiians played important roles in designing and implementing the details. But it would be a mistake to understand the Māhele simply as an act of colonization pressed upon Hawaii from the outside.[1] In both its conception and its implementation, the Māhele had the support of the indigenous Hawaiian governing class.

The story of Hawaii complicates the conventional account of colonial land tenure reform. Why did the land tenure reform movement of the late nineteenth and early twentieth centuries receive its earliest implementation in, of all places, Hawaii? Why did the Hawaiians do this to themselves? What did they hope to gain from it?

THE MOST INDUSTRIOUS PEOPLE

The Hawaiians were skilled farmers. The first Europeans to reach Hawaii, James Cook and his colleagues, marveled at what Cook's lieutenant James King described as "regular & extensive plantations" and "cultivated ground as far as they could see." King concluded that "it is hardly possible that this Country can be better cultivated or made to yield a greater sustenance for the inhabitants." By the 1790s Hawaii was already known as a place where American and European ships could load up with local fruits and vegetables on their way across the Pacific. The British explorer George Vancouver did just that in Maui in 1793. Archibald Menzies, the botanist accompanying Vancouver, was amazed that even steep slopes were "cultivated & watered with great neatness and industry, even the shelving cliffs of Rocks were planted with esculent [edible] roots, banked in & watered by aqueducts from the Rivulet with as much art as if their level had been taken by the most ingenious Engineer." Menzies reported that "the indefatigable labor in making these little fields in so rugged a situation, the care & industry with which they were transplanted watered & kept in order surpassed any thing of the kind we had ever seen before."[2]

Praise for Hawaiian agricultural skill quickly became a common theme in early nineteenth-century British and American travel narratives. The Scottish seaman Archibald Campbell, who visited Oahu in the first decade of the century, thought that Hawaiian irrigation systems were built with such "great labour and ingenuity" that the Hawaiians "are certainly the most industrious people I ever saw." When the English missionary William Ellis toured the Big Island in 1823, he found fields "planted with bananas, sweet potatoes, mountain taro, tapa trees, melons and sugar-cane, flourishing luxuriantly in every direction." In 1825 the British government sent HMS *Blonde* to Hawaii to return the bodies of the Hawaiian king and queen, who had died of measles while visiting England. One officer of the *Blonde* reported that irrigation at Maui "is managed with great care and skill"; the ship's botanist thought Lahaina, the island's largest town, "looked like a well cultivated garden"; and the artist aboard the *Blonde* pronounced the town "in an excellent state of cultivation."[3] It was well known among foreign visitors and their readership in Europe and the United States that the Hawaiians were an agricultural people.

Contact with whites had profound effects on Hawaiian farming, effects that ran in both directions. Incoming ships provided new markets for agricultural goods, which stimulated production. Those same ships, however, brought microorganisms that killed Hawaiians in enormous numbers. By the 1820s, depopulation had resulted in the abandonment of many fields. The sandalwood trade further depleted the labor supply, by causing many survivors to give up agriculture. The French shipmaster Auguste Duhaut-Cilly, trading in Hawaii in the late 1820s, found "large stretches of land where the remains of dikes, already reduced almost to ground level, show in an incontestable way that here there once were cultivated fields."[4] By the middle of the century such observations would cause many whites to write less favorably about Hawaiian agriculture, and that dim view of Hawaiian farming would provide ammunition for proponents of land tenure reform. But despite such criticism, there was no doubt among whites that Hawaiians were farmers.

That knowledge was important, because it predisposed Anglo-Americans to think of the Hawaiians as the owners of their land. Even the settler press in Hawaii conceded that the Hawaiians owned their land. Although settlers desperately needed land, the *Polynesian* acknowledged, to compel Hawaiians to give it up "would be a shocking morality."[5] Whites recognized Hawaiian property rights in land, because they had so much evidence of Hawaiian agriculture.

Educated visitors to Hawaii sometimes analogized Hawaiian land tenure to the feudal system that had once characterized Europe, and though the comparison was not perfect, it was close. No one in Hawaii "owned" land in the sense in which the word was used in nineteenth-century Europe and the United States. *Maka'āinana,* or commoners, had rights to use zones of land allocated by *ali'i,* or chiefs, in exchange for providing labor and agricultural products to the ali'i. (Rights to use land were not contingent on military service, as in feudal Europe.) The maka'āinana were supervised by lesser chiefs, called *konohiki,* who were accountable to the ali'i. The rights of the maka'āinana were perpetual, and handed down from generation to generation, so long as the maka'āinana satisfied the demands of the konohiki and ali'i. Maka'āinana were not tied to the land (this was another difference between Hawaiian land tenure and European feudalism); they could move to land given them by a different chief. No one's property rights were capable of being sold, however—neither the commoners' nor the chiefs'.[6]

When behavior was appropriate on both sides, patterns of land use seem to have been very stable. "In the old days," recalled the mid-nineteenth-century Hawaiian historian Samuel Kamakau, "the lands were divided up according to what was proper for the chiefs, the lesser chiefs, the prominent people, and the people in general to have. Each family clearly understood what was 'their' land and 'their' birthplace." The same knowledge was kept by the chiefs, who "knew what lands they had given to this or that person, and the obligations that went with each portion of the land."[7]

This system could be exploited by opportunistic konohiki or ali'i, however, and Kamakau also recalled that such exploitation was not unusual. "If a chief became angry with a commoner he would dispossess him and leave him landless," Kamakau explained. "It was not for a commoner to do as he liked as if what he had was his own. If a chief saw that a man was becoming affluent, was a man of importance in the back country, had built him a good house, and had several men under him, the chief would take everything away from him and seize the land, leaving the man with only the clothes on his back." Foreign critics of Hawaiian land tenure seized upon such accounts as evidence of the system's utter backwardness. "Not a common man owned a foot of the soil," insisted the pastor T. Dwight Hunt. "Not one could claim for his own the food he cultivated, the garment he wore, or the house he reared. All that grew upon the land, all that swam in the sea, all that was made or reared by the hand of man, could be seized and appropriated by the reigning chiefs."[8]

Some foreign observers were more positive about Hawaiian land tenure. The missionary William Ellis found the Hawaiians to possess "a kind of traditional code" governing the rights of property, a set of rules "which are well understood, and usually acted upon. The portion of personal labour due from a tenant to his chief is fixed by custom, and a chief would be justified in banishing the person who should refuse it when required; on the other hand, were a chief to banish a man who had rendered it, and paid the stipulated rent, his conduct would be contrary to their opinions of right, and if the man complained to the governor or the king, and no other charge was brought against him, he would most likely be reinstated." Recently historians sympathetic to traditional Hawaiian ways have likewise tended to describe Hawaiian land tenure as a well-ordered system of reciprocal obligations, which implies that incidents of exploitation by chiefs were rare.[9] In the absence of any quantitative evidence on this point, there is no way to tell who is right.

At the top of the pyramid, above the ali'i, was the king, who allocated land to the ali'i. The king was in principle an absolute monarch. As Kamehameha III proclaimed shortly after assuming power, "death and life, to disapprove and to approve, all pleasures, all laws, and all actions in the land, are mine." The nineteenth-century Hawaiian scholar and government official David Malo described a world in which "every thing went according to the will or whim of the king, whether it concerned land, or people, or anything else—not according to law." Kings sometimes seized crops or pigs belonging to commoners, Malo reported, and even confiscated commoners' land.[10] Again, recent historians have suggested that kings in fact were more restrained than accounts like Malo's indicate, and again there is not enough evidence to resolve the issue one way or the other.

Early white settlers in Hawaii inserted themselves into this system. Some received land grants from the king under circumstances suggesting that the king meant to treat them as ali'i. In the first decade of the nineteenth century, for example, the American adventurer Samuel Patterson received a tract on Oahu from Kamehameha I. "On looking the land over we found it produced numerous kinds of vegetables," Patterson related. "We then returned to the emperor and told him we were delighted with our present. He then gave us a canoe and servants to wait on us, and to till our ground, and told us to take wives of any women we saw on the island, excepting the chiefs' wives." The Scottish sailor Archibald Campbell had a similar experience, when Kamehameha I granted him sixty acres near the present site of Pearl Harbor. "My farm, called Wymannoo, was upon the east side of the river, four or five miles from its mouth," Campbell explained. "Fifteen people, with their families, resided upon it, who cultivated the ground as my servants."[11] With grants like these, Kamehameha seems to have been assimilating white visitors into the traditional hierarchy of land tenure. Patterson and Campbell, like other ali'i, enjoyed the right to demand a certain amount of labor and of crops from the commoners who worked "their" land.

In the 1810s and 1820s, as the white population increased, kings continued granting parcels to white settlers, especially as a form of compensation for services rendered. These later grants were apparently outside the traditional labor hierarchy: white grantees had no right to the labor of commoners on the land, but neither did they owe any labor to anyone higher up the ladder. By 1844 the American missionary-turned-government-official Gerrit Judd found 125 such grants recorded with the Hawaiian Treasury, most to Americans and Britons, and he presumed that many more remained unrecorded.[12]

All of these grants to foreigners, regardless of the details, were grants under traditional Hawaiian principles of land tenure. The grants were revocable at any time. The land could not be sold. In these respects, foreigners were in the same position as Hawaiians.

Of course, foreign residents of Hawaii were in a very different position from that of landholders in their countries of origin. In Britain, in the United States, and in all the other places from which white settlers had come, landholders had the power to sell their land, and they had little reason to worry about government expropriation. By the 1830s the inability to own land in fee simple absolute—that is, to own land in the Anglo-American sense—was a major source of complaint among the foreign residents of Hawaii. This was in part a concern to preserve their own investments. Many had built houses, planted farms, and so on, and they feared that all might be lost. This fear was particularly sharp among foreigners who had extended credit to the king or to the chiefs. In the early nineteenth century, Hawaiian elites ran up considerable debts in the sandalwood trade and in purchasing ships and other things manufactured by whites. Their white creditors were nervous that the king or the chiefs might drive them out of Hawaii, and reclaim their farms and houses, as a way of avoiding having to pay these debts. Their apprehensions reached such a pitch that in 1831, when Hawaiian soldiers disrupted two whites playing billiards, twenty-six foreign residents of Oahu signed a petition claiming the incident was intended "to drive us to desperation and induce us to leave the islands as the best means of paying the debts due to us."[13] But one did not have to be a creditor of the Hawaiian elite to want to leave one's home to one's children, or to want to sell one's land upon leaving Hawaii. The desire for fee simple ownership was pervasive among the settlers.

Many of the complaints about the impossibility of fee simple ownership, however, focused not on recouping past investment but on encouraging future investment. White settlers in Hawaii wanted to attract more white settlers, for economic reasons (more settlers would raise the value of their land) and for cultural reasons (for most settlers, more whites would make Hawaii a more pleasant place to live). For the large majority of the foreign residents of Hawaii, real estate development unambiguously represented progress. The inability to own land in the full Euro-American sense, they feared, was deterring white settlement and white investment. "Foreigners who would be glad to engage in agricultural labors, requiring a great outlay of capital, are prevented by the certainty that if any malady, or any motive whatever, should induce them to leave the country, they would lose at once the fruit of their labors," observed Théodore-Adolphe Barrot, who stopped off in Hawaii in 1836 on the way to the Philippines to serve as French consul. "Consequently, agriculture has made no progress, and instead of immense establishments which a more enlarged policy would have caused to spring up, no other cultivation is seen on the fertile plains of the Sandwich Islands than that of the taro." Gorham Gilman, who arrived in Honolulu from Maine in 1841, noted that "it has always been the policy of the Govt never to alienate their title to the soil—the fruits of this short sighted policy is obvious cramping investment—& retarding improvements."[14] By the 1840s, white residents of Hawaii were making the same complaint over and over—that the government's refusal to permit them to own land in fee simple was bottling up development.

In the 1830s, in response to pressures from British residents of Hawaii, the British government tried to secure by treaty the right to fee simple land ownership, but the Hawaiian government refused. The government of the United States tried the same tactic in the 1840s, but with no greater success. Kamehameha III explained during one discussion of a British resident's land claim, "We indeed wish to give Foreigners lands the same as natives and so they were granted, but to the natives they are revertable and the foreigners would insist that they have them for ever." From the perspective of the Hawaiian governing elite, the retention of traditional land tenure served several goals: it prevented the number of foreign residents from growing unmanageably large, it allowed the king and the chiefs to retain their traditional control over the allocation of land, and—not least—it ensured that the beneficiaries of any rise in land values would be Hawaiian, not foreign. The minutes of Hawaii's Privy Council relate that "the King and Chiefs laughed very heartily" on at least one occasion, while contemplating the desire of white residents to own land in fee simple, "remarking,—so they think we are fools—that we know not the value of our own lands." Before the Māhele, the greatest concession the government would make was to permit leases for periods as long as fifty years. Even then, the government was careful to specify that leases near the upper end of that range would be obtainable only at higher rents.[15]

The more reflective among the settlers came to a grudging admiration for what was, after all, a logical response to the danger posed by white immigration. "Should the number and wealth of the foreign population increase in an excessive ratio compared with that of the native," one white editorialist acknowledged, "the result would be nearly the same as if another government held the reins of state." When the American naval officer Henry Wise visited Hawaii in the late 1840s, he recognized that Kamehameha and the chiefs "are much too shrewd not to perceive, with prophetic vision, that the very moment the lands are thrown open to foreign enterprise and competition, a preponderating influence will be acquired by the wealth and intelligence of foreigners themselves, [and] the lands will slip like water through the hands of the chiefs."[16] The Hawaiian governing elite included some men who were aware of the course of colonization in other parts of the world. They understood the value of maintaining traditional Hawaiian land tenure.

Many, perhaps all, indigenous societies would have benefited from the same strategy, but it required a sufficient level of political organization to implement, and Hawaii was one of very few places in the non-European world where political authority was not fragmented among several small tribes. On the North Island of New Zealand, Maori tribes were able to organize so as to prevent land sales to whites for a decade or two in the mid-nineteenth century, but that coalition fell apart after the colonial government reorganized the land market to make it easier for dissident tribe members to sell as individuals. In the mid-eighteenth century, the Creeks and Cherokees in colonial North America worked toward developing a mutual land sale policy, and they discussed the issue with representatives of other tribes as well. Within a few years, however, the Cherokees offered to sell to the colony of Georgia land claimed by the Creeks.[17] In many societies, including in North America and New Zealand, individual tribes often lacked the capacity to prevent even their own members from selling land to whites, because political power was so widely dispersed. Organization on a larger scale was even harder to achieve. An indigenous polity had to be relatively large and relatively hierarchical for the Hawaii strategy to work. Few were. Tonga was one such polity—like Hawaii, Tonga was governed by a single king and many chiefs, and they were able to prohibit land sales to non-Tongans throughout the nineteenth century. But Hawaii and Tonga were unusual in this respect.

From the perspective of the settlers most directly affected, this insistence on holding on to the land looked like yet another example of the tyranny of the Hawaiian elite. "The Government is a feudal despotism," thundered the Briton Richard Charlton, whose dispute with the government over his rights to land was one of the major issues of Hawaiian foreign relations off and on between the late 1820s and the early 1840s. "Large tracts of valuable land lie waste, as the common people have no encouragement to cultivate it; if a man should get a piece of ground in good order, he would be certain that the King or some of the chiefs would take it from him." The British trader John Turnbull declared that "the despotism and wantonness of command in the chiefs is only equalled by the correspondent timidity and submission of the people." He drew a more general lesson from his years in Hawaii. "Philosophers are much mistaken who build systems of natural liberty," Turnbull concluded. "Rousseau's savage, a being who roves the woods according to his own will, exists no where but in his writings."[18]

As the white population of the islands increased, foreign residents' desire to own property by Anglo-American tenure increasingly came into conflict with the Hawaiian government's policy of making land grants only according to Hawaiian tenure. One of these forces would have to give way. As in most settler societies throughout the world, it was the settlers' desire that would prevail. Beginning in the 1840s, Hawaii would radically reorganize its property system, in the series of events that would come to be called the Māhele.

THE MĀHELE

Hawaii reorganized its government before it revised its property system. The Constitution of 1840, Hawaii's first written constitution, established a constitutional monarchy on the British model, with a bicameral legislature consisting of a House of Nobles and an elected chamber. Within a few years Hawaii had a Supreme Court and a Privy Council, as well as ministries of foreign relations and finance, among others. In its details, the form of the government was clearly influenced by the British and American missionaries who had taught the Hawaiians who drafted the constitution, but that influence extended even more deeply, to the tacit political theory underlying the constitution. Before 1840 the government of Hawaii did not exist as a set of institutions independent of the men who happened to occupy positions of leadership at any given time. For example, before 1840 there was no distinction between land belonging to the king and land belonging to the government, because there was no such institution as "the government" separate from the person of the king that was capable of holding land. The Constitution of 1840 changed that, by importing from Europe and the United States a conception of the government as an abstract entity, as distinguished from the personal identities of the king and other office holders. The Constitution made this distinction explicit as to property. It provided that the king "shall have the direction of the government property." In the next sentence, the Constitution stated: "He also shall retain his own private lands." For the first time, Hawaiian law distinguished between the king's land and the government's land, a difference that would prove to be important in later years.[19]

Kamehameha III quickly began hiring foreigners to staff this new government. By 1844 the Hawaiian government included six men from the United States, six from Britain, one from France, and one from Denmark. By 1851 these fourteen had grown to 48. "Were it not for the foreigners living under his jurisdiction he would require no Foreign Officers," Kamehameha III explained to the British admiral George Seymour in 1846. "He could manage his own subjects very easily,—even his word was always enough for them, but foreigners with great cunning and perseverance often sought to involve him in difficulty, and . . . by experience he found that he could not get along, but by appointing foreigners to cope with them." These men were a mixed lot. George Brown, the United States consul in Hawaii in the mid-1840s, did not think highly of them. "I don't believe a more stupid if not unprincipled set, ever surrounded a throne, than the King's advisors here," he informed a friend back home in Massachusetts. "There will be some queer developments by and by." Some were lawyers, some ex-missionaries, some adventurers; probably none would have become high-ranking government officials had they not moved to Hawaii. But whatever their faults, they swore their allegiance to Kamehameha, and they (or at least the ones who figured prominently in land tenure reform) seem to have been interested in advancing what they viewed as the best interests of Hawaii. Some were motivated by a missionary-like enthusiasm. Gerrit Judd, who left his post as a missionary physician to serve "the Dynasty of the King my Master" Kamehameha, declared his hope that with his assistance an independent Hawaii could "raise out of the aboriginal population of this distant part of the Earth a Government that could evince reason and could conduct its affairs upon the principles of the Law of Nations and could apply the Code of civilized administrations in its transactions."[20] These white advisors would play a crucial role in the Māhele.

Strictly speaking, the Māhele was a single event that took place in 1848, but colloquially the term has come to describe a process that consisted of five separate events between 1845 and 1855. The first, in 1845, was the creation of a Board of Commissioners to Quiet Land Titles. The statute creating the Land Commission, as it came to be called, explained that the commission was "to be a board for the investigation and final ascertainment of all claims of private individuals, whether natives or foreigners, to any landed property acquired anterior to the passage of this act." Once the Land Commission published a notice of its existence in the newspaper, any person, Hawaiian or foreign, with any claim to land, had to file that claim with the commission within two years. All claims not filed by the deadline, February 1848, would be forever barred. Once a claim had been confirmed, the claimant could obtain a written title, upon paying a fee to the government.[21]

The Land Commission had no power to change the law or to grant rights where none had existed previously. "The true object" of the commission, the *Polynesian* explained to a readership that must have included many foreign land claimants, "is to raise order and security out of the present involved and confused system of titles and tenures, and by putting all on a uniform and correct basis, give a wholesome spur to the landed interest of the country." The claims that the commission would hear were still, as always, founded on a grant from a chief or from the king directly, and they were still revocable at the chief's or king's option. The purpose of the commission was only to clarify, and to write down, which land had been granted to whom.[22]

There was an enormous mismatch, however, between the Land Commission's narrow ostensible purpose and the broad scope of its actual power, and that mismatch suggests quite strongly that other goals were at work beyond simply tidying up Hawaii's land titles or resolving disputes between competing claimants to the same land. The commission was charged, not just with cases where two people claimed the same land, and not just with land claims from foreigners, but with converting *all* the land in Hawaii from an oral tenure to a scheme of written titles, even land that had been uncontroversially used by particular Hawaiian families for as long as anyone could remember. This was a massive transformation of the Hawaiian property system, for the purpose of creating a formal written record of who owned what, on every square foot of every island. Such a major undertaking was hardly necessary merely to resolve existing conflicts or even to prevent new ones. Something else was going on.

The second of the events constituting the Māhele was the Māhele proper, the great division of land between the king and the chiefs. Between January and March 1848, Kamehameha III reached more than 240 agreements with individual ali'i and konohiki, each of which divided lands between the king and a chief. The chiefs were then to submit claims to the Land Commission for their parcels.

The third event was another important land division. In March 1848, after completing the division between the chiefs' land and his own, Kamehameha signed two documents in which he divided his own land into two kinds, a larger portion that would be owned by the Hawaiian government, and a smaller portion he would own in his personal capacity.

The final two events took place in 1850. In July the legislature for the first time allowed foreigners to acquire land in fee simple. This measure appears to have been the only segment of the Māhele that aroused significant domestic opposition. When the idea was first suggested by foreign-born officials within the Hawaiian government in the mid-1840s, it drew petitions of protest from maka'āinana, or commoners, throughout Hawaii, who feared they would be turned off the land by white purchasers. "You chiefs must not sell the land to the white men," insisted more than three hundred citizens of Kona, on the Big Island. "If the chiefs are to open this door of the government as an entrance way for the foreigners to come into Hawaii, then you will see the Hawaiian people going from place to place in this world like flies." Three hundred and one residents of Lāna'i pleaded with the government not "to open the doors for the coming in of foreigners. . . . We are afraid that the wise will step on the ignorant, the same as America and other lands,—on you and on us." A similar group from Maui offered a prediction of the consequences of opening up land sales to foreigners, a prediction that turned out to be quite accurate.

"Foreigners come on shore with cash ready to purchase land," they despaired, "but we have not the means to purchase lands; the native is disabled like one who has long been afflicted with a disease upon his back. We have lived under the chiefs, thinking to do whatever they desired, but not according as we thought; hence we are not prepared to compete with foreigners. If you, the chiefs, decided immediately to sell land to foreigners, we shall immediately be overcome. If a large number of foreigners dwell in this kingdom, some kingdom will increase in strength upon these islands; but our happiness will not increase; we, to whom the land has belonged from the beginning, will dwindle away."[23] The proposal to allow foreigners to purchase land revealed a division along class lines. The chiefs supported it; the opposition came from the makaʻāinana.

That same class conflict over the same issue reappeared in 1850, when after years of discussion land purchasing was finally opened up to foreigners. In the legislature the proposal had the unanimous support of the House of Nobles, but the other house, the one composed of elected representatives, opposed the measure at first, because, as one official explained, "they were afraid the foreigners . . . would own all the lands and some day there would be trouble." Ukeke, one of the representatives, noted that he opposed allowing foreigners to buy land "because my constituents the common people have requested me." Even after the measure passed, the settler press acknowledged that opponents had grounds for concern. "We know that it met with strong opposition from the immediate representatives of the people in the legislature," the *Polynesian* editorialized, "and that the opinion is quite prevalent among the natives that they will suffer in their rights, from want of skill and ability to compete with the foreigner. This is a natural fear, and one that should not be treated with contempt."[24]

In August 1850, finally, the Kuleana Act was enacted. A *kuleana* means a right or an interest; in the Kuleana Act, it referred to the rights of makaʻāinana in the land that they used. The act granted fee simple titles to commoners "who occupy and improve any portion" of land belonging to the government, to the king, or to a chief, "for the land they so occupy and improve." Before 1850, makaʻāinana who filed an appropriate claim with the Land Commission had the right to continue to use such land, subject to the traditional labor and produce owed to the konohiki, but not the right to sell it. After 1850, maka'āinana had the full bundle of rights associated with fee simple ownership, including the right to sell, and were freed from any obligations to the konohiki. "The Konohiki has no claim upon the tenant," the missionary Richard Armstrong exulted when the measure was approved by the Privy Council. "Each man will be his own Konohiki."[25] This freedom, and particularly the right to sell, would prove to be a mixed blessing.

The Land Commission received approximately 13,500 claims by the 1848 deadline. When it wound up its work in 1855 it had (in round numbers) granted 9,300, rejected 1,500 as unfounded, deemed another 1,500 to be duplicates of other claims, and concluded that the remaining 1,200 had been abandoned by the filers. The large majority of grants were to maka'āinana, or commoners, who constituted the large majority of the population. There were 12,000 claims filed by maka'āinana, at a time when the total number of maka'āinana was roughly 72,000, which works out to approximately one claim for every six people. Many of these claims were filed by men on behalf of families, so the number of maka'āinana who missed the opportunity to file a claim was not as large as five in six, but it nevertheless seems to have been substantial. Because many of the maka'āinana were illiterate (Hawaii lacked writing before European contact) and many lived in remote areas, many simply missed the 1848 deadline. Similar problems of communication and translation over great distances would later bedevil the parallel schemes of land tenure reform in New Zealand and the United States. After 1848 the legislature refused to extend the deadline for maka'āinana, despite several petitions asking for an extension. Chiefs who missed the deadline, by contrast, were granted a series of extensions, the last of which did not expire until 1895.[26]

In many cases maka'āinana refused to submit claims, or renounced claims they had already filed, because they preferred to continue living under traditional principles of land tenure. Such commoners inadvertently left themselves in a precarious position. When the land was sold, whether by the government, the king, or a chief, the purchaser had no obligation to respect the traditional rights of maka'āinana who had not received grants from the Land Commission. In other cases, ali'i and konohiki threatened their tenants in order to prevent them from filing claims with the commission.[27]

Government officials were well aware of these obstacles preventing many makaʻāinana from submitting claims. Some tried to encourage the filing of claims. In December 1847, with only two months left to go before the deadline, Chief Justice William Lee wrote to five ministers on the Big Island and three on Kauai, urging them to exhort Hawaiians to submit their land claims. "I learn with great pain," Lee declared in his letters to the Big Island ministers, "that there are not a dozen native claims received from the whole Island of Hawaii, while from the smaller islands of Maui and Oahu we have nearly 1200." The following month, as the deadline drew nearer and he heard reports that certain chiefs were preventing their makaʻāinana from filing claims, Lee insisted that "no Chief or Konohiki will have land awarded to him, except upon the condition of respecting, *to the fullest extent,* the rights of the tenants."[28] But Lee was whistling in the wind. Neither he nor the Land Commission had any authority to protect the rights of anyone who did not submit a claim.

Because the Land Commission confirmed existing rights rather than granting new ones, and because Hawaii was a highly stratified society, grants to chiefs were far larger than grants to commoners. In one large sample, the mean size of grants to makaʻāinana was 2.7 acres. The mean size of grants to konohiki was 74 acres; to aliʻi, 1,523 acres; and to foreigners, 141 acres. When the Māhele was finished, property ownership in Hawaii was no more egalitarian than it had been before. The chiefs ended up with 1.6 million acres of land. The government got 1.5 million acres. The king, in his personal capacity, received nearly 1 million. And the makaʻāinana, the vast majority of the population, ended up with 29,000 acres.[29]

In only a decade the independent Kingdom of Hawaii had transformed its system of land tenure. Before 1845 all the land in Hawaii was nominally owned by the king and in practice was allocated by chiefs to commoners in the form of grants revocable at the chiefs' will, in return for which the commoners were obliged to provide the chiefs with labor and produce. These rights were inalienable, whether to foreigners or to other Hawaiians. After 1855 everything had changed. Now land was held in fee simple,

4. Kamehameha III, king of Hawaii from 1825 until his death in 1854, was the architect of both phases of the kingdom's land policy. Before 1850, Kamehameha refused to modify traditional Hawaiian land tenure to allow foreigners to acquire land in fee simple, despite strong pressure from the British and American residents of Hawaii. At midcentury, however, Kamehameha authorized the series of events known as the Māhele, during which the kingdom's land was converted to Anglo-American tenure and opened for purchase by foreigners. PP97-7, negative 16,748, Hawaii State Archives.

just like in Britain or the United States. Land could be sold by anyone to anyone, whether foreigner, commoner, chief, or the king. The old land-related obligations between commoners and chiefs had ceased to exist. Rights to land were no longer revocable by the king. There had been created a new landowner—the government, as distinct from the person of the king—and the government quickly became a major seller of land. All these changes had been encouraged by the Britons and Americans holding office in the Hawaiian government, but they had been adopted willingly by the Hawaiian governing elite. The only significant opposition came from commoners, who feared—rightly, as it turned out—that land tenure reform posed the risk that foreigners would acquire a disproportionate share of the land.

What motivated all this change? Why were Hawaiian elites so ready to adopt Anglo-American land tenure?

ANNEXATION IS THOUGHT TO BE VERY NEAR

Long before the Māhele, there was a widely held belief among the white residents of Hawaii that traditional Hawaiian land tenure provided little incentive for hard work. "One of the strongest inducements to labor—that of a right of property—is entirely unknown," affirmed the missionary C. S. Stewart, who lived in Hawaii in the 1820s. "Two-thirds of the proceeds of anything a native brings to the market, unless by stealth, must be given to his chief; and, not unfrequently, the whole is unhesitatingly taken from him." Nor, Stewart insisted, did commoners have any incentive to accumulate wealth. "Any increase of stock, beyond that necessary to meet the usual taxes, is liable to be swept off at any hour; and that, perhaps, without any direct authority from a king or chief, but at the caprice of some one in their service." Stewart then recounted a story circulating among the foreign residents of Oahu, a tale that would be repeated by other critics of Hawaiian land tenure. A poor Hawaiian "by some means obtained the possession of a pig, when too small to make a meal for his family. He secreted it at a distance from his house, and fed it till it had grown to a size sufficient to afford the desired repast. It was then killed, and put into an oven, with the same precaution of secrecy; but when almost prepared for appetites whetted by long anticipation to an exquisite keenness, a caterer of the royal household unhappily came near, and, attracted to the spot by the savory fumes of the baking pile, deliberately took a seat till the animal was cooked, and then bore off the promised banquet without ceremony or apology!" The pig, whisked away at the last moment, was a metaphor for the fruits of one's labor. Without private property in the Anglo-American style, Anglo-Americans often asserted in the years before the Māhele, Hawaiians had little incentive to be industrious.[30]

That view remained the conventional wisdom among white residents in Hawaii at the time of the Māhele. In 1846 Robert Wyllie, Hawaii's minister of foreign relations, circulated a questionnaire to missionaries throughout the islands. A few of the questions concerned the "indolence and indifference" of the natives, and one requested the missionaries' advice as to "the best means of abolishing that indolence and indifference, and introducing habits of general industry." Almost every respondent suggested giving Hawaiians fee simple title to their land. The settler press editorialized repeatedly on the same theme. "It is impossible at present to predict the amount of prosperity which would result to the nation from changing the present feudal tenure of lands to the allodial," asserted the *Polynesian* in one representative issue, "but from the greater security and better definement of property, the inducements to enterprise which such a change would bring about, it would undoubtedly lead to a great improvement in the agricultural industry of the kingdom."[31]

The argument was also made again and again by the foreigners within the government: fee simple title was the surest way to turn Hawaiians from indolence to industry. William Lee was a tireless propagandist for land tenure reform, writing letter after letter in support of the Māhele to other white residents. "The present system of landed tenures in this Kingdom rests upon the nation like a mountain, pressing and crushing them to the very earth," Lee declared in one letter. "Remove it, and the fettered resources and depressed energies of the nation will rise, and cover the land with prosperity and plenty. Unless the people—the real cultivators of the soil, can have an absolute and independent right in their lands—unless they can be protected in those rights, and have what they raise as their own—they will inevitably waste away." He told another correspondent: "Before the people of Hawaii can prosper and thrive I am firmly convinced that this feudal system of landed tenures must come to an end." Lee was not a missionary in the religious sense—he was a lawyer—but when it came to land tenure reform he was very much like a missionary in his zeal to reform Hawaiian practices for what he was certain was the benefit of Hawaiians. "This silent and bloodless revolution in the landed tenures of Your Kingdom," he reported to Kamehameha, "will be the most blessed change that has ever fallen to the lot of Your Nation. It will remove the mountain of depression that has hitherto rested upon the productiveness of your soil."[32] Lee may have been more enthusiastic than the rest of the foreigners in Hawaii, but the substance of his views was typical. Whites' most commonly expressed reason for supporting land tenure reform was the hope that fee simple titles, and the ensuing ability of commoners to keep the benefits of their labor, would encourage Hawaiians to work harder.

Foreign residents of Hawaii of course had a personal stake in the matter: a thriving economy, coupled with the ability to own land themselves, would allow them to make their fortunes. They accordingly viewed traditional land tenure not just as a disincentive to local labor, but also as a deterrent to the foreign investment whites knew would be needed before agricultural production could expand significantly. This was, in part, a matter of mixing foreign capital with local labor. "Foreigners will never bring capital to your islands unless they can make a good profit upon that capital," Wyllie lectured Kamehameha in 1847. "To enable them to do so, your native subjects must have land to cultivate . . . and they must be sure that what they work for and what they produce will not and cannot be taken from them." It was also, in part, a matter of inducing foreigners to settle in Hawaii themselves. Large-scale land transfer to whites "need not prejudice the natives," insisted the *Polynesian.* "On the contrary, it will benefit them, not only by enhancing the value of their lands, but it is the surest means of providing a market for all they can produce, and of encouraging them, by influence and example, to labor more steadily."[33]

Whites often expressed a distaste for the inequality that characterized Hawaiian political and social life, and this provided Hawaii's foreign community with a second motivation for the Māhele. The Americans, in particular, were horrified at the power the king and the chiefs could exercise over commoners. "There *must grow up a middle class, who shall be farmers, tillers of the soil, or there is no salvation for this nation,*" William Lee declared in one of his many letters advocating reform. "My sympathies are all with the mass—the poor, Konohiki-ridden mass of common Kanakas, and my anxiety to have them send in their claims, and get their rights committed to writing, is beyond expression." As chief justice, Lee wasted no time in upholding the new written rights of the maka'āinana against claims by others, even the claims of foreigners based on grants from the king. "The people's lands were secured to them by the Constitution and laws of the Kingdom, and no power can convey them away, not even that of royalty itself," Lee affirmed in one of the first reported cases of the Hawaii Supreme Court. Lee was hardly alone in his disapproval of the Hawaiian aristocracy. The settler press acknowledged that among foreign residents there was a widespread "preference in favor of small farmers," and argued that the traditional hierarchy was not just inefficient but a "baneful influence upon the moral welfare of the people" because of the power some Hawaiians wielded over others.[34] British and American reformers could sincerely view themselves as genuine progressives, on the side of the common Hawaiian, seeking to break up an obsolete and tyrannical political structure and in its place introduce a more egalitarian way of life.

This view was unlikely to be held by many Hawaiian elites themselves, and it may even have been risky for other Hawaiians to express it out loud. The intellectual and government official David Malo, one of the most westernized Hawaiians at midcentury, was afraid to admit publicly that he too supported land tenure reform as a method of reducing the power of the Hawaiian aristocracy over the commoners. If land could be owned in fee simple, he reasoned in a letter to the missionary William Richards, "this high handedness exercised by the chiefs would cease." But after making an eloquent case for reform, he promptly pleaded with Richards: "Don't mention that I have urged you to do this."[35]

Although members of the Hawaiian governing elite would have had little interest in this sort of egalitarian political reform, they had an interest in economic reform. They too stood to gain from increased agricultural productivity. They were major landowners, so they would benefit from any general rise in land values, and the ability to sell their land (especially to foreigners) would allow them to capitalize on an asset that had previously been unmonetizable. Some, moreover, were government officials. They had an interest in expanding the revenues received by the government, to the extent those revenues could be derived from people other than themselves. Land tenure reform raised this possibility, by abandoning the old in-kind taxes, the labor and produce received from makaʻainana, and replacing them with property taxes payable in money and with the revenue from government land sales. The prospect of reorganizing the kingdom's public finance in this way was discussed in the Hawaiian press. From such measures, Interior Minister Gerrit Judd earnestly hoped, "the revenue may eventually be so far improved as not only to provide for the current expenditure upon its present scale, but for an increase of the present low salaries allowed to public officers."[36] Among those public officers were some of the Hawaiian nobility, who no doubt agreed.

The king stood to profit most of all from land tenure reform. He was simultaneously the largest landowner and the largest consumer of tax revenue, so he would gain more than any chief from a rise in property values, from the ability to sell land to foreigners, and from an increase in government revenue. Kamehameha seems to have been well aware of these prospects. In December 1847, in the midst of a discussion of the impending Māhele, Judd noted: "King wishes to sell & rent for himself to raise money for his own use."[37] From Kamehameha's perspective, land tenure reform offered a chance to be free from the constraints of traditional Hawaiian public finance, as it would open up a private revenue stream that could be expected to dwarf the existing public treasury.

The Hawaiian elite thus had some enduring reasons to undertake land tenure reform. But why did that reform take place in the 1840s rather than before or after? These motivations for the Māhele were all securely in place long before the Māhele occurred. Foreigners had been complaining about the inefficiencies and inequalities of traditional Hawaiian land tenure, and trying to persuade the Hawaiian elite to change their property system, for decades. Whatever fiscal benefits the king and the chiefs might have anticipated from reform in the 1840s could just as easily have been anticipated in the 1820s, or, for that matter, in the 1860s. What happened in the 1840s to make these benefits more salient?

The answer is that the Hawaiian governing elite had good reason to believe that Hawaii would not remain independent for long. In 1840 Britain assumed sovereignty over New Zealand. In 1842 France assumed sovereignty over Tahiti and the Marquesas. In Hawaii, members of the nobility knew of these developments and were concerned that Hawaii might be next. In August 1842, after a conversation with Kekuanaoa, the governor of Oahu, the missionary Stephen Reynolds noted in his diary that "Kekuanaoa asked me about France taking possession of Marquesas Islands & seemed much alarmed thinking they would come here." Queen Pomare of Tahiti corresponded with Kamehameha in 1844 and 1845. "I have frequently heard of your troubles and of the death of your Government and of your grief," Kamehameha commiserated with Pomare, "but I don't have the power within me to help you."[38] Accounts of events elsewhere in the Pacific were published in Hawaiian newspapers. In Hawaii in the early 1840s, annexation by a foreign power seemed imminent.

Britain and France had recently been sending warships to Hawaii, which reinforced the fear among Hawaiian elites that their turn was coming soon. When the United States Exploring Expedition arrived in Hawaii in 1840, Charles Wilkes, the expedition's commander, found that Kamehameha was already nervous about antagonizing the foreign residents of Hawaii, for fear that one of these ships would eventually bear foreigners who would annex the kingdom in retaliation for something he had done.[39]

Indeed, for a few months in 1843 Hawaii actually was annexed, by Britain. Lord George Paulet, the commander of a single British frigate, thinking he was protecting the property interests of British residents of Hawaii, forced Kamehameha to relinquish his kingdom to Britain. When news reached London, the imperial government promptly ordered Paulet to give the kingdom back. Paulet, having governed since February, returned sovereignty to Kamehameha in July.[40] The episode seems farcical in retrospect, but it could not have been amusing to the Hawaiian governing elite, who for a time saw their sovereign power vanish and who must have been nervous about their landholdings as well.

For years afterward, Hawaiians heard recurring rumors of impending foreign annexation. French sailors rampaged through Honolulu in the summer of 1849, destroying government property before returning to their ship and sailing away. A few months later, the Privy Council discussed a letter recently received from San Francisco, describing shadowy plans circulating in California to overthrow the Hawaiian government.

"Annexation is thought to be very near at hand," Chief Justice William Lee confided in 1854, "& expectation is on tip toe for its arrival. It is generally thought that it will take place in a month." Charles de Varigny, a Frenchman who lived in Hawaii in the 1850s and 1860s (and who was Hawaii's finance minister for a few years in the 1860s), recalled in his memoirs feeling how "the great maritime powers, France, England, and the United States of America, watch Hawaii with jealous eyes."[41] The genuine threat of colonization was a constant presence in Hawaii, from the early 1840s onward.

In this climate, the Hawaiian elite did the rational thing: they began making plans to protect their property in the event they had to give up their sovereignty. They knew they could not resist a colonizer's overwhelming military advantage; that much had been demonstrated in 1843, when a single British ship annexed the kingdom. They began instead to put their affairs in order.

A couple of the Americans working in Kamehameha's government, John Ricord and William Lee, were lawyers. Lee was in the habit of quoting Mansfield, Story, and Kent, apparently extemporaneously, in his jury charges. Kamehameha's other foreign advisors were not as well-read as Lee, but Lee, at least, was sophisticated enough to know the basic legal history of previous American territorial expansions, and others may have been as well. They would most likely have known that when the United States assumed sovereignty over new areas, the U.S. government recognized preexisting property rights derived from earlier sovereigns.[42] After the Louisiana Purchase, for instance, existing property owners, based on grants from France and Spain, got to keep their land. The United States likewise recognized Spanish land grants after the acquisition of Florida. If Hawaii were to be colonized by the United States, it would be prudent to put Hawaiian land titles into a form that resembled the titles recognized in these earlier expansions.

Some of Kamehameha's American advisors would most likely have also known that land possessed by American Indians, land that had never been formally granted to the Indians by the United States or any of its European colonial predecessors, received a far lesser degree of protection when the United States took over a new territory. Under U.S. law, the Indians were deemed to hold merely an ambiguous "right of occupancy" in such land, a right that might not be strong enough to withstand foreign conquest.[43] And in some cases, where Indian tribes had fought wars against the United States or its colonial predecessors, the United States had claimed the tribes' land by right of conquest. The best-known example had taken place after the American Revolution, when the new federal government had confiscated land possessed by many of the tribes who had fought on behalf of Britain. The lesson here was obvious. Traditional Hawaiian land tenure looked more like American Indian tenure than it resembled the written grants of France or Spain. To preserve its property in the event of colonization, the Hawaiian elite ought to convert its system of land tenure, ahead of time, to a form more likely to be respected by the United States.

British and French land policies were less clear. Kamehameha's advisors would most likely have been aware that in 1840 Britain annexed New Zealand in a treaty that recognized an undefined category of Maori property rights in land, and that the 1842 document establishing French sovereignty over Tahiti likewise preserved Tahitian land possessions. They might also have known, however, that in colonizing Australia a few decades earlier, the British had not recognized Aboriginal Australians as owners of their land at all, but had simply taken the land and doled it out to Britons. This uneven record suggested that unless Hawaii converted its system of land tenure, the Hawaiian elite was no more likely to retain its landholdings in a British Hawaii or a French Hawaii than in an American Hawaii. Each of the potential colonizers tended to draw a distinction between land owned under a customary indigenous property system and land owned under a European-style system, in which rights were evidenced by written grants emanating from a sovereign. Where land was owned in traditional tenure, the colonized nation ran a considerable risk that traditional property rights might not be recognized by the colonizer, and that land might accordingly be confiscated by the colonial government. Where land was owned in fee simple, however, the colonizer was far more likely to respect the property rights of the colonized.

Understandably, Hawaiian elites were very interested in this information. At a Privy Council meeting in 1847, Kamehameha asked: "If his lands were merely entered in a Book, the Government lands also in a Book, and all private allodial titles in a Book, if a Foreign Power should take the Islands what lands would they respect. Would they take possession of his lands?" He recalled an earlier instance of a monarch who had lost his power, on the other side of the world: "During the French Revolution were not the King's lands confiscated?" William Lee responded with an accurate picture of American land policy in earlier territorial expansions: "Except in the case of resistance to, & conquest by, any foreign power," he explained, "the King's right to his private lands would be respected." Robert Wyllie added that the French Revolution was a very different case: Louis XVI's lands "were confiscated, but that was by the King's own rebellious subjects," not by a foreign colonizer. Protecting his own land in the event of a foreign takeover was of paramount importance to Kamehameha. "Unless it were so," he told his Privy Council—unless he could be confident of retaining his land under a foreign sovereign—"he would prefer having no lands whatever."[44]

Two aspects of Lee's advice deserve emphasis. First, if Hawaii were to fight a war against a colonizer, the land in Hawaii was liable to be confiscated by the conqueror, particularly land belonging to people who participated in the fighting. The king would of course be a particularly conspicuous combatant were he to lead Hawaiian resistance to colonization, so his land would be particularly at risk. This consideration counseled against offering armed resistance to colonization if resistance seemed likely to fail, as it surely did.

Second, Lee might well have placed an emphasis on the word *private* when he explained that Kamehameha's private lands would be respected. An incoming colonial government would be certain to claim ownership of any land belonging to the Hawaiian government. (The United States government, for example, had assumed ownership of all the land in the Louisiana Purchase territory that had previously been owned by the government of France.) For that reason it was crucial to Kamehameha's planning that his own private land be clearly separated from the government's land. He knew this very well. After Lee gave his response, "the King observed that he would prefer that his private lands should be registered not in a separate Book, but in the same Book as all other Allodial Titles, and that the only separate Book, should be that of the Government Lands." This was a shrewd idea, and one that the Privy Council immediately adopted. Kamehameha was worried, reasonably enough, that an incoming colonizer might consider his land more "public" than "private." If the written evidence of the king's private domain differed in any way from the written evidence of the land belonging to other Hawaiians, that would offer a ground for distinguishing between the king and everyone else, and thus for placing the king's land on the "public" side of the line. Kamehameha was suggesting that steps be taken to depict the true distinction as being between government land and private land, regardless of the identity of the owner.

When Kamehameha suggested that he might "prefer having no lands whatever" if he could not be sure of retaining his land after colonization, he may have been suggesting a clever alternative strategy. If Lee had been unable to reassure him that denominating his land as "private" would allow him to keep it after colonization, a second-best plan would have been for Kamehameha to formally divest himself of all his landholdings, most likely by conveying parcels to individual ali'i. Before colonization, the traditional Hawaiian social structure would most likely have allowed Kamehameha to go on living as before, with an implicit understanding from the ali'i that although they were now the formal owners of the land, they were merely keeping it for the king. Should colonization occur, there would be no land for the new sovereign to confiscate, because Kamehameha would not own any land. Even if he were actually using the land, the ali'i would be the owners. This alternative was never seriously explored, probably because Lee and Kamehameha were confident that a division between government land and the king's private land was enough to do the trick.

A clear division between these two categories of land—government land and the king's private domain—was thus a crucial component of Hawaiian planning for what appeared to be imminent colonization. In 1847, when the Land Commissioners published the principles that would guide its decisions, this distinction was one of them. The Land Commission explained that in the Constitution of 1840, "the government or body politic and the King are for the first time, contradistinguished." The king still controlled the public lands, but only in his capacity as the head of the government, "and from these is contradistinguished his own private lands," which he owned in his personal capacity, like any landowner. When members of the government mistakenly asserted, as Robert Wyllie did, that "the King as an Individual and as the Head of the Nation should be regarded as one," or, as Kekuanaoa did, that "the King & Government ought to be considered the same," Lee stepped in immediately to correct them. It was a "great error" to believe that "the King & Government were *one* in their lands," he informed Wyllie. "The constitution recognises no such unity of property." To Kekuanaoa he replied: "The King and Government were one and the same in most things, but not in every thing. From the Constitution it seemed clear that in property the King and Government were two separate and distinct persons." In preparing for Kamehameha's future, it was crucial to be sure that "the King's lands and the Government's interest in lands are clearly treated as separate and distinct."[45]

The importance of clarity on this point was especially evident when the Hawaiian legislature formally accepted the division of land between the king and the government. Some legislators were not entirely sure what had taken place, so Gerrit Judd provided an account. Kamehameha "reserved unto his own private use a portion of the lands which are set out in this Act," Judd related. "The rest of the lands he has given to the Chiefs and people which constitute the Government." And then Judd told the legislature why: "If no explanation of this kind is made, it will mix matters later on, and some of the foreigners will come later on and say they have an interest in the lands too."[46] The Hawaiian government was doing its best to make the new land tenure arrangements as legible as possible, to protect the king's property after colonization.

For other Hawaiians, the task of preparing to be colonized was simpler. To protect their property, all they could do was obtain written titles from the Hawaiian government and hope for the best. In the event of colonization, Wyllie recognized, "all the natives, high and low, become hewers of wood and drawers of water. In such a case, it is only private property that is respected, and therefore it would be wise to put every native family throughout the Islands, in possession of a good piece of land, in fee simple, as soon as possible."[47] Even if Hawaiians would become a lower caste in an American (or British or French) Hawaii, the hope was that they would at least be able to hold on to their land. With some advance planning, and with some legal advice from Kamehameha's foreign assistants, Hawaiians might place themselves in a better position than the indigenous peoples previously colonized by white powers.

The Māhele, then, was a kind of vaccine. By adopting one particular aspect of the colonizer's law, the Hawaiian elite was inoculating itself against the catastrophic consequences of colonization. Even under a foreign sovereign, they hoped, they would still own vast tracts of land; they would still be an elite.

THE AMERICAN FASHION

The plan worked, in some respects. The Māhele, considered as a device to protect the landholdings of the Hawaiian elite, achieved much of what it was intended to achieve. Colonization did not come until the 1890s, but when the United States took over, it did indeed recognize the property rights that had been formalized during the Māhele. Much of this land was still owned by the descendants of the chiefs who had received fee simple title two generations before. By then many of the original Māhele awards had been subdivided among children and grandchildren, and there had been some intermarriage between Hawaiians and non-Hawaiians, but even in the mid-1930s there were still native Hawaiians who owned tens of thousands of acres of land in fee simple.[48]

Had the Māhele never occurred—had Hawaii retained its traditional system of land tenure through the 1890s—it is extremely unlikely that the United States would have recognized these massive estates. Rather, upon annexation the federal government would have become the fee simple owner of all the land in Hawaii. Hawaiians would have been deemed to hold their land by right of occupancy, the same tenure accorded to the indigenous inhabitants of the mainland. The federal government was then in the midst of allotting Indian reservations, and it would probably have done the same in Hawaii. The government would have given the chiefs no particular solicitude during this process; as on the mainland, the chiefs would have received the same allotments as everyone else. For the aristocratic Hawaiian families who managed to keep their landholdings intact through the nineteenth century, the Māhele was thus a tremendous success. By converting from Hawaiian to Anglo-American land tenure they saved their land.

In some respects, however, the Māhele failed to work as planned. Most obviously, it allowed Hawaiian landowners, who were often land-rich but cash-poor, to sell their land to foreigners, and many did. Within a few months of the enactment of the statute that allowed foreigners to buy land, there was already a thriving market. "Real Estate has advanced to a high figure, and has not yet reached its height," William Lee reported in December 1850. "All of Waikiki Plain has been divided into lots 100ft x 150ft and sold at auction, at an average price of over $100 per lot. The 5 lots owned by us, I have been offered $500 for." A few months later, Lee related that he had purchased a twenty-seven-acre farm up in the mountains from Governor Kekuanaoa for $2,000. "Lands adapted to the cultivation of Sugar Cane, coffee, potatoes, etc., are daily increasing in value," he explained. The missionaries jumped in as well. Elias Bond, for instance, noted in his journal around 1850 that he had bought a tract in Halaula for his brother, whom he hoped would come from Maine "to start a farm to give the natives employment." By the early 1850s even Americans on the mainland were buying up Hawaiian land as an investment.[49] Some of these purchases were from the government, but many were from private landowners newly empowered by the Māhele to sell.

Within a decade or two, it was already a commonplace among English-speaking travelers to Hawaii that Americans had bought most of the good land. Mark Twain visited in 1866 and discovered that "Americans . . . own the great sugar plantations; they own the cattle ranches; they own their share of the mercantile depots." Charles Nordhoff's 1874 tourist guide agreed that "almost all the sugar-plantations—the most productive and valuable property on the Islands—are owned by Americans; and the same is true of the greater number of stock farms." Nordhoff concluded, "If our flag flew over Honolulu we could hardly expect to have a more complete monopoly of Hawaiian commerce than we already enjoy." English lawyer Hugh Wilkinson was disappointed when he arrived in Hono-

5. *No. 1: View of Honolulu from the Harbor* (ca. 1854). Sketch by Paul Emmert, engraving by G. H. Burgess, lithograph by Britton and Rey. Within a few years of the Māhele, much of the best land in Hawaii had been purchased by white Americans. This mid-1850s view of Honolulu emphasizes commercial buildings and churches in the American style. LC-USZ62-52238, Library of Congress.

lulu in 1881, because his hoped-for exoticism had vanished. All he found were "churches, chapels, homes and meeting-houses, libraries, schools and colleges galore! The town is laid in squares, after the American fashion."[50] By the time of annexation, a half century after the Māhele, the Hawaiian aristocracy had already sold off much of its land. The Māhele protected what was left, but the Māhele had also enabled the sales.

Indeed, the Māhele stood in a complicated relationship with annexation. On the one hand, had foreigners not been allowed to purchase land, annexation might have come sooner. The foreign community in Hawaii was steadily growing at midcentury, and the pressure to purchase land might have become so great as to encourage, sometime in the middle of the century, the sort of white revolution that eventually took place in the 1890s. On the other hand, by permitting foreigners to purchase land, Hawaiians inadvertently facilitated their own annexation. The Māhele led to the formation of a class of wealthy American landowners who became the driving force behind the overthrow of the Hawaiian monarchy. Hawaii would likely have been colonized with or without the Māhele, and it is hard to say whether the Māhele accelerated annexation or retarded it.

The Māhele failed most conspicuously in the case of the royal family, but for reasons that its framers could not have anticipated. Kamehameha III emerged from the Māhele with a private domain of nearly a million acres. He died in 1854; the successor to his crown and to his lands was his adopted son Alexander Liholiho, who became Kamehameha IV. Nine years later, Kamehameha IV died, leaving a widow, Queen Emma, but no children and no will. His older brother became Kamehameha V. A dispute soon arose between Emma and Kamehameha V over the status of the king's private domain. Emma argued that for purposes of inheritance the land once possessed by her husband in his personal capacity should be treated as ordinary private property, just like land possessed by any other person in Hawaii. Such treatment would have entitled her under Hawaiian intestacy law to the standard widow's share: one half of the land in fee simple, and dower (a life estate) in the other half. Kamehameha V argued that as the successor to the crown he was entitled to all the land possessed by the former king. In 1864 the dispute was submitted to the Supreme Court of Hawaii, which split the difference. Emma, the court held, was entitled to the ordinary dower rights of a widow, but not to fee simple title in any of the land. The court determined that the king's private domain was unlike ordinary private land, in that inheritance was limited to successors to the throne. While a king was alive, he could do anything with his private domain that a private landowner could do: he could sell the land, or lease it, or alienate it any way he chose. But the one thing he could not do was convey it upon his death to someone other than the next king.[51]

With this decision, the Supreme Court undid much of what had been done in the Māhele with respect to the king's land. The aim of Kamehameha III had been to make land owned in his personal capacity resemble ordinary privately owned land as closely as possible, to ensure that an incoming colonizer would treat it that way. Now, however, the king's private domain was clearly marked as different from other people's private land, and in a way that made it look quasi-public, because (unless sold during a king's lifetime) it would follow the Hawaiian monarchy forever. This was exactly what Kamehameha III did *not* want to do. The Supreme Court's opinion rests on an implausible reading of the events of the late 1840s. It can only be justified as a practical expedient—perhaps to avoid unduly antagonizing the new king, Kamehameha V, or perhaps to ensure that the royal private domain would not be dissipated over the generations.

The Supreme Court's decision led to an even more surprising event the following year. The kingdom's legislature, evidently emboldened by the court's opinion, passed a statute providing that the king's private domain would thenceforth be inalienable (except for leases not exceeding thirty years) and would descend intact to subsequent monarchs forever.[52] With this step, the king's private lands now looked more like public land than private. Now the government was protected against land losses caused by an improvident monarch, but the monarch was no longer protected against expropriation in the event of colonization.

Sure enough, when colonization came, expropriation of the monarchy's private domain followed. Upon annexation, the United States respected the Māhele-derived land titles of everyone except the monarch then in place, Queen Liliuokalani. The United States deemed her land to be public, not private, and the federal government accordingly assumed ownership of it, just as it did with land once owned by the Hawaiian government. When Liliuokalani challenged this decision in the Court of Claims, the court disposed of her claim with little trouble. The Court of Claims found that the Hawaii Supreme Court, in its 1864 resolution of the dispute between Emma and Kamehameha V, had fashioned a royal private domain that was "limited as to possession and descent by conditions abhorrent to a fee-simple estate absolute." "It is clear from the opinion," the Court of Claims continued, "that the crown lands were treated not as the king's private property in the strict sense of the term. While possessing certain attributes pertaining to fee-simple estates, such as unrestricted power of alienation and incumbrance, there were likewise enough conditions surrounding the tenure to clearly characterize it as one pertaining to the support and maintenance of the Crown, as distinct from the person of the Sovereign. They belonged to the office and not to the individual." That conclusion was reinforced by the 1865 statute, which the court found "expressly divested the King of whatever legal title or possession he theretofore had in or to the Crown lands." In short, "the Hawaiian Government in 1865 by its own legislation determined what the court is now asked to determine."⁵³ The royal private domain had become public land, not private, and as public land it was ceded to the United States upon annexation. The worst nightmares of Kamehameha III had come true.

The Māhele thus failed in some important respects, but it was a genuine success from the perspective of many of its intended beneficiaries. The Hawaiian royal family lost its land to the government of the United States, but only because the other two branches of the Hawaiian government left the monarchy exposed to expropriation, many years after the Māhele was over. Many Hawaiian aristocratic families also lost their land to whites, but that was not due to annexation either; it was because they sold it. The Māhele did not provide much land to Hawaiian commoners, but it was not supposed to. The Māhele was a means by which the Hawaiian elite hoped to preserve its eliteness under colonial rule, by holding on to its land. In that sense, it worked.

The Hawaiian elite could not have carried out this plan had the United States and the other potential colonial powers treated Hawaii as terra nullius, as Britain had treated Australia. The presence of agriculture in Hawaii before European contact was thus a prerequisite to the Māhele. Nor could Hawaiians have carried out the plan had they been divided into several small political units like the Maori. A second prerequisite was the unification of Hawaii under a single monarch. Agriculture and a high degree of political organization allowed the Hawaiians to hold on to much of their land. The importance of these two factors can be seen especially clearly by comparing the fate of Hawaiians to that of an indigenous people who encountered whites in significant numbers at approximately the same time but who possessed neither agriculture nor much political organization—the Indians of California.

⊶⊷⊷⊶

chapter five

California

Terra Nullius by Default

CALIFORNIA IS THE ONLY part of the United States the federal government formally treated as terra nullius. That was less an intentional decision than a by-product of events: the government negotiated land cession treaties with many of the California tribes in 1851 and 1852, but the Senate refused to ratify those treaties and the government never bothered to secure new ones. Indians in California, like Aboriginal Australians, ended up with no recognized property rights in their land. That would not change for more than a century.

The colonization of California thus raises the same questions raised by the colonization of Australia. Why did California end up with an Indian land policy different from that for the rest of the United States? And why did California's anomalous status last so long?

THE LOWEST SPECIMENS OF HUMANITY

The early English-speaking visitors to California tended to perceive the Indians of California as extremely primitive. "All the various tribes of this country, are found in their aboriginal state of barbarism, as perfectly wild and timid, as the herds of beasts, with which they are surrounded," reported the Ohio lawyer Lansford Hastings, who traveled around California in 1843 and 1844. "They do not even build huts, nor do they wear any kind of clothing; being mere children of nature." This impression only grew stronger with repeated contact: the California Indians were "semi-barbarians," they were "brutes"; they were "wild children of the forest . . . their life, aimless and brutal; and their enjoyments, nothing above those of the beasts."[1]

Measured by any criterion of nineteenth-century Anglo-American civilization, the Indians were consistently found wanting. They were "indolent and averse from labor of every kind." They were "thievish, ungrateful, and dirty and lazy to an excess." Digging for gold on the American River in 1849, the minister (and temporary miner) Daniel Woods could discern simply by watching them that the local Indians "are very coarse and indolent" and that they "are uncivilized, and possess few of the arts of life."[2]

Perhaps their most commonly perceived shortcoming was their lack of agriculture. "The sustenance of the Indians appears to be now, as it always has been, principally grasshoppers, clover, acorns and the nut of the sugar pine, varied with fish when in season," the miner Pringle Shaw discovered. Some Indians had learned to farm from Europeans—there were agricultural villages along the coast near the former Spanish missions, and near John Sutter's inland settlement—and some tribes may have planted crops even before European contact, but these were a distinct minority at midcentury. Many white observers emphasized the Indians' dependence on roots and acorns—the Paiute and Shoshone of eastern California were widely called "Diggers" for this reason. Others more luridly focused on the Indians' sources of protein. "The way they caught grasshoppers and ate them would turn the stomach of anyone," one settler gasped. "Grasshoppers, snails and wasps are favorite delicacies with them," explained Hinton Rowan Helper, who would become famous as a southern abolitionist once he returned from California to North Carolina in the mid-1850s. "They have a particular relish for a certain little animal, which the Bible tells us greatly afflicted the Egyptians in the days of Pharaoh." Along the Humboldt River, the miner David Leeper found that the Indians "seemed to subsist mainly on the fat black crickets of the valley and the plenitude of their own vermin." California Indians in fact ate a wide variety of wild plants and animals, many of which, like fish and rabbits, were quite familiar to Anglo-Americans and so figured less prominently in the accounts of travelers.[3] But it was nevertheless true that most of the Indians in California were not farmers.

Indeed, a near consensus soon developed among white Californians that the state's Indians were, as the minister Horace Bushnell put it, "about the lowest specimens of humanity found upon the earth." They were consistently ranked below the other Indians of North America. Some put them even lower. At a time when Aboriginal Australians were commonly viewed in the English-speaking world as the absolute bottom in the scale of civilization, the Scottish traveler J. D. Borthwick found the Indians of California "very little less degraded and uncivilisable than the blacks of New South Wales." The American historian and lawyer Robert Greenhow, after reading many of the early travelers' accounts, concluded that "the aborigines of California are placed, by those who have had the best opportunity of studying their character and disposition, with the Hottentots, the Patagonians, and the Australians, among the lowest of the human race." The Yale botanist William Henry Brewer, who traveled throughout the state for four years as part of the Geological Survey of California, made a similar comparison perhaps more readily understood by Americans. "These Indians are very dark," he noted, "black as our darkest mulattoes, and not as intelligent looking as the negro."[4]

Emigrants from the eastern United States were repeatedly disappointed that the natives of California did not match their expectations of what Indians should be like, expectations formed from books rather than personal experience. In California the Indians were "neither brave nor bold, generous nor spirited," complained Franklin Tuthill. They lacked "the noble characteristics that, with a slight coloring of romance, make heroes of the red men of the Atlantic slopes, and win for them our ready sympathy. We hear of no orators among them, no bold braves terribly resenting and contesting to the last the usurpations of the whites." Easterners were comparing living Indians in California to romanticized eastern Indians of the distant past. But they were still disappointed. "It is universally conceded that the California Indians possess but few, if any, of those nobly daring traits of character which have distinguished the savage tribes of the Atlantic States, from the days of King Philip down to the notorious Billy

Bowlegs," one emigrant from Massachusetts reported. "They are deficient in all those manly arts which have given measurable immortality to the Cherokees." Children's novelist Alice Bradley Haven summed up this disappointment in her 1853 account of a westbound family. To young Sam, accompanying his father to the gold mines, "the natives seemed much more like children than grown up men, just as he had read about them in books of travel. He did not think they came up to his idea of the North American Indians, found by the first settlers on the Atlantic coast. To [his brother] Ben and himself, King Philip and his followers had always seemed finely formed, stern and resolute braves,—it would be hard to transform the thoughtless, degraded Californian natives into warriors, even in imagination."[5]

Dirty, lazy, ugly, stupid, subsisting on vermin rather than agriculture—the local Indians seemed to many white Californians more like animals than noble savages. "The only thing that can be called *human* in the appearance of the digger Indians of the Sierra Nevada is their resemblance to the sons of Adam," James Carson insisted. "I have made these class of beings a study and in them I find but few traits belonging to the human family." The English traveler William Kelly made the comparison even more specific. "In natural conformation the Digger Indian is very few degrees removed from the orang-outang," he reasoned; "not much above its stature, having the same compressed physiognomy, a low forehead, with little or no space between the eyebrows and roots of the hair. He is altogether devoid of resources, possessing little beyond the instinctive cunning of the monkey." Others made the same point inadvertently. American military commander R. B. Mason, in Monterey in 1848, found "a great many people and Indians," as if these were two separate species. The painter William M'Ilvaine, sketching scenes of the gold rush, feared "the grizzly bears and wild Indians." Silas Weston, who took time off from his job as a grammar school principal in Providence, Rhode Island, to try his luck in the mines, was likewise nervous about "encountering grizzly bears and the Indians, many of which infest this region of the country."[6] In such accounts one senses an unspoken and perhaps unconscious hesitation as to whether to classify the Indians as fully human, an uncertainty that had not existed with respect to Indians in other parts of the United States.

The line between humans and animals was not as distinct in the mid-nineteenth century as it had once been. Darwin's *Origin of Species* was published in 1859, in an intellectual climate in which evolution was being discussed more earnestly than ever before. It would not be long before criminologists would begin finding animal-like characteristics in criminals. The Indians of California were thus of considerable interest to those who believed they were studying man from a newly scientific point of view. In his 1852 treatise *Comparative Physiognomy; or, Resemblances Between Men and Animals,* James Redfield explained that the California Indians have a footprint "so like that of the grizzly bear, that it can only be distinguished by the size. The ball of the foot is more deeply indented in the ground in consequence of their treading more heavily on that part of the foot, like an animal." Redfield noted, "They are thought by some to be a link between man and brute, as if it were possible for such a link to exist. And why is this? It is because their resemblance to the bear has degenerated to that of the hog. They subsist entirely on roots and acorns, refusing flesh, and having no knowledge of agriculture." The social Darwinist Charles Loring Brace saw them as a confirmation of the truth of natural selection. "For centuries beyond reckoning," he reasoned, "this low and degraded tribe has lived in a state of unchanging barbarism, suited to its surroundings, and therefore continuing to exist. . . . The fossil Indians have not 'developed,' because it was not necessary in their 'struggle for existence.'"[7]

The struggle for existence became far more difficult in the late 1840s, when Anglo-Americans began arriving in California in significant numbers. The United States was of course not the first nation to colonize California. The Spanish had established missions along the coast beginning in the middle of the eighteenth century. By the early nineteenth century, many members of coastal tribes lived in or near these missions. Nominal sovereignty over California passed to Mexico in 1821, when Mexico gained its independence from Spain. Before the 1840s, however, the non-Indian population of California remained very small—by one estimate, as late as 1845 there were fewer than 4,000 non-Indians in California.[8] By 1850 there were 93,000, and by 1860 the census counted 380,000. Most of them had come from the eastern United States.

The new Californians of the late 1840s did not attempt to purchase land from the Indians. They tended instead either to occupy areas that seemed unused or to expel Indians from areas they desired. As in Australia, the long tradition of associating agriculture with property rights in land predisposed Anglo-Americans to consider the Indians as lacking any rights they were bound to respect. The California Indians, like Aboriginal Australians, were weak military opponents. They were at a considerable technological disadvantage relative to the settlers, and they were fragmented into small groups that spoke mutually unintelligible languages, which posed an insuperable obstacle to the formation of intertribal alliances.[9] The early Anglo-American settlers in California were thus both willing and able to acquire land without obtaining the Indians' consent.

By the 1840s the government of the United States had a long history of purchasing land from small nonagricultural tribes. Actual conditions on the frontier often diverged from formal policy, and that policy itself was not always benign, but had American government officials been in California by the late 1840s, they might have restrained at least some of the early settlers from taking the Indians' land. The United States did not acquire formal sovereignty over California, however, until 1848. No representatives of the federal government reached California until late 1849. For the first few years of significant white emigration, the settlers were largely outside the federal government's control.

There was little, therefore, to prevent the early settlers from mistreating the Indians. In 1846 the expedition led by John Frémont found a group of settlers at Deer Creek who had already so antagonized the Indians that they feared a massacre. Frémont refused to intervene on behalf of the government, but he did allow his men to take a temporary leave from government employ to participate as private individuals in the slaughter of nearly two hundred Indians. Most of the Anglo-Americans in Monterey in 1847, reported the naval officer Henry Wise, were rough men who "had passed the greater portion of their lives as trappers and hunters." They were "men who wouldn't stick at scalping an Indian. . . . In truth," Wise concluded, "the natives had good reason to regard them with terror." By 1847 the military captain Henry Naglee was urging upon his superior officers "the necessity of publishing some decree forbidding all persons from trespassing upon the Indians," for fear of being "forced into an interminable indian warfare."[10]

The discovery of gold, and the resulting influx of whites into northern California, only made matters worse. "The whites were strong, and drove the red man into the mountains, and for the crime of having *tried* to defend their homes and offspring, they are placed under a ban, and hunted down like wild beasts," John Letts reported from Placerville. Many Indians, after losing their accustomed places to live and gather food, were employed by gold miners.[11]

Many more were captured and sold into slavery. Indian slavery predated significant Anglo-American immigration. English-speaking settlers, many of whom were from slave states, took naturally to this system. On Frémont's 1843 expedition to California, Kit Carson "bought an Indian boy of about twelve to fourteen years for forty dollars," Frémont's cartographer noted in his diary. "He belongs to the Paiute Nation, which subsists only on mice, locusts, and roots, and such a life as the present must please him very much." Even after slavery was formally abolished in California in 1850, Indian slavery remained common. "The process is, to raise a posse and drive in as many of the untamed natives as are requisite, and compel them to assist in working the land," explained the miner James Delavan. "No doubt all these respectable proprietors are *Wilmot proviso* men, and eschew slavery," Delavan scoffed, "but their mode of recruiting the number of their laborers is something more exceptionable, than if they obtained their supplies from the far-famed slave market at Washington." Indian slavery remained a subject of newspaper comment in San Francisco well into the 1860s.[12]

In an atmosphere in which Indians were being hunted down and enslaved, there was little sentiment for recognizing Indian property rights in land. Occasional voices *were* raised in the Indians' defense. The naval lieutenant Joseph Revere, Paul's grandson, arrived in San Francisco in early 1849 to discover that "lots were being staked off and sold at auction in every direction and fabulous sums paid for them," without any regard to whether the land had previously been possessed by Indians. Despite their evident shortcomings, Revere declared, "we find them nevertheless upon their native soil, to which they hold an equitable title derived directly

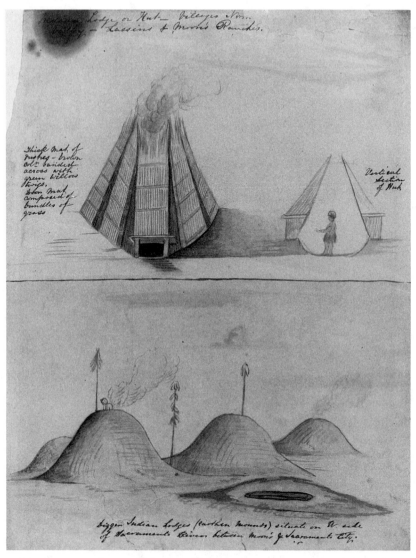

6. The Americans who swarmed into California in the late 1840s perceived the local Indians to be far less advanced in the arts of civilization than Indians elsewhere in the United States, as this drawing (ca. 1850) of "Digger" Indian dwellings suggests. Gold miners and other new arrivals in California did not respect Indian property rights. In the end, neither did the federal government. 1963.002:0285-B, Bancroft Library, University of California, Berkeley.

from the Almighty." He did not suggest that Indians ought to have equal rights with whites—he thought the idea "would be more absurd than to grant such rights to children under ten years of age"—but he did propose allowing them to hold land in limited quantities. Even John Frémont recognized that the California Indians had connections to specific areas of land. "The Indians of this country finding their food where they lived were not nomadic," he noted in his journal in 1845. "They were not disposed to range, and seemed unaccustomed to intrude upon the grounds which usage probably made the possession of other tribes." But such hints of support for Indian property rights were unusual. Most of the early English-speaking settlers, John Yates recalled, viewed the Indians "as a herd of brutes, framed only by the Almighty to fill up a vacuum in creation, and destined to be abused and trampled upon by the civilised and more enlightened members of the human family."[13] By the time the federal government arrived in 1849, there were already tens of thousands of white Californians occupying land without the consent of the Indians.

TREATIES

When the Mexican War ended in 1848, the government of the United States assumed sovereignty over a great many Indians about whom federal officials knew almost nothing. As William Medill, the commissioner of Indian affairs, admitted with some understatement, "the knowledge possessed by this office of the character, habits and location, of the various tribes within these territories, is too limited to justify it in making any specific recommendations as to the measures which should be adopted at this time." The status of Indian property rights was of major importance to the government, so the office immediately asked each of its agents to transmit information "embracing the names of the tribes, their location, the probable extent of territory owned or claimed by each respectively, [and] the tenure by which they claim it."[14] Other parts of the government were meanwhile doing the same thing. The State Department appointed the former congressman Thomas Butler King in early 1849 as a special agent to California, with the task of gathering a wide range of information about the area. A few months later the State and Interior Departments jointly sent the lawyer William Carey Jones, John Frémont's brother-in-law, to report specifically on the question of land titles.

Because of the great distance between the east and west coasts, however, and because of the difficulties of traveling around California to learn about the various tribes, it would not be until 1850 that the federal government received any useful information from these sources. As it turned out, the government's informants contradicted one another in virtually every respect.

Adam Johnston, sent by the Office of Indian Affairs, reported in early 1850 that the Indians residing in the vicinity of the old Spanish missions, near the Pacific coast, were "in general stupid, indolent, and ignorant, and in intellect far inferior to any of the tribes east of the Rocky mountains." They did not consider themselves owners of the ranchos on which they resided, Johnston explained. Rather, "they think themselves the property of the owners" of the ranchos, "as much as does the negro of the south to the owner of his cotton plantation. Indeed, the owner of a rancho looks upon them as his property." As for the land embraced within the missions themselves, Johnston observed, it had originally been granted by Spain to the Jesuits for the purpose of converting the Indians. When the Mexican government had secularized the missions in the 1830s, the land reverted to the Mexican government, to be held in trust for the Indians. Under the Treaty of Guadalupe Hidalgo, the government of the United States now stood in the shoes of the Mexican government with respect to this land: as Johnston saw it, therefore, the federal government was now the owner of the mission land, as trustee for the Indians.[15]

Johnston sent another report several months later, concerning several of the tribes farther inland, in the Sacramento valley. These Indians "all subsist on roots and grass-seeds from the earth, acorns and pine-seeds from the trees, and fish from the streams," he observed. Johnston found that these Indians, unlike the Indians along the coast, seemed to have a vague sense that they owned their land. "They have an indefinite idea of their right to the soil," he concluded, "and they complain that the *pale faces* are overrunning their country and destroying their means of subsistence. The immigrants are trampling down and feeding their grass and the miners are destroying their fish dams. For this they claim some remuneration—not in money, for they know nothing of its value, but in the shape of clothing and food." Johnston offered no explicit view as to whether such a claim was justified, but the tone of his report suggests that he thought it was. Land near the coast had been granted to non-Indians by Spain, thus terminating whatever rights the Indians had once possessed, Johnston seems to have concluded, but the same was not true of the land in the Sacramento valley, which was being trespassed upon by Anglo-Americans without any formal grant from a previous sovereign or any other extinguishment of the Indians' property rights.[16]

Thomas Butler King, meanwhile, was reporting something different. By King's own account he met only the tribes in the foothills of the Sierra Nevada, near the gold mines, but he drew conclusions he deemed applicable to all the Indians in California. The Indians "have never pretended to hold any interest in the soil," he informed the State Department, "nor have they been treated by the Spanish or American immigrants as possessing any." The latter half of this claim was certainly true, but the former contradicted Johnston's contemporaneous account. King was, in any event, more interested in how previous sovereigns had dealt with the Indians than in the Indians' opinion of their own rights. "The Mexican government never treated with them for the purchase of land, or the relinquishment of any claim to it whatever," he continued. "They are lazy, idle to the last degree, and, although they are said to be willing to give their services to any one who will provide them with blankets, beef, and bread, it is with much difficulty they can be made to perform labor enough to reward their employers for these very limited means of comfort."[17] King elaborated no further, but his account would most likely have been read to justify the United States in ignoring any claim of property rights on the part of Indians, on the ground that the government of the United States had assumed all rights held by the government of Mexico, including ownership of all the land the Mexican government had formerly owned. If Mexico had not acknowledged any property rights on the part of the Indians, then the United States, as Mexico's successor, need not either.

King's report was published nearly contemporaneously with that of William Carey Jones, who had been instructed to limit his inquiry to matters relating to land titles, and who accordingly had much more to say than either Johnston or King about the status of Indian property rights. Under Spanish colonial law, Jones told the government, the Indians had "a *right* to as much land as they need for their habitations, for tillage, and for pasturage." The Spanish had in fact secured such land for the Indians they were able to persuade to settle in the communities associated with the missions, Jones explained. "The early laws were so tender of these rights of the Indians," he continued, "that they forbade the allotment of lands to the Spaniards, and especially the rearing of stock, where it might interfere with the tillage of the Indians."

Jones concluded that under Spanish rule, "the Indians in California were always supposed to have a certain property or interest in the missions." Some individual Indians and some communities of Indians had received direct grants of land from the Spanish government, and these individuals and communities owned their land just as any white person or group would, but the property rights of Indians were broader than that. Even "apart from any direct grant, they have always been reckoned to have a right of settlement" on the land associated with the missions; "and we shall find that all the plans that have been adopted for the secularization of the missions" under Mexican rule "have contemplated, recognised, and provided for this right." This rule was not always followed to the letter, Jones acknowledged, "but the law itself has constantly asserted the rights of the Indians to habitations, and sufficient fields for their support." In short, he summarized, "I understand the law to be, that wherever Indian settlements are established, and they till the ground, they have a right of occupancy in the land which they need and use; and whenever a grant is made which includes such settlements, the grant is subject to such occupancy. The right of occupancy, however—at least when on private estates—is not transferable; but whenever the Indians abandon it, the title of the owner becomes perfect."

The Spanish law Jones described was very similar to American law, which also recognized an Indian right of occupancy, although the American version applied to all land occupied by Indians, not just land under cultivation. The American right of occupancy likewise survived a grant of the underlying title to a private party, likewise terminated upon abandonment, and was likewise nontransferable except to the government. In Jones's view, the United States would suffer little inconvenience in continuing to recognize such a property right in the Indians, because "the number of subjugated Indians is now too small, and the land they occupy too insignificant in amount, for their protection, to the extent of the law, to cause any considerable molestation." He might have added that the United States, standing in the shoes of the government of Mexico, assumed only those property rights claimed by Mexico, so if the Mexican government had recognized a right of occupancy in the Indians, the United States would be bound to do so as well.

Jones's account of Indian property rights was, for the era, unusually long and quite sympathetic to the Indians. At the end, however, he tacked on one last sentence: "In the wild or wandering tribes, the Spanish law does not recognise any title whatever to the soil."[18] Jones meant his sympathetic account to apply only to the "civilized" Indians settled near the former missions. The Indians in the gold-mining regions would have no property rights at all. In drawing this distinction, Jones ended up with a conclusion precisely the opposite of the one offered by Adam Johnston. Johnston had informed the government that the mission Indians lacked any property rights but the inland Indians deserved compensation for losing their land to Anglo-Americans. In Jones's view, it was the inland Indians who lacked property rights, and the mission Indians who would be entitled to compensation.

To make matters even more complicated, in 1849 the United States Army was still governing California, and the Army was conducting its own inquiry into the property rights of the Indians. The result was a report written by the lawyer Henry W. Halleck, who would later earn a mixed reputation as a Union general in the Civil War, but who in 1849 was secretary of state in the military government of California. Halleck concluded that under Mexican law the missions were owned by the government, and that the United States, as Mexico's successor, was now the owner. Mexico had granted some land to the Indians, Halleck recognized, but those grants "were merely for the use of themselves and their descendants" and could not be alienated by the Indians.[19] Once abandoned, the land would revert to the government. Halleck's advice was thus inconsistent with that provided by Jones, whose view was that Mexican grants to the Indians conveyed the same rights as Mexican grants to non-Indians.

All this cacophony presented the government, in principle, with four options. First, the government might have deemed itself the owner of all the land in California (or some of it) on the theory that the California Indians (or some of them) were too primitive to have acquired any property rights. Second, the government might have deemed itself the owner of all the land (or some of it) on the theory that it now stood in the shoes of the Mexican government, which before 1848 had considered itself the owner of all the land (or some of it). Third, the government might have accorded the Indians a right of occupancy in the land, on the theory that the Mexican government had accorded the Indians such a right before 1848, and that the United States, as Mexico's successor, was bound to recognize this right. Finally, the government might have accorded the Indians a right of occupancy in the land, on the theory that such had been the policy of the United States with respect to Indians everywhere else, and that this policy should not be affected by anything the Mexican government had done.

In practice, the debate over the relationship between the California Indians and their land never reached this level of detail. The Senate in effect chose the fourth option, by reverting to the long-standing custom of appointing commissioners to treat with the Indians, both in the missions and inland, for the purchase of their land, a course of action recommended by none of its four informants—neither Johnston, King, Jones, nor Halleck.

The appointment of commissioners gave rise to some controversy in the Senate, a clash that previewed what was to come two years later. California was already a state by the time the issue reached the Senate in 1850, so the debate was dominated by California's two senators, John Frémont and William Gwin. In September 1850, in his very first week as a senator, Frémont introduced a bill "to preserve peace with the Indian tribes in California, by extinguishing their territorial claims in the gold mine districts." The bill was referred to the Senate Committee on Indian Affairs, which came back a few days later with a much expanded bill authorizing the appointment of commissioners to treat with all the Indian tribes in the state, not just those living near the gold mines, and appropriating $100,000 for the purpose. David Rice Atchison of Missouri, speaking on behalf of the Committee on Indian Affairs, acknowledged that the committee was "entirely unable to communicate to the Senate the information which will perhaps be required. We do not know the number of tribes of Indians within the limits of the State of California, nor do we know the number of Indians nor the kind of title by which they hold the lands in the State of California." On the latter point, the reports from the government's four informants had been distinctly unhelpful. The Senate, Atchison suggested, would be better served by relying on the firsthand knowledge of California's two senators, Frémont and Gwin.

Frémont argued that under Spanish law the Indians had been accorded stronger property rights than British and American law had recognized as belonging to Indians in the eastern United States. "The general policy of Spain, in her Indian relations, was the same as that which was afterwards adopted by all Europe and recognized by the United States," Frémont declared. "The Indian right of occupancy was respected, but the ultimate dominion remained in the Crown." Such had been the Supreme Court's view in *Johnson v. M'Intosh:* John Marshall's opinion had cited the right of occupancy as a pan-European concept, adopted by all the nations colonizing America, including Spain. That view alone, if accepted, would have committed the government to extinguishing the California Indians' right of occupancy by treaty, just as it had extinguished the right of occupancy of Indians elsewhere in the United States. But the rights of California Indians were even greater than those possessed by Indians elsewhere, Frémont insisted, in that under Spanish law, the Indians had been allowed not just to occupy their land but to sell it to private parties. This was also consistent with the view of the Supreme Court, which in *Mitchel v. United States* had recognized the validity of Florida land titles derived from conveyances by Indian tribes to private parties while Florida was a Spanish colony.[20] Frémont concluded with an emphatic appeal in favor of the necessity of purchasing the California Indians' land. "Spanish law clearly and absolutely secured to Indians fixed rights of property in the lands they occupy, beyond what is admitted by this Government in its relations with its own domestic tribes," he argued. Implicit in the argument, although never expressly stated by Frémont, was that the United States, as the successor to whatever rights were once possessed by Spain, obtained the land in California subject to any claims that would have been recognized under Spanish law. "In California," he continued, "we are at this moment invading these rights. We hold there by the strong hand alone. . . . Our occupation is in conflict with theirs, and it is to render this occupation legal and equitable, and to preserve the peace, that I have introduced this bill."

William Gwin, California's other senator, disagreed. Gwin had much less knowledge of local conditions than Frémont. Frémont had been in California on and off since the early 1840s; he had met Indians and Spanish-speaking whites throughout the state. Gwin, by contrast, was a former congressman from Mississippi who had only arrived in California in 1849. He had been in the state but a year before moving to Washington to serve as a senator. Gwin was most likely accurately representing the views of the Anglo settler community when he denied that the state's Indians had any property rights in the land. "With regard to the title which Indians may have to tracts of land in California," Gwin declared, "they are disputed. They are not recognized as having any titles there by the Mexican law. That is the impression of the population of California." Rather than appointing commissioners to treat with the Indians, Gwin suggested, Congress should appoint commissioners to investigate whether the Indians had any property rights in the first place. Gwin's idea may well have been primarily intended as a stalling tactic, as Congress had just received the reports of four federal employees on exactly that topic.[21]

In the end, Congress enacted two statutes that collectively endorsed Frémont's side of the argument. In one, Congress authorized the president to appoint three Indian agents for the California tribes, but said nothing about what those agents were supposed to do. In the annual appropriation bill for the Office of Indian Affairs, meanwhile, Congress budgeted $25,000 "to enable the President to hold treaties with the various Indian tribes in the State of California."[22] Read together, the two statutes authorized the agents, at least implicitly, to buy land from the Indians. That is how the Office of Indian Affairs interpreted the statutes, and it is how the Senate would interpret them two years later in the course of rejecting the resulting treaties. The appropriation, however, was only a quarter of that suggested by the Senate Committee on Indian Affairs. The inadequacy of the agents' budget would prove to be extremely important.

The Office of Indian Affairs wasted no time. Within a couple of weeks three men were appointed as treaty commissioners—Redick McKee, George Barbour, and Oliver Wozencraft. None had any knowledge of the California Indians, or indeed of any Indians, and only one had ever been to California before. McKee was a merchant in Virginia and an acquaintance of Alexander Stuart, the secretary of the interior. Barbour was a former government official from Kentucky. Wozencraft was a physician who had migrated from Louisiana to California during the gold rush. None had any obvious qualifications for the task, apart from the one that really mattered: each was active in his state's Whig Party, the party of President Millard Fillmore.[23]

The three commissioners arrived in San Francisco in January 1851, only to discover that the job would be far more difficult than anyone in Washington had envisioned. The Indians were desperately poor and were scattered in small groups throughout an enormous area, separated by mountains and rivers. In many areas, whites and Indians were effectively at war. Making matters worse, the commissioners were unsure of their own authority. "As regards the Indian title to lands," they wrote home in February, were they supposed "to recognise even a possessory or usufructuary right in them or not, to any particular portion of the territory, before such lands as may be necessary for their subsistence shall have been set apart for their use?" Did they have the power to appoint agents to manage trade with the tribes? Most important of all, they asked, could they establish military posts throughout the state, to ensure that whites and Indians alike complied with whatever treaty provisions they could secure? Without some mechanism of enforcement, they predicted, "treaties would be of little service, as they would be violated as often as made, and continual warfare kept up until the Indians would be annihilated, at the sacrifice of many valuable lives and the loss of much property on the part of the whites."[24]

The first of these questions, about the legal status of the Indians' property rights, would never be answered by the Office of Indian Affairs, but the answer made little difference. The commissioners seem to have been primarily interested in reserving zones of land for the Indians as sanctuaries from the aggressions of whites, and in opening up the rest of California for white settlement, regardless of how lawyers might categorize the Indians' property rights. Before McKee set out to meet the Indians, he met with a group of ministers in San Francisco to explain his goals: "to colonize them on reservations, and place them under competent tutors, appointed by government, who should teach them husbandry and mechanics, and protect them against the rum-selling, extortionary, peddling fraternity of mean white men." William Taylor, one of the ministers at that meeting, recalled that everyone present agreed with McKee's plan. In his view, Taylor declared, the idea of establishing reservations marked a great advance over previous methods of managing relations with the Indians.[25]

In this respect, Taylor and the three treaty commissioners reflected a broader trend in thought. By the middle of the nineteenth century, whites with an interest in the welfare of Indians were turning toward the idea of the reservation. The West had once seemed virtually infinite, with room enough for all the Indians displaced by white settlement in the East, but by the mid-1840s the West was looking much smaller. Many whites who considered themselves humanitarians began to argue that the reservation was the Indians' last hope—that they would soon be extinct if they were not moved out of the way of white settlers. Others argued that reservations offered the Indians the possibility of a permanent land tenure, or at least a tenure that would last longer than anything they could reasonably anticipate while they remained in the path of white settlement. Still others noted the educational benefits of gathering the Indians in reservations, where they might be taught Christianity, agriculture, work discipline—all the practices that made up what whites tended to think of as civilization. For all these reasons, federal Indian policy turned to the reservation in the early 1850s, and California was one of the first places where the policy would be implemented on a large scale.[26]

The three treaty commissioners began their work in the San Joaquin valley. In March 1851 they signed their first treaty, with six tribes gathered near Stockton. "We gave them all the land they asked for," McKee reported, "not considering it of any real value to the government, or to the whites in the neighborhood, except at one or two points where ferries have been established." Members of the tribes soon moved to their new reservation. Six weeks later, still on the San Joaquin River, the commissioners signed their second treaty, with sixteen more tribes, who were allocated a reservation the commissioners estimated to be approximately fifty miles long and fifteen miles wide, with "occasional strips of tolerably good farming land," for a population they guessed was somewhere between two and three thousand. They already knew, however, that no words on paper could prevent whites and Indians from attacking one another. For that, they needed money and military force, two things they had little of. "That the peace and security of a frontier of nearly two hundred miles depends upon our ability to keep the Indians in good humor by liberal appropriations for their subsistence, there can be no doubt," McKee wrote back to Washington shortly after concluding the second treaty. "How this is to be done by means of a pitiful grant of $25,000, is beyond my arithmetic."[27]

The commissioners soon realized that California was so large, and the Indian tribes so scattered, that they would have to split up if they hoped to cover the whole state. Their eagerness to part ways may also have been motivated by antipathy between Wozencraft and McKee. Wozencraft privately thought McKee "a hypocritical old scoundrel" who preached temperance to the Indians while sneaking regular drinks. McKee, for his part, considered Wozencraft "a man of little character, and bad habits." McKee took the northern part of the state, Wozencraft the middle, and Barbour the south. By January 1852 they were finished. McKee had negotiated four treaties, Wozencraft eight, and Barbour four more. Added to the first two treaties they negotiated as a team, the three men concluded eighteen agreements with a total of what they perceived to be 139 Indian tribes. All told, the signatory tribes ceded an ambiguously defined area in exchange for reservations amounting to approximately 11,700 square miles, or about 7.5 percent of the state.[28]

There must have been a great deal of misunderstanding on both sides. The commissioners, with no prior knowledge of California Indians and under pressure to produce signed documents without delay, were not especially careful in choosing their treaty partners. Anthropologists have been able to identify only 67 of the 139 "tribes" whose ostensible representatives signed the treaties. Of the rest, 45 were names of villages, 14 were duplicate names spelled differently, and the other 13 either were personal names or remain utter mysteries. More than 175 tribes known to anthropologists, meanwhile, were not included in the treaties. None of the treaties defined the boundaries of the land that was being ceded, because the commissioners did not know which tribes possessed which land. Instead, each treaty simply included a general clause in which the Indians relinquished to the United States "all the right, title, claim, or interest, of whatsoever character, that they, or either of them may have had, or now hold, in and to any lands in the limits of the State of California." (This wording comes from the first treaty. Each of the subsequent treaties had a version of it.) The commissioners seem to have been under the impression that they had purchased virtually all the land in the state, but as the number of tribes they did not meet far exceeds the number they did, this assumption must have been incorrect.[29]

Many of the Indians were no doubt equally confused. None of the ostensible sellers had ever been asked to sell land before: the commissioners were proposing a transaction that had no precontact Indian counterpart. Explanation on the part of the commissioners was hindered by the multitude of Indian languages and the lack of adequate translators. McKee's interpreter was the lawyer George Gibbs, who while in Oregon had learned Chinook, the intercultural jargon of the Northwest. As Gibbs admitted, however, his Chinook was of no help in speaking with some of the tribes he and McKee encountered in California. Barbour's journal brims with confidence that the Indians with whom he treated understood and readily accepted his proposed terms, but Barbour had even less knowledge of their languages than did Gibbs. His own view, expressed after his tour of the southern tribes, was that "the Indians of California, I believe without exception, are all great rogues and robbers," and that "like all other wild savages, they may be said to be an extremely ignorant, vicious, and faithless people."[30] He had little motive to inquire too closely into the Indians' perception of the treaties.

Even when the terms of the treaties were mutually understood, the Indians were under considerable duress. In some cases tribes were threatened with military attack if they refused to meet with the commissioners. Once the meeting was under way, the Indians' apprehension of the consequences of not accepting the terms proposed may well have been heightened by the military escort that accompanied the commissioners.[31] The California treaties were not a model of voluntary transacting.

The Indians, in any event, were in no position to decline an offer of protection. Many were starving after having been driven from their accustomed homes, and some of the treaties included promises of government-supplied beef and flour for two years. "Without some such provisions," Barbour explained, "the commissioners, as well as every intelligent man in California, knows that no treaty made with those Indians would be observed by them." Settlers were killing Indians in large numbers, and the treaties promised safety in areas that would be off-limits to white occupation. As Wozencraft summarized one of his negotiations, "the Indians complained very much" about the reservation to which they would be moved, "and only consented to go that they might have a home in which they would be protected from the white man."[32] The situation of many California Indians was so dire by 1851 that they would likely have grasped at just about anything offered by the federal government.

THE MOST FLAGRANT CASE

As they neared the end of their travels, the three treaty commissioners were sure they had laid the foundation for harmonious settler–Indian relations in the future. "The preliminaries of a great work have been begun and accomplished, the consummation of which *is within reach*, and will result in peace and quiet to the people, and permanent security of life and property," Wozencraft exclaimed in the fall of 1851. "The resources of a vast extent of country will be developed; its aborigines will become useful husbandmen—and this at an expense to the government much smaller than would be incurred in taking life." McKee thought that one of his treaties, signed in Scott's Valley, "will be remembered, by both white and red men, long after the immediate parties to the arrangement have left the stage."[33] The commissioners' own letters home, however, suggested two reasons their confidence was misplaced.

First, the treaties committed the government to an expenditure of far more money than Congress had authorized. The commissioners had been sent west with a budget of $25,000, to which Congress later added another $25,000. By the summer of 1851, when their work was only about half done, McKee was already reporting that the cost of the treaties would "be pretty large—probably two to three hundred thousand dollars for the first year," mostly for the emergency supplies of food he and his colleagues were promising to the signatory tribes. McKee was certain that "if they shall require even half a million, you may still be assured they are the cheapest treaties ever made by this government," because "the largest estimate will fall below the cost of a *California Indian war,* if one should unhappily become general, even of three months' duration."[34] The commissioners repeatedly pointed out that Indians throughout the state were on the verge of starvation, and that there was no chance of securing treaties without providing food. But the unexpected cost of the treaties began to raise eyebrows in Washington. By the time they were finished, the commissioners had entered into treaties that committed the government to spending more than $700,000 on the California Indians. They had spent their budget nearly fifteen times over.

Even more damaging, however, was the strength of the opposition to the treaties among white Californians. In some locations there were already many whites living within the boundaries of the reservations the commissioners drew on paper. As they traveled around the state, the commissioners had considerable trouble persuading these settlers to leave. In other areas, they struggled to create reservations that would not encompass land already claimed by whites. "I foresee great difficulties in arranging for an Indian reservation," McKee lamented in Shasta County. On the only land suitable for farming, "squatters' tents and cabins may be seen on almost every little patch or strip." By the winter of 1851–52, as the commissioners signed the last of the treaties, they were aware that white public opinion in California was turning against them. In the local press, McKee reported, they could read repeated accusations "that we had given the Indians large bodies of the finest farming and mineral lands in the State, to the great prejudice of the white settlers." McKee insisted these charges were untrue, and he even met with members of the state legislature to assure them that plenty of good land was left for whites, but the general impression among Californians was that the commissioners had been far too generous in allocating reservations. "The attacks upon us and our policy, in the Assembly, have been quite *savage*," McKee complained in early 1852.[35]

Letters began to arrive in Washington from settlers with claims located within the reservations created by the treaties. Farmers argued that they had invested years of work and thousands of dollars in building houses and cultivating land, "without the most remote suspicion that the point selected by us would fall within any reservation." Miners contended that it would be unfair, after they had undertaken the expense of locating minerals, if they were to be barred from extracting them, simply because land containing the minerals had been newly included in a reservation.[36] Such tales of hardship, combined with the more diffuse but perhaps more widely held feeling that settlement would be bottled up in the future due to the disproportionately large areas reserved for the Indians, gave rise to a flurry of settler criticism of the treaties.

This sort of criticism was hardly unique to California. Settlers on the frontier had always criticized the federal government for allocating too much land to the Indians and not leaving enough for white settlement, and indeed previous treaties with Indian tribes farther east had required settlers on the wrong side of the line to relocate. On other frontiers, however, the settlers aggrieved by an Indian treaty had typically lacked the power to do much about it. The federal government had set aside areas for Indians before there was a significant local white population, while the places in question were still territories controlled directly by the executive branch of the federal government, through appointed territorial governors. California, by contrast, had seen such rapid immigration that it was already a state. It had an elected government of its own, answerable to the settlers, not to the Interior Department. It had two senators in Congress, who could influence votes on whether to ratify Indian treaties. In attempting to manage the Indians of California, the federal government faced an opponent—the state government—more formidable than it faced elsewhere.

In early 1852, as the treaties came before the U.S. Senate, both houses of the California legislature voted overwhelmingly to instruct the state's two

senators to oppose ratification. The treaty commissioners "have undertaken to assign no inconsiderable portion" of the state's best agricultural
land "to the Indian tribes," people "wholly incapable, by habit or taste, of
appreciating its value," charged the majority report of a special committee
of the state Senate. A better policy, the report concluded, would be "to remove all Indian tribes beyond the limits of the State," so as to open up all
that land for white settlement. Redick McKee, still in San Francisco, continued to defend his work. "As to removing and colonizing the tribes of
California beyond the limits of the State, the idea is simply ridiculous," he
pointed out. "We have no vacant district or country to send them to."[37]
But members of the state legislature, who no doubt had a good sense of
the views of their constituents, were more interested in ridding the state of
Indians than in the details of where those Indians would go.

There were thirty-one states in 1852, so California, the newest, had only
two out of sixty-two senators, and an even smaller proportion of representatives. Elected officials from the other thirty states had a general preference for advancing the welfare of whites over that of Indians, however,
and probably more to the point, many were deeply disturbed that the
treaty commissioners had spent so much of the government's money before even finding out whether their treaties would be ratified. When Representative Joseph McCorkle of California proposed an appropriation
of an additional $520,000 to enable the Interior Department to pay
debts the commissioners had contracted in supplying the Indians with
food—McCorkle was representing the contractors, who were holding paper promises that would be worthless if not backed by an appropriation—
the proposal attracted indignant opposition. The commissioners "tran-
scended their authority," insisted George Houston of Alabama, "by agreeing to execute treaties before they were ratified by the Senate." Harry Hib-
bard of Massachusetts was flabbergasted that given a budget of $50,000
"the commissioners have gone on, and expended over $500,000. That is
the astounding fact." Even McCorkle, who had to defend the commissioners' conduct if the contractors were to be paid, characterized them as
"innocent and immaculate commissioners" who, in their zeal to follow
the biblical injunction to clothe the naked and feed the hungry, had "set
about clothing these savages who had never known before the luxury of a

shirt, and feeding them beef, where, for generations, they had subsisted on roots and acorns."[38] In Congress, the status of the treaties was intertwined, from the beginning, with the need to reimpose limits on an Indian Office that was widely perceived to be spinning out of control.

The Senate rejected the treaties in executive session in July. There appears to be no surviving account of the debate, if there was a debate, but the Senate's subsequent discussion of the issue suggests that the commissioners' overspending was a serious concern, particularly because the commissioners had spent the money to comply with the terms of treaties before they could be ratified. "Why, our Indian agents make treaties with the Indians in California, and while they are yet inchoate, before they are submitted to the Government here for ratification, the Indian agents go on and purchase beef for these Indians, as it is alleged, to the value of $1,000,000," declared Wisconsin senator Isaac Walker, with only some exaggeration. "Was ever such a thing heard of before?" David Rice Atchison of Missouri found the commissioners' behavior so extraordinary that he wondered: "Were these officers so ignorant, or was this done because they were so corrupt? One or the other must be true." Lewis Cass, from Michigan, was the senator with the most experience in Indian affairs, having been Andrew Jackson's secretary of war, back when the Office of Indian Affairs was part of the War Department. "This is the most flagrant case which has taken place in my day, connected with our Indian affairs," Cass fumed. "Here was one Indian commission directed to make a treaty or treaties with the Indians in California, and an appropriation, I understand, of $50,000 was put at their disposal to defray their expenses. I have not a doubt that in the instructions of the Department they were expressly directed not to exceed that amount. I have no doubt of that. They had probably a standing instruction on that subject. The commissioners have gone on and made contracts to the amount of almost $1,000,000. They have not only undertaken to make expenditures connected with the collection of the Indians, but they have anticipated the ratification of their own treaty, and carried it into effect."[39] Much of the Senate opposition to the treaties was prompted by the desire to make sure that such a thing would never happen again.

As to the merits of the treaties themselves, it is likely that many senators deferred to the views of the California delegation that the commissioners had been far too generous in allocating land to the Indians. "I was opposed to the ratification of the treaties, because they retained a great many reservations for the Indians in the midst of the white population," explained John Weller, John Frémont's successor as senator from California. "I knew that it would be utterly impossible to secure to the Indians the undisturbed possession of the reservations proposed to be set off to them." Senators from other states lacked any firsthand knowledge about circumstances in far-off California, and in any event they had no incentive to disagree. Interior Secretary Alexander Stuart reported at the end of the year that the Senate rejected the California treaties "not so much on account of objections to their details as to the leading principles embraced in them, which secured particular districts of country for the exclusive occupancy of the Indians." Stuart's meaning is not entirely clear, but he seems to have been suggesting that senators objected to the *concept* of the Indian reservation rather than the size and location of the particular reservations delineated in the treaties. This view seems implausible, however, in light of the Senate's ratification soon after of many other Indian treaties from other parts of the country, many of which included Indian reservations on land less coveted by white settlers. It is more likely that California's senators persuaded their colleagues that these particular reservations were simply too big and located too close to white population centers.[40]

Underlying the rejection of the treaties was the widely shared view that the question of where the California Indians would live was only of temporary importance because before long they would all be dead. The Indian population of California had been declining ever since whites arrived. "There is a great natural law which drives us forward," the minister Sylvester Woodbridge sermonized, just as the treaty commissioners were beginning their work. "Sentimentalists may prate and groan over its existence—over the extermination of the savage tribes that perish by our vices, our poisons, our diseases,—but the fact is an iron necessity." Some of the eastern tribes had demonstrated their capacity to adapt to Euro-American ways of life and thus maintain their population, but the California Indians were generally viewed as too primitive to do the same. Whatever arrangements the government might adopt for housing them "is a question only of humanity or temporary policy," concluded one observer shortly after the Senate rejected the treaties. "The period cannot be very remote when they will be swept before the restless tide of emigration."[41]

In retrospect, it seems clear enough that this restless tide, this natural law, was helped along by some all-too-human actions. A contemporary editorial in a Sacramento newspaper declared, "The fate of the Indian is fixed. He must be annihilated by the advance of the white man; by the diseases, and, to them, the evils of civilization. But the work should not have been commenced at so early a day by the deadly rifle." California's first governor, Peter Burnett, predicted in his annual message for 1851 that "a war of extermination will continue to be waged between the races, until the Indian race becomes extinct." Burnett, no doubt like many of the Californians he represented, understood the war of extermination to be a kind of natural process. "While we cannot anticipate this result but with painful regret," he concluded, "the inevitable destiny of the race is beyond the power or wisdom of man to avert."[42] Maybe Burnett was being disingenuous, but maybe not: certainly events to that point suggested that the government would have considerable trouble if it ever really tried to prevent whites from killing Indians and taking their land. Either way, the assumed imminent extinction of the Indians made the treaties seem less important than they would have been otherwise.

MORE VILIFIED AND LESS UNDERSTOOD

Once the treaties had been rejected, many assumed that new ones would have to be negotiated. "The treaties have all to be made over again," Lewis Cass lamented on the floor of the Senate a month after the vote. John Bell of Tennessee, like Cass a former secretary of war at a time when Indian affairs were the responsibility of the War Department, agreed that "some new treaties will have to be made with the Indians" of California.[43] But none ever were. In the summer of 1852 the Senate also rejected a group of land cession treaties with Indian tribes in Oregon. These were renegotiated and ratified a few years later. But nothing of the kind was ever attempted in California.

Instead, the position of the Indians grew even more precarious. Edward Beale, the federal government's newly appointed superintendent of Indian affairs for California, arrived in late 1852 to find the situation worse than he had expected. "Our laws and policy with respect to Indians have been neglected or violated," he reported back to Washington. The Indians "are driven from their homes and deprived of their hunting-grounds and fishing-waters at the discretion of the whites; and when they come back to these grounds and waters to get the means of subsistence, and also when they take cattle and stock from the inhabitants for food, they are often killed." He blamed the rejection of the treaties, which would have provided the Indians with havens from white persecution. "Now the Indians remain without practical protection from law or treaties," Beale concluded, "and the government officers have to do the best they can to save them from death by massacre or starvation."[44]

Reports of Indian suffering came from all over the state. From Grass Valley, near Sacramento, the *San Francisco Herald* reported that "the whites encroach upon them here day by day, and in a year from now they will have no place even to gather acorns. They are wretchedly poor, and hunger drives them to the commission of crime." In the area near Lake Tahoe, the Indian agent E. A. Stevenson observed, "the poverty and misery that now exists among these Indians is beyond description." The historian and early ethnologist John Russell Bartlett spent the winter of 1852–53 in Los Angeles, where he found the local Indians "a miserable squalid-looking set, squatting or lying about the corners of the streets, without occupation. They have no means of obtaining a living, as their lands are all taken from them." The judge Benjamin Ignatius Hayes recorded in his diary his inability to help the Indians of San Juan Capistrano, who came to him when whites took their small lots and stole their water: "What could *I* do for them? Nothing." The Indians simply had no property rights the law would enforce. Throughout southern California, government agent Benjamin Wilson found "utter demoralization and ruin." (The government did not help matters when in late 1852 it sent a shipment of presents for the Indians consisting largely of blankets. "The greater part of the goods are intirely useless," Wilson complained. "What our Indians want is something to eat.") Conflicts over resources between Indians and whites intensified, resulting in a series of massacres of entire Indian villages—men, women, and children.[45]

Faced with this disaster, federal officials scrambled to find land on which to relocate the Indians, while there were still Indians to relocate. "Unless they can be gathered together, and placed under military protection," John Weller warned, "we shall have a bloody war, which will result in the extermination of the race. The Indians should be withdrawn as much as possible from the white population." The difficulty, Beale reported, was that all the good land was already taken. "It is impossible to find, at this time, any extent of country either unclaimed by Spanish grants or free from white settlers," he explained in the fall of 1853. "Between the southern boundaries of this State, and as far north as I have any knowledge, there is not sufficient land for a single reservation of the quality required." Beale nevertheless managed to establish a 75,000-acre reservation in the Tejon Pass north of Los Angeles in September 1853, a tract encompassed within an area ten times as large that had been reserved to the local Indians in one of the rejected treaties. (The Tejon reservation would be reduced to 25,000 acres in 1855 and then abandoned in 1864, by which time much of the land was owned by Beale himself.) By 1856 California had four Indian reservations, all on land far from white population centers.[46]

These reservations, and the others that would be created later, were carved out of land owned by the federal government, not by the Indians. After the rejection of the eighteen treaties, it would be a very long time before there was any substantial interest among whites in recognizing any Indian property rights in California. The reservations themselves most likely contributed to this lack of interest: by removing Indians from the view of most white Californians, the reservations made it possible for most whites to stop thinking about the Indians' welfare or their legal rights. By 1870 even a sympathetic observer like Edward Chever could conclude that "the present policy of removing Indians from disputed lands, and settling them upon reservations, is perhaps the best thing that can be done."[47]

The reservations were dismal places. "It is useless to draw distinctions" among them, one federal official admitted in 1859. "One reservation is as bad as another." Before the reservations were established, many Indians had lived and worked among whites, as laborers and domestic servants. "The men work discharging the boats," explained the Weaverville merchant Franklin Buck, "& the girls are employed as servers in the public houses & they do first rate." This form of intercultural contact remained common even after the reservations were up and running.[48] But when many of the Indians were moved largely out of sight, the question of Indian property rights moved largely out of mind.

The anomalous status of the California Indians—the only Indians in the United States not recognized as possessing some sort of property rights in their land—was never completely forgotten. In 1860 a joint committee of the state legislature had the gall to blame the recent war with the Indians of Mendocino County on the federal government's failure to ratify the treaties of 1851–52. "On the east of the Rocky Mountains, our government has bound itself by treaties, to appropriate some twelve millions of dollars, in annuities, to various tribes, in payment for their lands," the joint committee pointed out. "The government has also provided a 'Trust Fund' for the Indians, of about six millions of dollars. The Cherokees, alone, have about one million six hundred thousand dollars invested. It appears that the natural rights of the Indians on the Pacific coast are alone disregarded by the General Government."[49] Through the 1860s and 1870s there were always critics of the government's treatment of California as terra nullius.

To be sure, not everyone thought terra nullius a bad thing. Robert Stevens, sent by the Office of Indian Affairs in the late 1860s to report on the California reservations, reminded the Office that "there have been no formal ratified treaties with the Indians, or extinguishment of title in this State, any more than by the inherent extinguishment conferred by the natural rights of man, evolved in the necessities of the continually incoming emigrants, who wish to occupy and develop the soil." Stevens thought the absence of Indian property rights was just fine. "The men of the past must give way to the men of the present; to a race superior in adaptation to their surroundings," he reasoned. "After all, nations die like men." But terra nullius was typically mentioned in order to be deplored, and to urge the government to treat the California Indians like Indians elsewhere. "It has been the melancholy fate of the California Indians," concluded the early ethnographer Stephen Powers, "to be more vilified and less understood than any other of the American aborigines."[50]

In an earlier era, these misgivings about terra nullius might eventually have prompted the government to draft treaties in order to align California with the rest of the United States, at least as a formal legal matter. By the middle of the nineteenth century, however, many whites, even those with the most sympathy for the Indians, were beginning to doubt the usefulness of treaties. As it became increasingly clear that many of the Indian treaties were in fact forced by the government upon unwilling tribes, even the tribes' white defenders began to concede that the treaties lacked much point. In 1871 Congress put a formal end to the institution of the Indian treaty. Indians outside of California were still deemed to possess a right of occupancy in their unceded land, and the government thus continued to acquire land with the ostensible consent of Indian tribes, but that formal consent was no longer manifested in documents called treaties.[51] The abolition of the Indian treaty weakened any pressure that might otherwise have existed to renegotiate land cession treaties with the California Indians.

As a result, terra nullius remained in place for a long time. In 1927, after white sympathies began to shift toward the Indians, the California legislature authorized the state's attorney general to bring suit against the United States on behalf of all California Indians to seek redress for the failure of the United States to purchase the Indians' land. Congress authorized such a suit the following year, in a statute that imposed some strict limits on the amount of compensation that would be available. The suit was filed in 1929. It would not be resolved until 1964—the litigation is a fascinating story in its own right—with a settlement in which the government paid $29 million in exchange for the Indians' agreement to be barred from any future claims.[52] This was not a large sum when distributed among all the surviving Indians of California, but it was far more than they could ever have hoped to receive in the nineteenth century.

In the end, California was to the United States what Australia had been to Britain: a departure from the ordinary policy of formally respecting the property rights of indigenous people. As in Australia, the adoption of terra nullius was caused by a combination of two factors. First was the perception that the indigenous inhabitants were more primitive than other in-digenous people—that they lived in small groups, that they would be no military match for settlers, and that they were not farmers. This factor was identical in California and Australia. The second factor was the timing of the government's involvement in settlement, but the timing was different in the two cases. In Australia, the imperial government was committed *a priori* to a policy of terra nullius, and got there early enough to prevent settlers from engaging in purchases. In California, by contrast, the federal government was committed *a priori* to a policy of purchasing land, but it got there too late. By the time land cession treaties could be negotiated, there were already tens of thousands of white settlers on the Indians' land, and those settlers were represented by elected members of Congress with enough leverage to prevent the treaties from being ratified.

chapter six

British Columbia

Terra Nullius as Kindness

B RITISH COLUMBIA WAS THE only part of Canada the British treated as terra nullius. Except in a handful of early instances on Vancouver Island, whites did not acquire land from native tribes by treaty. Rather, as in Australia, the government simply allocated the land to settlers without obtaining the consent of its previous occupants. The law would remain the same in British Columbia for almost 150 years, until near the end of the twentieth century.[1]

Today, from the perspective of indigenous people or anyone who sympathizes with them, the land policy pursued in British Columbia seems self-evidently worse by any measure—less humane, more miserly, and so on—than that followed in the rest of Canada. Historians trying to explain British Columbia's anomalous status have accordingly focused on the inhumane and miserly motives of settlers and government officials in the colony. Such motives were certainly plentiful. Settlers wanted land. They often had scorn for the indigenous people they encountered. They believed that valuable land was being wasted because its indigenous inhabitants were not using it as intensively as settlers would. Colonial governors, although appointed from Britain, had to maintain the goodwill of the settlers, and the colony was so far from London that the Colonial Office could not do much to prevent local views from becoming local policy.

Money was short, so the public funds that might have been used to purchase land were always needed for something else. All these factors were present in abundance in British Columbia, and they no doubt contributed something to the policy of terra nullius.[2]

The difficulty in stopping here as an explanation of terra nullius, however, is that all these factors were present in abundance in *every* colony, including the ones that did not adopt terra nullius. Settlers everywhere wanted land. There was no group of indigenous people they considered their equals. Settlers always thought they could use the land better than the natives were using it. Officials in every colony had to reckon with settler opinion. All of the colonies were far enough from London or Washington to make oversight loose at best. There were always plenty of other things on which to spend public money. What was it about British Columbia, then, that made it different?

A PEOPLE SO DISTANT AND SO IMPERFECTLY KNOWN

James Cook and his crew, the first Britons to reach what would become British Columbia, discovered that the residents had a keen appreciation of what they owned. "No people had higher Ideas of exclusive property," explained James King, who was with Cook at Nootka Sound, on the west coast of Vancouver Island, in 1778. "They made the Captain pay for the grass which he cut at the Village, although useless to themselves." They also demanded payment for wood and water, but Cook's men refused to comply, as Cook later discovered to his embarrassment. "I have no w[h]ere met with Indians who had such high notion of every thing the Country produced being their exclusive property as these," Cook noted in his journal. "The very wood and water we took on board they at first wanted us to pay for, and we had certainly done it, had I been upon the spot when the demands were made; but as I never happened to be there the workmen took but little notice of their importunities." Charles Clerke, Cook's second in command, observed that the Nootkans even "look'd upon us [as] so far their property as to be entitled to a right of monopolizing all kind of Exchanges with us to themselves." They accordingly charged other tribes a percentage for allowing them to trade with Cook's crew.[3]

The early European visitors after Cook repeated this pattern: they took notice of some indigenous property rights and ignored others. The English trader John Meares arrived in Nootka Sound in 1788 and built a house on a plot of land he claimed to have purchased from the chief Maquinna.[4] As one contemporary defender of British claims to the Northwest argued, such purchases were necessary because "Common Sense must evince that Europeans, visiting Countries *already inhabited,* can acquire *no right* in *such Countries* but from the *good will* of the *Friendly Inhabitants.*" The botanist José Mariano Moziño was at Nootka Sound in 1792, as part of a Spanish expedition, and observed that the Nootkans, "like all the other inhabitants of this archipelago, dispute with arms the right of fishing in their respective districts; and they believe that foreigners violate this public right when they sail into these areas for that purpose." Other visitors, however, seem to have commandeered local resources without much thought for whether they were owned. The Boston trader John Boit purchased furs and fish along the northwest coast in the mid-1790s, but his log indicates in the next sentence that he sent "a party well arm'd on Shore after Wood & Water," a notation suggesting he had no intention of paying for these, too. The British naval commander William Broughton spent the spring of 1796 repairing his ship in Nootka Sound. His account mentions building a wharf on shore but says nothing about how the rights to use the land and the wood were acquired.[5] In the early years of contact, the rules of the game appear to have been improvised upon each encounter.

The rules remained fluid for some time. Until the 1840s virtually the only whites in the area were fur traders. They were interested in furs, not settlement, so they only wanted enough land in any one location to build a trading post and a few houses. As the local residents tended to welcome the opportunities for trade, and as the traders' real estate demands were very small relative to the amount of available land, neither side had much need to worry about exactly who owned what, at least not explicitly. Traders simply built their posts in ways that facilitated defense against armed attack, and then hoped for the best.[6]

The traders must have known, however, from the experience of eastern North America, that the future was likely to bring permanent white settlers and that the informality of property arrangements could not last forever. Some of the early traders cautioned that when whites arrived in the Northwest they would encounter already-functioning systems of property. "The people of every village have a certain extent of country, which they consider their own, and in which they may hunt and fish," noted Daniel Harmon, a fur trader on the mainland west of the Rockies in the first two decades of the nineteenth century. Harmon explained that villagers "may not transcend these bounds, without purchasing the privilege of those who claim the land." The trader William Brown observed in the 1820s that the Gitksan and Wet'suwet'en divided their territories into hunting areas, each under the control of a single person acting as custodian for an extended family.[7] Still, before formal colonization, and without any permanent white inhabitants, the British had no reason to formulate an explicit land policy.

It was not until 1849, when Vancouver Island became a British colony, that there was much need to think about indigenous property rights. (Mainland British Columbia was formally colonized in 1858, and the two colonies were merged in 1866.) The task of colonization was delegated to the Hudson's Bay Company, which was granted all the Crown's rights in Vancouver Island, in the expectation that the company, which already had a fort at the southern tip of the island, could make progress faster than the government could. The company's charter deliberately said nothing about Indians or land. "With regard to the Indians," the Colonial Office explained, "it has been thought on the whole the better course to make no stipulations respecting them in the grant. Little is in fact known of the natives of that island by the Company or by any one else. Whether they are numerous or few, strong or weak; whether or not they use the land for such purposes as would render the reservation of a large portion of it for their use important or not, are questions which we have not the full materials to answer. Under these circumstances any provisions that could be made for a people so distant and so imperfectly known, might turn out impediments in the way of colonization, without any real advantage to themselves." Without any knowledge of how many Indians lived on Vancouver Island or how they used the land, the government could not know whether they had any property rights Britons were bound to respect. The Colonial Office was careful to remind the Hudson's Bay Company that if the government had to buy the Indians' land the Company had to buy it as well. "In parting with the land of the island Her Majesty parts only with her own right therein," the Company was warned, and so "whatever measures she was bound to take in order to extinguish the Indian title are equally obligatory on the Company."[8]

The grant of Vancouver Island to the Hudson's Bay Company had its critics, who alleged that the Company was less likely to have the Indians' welfare in mind than the government would be. The Aborigines Protection Society declared its alarm "at the prospect before the unhappy Aborigines, under the sway of a body like the Hudson's Bay Company" and worried that the charter's failure to instruct the Company how to treat the Indians left them "completely at the mercy of an interested and irresponsible corporation." The prevailing view within the government, however, was that the Indians could not lose anything from the grant. "The Company from their position were better acquainted with the Indian races than any other persons," Earl Grey, secretary of state for the colonies, recalled a few years later. In any event, he concluded, "the charter cannot, of course, interfere with the rights of the aborigines."[9] If the Indians of Vancouver Island owned their land as against the British government, they owned it just as much as against the Hudson's Bay Company.

Thus it was the Hudson's Bay Company, not the British government, that had the initial responsibility for establishing Indian land policy in the area that would become British Columbia. The company had considerable experience dealing with the tribes of eastern North America, so company officials knew the long history of acquiring Indians' land by purchase. They doubtless knew of recent events in the South Pacific: they were aware that New Zealand was likewise in the midst of being acquired from the Maori by purchase, but they probably also knew that Aboriginal Australians had been accorded no property rights. In deciding whether to recognize indigenous property rights on Vancouver Island, the men of the

Hudson's Bay Company had a choice of two models. Were the local Indians as primitive as Aboriginal Australians were perceived to be? Or were they as advanced as the Maori and the Indians of eastern North America?

Many of the early fur traders were impressed by the intelligence of the people they encountered in the Northwest. The American ship captain John D'Wolf traded with "a great number of the Indians" at the northern end of Vancouver Island in 1805 and found them "exceedingly sharp in all their intercourse with us. . . . They were a very stout and robust people," D'Wolf recalled years later, "and in some things not destitute of skill." The naturalist John Schouler was employed by the Hudson's Bay Company in the late 1820s. "The N.W. Indians, especially the coast tribes, have made considerable progress in the rude arts of savage life," he reported. "Their canoes are constructed with much skill; their houses, being for permanent residence, have been erected with some forethought and attention to comfort; and their fishing apparatus and articles of domestic economy are far more numerous and elaborate than can be found in the temporary lodge of hunting tribes."[10]

Positive accounts like these persisted throughout the early years of colonization. One missionary found the northwestern tribes "superior to most other civilized nations" and lavished particular praise on the residents of the Queen Charlotte Islands, whom he described as "physically and mentally regarded, as fine a race of men as can be met with." He paid them the highest compliment: "They may truly be styled the 'Anglo-Saxons' of this coast." The merchant Gilbert Sproat had a similar view of one of the tribes on Vancouver Island. "Compared with the manners of English rustics or mechanics," he concluded, "the manners of the Aht natives are somewhat dignified."[11]

This view, however, was hardly unanimous. Thomas Manby, a midshipman on George Vancouver's expedition in the 1790s, found the northwestern Indians "the nastyest race of people under the sun." By the middle of the nineteenth century, whites frequently depicted First Nations as utter savages with scarcely any prospects for improvement. Charles Wilson, one of the Britons responsible for mapping the boundary between the British and American possessions in the Northwest, reported that "the tribes eat human flesh on certain occasions & generally prefer it in a putrid state." The Anglican bishop George Hills, invited into a local house, was disgusted by "the damp and filthy ground. Fish & decayed flesh render unbearable the atmosphere, they are eaten up by vermin and dirt." By 1862, when the discovery of gold sparked British interest in mainland British Columbia, a guide for prospective miners summed up a widespread feeling among white settlers: "The native tribes of Vancouver's Island and British Columbia are as savage, treacherous, inhospitable, and cunning as any to be found on the two continents of America."[12] As the white population increased, dark portrayals like these seem to have grown more common.

Some whites saw the Indians of British Columbia as irredeemably savage. Others saw them as nearly English in their capacity for civilization. By the 1860s there was a middle ground as well—the view that the Indians' present degraded state was not natural but an artifact of contact with Europeans, and that there was little to be learned about the true nature of the Indian from present-day observation. It was generally accepted among whites that the Indian population had plummeted from disease since contact. Indians still alive were afflicted with diseases and liquor brought by whites. Whatever Indians had once been like, they were no longer that way. It made little difference in any event, many pointed out, because if the indigenous population continued its sharp decline there would soon be no Indians left. Of course, this was not the only conclusion to be drawn. Others urged the need to save Indian lives before it was too late and the northwestern tribes had been driven to extinction like many tribes in the east. One correspondent to the *Victoria Gazette* argued that with some clothing and a little education the aboriginal children of Victoria "would appear as clean and neat as the children from the cotton mills from Lancashire. These Indian children could be trained to civilized habits."[13] Whites in British Columbia held heterogeneous opinions about Indians. There was no consensus as to their present level of civilization or their capacity for moving to a higher level.

On whether to recognize Indian property rights in land, the most relevant white observations were of Indian land use, but white opinion was not unanimous on this point either. The northwestern tribes supported themselves primarily by fishing, hunting, and gathering berries and other uncultivated plants. Maximizing the yield of food required villages to shift locations according to a seasonal cycle, within territories acknowledged to belong to the tribe. Some of the earliest white observers recognized this pattern. On the northwest coast in the 1780s the British naval captain Nathaniel Portlock reported seeing temporary summer camps and more permanent winter houses. In the early 1790s the Boston merchant John Hoskins noticed that the Haida "during the summer season live in scattered huts for the benefit of fishing . . . but their head villages," where they lived in the winter, "are neatly and regularly built." Charles Bishop, captain of a fur trading ship that encountered the Haida and the Tsimshian in 1795, saw the same cycle.[14]

Other white observers, less interested in understanding than in criticizing, saw the local tribes as primitive nomads. "They seem to have no permanent or fixd habitations," declared Archibald Menzies, the botanist accompanying Vancouver, "but wander about from place to place just as the whim or necessity of the moment impells them." The early settler Gabriel Franchère, in the Northwest from 1811 to 1814, believed that the tribes of what would become mainland British Columbia "do not dwell in villages . . . but are nomads, like the Tartars and the Arabs of the desert."[15] As with their more general views of the Indians, whites were of two minds with respect to Indian land use from the beginning.

The one point on which whites agreed was that the northwestern Indians lacked agriculture before white contact. John Jewitt was a blacksmith aboard an American trading ship. His captivity narrative of his years among the Nootkans was probably the most widely read account of Vancouver Island in the early nineteenth-century United States. "Their mode of living is very simple," Jewitt reported, "their food consisting almost wholly of fish, or fish spawn fresh or dried, the blubber of the whale, seal, or sea-cow, muscles [sic], clams, and berries of various kinds." Such descriptions of nonfarming Indians soon became commonplace. At times the absence of agriculture was a ground for criticism: the artist Paul Kane, for example, thought the fishing in Victoria so easy that local tribes had never learned the value of work and had accordingly become "the laziest race of people in the world." Other observers more charitably pointed out that aboriginal food-gathering practices were as well suited for local conditions as English practices were for England. "Salmon are *harvested*," insisted one writer, "and garnered by the savages in North-West America as we in the civilised world reap the 'golden grain' and store it for winter use."[16] But whether good or bad, there was no doubt that the aboriginal inhabitants of the land that would become British Columbia did not practice agriculture before whites arrived.

In Australia, the absence of agriculture had been one of the primary reasons the British government refused to recognize any Aboriginal property rights in land. Had colonization preceded contact in British Columbia as in Australia, British Columbia might have been treated as terra nullius for the same reason. By the time the British colonized the northwest coast, however, fur traders had been interacting with indigenous people for more than half a century. In many places, the traders had taught the Indians how to farm. Tribes had passed this knowledge along to other tribes. By 1835 the Hudson's Bay Company factor John Work found "a considerable quantity of potatoes" being grown by the Haida in the Queen Charlotte Islands. By the 1840s potatoes were being grown all over the coast and on the mainland as well. Scouting out the prospects of farming on Vancouver Island in 1842, James Douglas was optimistic, because he had firsthand evidence of the fertility of the soil. "We are certain that potatoes thrive, and grow to a large size," he explained, "as the Indians have many small fields in cultivation which appear to repay the labour bestowed upon them."[17] The Indians had once lacked agriculture, but they acquired it before they were colonized by Britain, and it seems to have continued spreading afterward. If the decision to recognize Indian property rights had been made in 1800, the Indians' lack of agriculture might have implied an absence of property rights, as in Australia. By the middle of the century, however, many of the Indians were farmers, as in eastern North America and New Zealand. Once again, there was no easy answer.

In 1849, then, when the Hudson's Bay Company had to decide whether to purchase land from the tribes of Vancouver Island, the facts before it permitted a decision either way. Some Britons thought First Nations were as nearly civilized as the Maori; others found them as primitive as Aboriginal Australians; and still others thought they might have degenerated from the former to the latter as a result of contact with whites. Some Britons saw farmers and fishermen with recurring seasonal patterns of land use; others saw nomads with no connection to any particular area of land. There were no Britons already residing on Vancouver Island with claims to land that depended on a prior purchase, but neither were there any prior British residents with a claim based on the occupation of seemingly vacant land, so there were no vested interests in either direction. The government had provided no guidance. In setting land policy, the Hudson's Bay Company had virtually unconstrained discretion.

FROM TREATIES TO TERRA NULLIUS

That discretion would be exercised by James Douglas, the Hudson's Bay Company's chief factor on Vancouver Island. Douglas, virtually a lifelong company employee, had lived among the northwestern Indians for two decades. He had been one of the founders of Fort Victoria in 1843. Few Britons, if any, knew more about the Indians of Vancouver Island than Douglas did. In 1849, as formal colonization began, strictly speaking he represented the Hudson's Bay Company rather than the British government, but in practice his authority was unchallenged. The government's nominal representative as governor was the lawyer Richard Blanshard, who had little prior knowledge of the area and who did not even arrive until March 1850. A year later he was gone. In early 1851, recalled one early settler, "[Blanshard] told me he was so disgusted with his position that he had sent his resignation, as he had no power or authority, as it was all Hudson Bay authority and his was not recognized, and no power to support his position." Had he been able to wield power, Blanshard would most likely have had little influence over Indian land policy in any event, because whatever property rights the government possessed in Vancouver Island had already been granted to the Hudson's Bay Company. Blanshard carried a list of instructions from the government, telling him in some detail what he was supposed to do on a wide variety of matters, but none of the instructions said a word about the Indians or their land.[18] When Blanshard returned to England, the government simply appointed Douglas as governor, an act that brought his formal authority into congruence with the actual authority he exercised from the beginning.

In September 1849, soon after he learned that the government had granted the island to the Hudson's Bay Company, Douglas announced his intention to begin negotiating with the tribes around Victoria. "Some arrangement should be made as soon as possible with the native Tribes for the purchase of their lands," he reported back to the company's headquarters in London. He wanted to spread the purchase price over as long a period as possible, to prevent the Indians from dissipating the proceeds of a sale and to ensure that they would have an ongoing incentive to avoid violence. "I would recommend payment being made in the Shape of an annual allowance instead of the whole sum being given at one time," he explained. "They will thus derive a permanent benefit from the sale of their lands and the Colony will have a degree of security [for] their future good behavior." Douglas was most likely aware that over the past two centuries many of the eastern tribes had sold land for less permanent goods, only to find themselves, not long after, without land or anything left from the sale. He would also have known that some of the recurring wars between settlers and Indians had been caused by conflict over land transactions—sales the Indians justifiably believed to have been infected with fraud. Even before his first purchase, Douglas was looking for ways of preventing these outcomes.

Douglas was planning to supplement his program of land purchasing with a policy of reserves. "I would also recommend," he informed the company, "equally as a measure of justice, and from a regard to the future peace of the colony, that the Indians' Fisheries, Village Sites and Fields, should be reserved for their benefit and fully secured to them by law."[19] Land purchasing in the east had often caused the utter disruption of traditional Indian life, with dire consequences directly for Indians and sometimes indirectly, because of the resulting intersocietal violence, for settlers. Douglas was searching for a way of heading off this outcome as well.

Neither of these ideas was original. Both represented progressive white thought in North America at midcentury, and both were then being carried out by the government of the United States. Reserves in particular—usually called "reservations" in the United States—were just becoming a standard feature of U.S. Indian treaties and were being hailed by many who considered themselves humanitarians as the most effective way, or even the only way, of protecting the Indians from extinction.[20] James Douglas was a fur trader on Vancouver Island, far from the eastern intellectuals who were speaking and writing in favor of the reservation, but his views of Indian land policy were in line with theirs.

Douglas's plan to purchase land seems to have been widely known on Vancouver Island. A month after he sent his letter to London, he received a complaint from Walter Colquhoun Grant, the first noncompany settler to arrive in the new colony, that Indians were setting fires in the woods around Victoria in order to clear away the underbrush, to make it easier to gather fruit. Grant had a solution: when the Hudson's Bay Company bought land from the Indians, it should deduct from the annual payments a sum proportionate to the number of fires.[21] This plan was never implemented, but the fact that it was even proposed, well before anyone in London had approved of the idea of purchasing land, suggests a general awareness among the small number of Britons on Vancouver Island that Douglas intended to acknowledge the Indians as possessing some kind of purchasable property right in their land.

The Hudson's Bay Company approved Douglas's proposed purchases in a letter that arrived in Victoria in early 1850. Archibald Barclay, the company's secretary, had some modifications to Douglas's plan. "You are to consider the natives as the rightful possessors of such lands only as they occupied by cultivation, or had houses built on, at the time when the Island came under the undivided sovereignty of Great Britain in 1846," Barclay instructed Douglas. Britain and the United States had both claimed the Northwest until the 1846 Treaty of Washington set the border at the 49th parallel. By limiting Indian property rights to farmland and house lots occupied as of 1846, the company would be denying the Indians rights to most of Vancouver Island. "All other land," Barclay continued, "is to be regarded as waste, and applicable to the purposes of colonization." As Barclay used it, the word *waste* referred to land that was unoccupied and therefore unowned. The large majority of Vancouver Island was thus to be "applicable to the purposes of colonization"—that is, free for granting to settlers.[22]

Barclay's position was at odds with the law governing New Zealand and the earlier-colonized eastern parts of British North America, where the

7. A Songhees woman carries a basket of fish in this photograph by the prolific Victoria photographer Frederick Dally. Although fish was the staple food of the Songhees and the other tribes of the northwest coast, many of the tribes of British Columbia learned agriculture from white fur traders before British Columbia was formally colonized, a factor that most likely caused the Hudson's Bay Company to enter into land cession treaties with the tribes in southern Vancouver Island in the early 1850s. Photo F-08291 (ca. 1860), British Columbia Archives.

British drew no such distinction between indigenous property rights in different types of land. Douglas ignored it. He soon began buying large tracts without reference to how they were used as of 1846. As in New Zealand and eastern North America, the price of land was low enough, and the need to avoid antagonizing indigenous people was sufficiently pressing, that a distinction between categories of land was not worth the effort of making.

Barclay's letter to Douglas included a second instruction that Douglas *would* follow, one that represented a continuation of British land policy in other colonies. "The uncivilized inhabitants of any country have but a qualified dominion over it, or a right of occupancy only," Barclay reminded Douglas, quoting a recent report of a committee of the House of Commons. "They cannot grant to individuals, not of their own tribe, any portion of it, for the simple reason that they have not themselves any individual property in it." Only the government had the power to purchase land from indigenous people. This principle had been followed in British North America since 1763, in the United States since independence, and, except for a brief period, in New Zealand since formal colonization in 1840. On Vancouver Island, the Hudson's Bay Company had been granted the government's exclusive power to purchase land. Douglas was accordingly instructed not to allow the Indians to sell land to anyone else.[23]

Douglas began buying land immediately after receiving Barclay's letter. Between April 29 and May 1 he concluded nine treaties with tribes inhabiting the southern end of Vancouver Island. In each treaty, the selling tribe agreed to cede an area of land in exchange for an amount of money specified in British pounds. Douglas in fact provided the tribes with goods rather than currency, which would not have been useful for most indigenous people in 1850. Each of the nine treaties included a clause reserving to the selling tribe its "village sites and enclosed fields," as well as "liberty to hunt over the unoccupied lands" conveyed in the treaty, and the right "to carry on our fisheries as formerly." The language of the treaties was copied from a form Barclay sent to Douglas, which was in turn copied from a document recently used to purchase Maori land in New Zealand. Barclay sent Douglas the form several months *after* Douglas negotiated the treaties, a sequence of events suggesting that the sellers' consent was obtained well before the treaties were drafted, and thus that their precise wording was perhaps not of major importance to either side. Douglas's account of the treaties, written before he ever received Barclay's form, suggests that the substance of the agreements was in any event quite close to the language proposed by Barclay.[24]

Buying the land turned out to be "rather a troublesome business,"

Douglas reported a few days after completing the series of conferences with the Indians. His plan of annual payments to the tribes "was so generally disliked" by the Indians "that I yielded to their wishes and paid the sum at once." Insisting on full payment was probably a wise decision on the part of the sellers. Tribes in the eastern United States had long complained of unfulfilled treaty promises. Had they known, the indigenous people of Vancouver Island might reasonably have feared to put the same kind of trust in the Hudson's Bay Company. Paying in full was not much of a hardship for the colonial government, because prices were not high— on average about fifteen shillings in goods per head of household, to a total number of recipients that did not exceed a few hundred.[25] There would be only five more purchases, two in 1851, two more in 1852, and then the last in 1854, all from tribes in southern Vancouver Island, and all with similar terms.

The residents of Vancouver Island had never sold land before, so it would be surprising if their understanding of the transactions matched Douglas's. The Saanich, for example, ostensibly conveyed about fifty square miles to the Hudson's Bay Company in the two 1852 treaties. Eighty years later, however, the descendants of the "sellers" insisted that the treaties had not conveyed any land at all. The South Saanich treaty, they said, had been signed by Indians who were not even members of the tribe. The North Saanich treaty had been signed by tribe members, but it had been intended only to settle a dispute over the right to cut timber from the land. According to Saanich oral tradition, at a time when there had been much conflict between the tribe and the British, Douglas invited them to a meeting on the beach, where he provided piles of blankets and a document written in English. He asked each Saanich man to place an "X" on the document. "One man spoke up after they discussed it, and said, 'I think James Douglas wants to keep the peace,' because they were after all almost in a state of war. . . . 'I think these are the sign of the cross.' He made the sign of the cross. . . . They thought it was just a sign of sincerity and honesty. It wasn't much later they found out actually they were signing their land away by putting those crosses out there. They didn't know what it said on that paper."[26] As in other colonies, the earliest land transactions were interpreted very differently by the two sides.

In purchasing land, Douglas was acting on behalf of the Hudson's Bay Company, not the government, but the Colonial Office approved of what Douglas was doing. In 1851 Douglas presented Richard Blanshard with a statement of the company's expenditures under the first nine treaties, an accounting that was necessary because under the terms of the grant there was a possibility the government would be required to reimburse the company's expenses when the grant expired. Blanshard had no complaint about the purchases. Rather, he took issue with the value Douglas had placed on the goods paid to the Indians, which he thought had been inflated in order to increase the company's eventual reimbursement from the government. In London, Benjamin Hawes, undersecretary in the Colonial Office, defended Blanshard's scrutiny of the bill in correspondence to the company's headquarters, but Hawes was careful to explain that Earl Grey "is far from wishing that unnecessary interference should take place with the proceedings of the Company in the acquisition of land from the Natives." A few years later, George Grey, one of Earl Grey's successors as colonial secretary, cited the Hudson's Bay Company's treatment of the Indians on Vancouver Island as a model of sound colonial administration. Edward Bulwer Lytton, one of George Grey's successors, said much the same thing in 1858. "I have to enjoin you to consider the best and most humane means of dealing with the Indians," he instructed Douglas. "It should be an invariable condition, in all bargains or treaties with the Natives for the cession of lands possessed by them, that subsistence should be supplied to them in some other shape."[27] In purchasing land, the company was fulfilling the hopes that had led the government to grant the island to the company in the first place.

There would be no purchases after 1854, and no purchases anywhere other than southern Vancouver Island. Part of the reason was the cost. Before the Hudson's Bay Company's grant expired in 1859, the company, not the government, was the entity entitled to purchase land. Company officials knew that the government would not help pay for the Indians' land. When Douglas became governor of Vancouver Island in 1851, his superiors at the company's headquarters in London reminded him that his money was coming from them, not from the government. "The Colony of Vancouver's Island must be self-supporting," they told him, "the only assistance to be expected from the Mother Country being protection against foreign aggression."[28] The Hudson's Bay Company was a profit-maximizing private firm with no interest in buying land unless it could expect to resell the land to settlers at a higher price. As there was never much emigration to Vancouver Island in the 1850s, the company had no reason to buy any more land.

When the Hudson's Bay Company's grant expired, land became the government's responsibility. White settlement was meanwhile increasing, so the colonial government had to seriously consider buying more land. Even before the grant expired, however, the Colonial Office made clear to Douglas that the colonial government could not expect any money from London. "Vancouver Island must of necessity find means for providing for its own civil administration," the Duke of Newcastle instructed Douglas in 1859. "Vancouver Island like other British communities however small must expect no assistance from without towards these ordinary and regular expenses of Her Government." Colonial officials tried to change this policy in later years, but with no success. In 1860 several members of the colonial legislature agreed, as one put it, that "the Indians have a right to be paid for their lands, but the Home Government must do it." The legislature accordingly sent a petition to the Duke of Newcastle, "praying for the aid of Her Majesty's Government in extinguishing the Indian title to the public lands in this Colony." The local press had little hope the petition would be granted. "Our impression is, we might just as well ask the London police to quell a fight on the Indian reserve," despaired the *British Colonist*. "We are already told, 'You must be self-supporting.' If such is the case, we will have to extinguish the title ourselves." Sure enough, the Duke of Newcastle brushed the petition aside. "I am fully sensible of the great importance of purchasing without loss of time the native title to the soil of Vancouver Island," he explained, "but the acquisition of the title is a purely colonial interest, and the Legislature must not entertain any expectation that the British taxpayer will be burthened to supply the funds." The Vancouver Island Legislative Council asked the imperial government again for a subsidy in 1864 but was rebuffed once again.[29] The colony was on its own.

The colony's want of money has been cited by some historians as a cause of the absence of land purchases after 1854, but it cannot be the only reason. In refusing to subsidize land purchasing on Vancouver Island, the imperial government was treating the colony the same way it treated its other colonies. Land purchasing had been locally funded in the eastern parts of British North America. It was being locally funded in New Zealand even as Vancouver Islanders pleaded for subsidies. Purchasing land on Vancouver Island would have been expensive, and the necessary negotiations would have been time-consuming, but in neither respect is there any obvious reason why land purchasing should have been more difficult on Vancouver Island than it was elsewhere, had Douglas been genuinely interested in trying.

Rather, some of Douglas's words and actions after the initial batch of treaties suggest that he was losing interest in purchasing land. As early as 1852 he reported to the Colonial Office that the Cowichan, one of the tribes on Vancouver Island, "live in several villages, each having a distinct chief," but that the chief "cannot be said to rule the community which acknowledges his supremacy, as there is no code of laws, nor do the chiefs possess the power or means of maintaining a regular government." The chiefs possessed only a "personal influence" with their followers. Douglas did not spell out the implications for land purchasing, but one likely implication was that chiefs lacked the authority to make commitments on the village's behalf, including commitments to sell land. This lack of authority would not have been an insuperable obstacle to land transactions in principle, but it would have made transactions much more cumbersome, because it would have required Douglas to negotiate with large numbers of tribe members, and perhaps all tribe members, for each purchase. Douglas's less scrupulous counterparts in the United States were satisfied to get a few Indian signatures on paper and not inquire too closely into the authority of the ostensible sellers, but Douglas seems to have been having second thoughts about the practice of land purchasing. Indeed, in the early 1860s the legislature twice appropriated funds to purchase land from the Cowichan, land for which there was great demand among white settlers, but Douglas never spent the money.[30]

Douglas's doubts about land purchasing reached the point of articulation in the late 1850s. They were prompted by a letter from Edward

Bulwer Lytton, secretary of state for the colonies, giving Douglas instructions on the occasion of his assumption of the governorship of the new colony of British Columbia. After covering a variety of other subjects, Lytton turned to "a few observations on the policy to be adopted towards the Indian Tribes." He inquired as to Douglas's views on whether "it might be feasible to settle them permanently in villages," where they might commence the process of civilization. Once they had been settled, "law and religion would become naturally introduced among the Red Men and contribute to their own security against the aggressions of immigrants"—that is, of whites. If Indians were participating in the colonial economy, meanwhile, they could be taxed by the government, which would provide a fund "which would be expended strictly and solely on their own wants and improvements."

Thus far Lytton's observations were not necessarily inconsistent with a policy of purchasing the Indians' land. The creation of Indian villages could have been accomplished any number of ways, one of which was to buy the Indians' current land and grant them new land in exchange. But Lytton then provided an example of what he had in mind. "Sir George Grey," he told Douglas, "has thus at the Cape been recently enabled to locate the Kafirs in Villages." Grey had not purchased land from the Xhosa. In practice, "locating the Kafirs in Villages" meant arresting their leaders, reducing their reserves, and forcibly transporting them to new locations to labor for the colonial government.[31] Upon receiving Lytton's suggestions, a person conversant with British colonial policy would have recognized that Lytton was suggesting that Douglas treat the new colony of British Columbia as terra nullius.

Douglas leapt at the chance. His lengthy and (for him) impassioned reply to Lytton makes clear that he had already been thinking along these lines. Not only would Lytton's plan be feasible, he declared, but it was "also the only plan which promises to result in the moral elevation of the native Indian races, in rescuing them from degradation, and protecting them from oppression and rapid decay." He announced his intention of implementing it at once. On Vancouver Island, where Indian reserves had already been marked out, he would lease to settlers the parts Indians were not using, without seeking the Indians' consent, and use the rental proceeds for the Indians' benefit. In British Columbia, where the colonial government could begin with a clean slate, unencumbered by previous land transactions, he would make "anticipatory reserves" of all the land the Indians were likely to need. "Those reserves should in all cases include their cultivated fields and village sites," he explained. The resulting native settlements would be made "entirely self-supporting, trusting for the means of doing so, to the voluntary contributions in labour or money of the natives themselves; and secondly, to the proceeds of the sale or lease of a part of the land reserved." This arrangement would not just be a money-saver for the colonial government but would promote "the well-being of the Indians themselves," who would become self-reliant and no longer depend on the mercy of the colonial state.[32] It was a plan that rested on terra nullius. If the Indians had property rights in their land, the government would have lacked the power to assign them to reserves or to grant the unreserved land to settlers.

In seizing the opportunity to implement a policy of terra nullius in the new colony of British Columbia, Douglas was acting upon humanitarian motives. To be sure, Douglas was not at all sentimental about American Indians. He considered them to be "in the earliest stage of savage life, when the untutored reason, darkened by ignorance is overcome by the fierce impulses of the passions, and the mere animal instincts given for the support and preservation of life hold absolute sway."[33] When he established Fort Victoria in 1843, he was apprehensive about the local residents, whom he viewed as "having as yet lost no trait of their natural barbarity." As governor of Vancouver Island he commiserated with Isaac Stevens, his counterpart to the south in the Washington Territory, about "the dangerous and unprincipled character of the Northern Indians" in his own colony.[34] Like virtually every other government official in North America at the time, Douglas believed that whites had traveled farther than Indians along civilization's path.

Like many of his contemporaries, however, Douglas also believed that it was the responsibility of whites to help the Indians catch up. To be a British or American humanitarian in the middle of the nineteenth century was not to believe that Indian ways of life were as good as Anglo-American ways. It was, rather, to believe that with proper training the

8. James Douglas, the first governor of British Columbia, gave the colony a land policy different from that of the rest of Canada. A man with a free black mother and a Swampy Cree wife, Douglas lived most of his life among the Indians of the Northwest and accordingly had more interest in their welfare than most colonial officials did. His decision in the late 1850s to stop recognizing aboriginal title and instead allocate reserves out of land newly deemed to be owned by the Crown was primarily motivated by his desire to avoid the harms to Indians caused by land purchasing in the United States, but tribes in British Columbia ended up no better off. Photo A-01231 (ca. 1860), British Columbia Archives.

Indians might one day be as civilized as Anglo-Americans. On this definition, Douglas was a humanitarian, and indeed he was well known for it. The Aborigines Protection Society, the leading British organization advocating on the behalf of indigenous people throughout the empire, praised Douglas in its journal for seeking "to act towards them the part of a friend and benefactor." While governor, Douglas was lauded for "his firm, yet mild and conciliatory policy," which had made settler–Indian relations far more harmonious than in the nearby American territories. Recent comparative historians of British Columbia and Washington/Oregon have tended to agree.[35]

Douglas's own personal background most likely contributed to that attitude. Douglas was half black, half white, the son of a Scottish sugar planter and a free black woman. After a childhood in Barbados and Guyana, Douglas was brought by his father to Glasgow at the age of eleven. He may well have had firsthand experience of being looked down upon for being a member of a racial minority. At eighteen Douglas indentured himself to the North West Company and moved to Canada, where he met his wife Amelia, the daughter of a Swampy Cree woman and North West Company trader, a man of Irish ancestry born in Quebec. Between the two of them, the Douglases embodied much of the empire.[36] This background may have played a part in Douglas's willingness to bridge racial differences to a greater degree than most of his colleagues.

When Lytton opened the door to a policy of not purchasing land in British Columbia, Douglas walked right through, because he had evidently been harboring doubts as to the long-term effects of land purchasing on indigenous people. He explained to Lytton that in the United States, Indian reservations were supported by the government "at an enormous expense," despite which "the Indians in those settlements are rapidly degenerating." The onset of colonization in British Columbia afforded an opportunity to escape "the great expense and the debasing influences of the American system."[37] Closer to home, Douglas could not have avoided seeing the poverty, alcoholism, and population decline of the tribes who had sold him the land around Victoria a few years before. Purchasing land from Indians, in Douglas's experience, had not been a way of advancing the Indians' welfare.

In thinking of land purchasing as harmful to Indians, Douglas was anticipating a line of thought that would grow common among white humanitarians in the United States a few years later. For whites who considered themselves enlightened humanitarians, the purchase of land from indigenous people was, in the 1850s, beginning to look like a tragic mistake. In North America, two centuries of acquiring land by purchase had only left Indians dead or desperately poor. Land was being purchased in the 1850s from Indians in the western United States and from Maori in New Zealand, and their prospects did not look any brighter. Purchasing land from indigenous people was for many at midcentury coming to seem a cruel policy that was quickly driving indigenous people to poverty or even extinction. Thoughtful, sympathetic whites were casting about for alternatives, for forward-looking methods of providing for the needs of indigenous people in the present and the future rather than backward-looking (and frequently token) compensation for land those people once possessed. These alternatives no longer seem as appealing as they once did, because we know that the results were no better, but there was a moment in the middle of the nineteenth century when it was possible for a well-meaning white person to think of terra nullius as the enlightened choice.

For centuries such people had been the *defenders* of land purchasing, against white critics more interested in obtaining land quickly and cheaply than in providing for the Indians' well-being, because any other method of transferring land from Indians to non-Indians only promised to leave the Indians worse off. Many of the nineteenth-century land purchases in the United States, however, were thinly veiled exercises of force. By the middle of the century, white humanitarians were beginning to have doubts about purchasing land. The Board of Indian Commissioners, a group of wealthy religious philanthropists appointed in 1869 by President Grant to oversee much of the government's relations with the tribes, concluded in its first annual report that the treaty system should be abandoned, and "uncivilized Indians" treated as wards of the government. The Episcopal bishop Henry Whipple, perhaps the best-known white American advocate for the Indians in the 1860s, thought the way treaties were negotiated was "one of those blunders which is worse than a crime. We recognize a wandering tribe as an independent and sovereign nation," Whipple argued. "We send ambassadors to make a treaty as with our equals, knowing that every provision of that treaty will be our own, that those with whom we make it cannot compel us to observe it." The Reverend T. S. Williamson agreed that "after treaties are solemnly made, we fulfil, modify or abrogate them as suits our own convenience."[38] After 250 years of buying land from the Indians, white Americans trying to take the Indians' point of view were beginning to wonder whether the whole idea had been wrong from the start.

The U.S. system of land purchasing was beginning to attract criticism from white humanitarians for a second reason as well. The system had been predicated on keeping whites and Indians apart. Land purchased from the Indians normally became, after some time, an area dominated by white settlement. Land left to the Indians tended to become a backwater of Indian poverty. By the later part of the century, many critics were pointing to the policy of separation as a failure. After centuries of separation, the Indians were poised on the brink of extinction. The only way to save them, many began to argue, was to assimilate them with whites. This was not a new way of thinking—many in Britain and in North America had been saying so for some time—but it acquired greater force in the United States in the later nineteenth century, where it would eventually give rise to the policy of dividing the reservations into individually owned plots of land.[39]

In Victoria, James Douglas was an early convert to both views—that the Indians would be best served by assimilating, and that land purchasing had only harmed them in the past. Instead of negotiating with Indians for land cessions, he told Lytton, he had a better plan. He would lay off adequate reserves for the Indians, give each family a distinct portion to cultivate, and give them moral and religious training, but in all other respects treat them the same way the government treated whites, "as rational beings, capable of acting and thinking for themselves." The Indians would be encouraged to earn money and to acquire property beyond their original reserves. Like whites, they would be "left, under the protection of the laws, to provide for their own maintenance and support."[40]

The Colonial Office gave Douglas its full approval. The Earl of Carnarvon, undersecretary for the colonies, replied immediately to Douglas's letter, to express his happiness "that your sentiments respecting the treatment of the native races are so much in accordance with my own." Carnarvon hoped only that "whilst making ample provision, under the arrangement proposed, for the future sustenance and improvement of the

Indian tribes," Douglas would not be *too* generous in laying out reserves, "so as to avoid checking at a future day, the progress of the white colonists."[41] That caution aside, Douglas received a green light to proceed with the new method of land acquisition.

He lost no time in beginning. Douglas first requested and secured permission from the Colonial Office to have new reserves in British Columbia conveyed from the government to himself, as governor, for him to hold in trust for the benefit of the Indians. This was a step that would have been impossible a few years earlier, because the government would not have been understood to possess the power to convey land it had not yet purchased from the Indians. Douglas next instructed R. C. Moody, his commissioner of land and works, to travel through British Columbia and mark out reserves of land for the Indians. "The extent of the Indian Reserves," Douglas ordered, were "to be defined as they may be severally pointed out by the Natives themselves." The Indians were to be the judges of what they owned. Surveyors were instructed to stake out "all Indian villages, burial places, reserves, etc., as they may be pointed out to you by the Indians themselves," and were told to "be very careful to satisfy the Indians so long as their claims are reasonable." Correspondence within the colonial government suggests that Douglas and his employees were optimistic about the new procedure. After centuries of mistreating indigenous people in various colonies, they must have thought, Britons had finally adopted a humane method of colonization. "I have never yet received, nor heard from any source whatever, a complaint from the Indians in reference to the extent of their boundaries," Moody reported proudly to Douglas in 1863, after two years of marking off reserves under the new plan. "In fact, in every case the wishes of the Indians are carefully consulted, and the bounds are widely extended beyond the limits marked out by themselves."[42] The new colony of British Columbia seemed to offer a new model of achieving harmonious settler–Indian relations.

Half of the new model involved replacing land purchasing with a policy of terra nullius. The other half involved assimilation, and in this respect Douglas was just as active. In the spring of 1862 a member of the Squamish tribe named Snat Stroutan asked to purchase one of the parcels of land offered for sale to settlers. Moody was not sure what to do.

Stroutan was apparently the first Indian in the colony who wished to buy land the same way whites did. Douglas could hardly have asked for a better opportunity to implement a policy of assimilation. The question presented "an interesting turning point in the history of the Indians of British Columbia," Moody explained to Douglas. He asked Douglas's permission "to receive the purchase money, procure him a title deed, and in all respects deal in the matter precisely as I would with a white man." Douglas gave his approval without hesitation. "There can be no objection," he told Moody, "to your selling lands to the Natives on the same terms as they are disposed of to any purchasers in the Colony whether British subjects or aliens." Within a couple of weeks, many of the Squamish had followed Stroutan in seeking land under the terms offered to white settlers. They were filing claims to some of the best land "along the river and elsewhere to considerable extent," Moody reported, and "such extent is likely to increase very considerably and very rapidly."[43] Douglas's vision, of Indian farmers owning land side by side with white farmers under the same property law, appeared to be on the verge of being realized.

Others in British Columbia shared Douglas's opinion that land purchasing had been inhumane. In the early Vancouver Island treaties, Walter Colquhoun Grant reckoned, the Hudson's Bay Company had traded one thousand blankets for two hundred square miles of land—a minuscule price, even allowing for a 100 percent markup on the value of the blankets to account for the cost of transporting them. The surveyor D. G. Mac-Donald thought it "folly to treat with the North American Indians in a formal matter, as they know nothing of legal terms."[44]

Perhaps the most thorough exponent of this view was the colonial merchant Gilbert Sproat, who had himself purported to purchase land in 1860 (in a transaction that lacked any legal effect because it was not on behalf of the government) from a group of Nootkans on the west coast of Vancouver Island. The deal was not quite consensual on the Nootkans' part: as one amused commentator described Sproat's account of the purchase, "their land was not forcibly taken from them; they were only obliged to sell it, notwithstanding their mild and reasonable protest." Years later, Sproat clearly felt some remorse about the event. "Is not a treaty between a powerful civilised nation and a few 'Blanket Savages' a sham," Sproat asked, "except as a record of certain arrangements which the Indians are supposed to have agreed to, but which have been in reality imposed upon them? They ignorantly break the 'treaty' and then are placed before the white people as 'treaty breakers.' Deficiency of foresight and inability to appreciate other than present tangible advantages, are leading and evident components of the moral habit of savages. May it not be said that we presume on their weakness and ignorance in making treaties with them, knowing all the time, as we do, that they would not agree to cede their (supposed) lands for a small sum, were they able to see all round the proposal as white men are able to do?"[45] In ceasing to purchase land from Indians, Douglas was thus conforming to the well-intentioned opinion of at least some of the white residents of the colony.

Similar complaints had been leveled for years in the United States against acquiring land by treaty. Indeed, the experiences of the United States and the eastern parts of British North America were, for some, the best evidence of the dreadful effects of land purchasing. Richard Blanshard, testifying before the House of Commons after serving two ineffectual years as the first governor of Vancouver Island, predicted with heavy sarcasm that if colonization were to take place there as it had in the United States, the Indians would soon be dead. "I believe it is what the United States' people call improving them," he suggested. "Improving them off the face of the land?" asked one MP. "Exactly so," Blanshard answered. Walter Colquhoun Grant declared that one could "proceed across the entire continent of America" and find "the aboriginal red man entirely extinct."[46] When Douglas switched to terra nullius as the foundation of colonial land policy, he could assume the support of at least some whites seeking to ensure that the Indians of British Columbia did not suffer the same fate.

James Douglas retired in 1864. As he looked back on his career, one can imagine his pride in having reorganized colonial policy regarding the land of indigenous people. No longer would the government buy land for a pittance, as it had done in other colonies, including in the early years of Vancouver Island. The recent history of North America had shown Douglas that land purchases only left the sellers destitute and sealed off from the benefits of white civilization, whether driven from their former land or forced to inhabit desperately poor reservations. But something new was happening in British Columbia. Under a policy of terra nullius, Indians were being allowed to choose their own land, both as reserves, for their traditional areas, and as parcels available for purchase, on the same terms as those available to whites. After centuries of failure, he may well have believed, Britons were finally getting colonization right.[47]

GROWLING ABOUT PAYMENT

Terra nullius did not appeal only to avowed humanitarians. It was equally attractive to whites interested in divesting the Indians of their land as quickly as possible, because it allowed them to dispense with the often difficult task of securing the Indians' consent to sales. "How much longer are we to be inflicted with the intolerable nuisance of having hundreds upon hundreds of hideous, half-naked, drunken savages, in our midst?" asked one resident of Victoria, who could not understand Douglas's refusal to take back the land he had once reserved for the Indians. "What a doctrine for this enlightened day! Keeping hordes of savages in the midst of a city for their own good!" The men Gilbert Sproat employed at his sawmill were of the opinion that Indians lacked any property rights in the land they occupied. "They considered that any right in the soil which these natives had as occupiers was partial and imperfect," Sproat recalled, because, "with the exception of hunting animals in the forests, plucking wild fruits, and cutting a few trees to make canoes and houses, the natives did not, in any civilized sense, occupy the land." Sproat agreed. "My own notion," he explained, was that "we might justify our occupation of Vancouver Island by the fact of all the land lying waste without prospect of improvement."[48] It is likely that many white British Columbians, like many other settlers on other frontiers, shared the view that the Indians had no property rights a civilized nation was bound to respect.

Others concluded that even if the Indians did have some rights to some land, Douglas had been far too generous in allowing the Indians to define the extent of their own reserves. "It will not be difficult for the reader to imagine the result of this palpably ill judged step," despaired the *British Columbian* shortly after Douglas retired. "Several millions of acres of the choicest prairie lands, in all conceivable forms and position, were laid off as the greed or caprice of the wandering Indian suggested." Indeed, "so extravagant were the Indians in their notions that in some instances, we are assured, the reserve amounts to about a thousand acres to each man!" The complaint lingered for many years: a small number of Indians had been allowed to lock up a disproportionately large amount of land, "to such an extent as seriously to retard settlement. And this is the legacy, in the form of an Indian policy, bequeathed to us by Sir James Douglas." As the *Cariboo Sentinel* put it, when Indian reserves threatened to block construction of a much-wanted railway line, "surely a small tribe of Indians do not need the whole of the Chilcoton valley."[49]

Douglas's successors as governor were career colonial officials who did not share his long experience in the Northwest. Arthur Kennedy, who took over on Vancouver Island, was between posts in Australia and Africa. Frederick Seymour, who became governor of British Columbia in 1864, came from the West Indies. Anthony Musgrave, who succeeded Seymour in 1869 (after Vancouver Island had been merged into British Columbia), was between posts in Newfoundland and Africa. None of these men was as interested as Douglas in the welfare of Indians. Seymour, for example, had been on the job only a few months when he informed the Colonial Office, to the dismay of Secretary of State for the Colonies Edward Cardwell, that in the event of war with the Indians he might "invite every white man to shoot each Indian he may meet. Such a proclamation would not be badly received here."[50]

In practice, authority over Indian land policy was delegated to Joseph Trutch, the colony's commissioner of lands and works, and, after 1871, its lieutenant governor. Trutch shared his superiors' dim view of the Indians. He agreed that Douglas had allocated them far too much land. "The Indians really have no right to the lands they claim, nor are they of any actual value or utility to them," he reasoned, "and I cannot see why they should either retain these lands to the prejudice of the general interests of the Colony, or be allowed to make a market of them either to Government or to individuals." Trutch instead favored reducing the size of the reserves unilaterally, by simply taking land back. The Indians "should be confirmed in the possession of such extents of lands only as are sufficient for their probable requirements for purposes of cultivation and pasturage," he concluded. "The remainder of the land now shut up in these reserves should be thrown open to pre-emption" by settlers.[51] Over the next several years, the colonial government did exactly that. Some of Douglas's reserves were made smaller. New reserves included much less land per capita than the reserves Douglas had created. The government stopped allowing Indians to acquire land on the same terms as whites. With the retirement of James Douglas, British Columbia's land policy changed dramatically.

One important component of that policy, however, did not change. Terra nullius—the view that the Indians had no property rights in land before such rights were granted by the colonial government—remained the basis of colonial land allocation. The government was able to grant land to settlers rather than Indians only because of the logically antecedent decision to vest ownership of the land in the government. If the government had never adopted terra nullius—if Douglas had stuck with the original view that land could not be settled before it was acquired from the Indians by treaty—the Indians might have been able to block the post-Douglas switch to more miserly reserves by refusing to sell land or by holding out for a better offer.

Had that happened, the governors after Douglas might have adopted terra nullius themselves, to be sure, but there are a few reasons to think that they would not have. In the 1860s such a change in land policy, for the transparent purpose of diminishing the amount of land available to Indians, would have raised eyebrows in the Colonial Office, which might well have intervened. After 1871, when British Columbia became part of Canada, such a change would have been viewed by Dominion officials with similar alarm. In the United States, meanwhile, relations between whites and Indians were at their darkest, probably even darker than in British Columbia, but no American territorial official had the nerve to declare a formal policy of terra nullius. For all the violence and settler trespassing that took place in the western United States, the American government continued to acquire land from Indian tribes (except in California) in transactions formally structured as contracts. If terra nullius never became law in the United States, it seems unlikely it would have become law in a post-Douglas British Columbia.

Terra nullius remained controversial for decades. Settler opinion in the aggregate may have favored terra nullius, but there were many whites, in Britain and in British Columbia, who called upon the government to resume acquiring Indian land by treaty.

In Britain the Aborigines Protection Society repeatedly petitioned the government to recognize Indian property rights in land and to purchase land from the Indians in voluntary transactions. "It is certain that the Indians regard their rights as natives as giving them a greater title to enjoy the riches of the country than can possibly be possessed either by the English Government or by foreign adventurers," insisted F. W. Chesson, the Society's secretary, in a letter to Edward Bulwer Lytton. "We would beg, therefore, most respectfully to suggest that the Native title should be recognized in British Columbia." In 1869, after five years of post-Douglas land policy, the Society forwarded to the Colonial Office and published a letter it had received from a settler in Victoria, deploring the absence of any recognition of Indian property rights. "They have *never* been paid for their land," the settler lamented, "their reserve has *not* been kept intact, and they have *no sort* of protection extended to them." This sort of lobbying had no effect on the Colonial Office, for reasons that may be best captured in an annotation made on one such petition by Undersecretary Herman Merivale. "These gentlemen are well meaning—at least some of them—& they represent a common & healthy British feeling," Merivale wrote; "but the worst of it is that 'protection of the aborigines' has become with them a 'technical profession.' They never see, or pretend to see, two sides of a case: consequently their practical suggestions, when they make any at all (which I must do them justice to say, is very seldom) are of a character which would probably cause some astonishment to people on the spot."[52]

Here Merivale was wrong, because many people on the spot—white British Columbians—were likewise pleading with the government to abandon terra nullius and acquire Indian land by treaty. "The Indians have a right to be paid for their land," the *British Colonist* editorialized, while Douglas was still in office. "There prevails among all the members of the tribes whose lands have been taken by the Government, a great amount of ill feeling toward the dominant race," the paper noted in 1863. "The cause of this animosity is simply the neglect of the Executive to make the natives compensation for the property we have appropriated belonging to them." The volume of this kind of criticism increased after Douglas retired and the colonial government became much stingier in allocating reserves. "Joseph bought the lands of the Egyptians for Pharaoh, but even Pharaoh gave the coin in return," recalled one correspondent to the *Colonist*. "The Government of Vancouver Island had better do the same thing." The *Nanaimo Gazette* accused colonial officials of treating the Indians like wild animals rather than human beings. "Is there a spot of ground on this Island that they can call their own, or even lawfully hold for the shortest term on the slightest of tenures?" the *Gazette* asked. "Are their persons or their property, little as the value of each may be, in reality protected?" Though Indians were "the original possessors of the soil," the *Mainland Guardian* recognized, "there can be no doubt that white settlers have shown very little respect for the prior possession by the Indians of the best locations, which have been seized by the Caucasian invaders."[53] Settler opinion was far from monolithic.

Some of the most vocal white proponents of Indian property rights were the missionaries. The missionary Charles Grandidier crusaded for Indian property rights from his arrival in British Columbia in 1873. "Before the settlement of this Province the natives were in possession of it," Grandidier declared in a letter to the *Victoria Standard*. "The whites came, took land, fenced it, and little by little hemmed the Indians in their small reservations." Other missionaries—men who, after living for extended periods among the Indians, could see matters from their converts' point of view—made similar arguments.[54]

Indeed, there may well have been more white sympathy for Indians than is suggested by the surviving documentary record, a record in which government officials have a disproportionate voice. Lucius Edelblute was an itinerant miner who followed the gold rushes in California and the Northwest, including in mainland British Columbia. Uneducated, half-literate, and dependent for his livelihood on access to land, Edelblute was exactly the sort of person most prone toward ignoring the rights of Indians. Yet Edelblute was also a Christian. "I bleave that wee are oll godolmtez [God almighty's] natural hand worke," he explained, "and thare is a loow [law] in natur which wee the inteligant should live by and dy by and ot [ought] never step out side of." The law was the Golden Rule: "to du unto oll mankind az wee wizh them to du untoo you." Edelblute was certain that whites had violated the Golden Rule in their treatment of the Indians. "It was a rong ide [idea]," he concluded, "to dizzolvd the frend Ship with the inainz [Indians] in the furzt setling uve a marica if that iz eny thing left for the poor indin it iz the white manz simphity."[55] There may have been other settlers like Edelblute for whom simple Christian charity required respect for the rights of Indians.

In lobbying for the resumption of land purchasing, white opponents of terra nullius were joined by many of the Indians themselves. Indians had always done what they could to enforce their own rights to land, from expelling trespassers to requesting compensation for land taken. By the 1860s many were complaining about terra nullius. "Everywhere the Indians are growling about payment for their land," reported the botanist Robert Brown, touring Vancouver Island in 1864. "When traveling or sitting round the camp fire with them they always appeal to me on that subject & I assure you that it is no easy matter to answer the question satisfactorily when an intelligent [Indian] looks up in your face and asks 'Had you no good land of your own that you come and deprive us of ours?'" On the mainland that same year, a group of Indians stole sacks of flour from a surveying party. Asked why, they responded: "You are in our country; you owe us bread." The Haida claimed to own the Queen Charlotte Islands, while at Alberni, according to an alarmed government employee, "the Indians in that locality claim the lands as their property, and threaten to molest parties occupying said land." Similar incidents took place all over British Columbia.[56]

In the 1870s, when British Columbia became a province of Canada, it became the only province that treated Indian land as terra nullius. Dominion officials seem to have been taken by surprise, and they too accordingly urged the government of British Columbia to resume acquiring Indian land by treaty. British Columbia "appears to be treating its Indian subjects with great harshness," the Earl of Dufferin, governor-general of Canada, reported to the Colonial Office in 1874. "It does not recognize any obligation to extinguish the Indian title." Dufferin returned to the theme in another dispatch a few weeks later. "The B.C.'s have evidently been behaving very badly," he complained, "and they certainly should be required to extinguish the Indian title before assuming possession of the lands, which is the universal principle observed in every province of the Dominion." But the government of British Columbia would not back down. "The Canadian treaty system as I understand it will hardly work here," Joseph Trutch informed the prime minister of Canada, John Macdonald. "We have never bought out any Indian claims to lands nor do they expect we should."[57] The government of Canada was powerless to intervene. Acquiring land from Indians was a provincial, not a Dominion, matter; all the government of Canada could do was to establish, with the British Columbian government, a weak and ultimately ineffectual joint commission to inquire into the Indians' land-related grievances.

As Trutch's defiant statement suggests, by the 1870s British Columbia officials were denying that land had *ever* been acquired from the Indians by treaty. Matthew Begbie, British Columbia's chief justice, conceded in 1872 that Douglas had made "some sort of arrangement" with tribes on Vancouver Island, but, Begbie declared, that arrangement was not a treaty. "I am not aware that it has been reduced to writing," he claimed. "I believe it has generally (where it exists) been in the form of a declaration of intentions by the local government." Begbie ought to have known better, and perhaps he did. The same could be said of the Justice of the Peace Alexander Caulfield Anderson, who insisted in the early 1880s that "no system of 'purchase of land' . . . has ever been countenanced here." The claim might have been true had it been made more narrowly. Strictly speaking, Douglas entered into his early land purchases on behalf of the Hudson's Bay Company, not the government. One could truthfully, if legalistically, say, as did B. W. Pearse, the province's chief commissioner of lands and works, that *the government* had never purchased land from the Indians of British Columbia, because the government had not been a party to any of Douglas's treaties.[58] But the men who governed British Columbia were making a broader claim than that—they were denying, wrongly, that Britons had ever recognized the Indians of British Columbia as owners of their land.

Indeed, in the 1880s, as Indian discontent over land issues mounted,

British Columbia officials took pains to repress any memory that there had ever been any treaties. On his way to hear the complaints of Indians along the Nass River, J. P. Planta was instructed by the province's attorney general to be particularly "careful to discountenance, should it arise, any claim of Indian title to Provincial lands." When such a claim did arise, the government denied that land had ever been purchased, in any part of Canada. At a government–Indian conference in 1887, John Wesley, speaking for a Nisga'a and Tsimshian delegation, demanded a treaty. "What do you mean by a treaty?" asked William Smithe, the province's premier.

Wesley: We want such a law as the law of England and the Dominion Government which made a treaty with the Indians.

Hon. Mr. Smithe: Where did you hear that?

Wesley: It is in the law books.

Hon. Mr. Smithe: Who told you so?

Wesley: There are a good many Indians that can read and write, and they are the ones who say this themselves.

Hon. Mr. Smithe: And they told you this, did they?

Wesley: Yes.

Hon. Mr. Smithe: Well, I should like them to produce the book that they read this in. I have never seen that book.

Wesley: We could not tell you the book just now; but we can probably find it for you if you really want to see it.

Hon. Mr. Smithe: There is no such law either English or Dominion that I know of; and the Indians, or their friends, have been misled on that point.[59]

Smithe was either deliberately lying or startlingly ignorant of Canadian history. East of British Columbia, Britons had been purchasing land from Indians since the seventeenth century. By the 1880s, however, government officials had either forgotten or no longer wished to remember.

As for the history of their own province, the views of John Helmcken were perhaps representative of official memory. Helmcken had arrived in Victoria in 1850 as a physician in the service of the Hudson's Bay Company. He married James Douglas's daughter. In later years he held a variety of political positions in the colony. Helmcken's adult life coincided with the early history of British Columbia. His recollection must have carried special weight, then, when in the 1880s he insisted that the early Douglas treaties had not been treaties at all. "Sir James Douglas had not bought the Indian title but had made a treaty of *amity* and *friendship* with the Indians about Victoria," Helmcken wrote in the *British Colonist*. "It matters not how the papers were made out; the Indians not having any legal right in the land could not give any conveyance of land. What they could give goodness only knows." If the Indians themselves remembered otherwise, that was only because white "misleaders and agitators" had "put their own cranky, socialistic, untenable, impracticable and unlawful notions into Indian heads."[60]

Seeking support for this view of events, Helmcken wrote to Joseph Mackay, to ask if Mackay remembered things the same way. Mackay was another old-timer, who had also been at Victoria in the employ of the Hudson's Bay Company almost from the beginning. "As to purchase, this was all moonshine," Helmcken wrote. "My feeling is, the blankets &c. were given to appease or make friends with the indians, in order that no trouble might arise in case settlers arrived upon the land. Why Douglas should have given such a document as he did is a conundrum. I suppose he had no legal advisor!"[61]

Mackay agreed. "Mr. Douglas made no purchase of the country from the Indians," he confirmed. "They were told that only such places as they had occupied and improved property belonged to them . . . and the rest of the country would be open for sale to white settlers." Douglas had paid the Indians with whom he had treated, but the payment was not for the land, Mackay recalled. Rather, it was intended as compensation for damage to the land that had already been caused by the Company's sheep and cattle.[62] Whether deliberately or not, the brief era of land purchasing had been re-remembered a few decades later as its opposite—as the origin of the policy of terra nullius.

chapter seven

Oregon and Washington

Compulsory Treaties

SOVEREIGNTY over the area north of California and south of Alaska—today, the American states of Oregon and Washington and the Canadian province of British Columbia—was not established until 1846, when the United States and Britain agreed to the current international boundary. Between 1818 and 1846 the two countries agreed not to interfere with settlement by citizens of either. In practice, before 1846 neither country tried to govern the area, for fear of antagonizing the other.

The white population of the area was negligible in 1818—it consisted of a handful of fur traders. By 1846, however, there were already thousands of white settlers in the southern part of the Oregon Territory, the present-day state of Oregon. (The Washington Territory would be split off from Oregon in 1853.) These early settlers entered a jurisdictional vacuum, in which neither Britain nor the United States had the power to prescribe rules for acquiring land. The early settlers, like their counterparts in New Zealand and California, were thus able to develop their own practices from the bottom up, practices that would be determined by their perceptions of, and their power relative to, the local tribes.

A LAZY, STUPID RACE OF PEOPLE

The earliest English-speaking settlers in the Oregon Territory tended to hold low opinions of the Indians. At Astoria, established on the Oregon coast in 1811 by employees of John Jacob Astor's Pacific Fur Company, the Indians "were the most uncouth-looking objects," the clerk Ross Cox recalled. "Their bodies besmeared with whale oil, gave them an appearance horribly disgusting. Then the women,—O ye gods!" As explorers and missionaries began to arrive in Oregon in the 1820s and 1830s, they expressed similar views. "The natives are inquisitive in the extreme, treacherous, and will pillage or murder when they can do it with impunity," the botanist David Douglas noted in 1825 on the banks of the Columbia River. The Methodist missionaries Daniel Lee and J. H. Frost, in Oregon in the 1830s, found the Indians "the most degraded human beings that we have met with in all our journeyings, taking them as a whole. There is not one among them that can be considered *virtuous.*"[1]

Many of the settlers who soon began arriving by the thousands felt the same way. The Indians of the Oregon Territory are "a sort of half human, half vegetable race," declared one guide for prospective emigrants. Another reported that the Wallawallas were "in general poor, indolent, and sordid, but avaricious," and that the Cayuses were "boisterous, saucy, and troublesome." Not all accounts were as bleak: the naturalist John Kirk Townsend thought the Oregon Indians were "almost universally, fine looking, robust men," who had been very friendly to him, "each of the chiefs taking us by the hand with great cordiality." But this was an unusually positive appraisal. By the 1850s, government surveyor A. N. Armstrong could sum up, in a single sentence, four decades of white observation of the Indians of the Northwest: "They are a lazy, stupid race of people."[2]

Contributing to this disdain was the fact that the tribes of Oregon, like those of British Columbia to the north and California to the south, did not practice agriculture before contact with whites. "None of these Indians cultivate any thing," the fur trader Joshua Pilcher reported in 1830. "They depend upon hunting and fishing." Early white accounts of indigenous diets suggest an environment rich in spontaneously growing plants and animals, especially fish. The Jesuit missionary Pierre-Jean de Smet, on the Columbia River in the 1840s, feared that "those who know not this territory may accuse me of exaggeration, when I affirm, that it would be as easy to count the pebbles so profusely scattered on the shores, as to sum up the number of different kinds of fish, which this western river furnishes for man's support." Inland, in southern Oregon, the trapper Peter Skene Ogden found the Shasta Indians "well in flesh" despite apparently subsisting largely on acorns.[3] But if one could live well in the Northwest without farming, the association of agriculture with civilization was too firmly a part of American thought to be dislodged by contrary examples.

By the time whites arrived, in any event, Indian economies were on the decline. The smallpox virus reached the Columbia River around 1780, killing approximately a third of the inhabitants, and that was just the first of a series of microorganisms that would devastate the tribes of the Northwest. By the mid-1830s, the missionary Samuel Parker found the Indian population on the lower Columbia "far less than I had expected, or what it was when Lewis and Clarke made their tour" thirty years before. As whites emigrated in increasing numbers, Parker concluded, the rate of Indian death was accelerating. "Since the year 1829, probably seven-eighths . . . have been swept away by disease." In an era before the causes of disease were well understood, no one was certain why this was happening. Parker blamed the Indians' method of treatment: "In the burning stage of the fever they plunged themselves into the river," he reasoned, "and continued in the water until the heat was allayed, and rarely survived the cold stage which followed." The fur trader John McLoughlin, a longtime resident of Oregon, pointed out that the onset of the fever in 1829 had coincided with the introduction of farming to the area, and concluded that some kind of poison must have been released from the soil when it was first plowed. But if the cause of these diseases was a mystery, their effect was not. "So many and so sudden were the deaths which occurred, that the shores were strewed with the unburied dead," Parker related. "Whole and large villages were depopulated; and some entire tribes have disappeared, the few remaining persons, if there were any, uniting themselves with other tribes. This great mortality extended not only from the vicinity of the Cascades to the shores of the Pacific, but far north and south." And this was just one of several epidemics. In 1843, when Overton Johnson and William Winter arrived in Oregon, they found "the bones of hundreds, perhaps thousands" of Indians in large piles. "And every isolated rock that rises out of the Columbia, is covered with the canoes of the dead," they explained in their guide for prospective emigrants. "They are nearly all gone." It quickly became the conventional wisdom among whites that the Indians of Oregon would soon be extinct.[4]

The missionaries, meanwhile, considered it part of their calling to teach agriculture to the survivors. By the 1840s, travelers were reporting thriving Indian farms in areas near missions. "They raise wheat, corn, potatoes, peas and a variety of vegetables," the emigrant Joel Palmer observed near the Umatilla River. Palmer was most likely among the Cayuses, who had been the recipients of nine years of Presbyterian missionary work by the time of Palmer's visit. Palmer took careful note of Indian agriculture—he would later become superintendent of Indian affairs for the Oregon Territory. The Wallawallas sold him potatoes they had grown, he explained, and elsewhere along the Columbia "the Indians were constantly paying us visits, furnishing us with vegetables" from their gardens. Other travelers found similar farms.[5] Indian land use had changed dramatically by the time there was a substantial white presence in Oregon.

In the early decades of white settlement, most Indians were nevertheless not farmers. Whites soon realized that the Indians of the Northwest, unlike some of the midwestern tribes, were not nomadic, despite their lack of agriculture. "They have no fixed habitations, and yet they are not, properly speaking, a wandering people," noted Charles Wilkes, the commander of the United States Exploring Expedition, which surveyed the northwest coast in 1841. "Nearly every month in the year they change their place of residence,—but the same month every year finds them regularly in the same place." Some settlers, at least, seem to have recognized that the Indians were moving seasonally, in accordance with fishing, hunting, and plant-growing cycles.[6] The result was a consensus view among whites about patterns of Indian land use: most Indians were not farmers, but Indian tribes controlled particular zones of land, within which tribe members had rights to use resources to the exclusion of members of other tribes.

That fact alone might have caused land policy to go in either direction. The absence of precontact agriculture tended toward terra nullius, as in Australia, California, and British Columbia, but the control tribes exercised over areas of land might, in other circumstances, have tended toward a policy of purchasing those areas. East of the Rockies, for example, the government of the United States was long accustomed to purchasing land from nonagricultural tribes. In Oregon, however, two additional factors pushed settlers toward terra nullius.

The first was that, as in California, settlers had the ability to establish a de facto land policy before the government arrived. The joint U.S.-British occupation of Oregon prevented either country from attempting to govern the area before the late 1840s, by which time there were already thousands of settlers in place. The United States government was hardly an effective or enthusiastic protector of Indians in the mid-nineteenth century, but it did have a modest record of preventing some settlers in other parts of the country from seizing the Indians' land. Before the late 1840s it could not play this role in Oregon. The local tribes, meanwhile, were so small and at such a technological disadvantage that they posed little threat. As in California, the early settlers of Oregon could simply begin occupying land without fear of reprisal.

The second factor pushing toward terra nullius was unique to Oregon. Although the U.S. government was far away and did not actually govern the area until the late 1840s, the settlers, most of whom were American, expected that the United States was likely to exercise sovereignty one day. Since at least the 1820s, the general assumption in Congress and the press had been that the Northwest would become part of the United States—perhaps not soon, but eventually.[7] Under American law, the federal government was the sole lawful purchaser of Indian land. Private purchasing was illegal. Had the early Oregon settlers *wanted* to purchase land from the Indians, therefore, they would not have been able to.

The settlers most likely knew this very well. In 1832, when a group of prospective emigrants inquired of Lewis Cass, the secretary of war, as to the legality of establishing a colony in Oregon, Cass responded with a warning. "Our laws make no provision for the occupation of the country, nor for any negotiation with the Indians for that purpose," he reminded the would-be land purchasers. "Congress alone can authorise the measure proposed." A skeptical magazine article made the same point, in mocking Hall Jackson Kelley's proposal to lead a caravan of settlers from New England to Oregon in the early 1830s. "When Mr. Kelly has gotten his gulls fairly to their nests, that is, to Oregon," the article asked, "how is he to obtain the land which he proposes to lay out for them, in lots of two hundred acres each? Does he mean to purchase it of the natives with the money with which the settlers will have so judiciously entrusted him? The laws of the United States expressly prohibit any such traffic between Indians and private individuals." Kelley himself was well aware of this problem: he spent years trying to persuade the government to delegate to him the power to purchase land. "The title of the whole country, and the exclusive right of occupation remains invested in the aborigines," he declared. "To take from them a part or the whole of their land, without an adequate remuneration, on the ground that the improvements in human affairs and the good of mankind require it, is wrong and utterly unjustifiable."[8] Kelley never did receive any delegation of the government's land-purchasing power, but he headed out for Oregon anyway, presumably planning to occupy land without buying it first.

In the 1830s and 1840s, then, even the most well-intentioned American emigrant would have realized that there was no point even trying to purchase land from the Indians, because no such purchase would have been recognized as valid by the federal government. As the Oregon lawyer Jessy Quinn Thornton complained in 1849, the territory's early settlers were "surrounded by restless tribes of Indians, who clamorously and insolently demanded of the immigrants pay for lands which the immigrants had neither the means nor the right to purchase."[9] By agreeing to the joint U.S.-British occupation of the Northwest, the U.S. government in effect required settlers to treat Oregon as terra nullius. Of course, many (and perhaps all) would have done so in any event. Their presence on land they knew they could not legally buy suggests they were untroubled by the prospect of failing to respect the Indians' property rights. But the government's inability to purchase land during the joint occupation only reinforced this tendency.

As a result, most of the settlers of the 1830s and 1840s simply occupied land without obtaining the consent of the Indians. Not all did—there were ways of obtaining permission that did not violate the law banning private purchases. Some of the earliest white emigrants married into Indian families and presumably acquired rights to land in the process. The schoolteacher Solomon Smith, for example, married a Clatsop woman named Celiast in 1834 and began farming soon after. Clatsop men helped him build his house, so tribe members probably did not object to Smith's farm. The missionaries convinced themselves, and perhaps some of the Indians as well, that the land occupied by the missions was a small price to pay for all the good they brought to Oregon.[10] These were methods of land acquisition, however, that obviously could not accommodate thousands of people who intended to reside in Oregon permanently. Most emigrants took land without the Indians' consent.

Peter Burnett was one of them. Burnett left his Missouri law practice for a farm near the Willamette River in 1843. As one of the first lawyers in the far west he went on to a career as a big fish in a small pond: in 1848, when the federal government organized a territorial supreme court, Burnett was appointed one of the justices, and two years later, after a move to California, he became the state's first governor. Many years later, in his memoirs, Burnett explained how he and his fellow settlers had acquired land in Oregon. "We went anywhere we pleased," he recalled, "settled down without any treaty or consultation with the Indians, and occupied our claims without their consent and without compensation." From the Indians' perspective, Burnett recognized, this pattern of land acquisition was something new. The Hudson's Bay Company had founded trading posts in Oregon for decades before Burnett arrived, but "the Indians soon saw that the company was a mere trading establishment, confined to a small space of land at each post, and was, in point of fact, advantageous to themselves." Individual fur trappers, most from Canada, had also predated Burnett's party, but "the few Canadian-French who were located in the Willamette Valley were mostly, if not entirely connected by marriage with the Indians, the Frenchmen having Indian wives, and were considered to some extent as a part of their own people." Burnett's party, by contrast, numbered nearly a thousand, intended to stay permanently, and consisted largely of married couples and their children, people who had no interest in intermarriage with the Indians. "When we, the American immigrants, came into what the Indians claimed as their own country, we were considerable in numbers," Burnett remembered, "and we came, not to establish trade with the Indians, but to take and settle the country exclusively for ourselves." Burnett realized that this difference was not lost on the Indians. "Every succeeding fall they found the white population about doubled, and our settlements continually extending, and rapidly encroaching more and more upon their pasture and camas grounds," he admitted. "They saw that we fenced in the best lands, excluding their horses from the grass, and our hogs ate up their camas. They instinctively saw annihilation before them."[11]

Most of the whites occupying land in Oregon probably gave little thought to whether their new farms could be reconciled with the property rights of Indians. When they did think about it, there doubtless seemed to be plenty of land available to all. As eastern cities grew more crowded than they had ever been, as working people increasingly lacked land of their own, it hardly seemed reasonable that a relatively small number of nonfarming Indians should lock up enormous areas of excellent agricultural land. The Indians of Oregon had a right "to hold so much of the land as was necessary for their subsistence, but no more," declared the *Workingman's Advocate,* a New York labor newspaper. "The people of any nation on the globe have a full and perfect right to go to any other nation, and to occupy any land that they can find unoccupied."[12] Emigrants to Oregon could implement a policy of terra nullius with a clear conscience.

By 1845, Elijah White discovered, the Indians of the Willamette Valley were "looking upon the rapid growth and increased strength of the whites with sorrowful countenances and sad hearts." White was the first federal agent charged with relations with the Indians of the Northwest; he was appointed even before the 1846 treaty establishing American sovereignty over Oregon. Already, he reported back to Washington, white settlers were arrogating so much land that many of the Indians "were becoming very bitter towards the Americans." White predicted trouble: "The present state of things between us and them," he concluded, "is peculiar, critical, unenviable, and dangerous, at least so far as peace and property are concerned."[13]

A few years later, White would be proven right.

RIGHTFUL OWNERS OF THE SOIL

The treaty dividing the Northwest between the United States and Britain, and confirming American sovereignty over the area encompassing the present-day states of Oregon and Washington, was signed in June 1846, but the Northwest was of so little practical importance to the federal government that it would be more than two years before Congress established a territorial government. The 1848 statute specifying the structure of that government assumed that the land within the Oregon Territory would have to be purchased from the Indians. It provided "that nothing in this act contained shall be construed to impair the rights of person or property now pertaining to the Indians in said Territory, so long as such rights shall remain unextinguished by treaty between the United States and such Indians."[14] The end of terra nullius appeared imminent.

There would be no further progress, however, for another two years, despite the pleas of settlers and Indians alike. Even before the territorial government was established, the white residents of Oregon petitioned Congress to send treaty commissioners to the Indians as soon as possible. For years they had been promising the Indians that one day "the United States would send agents, authorized and empowered to treat with them in relation to their claims to the soil of the country." The 1846 treaty with Britain had removed the last diplomatic obstacle to land purchasing, but still no agents had arrived. "These promises have been repeated so often, without being fulfilled, that the Indians have become exceedingly restless, distrustful and jealous," the settlers complained. The Indians "say, with great apparent reason, that their numbers are diminishing rapidly; that they are growing old, and will soon pass away, without receiving any compensation for their lands." This prospect was unwelcome from either a humanitarian or a military point of view; whether one sympathized with the Indians or feared them, it was unwise to let this grievance fester. The settlers would have bought the land themselves, they explained, correctly, "but we have no *power or right to treat with the Indian tribes.*"[15] All they could do was wait for federal land purchasers to come.

When Joseph Lane, the first governor of the Oregon Territory, arrived in early 1849, he immediately began lobbying the federal government to send purchasers. The Indians "say the whites have settled their country," he reported to Secretary of State John Clayton. "The white people have promised them from year to year and from time to time, that the United States Government would send out a Governor with presents for them, and Commissioners to purchase their lands and pay for them. They are anxious to sell, and the people are exceedingly sensitive on the subject." Lane urged the territorial legislature to send the same message to Congress. "The extinguishment of their title by purchase," he declared, "is a measure of the most vital importance to them."[16] But the federal government did nothing.

Some of the calls for land purchasing were motivated by a genuine desire to treat the Indians properly. As one correspondent to the Quaker magazine *The Friend* pointed out, the rate of emigration to Oregon was increasing so quickly that unless the government acted soon the Indians would be left landless. Some of the calls were motivated by the apprehension that the only alternative would be war. President James Polk included a request for Indian treaties in his annual message to Congress for 1848. Tension between settlers and the Cayuses had recently attracted national attention when a group of Cayuses killed the missionary Marcus Whitman and several others, including Whitman's wife. The cause of the violence, Polk recognized, was "the long delay of the United States in making them some trifling compensation, in such articles as they wanted, for the country now occupied by our emigrants."[17]

White residents of Oregon also had some self-interested motives to call for treaties. Once the Indians' land had been purchased, they hoped, the government would step in and move the Indians far away from them, just like Indians had been removed from the Southeast a decade earlier. "At present, the thinned and scattered fragments of once numerous tribes are intermingled with the whites," the Oregon legislature informed Congress in its memorial pleading for the appointment of federal land purchasers. "They are mutually annoying to each other."[18] White Oregonians were also eager to remove the clouds on settlers' land titles that were created by the lack of any formal grants from the government, clouds that could be dispelled only by entering into treaties with the Indians. Despite all these pressing reasons to negotiate land cession treaties, however, Congress did not take up the issue until 1850, two years after it established the territorial government, and four years after the United States acquired clear sovereignty.

Even then, Congress moved slowly. Bills to appoint treaty commissioners and appropriate money to buy land were introduced in both houses in January 1850, but no statute was enacted until June. The delay does not seem to have been caused by any controversy over whether treaties were desirable. No one disagreed with Senator John Bell of Tennessee when he pointed out that "there is scarcely an inhabitant" of Oregon "who can make any improvements, clear his land or build, with any confidence, because there is not an acre of land to which some of the Indian tribes do not set up a claim." When Bell asserted that "it is important to preserve peaceable relations with the Indians, and extinguish their title by giving them such compensation as Government may think reasonable, and to which the Indians may assent," no one spoke to the contrary. The bill's main proponent was Samuel Royal Thurston, the Oregon Territory's delegate in the House of Representatives, who reminded his colleagues that "although the white population in Oregon reaches about fifteen thousand, up to this time, the Indian title to a foot of land in that territory never has been extinguished. Consequently no man owns a foot of land in Oregon; but all of us are comparatively trespassers upon the soil." Again, no one disagreed. The statute Congress finally passed had no controversial provisions; it simply appropriated $25,000 and authorized the president to appoint one or more commissioners "to negotiate treaties with the several Indian tribes in the Territory of Oregon, for the extinguishment of their claims to lands lying west of the Cascade Mountains; and, if found expedient and practicable, for their removal east of said mountains."[19] The large majority of Oregon's white residents lived west of the Cascades, so there was no dispute that this was the land that needed to be purchased first. The statute scarcely differed from similar statutes appropriating money for land purchases from Indians in other parts of the country.

Why, then, did it take Congress four years for such a routine matter, four years during which both the whites and Indians of Oregon were anxiously waiting? One might conceivably interpret the delay as a clever way of reducing the purchase price, by stalling until the white population of the territory grew so large, and the Indian population so small, that the Indians would be willing to sell vast tracts of land for very little money. This possibility would be too far-fetched even to contemplate but for the fact that the same Congress, only three months after authorizing treaty negotiations and before any negotiations actually began, enacted another statute completely at odds with the first. In the Oregon Donation Act of 1850, Congress granted to every white adult in the Oregon Territory 320 acres of land, for free, once the land had been lived on and cultivated for four years.[20] The Donation Act tacitly presumed that the land was the government's to grant. It said nothing about any property rights in the land that might be possessed by Indians. Indeed, by encouraging settlers to move to Oregon and begin farming on land not yet purchased from Indians, the Donation Act undermined Indian property rights nearly as much as an explicit declaration of terra nullius would have.

Nevertheless, it seems unlikely that either the Donation Act or the four-year delay in authorizing Indian treaties was part of a covert plan to reduce the price of Indian land. There was so much white support for quick treaties that someone surely would have made this accusation had it appeared credible at the time. The incentives for delay were at least as strong in California, but there Congress moved much faster—the statute appropriating funds for land purchasing was enacted within months after Congress's receipt of reports on the status of Indian land. The more probable explanation for the delay with respect to Oregon is simply that the Oregon Territory was of little national importance, especially relative to California. The 1850 census found 93,000 white Californians but only 12,000 whites in the Oregon Territory. California had gold; Oregon did not. In Congress Oregon was a "Terra incognita," Samuel Royal Thurston complained to his wife. "The fame of Oregon, what she once had was now sleeping in forgetfulness, amidst the panegyrics of California."[21] Once the boundary with Britain was settled in 1846, Oregon would not form a significant part of the national political agenda for many years.

The preferences of a few thousand settlers and Indians in the most remote part of the continent were easily forgotten.

The Donation Act is most likely attributable to a similar lack of attention. Within Congress, the force behind the Donation Act was once again Thurston, the Oregon Territory's delegate, the same person who had pushed the treaty bill through Congress a few months before. He spent most of the first half of 1850 lobbying for the two bills simultaneously. Thurston and his constituents would have perceived no inconsistency between the two statutes. They wanted the government to purchase the Indians' land precisely so the land could then be granted to settlers. As Thurston pointed out, while campaigning for reelection soon after, "the extinguishment of the Indian title to land in Oregon" was "an obstruction in the way" of the government's ability to distribute land to white emigrants. Congress had already enacted similar statutes authorizing grants of land in other parts of the country to settlers, land that was already part of the public domain because the Indians' right of occupancy had been extinguished. Members of Congress may well have assumed that the Donation Act, like these earlier statutes, was meant to apply only to land that lay within the power of the government to grant. If so, however, this assumption was only implicit in the actual text of the statute, which contained no such limitation. Nor was any such limitation understood by white settlers, many of whom began setting up farms on land the government had not yet purchased from the Indians. It was not long before Anson Dart, the superintendent of Indian affairs in the Oregon Territory, was alarmed by "the awkward position in which our government is placed in Oregon." In the Donation Act, he hastened to inform the Office of Indian Affairs, the government had promised land to settlers, but "at the same time every acre of this land is owned and occupied by a people that the Government has always acknowledged to be the bonafide and rightful owners of the soil." Once the Indians found this out, Dart predicted, there would be trouble.[22]

Like Congress, the Office of Indian Affairs gave California a higher priority than Oregon in negotiating treaties. Congress appropriated money for the Oregon treaties in June 1850 and for the California treaties in September, but the Indian Office did not appoint any treaty commissioners for Oregon until October, only after the Office had already appointed commissioners for California.

The primary qualifications of the three men authorized to purchase land from the Oregon Indians—John Pollard Gaines, Alonzo Skinner, and Beverly Allen—were loyalty to the Whig Party and presence in Oregon. (In this respect they were no different from any of their contemporaries. Indian Office appointments were rooted in political patronage rather than knowledge of Indians. Once Franklin Pierce became president in 1853, the Office's representatives in the Northwest would all be Democrats.) Gaines was a one-term Whig member of Congress from Kentucky who had been elected in 1846 while incarcerated as a prisoner of war in Mexico City. His escape and return to the United States did not help his political career, as he lost his bid for reelection. Gaines was then appointed by Zachary Taylor as governor of the Oregon Territory, after the job was turned down by Taylor's first choice, another newly unemployed one-term Whig congressman, Abraham Lincoln. Gaines had only just arrived in Oregon when the responsibility for purchasing Indian land was added to his duties. Skinner and Allen were lawyers who had recently emigrated to Oregon.

In his instructions to the three treaty negotiators, A. S. Loughery, the acting commissioner of Indian affairs, admitted that the government knew very little about the Indians of the Northwest. "The information in the possession of this office is so limited," he conceded, "that nearly everything must be left to your discretion beyond what is here communicated, and even that may be found by you to be somewhat defective." The commissioners were responsible for an enormous area, all the land west of the Cascades between 42 and 49 degrees latitude—roughly the western third of the present-day states of Oregon and Washington. All this land was thought to be inhabited by numerous small tribes, which among them "set up claims to every portion of the territory." Loughery reminded the commissioners of their task. "The inhabitants complain that they have been there for several years and have been obliged to make settlements, improvements, &c., &c., and not one of them can claim a perfect title to any portion of the soil they occupy," he explained. "It is indispensable that this question be settled in some form or other." To that end, he added, "the object of the government is to extinguish the title of the Indians to all the lands, lying west of the Cascade mountains, and, if possible, to provide for the removal of the whole from the west to the east of the mountains." The purchase price was left to the discretion of the commissioners, but Loughery made plain his assumption that land so remote could not be worth very much. "In many cases it is presumed the consideration will be merely nominal," he reasoned, and even for the more valuable portions of the land, he expected a purchase price well below the ten cents per acre the government had paid for land farther east. The Indians were not to be compensated with money, but rather "in objects beneficial to the Indians," including "agricultural assistance, employment of blacksmiths and mechanics," and education.[23]

In April 1851 the three commissioners began their first negotiation, with the Santiam band of the Kalapuya tribe, a group numbering 155 people by their own count, who lived in the Willamette Valley. Gaines explained to the assembled Indians, through an interpreter, "Your G[rea]t Father, the President, has sent us among you, in order to show his love and care for you; and to treat with you for your lands, which you kindly allowed his white children to live upon and cultivate for many years." The Santiam replied that they would be pleased to sell their land, "except a small portion, which they wished to reserve to live upon." The commissioners had been charged with persuading the Indians to relocate east of the Cascades, but when they proposed such a move, the Santiam were decidedly against it. Their "hearts were upon that piece of land," declared Ti-a-can, their primary spokesman, "and they did not wish to leave it." This presented the commissioners with an unexpected problem, because much of the land the Santiam wished to retain had already been claimed by white settlers. Negotiations stalled for two days, until a compromise was reached: the commissioners agreed to the reservation the Santiam desired, and to include some money (not just goods and services) in the purchase price, but the Santiam would permit whites who had already claimed lots under the Donation Act to remain within the new reservation's boundaries. The result was the sale of a tract the commissioners estimated to be about eighty miles long and twenty miles wide, for a sum of $50,000 to be paid in twenty annual installments of $2,500, of which $500 would be in cash and the remaining $2,000 in goods, primarily clothing.[24]

Over the next month the commissioners reached five similar agreements with three other bands of the Kalapuyas and two bands of the Moolalle tribe. These groups were even smaller than the Santiam; they ranged in size from 44 to 65 people. All refused to move east of the Cascades, so the commissioners again agreed to reservations in the Willamette Valley, in exchange for the Indians' willingness to allow Donation Act claimants to stay within the reservations. These reservations were all located within the territory then occupied by the bands, except that of the Yamhill band of Kalapuyas, whose territory had been entirely claimed by settlers under the Donation Act. The Yamhill band agreed to move seven miles away, to unclaimed land. Taken together, the six treaties secured most of the Willamette Valley for white settlement.[25]

The commissioners recognized that they had failed to move the Indians east of the Cascades, as they had been instructed. "We exhausted every argument," they apologized to Luke Lea, the new commissioner of Indian affairs, "but the Indians, without any exception, manifested a fixed and settled determination not, under any circumstances, or for any consideration, to remove." The only alternative was to agree to reservations, but the commissioners assured Lea that the reservations would not impede white settlement. "We have, therefore, found ourselves compelled, against the wish of the government, as expressed in our instructions, to accede to reservations in the lands purchased," the commissioners explained. "That these reservations will cause any considerable annoyance to the whites we do not believe; they consist for the most part of ground unfitted for cultivation, but suited to the particular habits of the Indians." The Kalapuyas had been given "low and marshy spots," and the Moolalles would inhabit "the woody slopes of the Cascade mountains."[26]

The commissioners learned only afterward that their authority had been revoked two months before they concluded their first treaty. In February Congress had mandated that all Indian treaties be negotiated by the Indian Office's regular agents, not by commissioners specially appointed for the purpose.[27] This change was not motivated by anything the commissioners had done or failed to do; it was part of a broad reorganization of the Office of Indian Affairs prompted by the nation's dramatic territorial expansion in the late 1840s. The job of negotiating treaties accordingly shifted to Anson Dart, the superintendent of Indian affairs for the Oregon Territory, who concluded thirteen more treaties in the summer and fall of 1851. Dart identified ten of the sellers as small Chinook bands numbering 320 people all told, who conveyed a tract along the Pacific, north and south of the Columbia River, approximately one hundred miles long and sixty miles wide. Some of these bands had been so devastated by disease that they were left with only a few members each. Two of the remaining three treaties were with a group of four slightly larger bands, totaling 500 people, along the coast in the southwestern part of the territory. The last of the thirteen was with the Clackamas tribe in the part of the territory most thickly settled with whites, near the Columbia and Willamette Rivers. Dart was no more able to persuade the Indians to relocate than his predecessors had been. Reservations near white settlements would *help* the settlers, Dart explained to the Indian Office; the Indians were useful farm laborers, he noted, and they would soon die out in any event.[28]

All nineteen treaties, the thirteen negotiated by Dart and the six by the commissioners, were submitted to the Senate for ratification in the summer of 1852, but none was ratified. One of the two primary objections to the treaties, as with the California treaties, was that they established reservations so close to white settlers. In his annual message at the end of the year, President Millard Fillmore, speaking of California and Oregon simultaneously, suggested that "this provision, more than any other, it is believed, led to their rejection." The other objection, perhaps more important in Oregon, was to the size of some of the bands from which Dart had purchased land. "One of these treaties, for instance, has been negotiated with a tribe which consisted of two men and five women," complained George Smith Houston of Alabama; "another with a tribe numbering two men and seven women." Cyrus Dunham of Indiana was flabbergasted that the United States of America would treat, on a sovereign-to-sovereign basis, with such paltry collections of people. "It must strike everyone as extraordinary," he exclaimed, "that the Department should ask for appropriations for expenditure in making treaties with six, seven, or eight persons." Joseph Lane, the former governor of the Oregon Territory, was by then Oregon's delegate to the House of Representatives, and he pointed out that the territory's tribes could hardly be blamed for being so small. "I know the Indians are broken up into small bands," he protested, but "if they have but three people in their tribe or band, they claim the country which their fathers claimed, . . . and to extinguish their title it is necessary to treat with them, be they one or more." Lane was speaking on behalf of, not the tribes, but rather the settlers, who wanted treaties to firm up their land titles. "Towns and cities are being laid off upon Indian lands," he reminded Congress, "but the owners and proprietors cannot sell their town lots, giving any kind of conveyance, until the Indian right is extinguished."[29] But such protests did not move the Senate. The incongruity of a great nation meeting as equals with groups so small—and indeed being forced to make concessions of reservations—was too much to bear.

With the rejection of the 1851 treaties, relations between Indians and settlers in the Oregon Territory deteriorated even more. E. A. Starling, the government's Indian agent for the area around Puget Sound, reported in late 1852 that settlers, attracted by the land promised in the Donation Act, "are scattered over this part of Oregon in every direction," on land that had never been purchased from the Indians. Arthur Denny, for example, moved from Illinois to Oregon in 1851, and then to Puget Sound the following year, where he was one of the founders of the city of Seattle. He recalled that "the object of all who came to Oregon in early times was to avail themselves of the privilege of a donation claim." R. R. Thompson, the agent responsible for the central part of the territory, confessed the difficulty he faced in preventing white emigrants from seizing the Indians' best land. "Some settlers have selected claims which include the improvements and possessory rights of the Indians," he explained, and while he had been able to mediate the resulting disputes thus far, he was not optimistic about the future. George Gibbs, the lawyer who served as an interpreter in land cession negotiations up and down the west coast, was acutely aware of the problem. "The great primary source of evil in Oregon," he declared in early 1854, "is the donation act, in which, contrary to established usage and to natural right, the United States assumed to grant, absolutely, the land of the Indians without previous purchase from them.

It followed, as a necessary consequence, that as settlers poured in, the Indians were unceremoniously thrust from their homes and driven forth to shift for themselves." The combination of the Donation Act and the rejection of the 1851 treaties had created a regime of terra nullius, in which settlers were occupying land without regard to Indian property rights. "A consequence of this," Gibbs observed, "has been that a natural distrust has sprung up in their minds as to the good faith of the government or its agents in making treaties at all."[30]

Robert Hull, for example, began farming in Molalla, a town south of Portland, in 1848. "I was on my clame some time before I knew that I was on the Indians Camping ground," he explained a few years later, but he did not leave, "thinking that government would soon take them away." But they did not go away. Instead, Hull complained, "I have continually had to suffer from them ever since. Every fall they have stolen some of my Cabuge and potatoes." As the Indians took his crops, "they would tell me that I had stolen there land." Hull had become so exasperated that he was considering whether to "take the law into my own hands and shoot them down" the next time.[31] Similar conflicts were taking place on other settler farms.

No one could have been surprised when war broke out. In the Rogue River valley in southern Oregon, intermittent fighting between whites and Indians over rights to use land began in 1851 and lasted for several years, resulting in hundreds of deaths on both sides. "The whole press of Oregon Territory was urging a war of extermination," reported the farmer John Beeson, who fled southern Oregon in disgust at the slaughter. "The sum total of their religious and political faith consists in *Squatter Sovereignty*," Beeson charged of his fellow emigrants. "Men are heard to declare their determination to shoot the first Indian they see." Beeson was not exaggerating. After twenty Oregon families were killed in 1855, the whites of southern Oregon "declared a war of extermination" against the local tribes, wrote the Calvinist missionary George Atkinson, in an anxious letter back to his employer, the American Home Missionary Society. Anson Dart, who had negotiated the last thirteen of the nineteen treaties rejected by the Senate, bitterly pointed out that ratifying the treaties would have been far less expensive, by a factor of nearly one hundred, than fighting the ensuing war.[32]

Similar fighting took place in the newly organized Washington Territory in the mid-1850s, between white squatters and the Indians whose land they had occupied. The missionary Timothy Dwight Hunt toured the Washington Territory just before the violence broke out. Along the Cowlitz River he found American squatters "impudently settled over the fairest portions of the plain." He lamented "that in a few years, when the fertile banks of the Cowlitz should be cleared of their forests & made beautiful with homes & civilized farms, not an Indian would be left to spear a salmon in the stream, nor startle the dweller or traveller, or the timid fawn, with the whoop of the warrior or the shout of the hunter."[33] The Indians themselves could not afford to be as fatalistic.

Some of the army officers sent to the Northwest to fight the Indians recognized that terra nullius was at the root of the violence. From The Dalles, on the Columbia River, Major Benjamin Alvord expressed his hope in 1853 "that the Indian title to the land will be extinguished by treaty before further settlements are made." He regretted that the treaties of 1851 had not been ratified and hoped the Senate would not make the same mistake twice. "As many of the whites are now settling among them upon the bare sufferance of the Indians," he foresaw, "intrusions are likely to lead to collision and bloodshed." From the Washington Territory, Lieutenant Floyd Jones noted the same year that "the practice which exists throughout the Territory, of settlers taking from them their small potato patches, is clearly wrong, and should be stopped. A few years later," he predicted, "and the poor Indian will not have an inch of soil for his own use." The soldiers under these officers' command tended not to be as understanding. "To the Indians they were always a source of terror," the publisher Charles Prosch recalled, of the troops garrisoned at the four military stations on Puget Sound in the late 1850s. "The soldiers rarely met one without subjecting him to treatment more or less cruel. If he had money or valuables of any kind, they invariably robbed and beat him."[34] But some of the officers, at least, seem to have understood that the absence of recognized property rights was driving the Indians to desperation.

The Indian Office's field agents provided the same diagnosis and recommendation. Joel Palmer, sent to Oregon as superintendent in 1853, immediately requested permission to negotiate land cession treaties, and indeed began entering into such treaties before permission even arrived. "The doubts in my own mind as to my authority to negotiate treaties with the Indian tribes . . . has been a source of some indecision on my part," he explained to the Office, "but the necessity and urgency of the case seemed to demand this course." When the Indian Office instructed Palmer not to incur any treaty-related expenses until he had been specifically authorized to do so, he ordered his agents to substitute informal treaty arrangements for formal ones. While distributing the ordinary presents to Indian tribes, Palmer suggested, the agents should tell the Indians that the presents were "in consideration that the whites are occupying their country and is in just payment for their lands."[35]

Isaac Stevens, simultaneously the first governor of the Washington Territory and the Territory's first superintendent of Indian affairs, likewise found an "urgent necessity existing for treaties being immediately made with the Indians west of the Cascade mountains, in this Territory. For years they have been promised payment for their lands by the whites," he reminded George Manypenny, the commissioner of Indian affairs, but that payment had never come. Meanwhile, white settlement was only increasing, and the likelihood of violence was growing accordingly. Manypenny agreed. "With many of the tribes in Oregon and Washington," he urged in a letter forwarded to Congress in early 1854, "it appears to be absolutely necessary to speedily conclude treaties for the extinguishment of their claim to the lands now or recently occupied by them." The nonratification of the treaties, combined with the encouragement to settlement provided by the Donation Act, had produced a pointless war provoked by white trespassing. "The Indian tribes still claim title to the lands on which the whites have located, and which they are now cultivating," Manypenny concluded. "The jealousy which has resulted from this state of things has naturally led to repeated hostilities, resulting in the severe suffering, and, in some instances, the murder of the white settlers." He accordingly asked Congress to appropriate the funds necessary for purchasing the Indians' land.[36]

Congress quickly did just that: it appropriated $68,000 for land cession treaties in Oregon, and another $45,000 for treaties in Washington.[37] The federal land-purchasing program was back in business.

BETTER SIGN AND GET SOMETHING

The government bought up most of the Northwest in the next few years. Joel Palmer's two 1853 treaties with tribes near the Rogue River, although concluded before their authorization by Congress, were ratified shortly after. In each the government acquired land in southwestern Oregon in exchange for the annual provision of goods and a temporary reservation, from which the Indians would soon be removed. Once Congress appropriated funds for the purpose, Palmer concluded similar land cession treaties in all the parts of the territory with significant white settlement. By 1855 he had acquired about half of Oregon. "A country is now opened for white people to settle that is sufficiently large to form two States, as charming a country as any in North America," exulted David Newsom, who had recently emigrated from Illinois. The selling tribes would move to reservations, some within the areas they had ceded and others in unfamiliar portions of the territory.[38] Most of the rest of Oregon would be purchased in two major treaties in the early 1860s.

Similar events took place in the Washington Territory. Isaac Stevens began by purchasing the area around Puget Sound, the area most thickly settled by whites, in a series of treaties in late 1854 and early 1855. By the end of 1855 he had acquired nearly all of Washington except the southwest and northeast corners, which the government would purchase in the 1860s and 1870s.[39] As in Oregon, the purchase price consisted of the annual provision of goods, and the selling tribes were moved to reservations, some within the land they had ceded and some not.

The unratified 1851 treaties had been genuinely negotiated, by American government officials compelled to make concessions to Indian preferences in certain respects, but by the second round of treaties power relations in the Northwest had tipped in the direction of white settlers. The white population had increased and spread throughout the Northwest, whereas the Indian population had continued to decline from disease, particularly among the Washington tribes experiencing their first significant contact with whites. In central Washington, along the Yakima River, "the small-pox has destroyed great numbers of these tribes," one missionary reported in 1855. The river was "lined with the vestiges of former villages."[40]

Palmer and Stevens were thus able to impose terms of their own choosing. As Palmer explained in 1854 to a Kalapuyan group reluctant to move, "the whites are determined to settle on your land. We cannot prevent them and in a few years there will be no place left for you. Then what will you do? Will you live in the mountains like wolves?" A few days later the Indians sold the Willamette River Valley and agreed to let the government choose the location to which they would move. "It will be but a few years before the whole country is filled up with whites," Palmer threatened at another purchasing conference. "Then where will the Indian have his home?" Palmer depicted these treaties as more consensual in his own accounts. After treating with the Cow Creek band of the Umpqua tribe, for instance, he simply noted in his diary that "after learning their great desire to sell their country [he] made them a proposition which after a consultation among themselves they agreed to and a treaty was drawn up and signed in the evening."[41] He did not mention whether he himself had played any role in creating the Cow Creek band's great desire to sell their country.

Events in the Washington Territory followed a similar pattern. "If you do not accept the terms offered and sign this paper," Stevens threatened the Yakima chief Kamiakin at Walla Walla in 1855, "you will walk in blood knee deep." The early Puget Sound settler Ezra Meeker recalled that in the Point Elliott and Medicine Creek treaties—in the first of which Stevens purchased a large tract that now encompasses Seattle—"the whole proceeding was a farce." The text of the treaties was not negotiated, but was written in Stevens's office in Olympia, because American officials knew that "the Indians would sign anything presented to them." Years later, Meeker asked John Hiton, one of the Puyallup signatories at Medicine Creek, why he had put his name on the treaty. "What's the use for Indians to fight whites?" Hiton replied. "Whites get big guns; lots ammunition; kill all soldiers, more come; better sign and get something some other way."[42]

Hiton's assessment of Stevens's intentions was accurate. "The Indians have to be evicted," Stevens complained to the lawyer George Gibbs, while waiting for a shipment of goods he intended to give them in return. In a report to Secretary of War Jefferson Davis, Stevens urged "the importance of the most vigorous and decisive blows to get possession of the whole country east of the Sound now infested with the savages."[43] In the governor's office there was little pretense that the Indians were equal negotiating partners.

When Indians persisted in refusing to agree to terms dictated by Stevens, he simply walked away, secure in the knowledge that time was on the government's side. The longer the government waited, the more powerful it would grow relative to the Indians, and the easier it would be to secure the Indians' agreement to any given cession of land. Most tribes capitulated to the inevitable. At the two-day meeting leading to the Treaty of Point No Point, for example, Stevens acquired most of the Olympic Peninsula from the Clallam, Chemakum, and Skokomish Indians. According to the government's transcript of the meeting, on the first day the Skokomish were virtually unanimous in refusing the sale, but on the second day they all suddenly changed their minds. The transcript gives no account of why this happened, but it seems a fair inference that they realized, perhaps with some government assistance, they had no better choice. Stevens himself reported that such meetings normally ended with "the Indians, at the close, again expressing the utmost joy and satisfaction" with the resulting treaties. In fact, Indian dissatisfaction with the treaties gave rise to sporadic warfare between settlers and Indians throughout the Northwest in the late 1850s. Stevens interpreted the new spurt of violence as proof of Indian treachery, but some of the settlers knew better. "When we were likely to be overpowered by the Indians, the rightful owners of the land, for trespassing on their land," the government had finally purchased the land, Washington settler A. M. Collins told his brother back in Indiana. But the government had entered into the treaty "with the acknowledged intention of breaking it and now we have no protection" from the angry ostensible sellers.[44]

The Senate was yet again very slow to ratify some of these treaties. The army opposed the treaties while the war was still active, but the Senate's failure to ratify the treaties contributed to the anger felt by many of the

9. Isaac Stevens, the first governor of the Washington Territory and the territory's first superintendent of Indian affairs, purchased most of Washington in a series of treaties in 1854 and 1855. The terms of the treaties were written in Stevens's office and dictated to the tribes ostensibly consenting to the sale, who had little choice in the matter after suffering years of war and disease. LC-BH82-5175A, Library of Congress.

Indians, which in turn fueled the fighting. The Indian Office repeatedly urged the Senate to action. "The non-ratification of the treaties heretofore made to extinguish the title to the lands necessary for the occupancy and use of our citizens seems to have produced no little disappointment," Commissioner James Denver noted, with some understatement, in his annual report for 1857. "The continued extension of our settlements into their territory, without any compensation being made to them, is a constant source of dissatisfaction and hostile feeling." Denver's successor Charles Mix made the point more clearly the following year. "Intruded upon, ousted of their homes and possessions without any compensation, and deprived, in most cases, of their accustomed means of support," he pointed out, "it is not a matter of surprise that they have committed many depredations upon our citizens, and been exasperated to frequent acts of hostility."[45] Yet most of the 1855 treaties would not be ratified until 1859. In the years leading up to the Civil War, the complex affairs of a small number of people thousands of miles away, affairs with no bearing on the North–South division of power, had a hard time getting on the Senate's agenda. By the time the treaties were ratified, much of the land ostensibly being purchased had long since been possessed in practice by white settlers.

Once the Civil War began, the federal government devoted even less attention to the Pacific Northwest. Payment for land purchased in the 1855 treaties did not begin to reach any Indians until 1861. By 1870 few of the reservations contemplated by the treaties of the mid-1850s had yet been established, and many Indians complained that they were not receiving the annuities promised them in the treaties. What compensation did come was often inadequate. "There would not be half enough presents to go round," recalled the early Washington settler H. A. Smith. "Recipients of the government's bounty were put off with a tin pan, a pot metal ax, or a shoddy blanket that would hardly do for a mosquito bar. This is no exaggeration of facts. I have seen dozens of pot metal axes—especially manufactured for 'Indian communities' by villainous contractors—in the possession of the half nude savages, who wondered why they would not keep sharp." As in California, where no treaties had been ratified, many of the Indians of the Northwest, now landless, found work as laborers in the white economy. The government's agents in the field were political patronage appointees who had little or no experience interacting with Indians or interest in assisting them; indeed, many obtained their positions because of their military service in the Indian wars just a few years before.[46] Two decades after the American government had formally abandoned terra nullius in the Northwest, in favor of a policy of acquiring land by treaty, Indians experienced terra nullius, in practice, as strongly as ever.

Some of these treaties were with tribes no larger than the ones from whom land had been purchased in 1851; indeed, some were with the very same tribes for the very same land. The size of the land-ceding tribes proved no obstacle to ratification the second time around, but a sense of incongruity lingered. Something seemed not quite right about entering into a treaty with such minuscule nations. A decade and a half later, that feeling of disproportion was one of the factors that would cause Congress to put an end to the institution of the Indian treaty. "One of these treaties which has been made in Oregon was with the Umpquas," complained Aaron Augustus Sargent of California. "There are thirty-eight individuals, men, women, and children, all told, as shown by the census of the 'great nation' of Umpquas!" Groups so small and so impoverished intuitively felt less like sovereign nations than like wards of the federal government, to be regulated directly rather than negotiated with. In the Washington Territory, government officials sometimes created "tribes" on their own, by combining self-governing villages into larger political units for the purpose of entering into treaties.[47] Perhaps they were responding to the same feeling of incongruity that had motivated members of Congress to reject the first round of treaties, or perhaps they were prudently packaging the second round of treaties in a form that would be more appealing in Congress. Either way, the Northwest treaties of the 1850s gave rise to a feeling of unease on the part of government officials that in 1871 would contribute to the demise of the Indian treaty.

The Oregon and Washington treaties were emblematic of the era, in that virtually all of the Indian land cessions obtained by the United States in the middle of the nineteenth century were, to one degree or another, forced upon the tribes ostensibly consenting to the sale. Treaties retained the formal structure of negotiated agreements, but in substance they increasingly resembled acts of forcible conquest. "Suffice it to say, the right of the aborigines is more visionary than real," one lawyer admitted in the 1860s. "Treaties are made with them from time to time, and the United States has paid large sums in presents and annuities, for extinguishing their title to the public lands. Yet so weak is their tenure, that the President, in 1838, expelled them by military force from the east side of the Mississippi, assigning them hunting grounds beyond the abode of the white man." Just as the Indians had been removed from the Southeast in the 1830s, they had been removed from the parts of the Northwest most desired by whites in the 1850s. Both removals had been structured as voluntary agreements, but in the end both had been accomplished by force.[48]

As land was being "purchased" from the Indians of Oregon and Washington in these compulsory treaties, land was being taken outright, without even the pretense of contractual form, from the California Indians to the south and the British Columbia Indians to the north. There were some white residents of California and British Columbia who deplored the policy of terra nullius, but they were most likely greatly outnumbered by settlers content to accept government grants of land that had never been purchased from the Indians. In Oregon and Washington, by contrast, settlers had been clamoring for the purchase of Indian land for years. Through the 1850s the Indians of Oregon and Washington were serious military opponents, more serious than the Indians of California or British Columbia. As a result, there were many white residents of Oregon and Washington who favored purchasing land from the Indians in order to stave off war. Meanwhile, the governments of California and British Columbia had the power to grant land titles to white settlers despite the absence of treaties, but Oregon and Washington were still territories governed directly by the federal government, which remained formally committed to acquiring Indian land by treaty. As a result, the white residents of Oregon and Washington desperately wanted treaties in order to firm up their own land titles. Government officials in the two territories, responding to local political pressure, urged Congress to appropriate money to buy land, at a time when California's representatives in Congress were advocating precisely the opposite.

These compulsory treaties were of little or no benefit to the Indians of Oregon and Washington in the nineteenth century. They were in no better position, with treaties, than the Indians of California or British Columbia were without them. A century later, however, when white attitudes toward Indians had changed considerably, the treaties would be the basis for lawsuits successfully claiming Indian rights to natural resources in Oregon and Washington. The Indians of California and British Columbia, lacking such treaties, could not achieve anything comparable.

chapter eight

Fiji and Tonga

The Importance of Indigenous Political Organization

FIJI AND TONGA ARE SIMILAR in many ways. Both are large groups of small islands. The two nations are neighbors, or as close to neighbors as countries can be in the Pacific: they are close enough that Tongans and Fijians were each visiting the other long before Europeans arrived. In both Fiji and Tonga the soil is well suited for agriculture. Fiji has a land area more than twenty times larger than Tonga and has had a much larger population since white contact (and most likely before as well), but in most respects neither was a more likely destination than the other for prospective colonists. Considering only their location and their physical characteristics, it would have been hard to predict as of 1820 whether whites would purchase a greater percentage of Fiji or Tonga.

Fifty years later, the two groups of islands had diverged considerably. Europeans had purchased much of the good agricultural land in Fiji, but they had purchased none in Tonga. Fiji was on the cusp of being colonized—it would be formally annexed by Britain in 1874—while Tonga was not. As of 1870 one might reasonably have predicted that Fiji would become a settler colony like Hawaii or New Zealand, with an economy dominated by white-owned agriculture. Tonga, by contrast, seemed likely to remain Tongan.

Twenty years after that, Tonga indeed remained Tongan, but Fiji, surprisingly enough, remained largely Fijian. The white acquisition of land in Fiji came to an abrupt halt. White purchasers of the past were forced to undo their more dubious transactions and renounce their claims to much of the land. The flow of white emigrants to Fiji slowed to a trickle. Fiji was a British colony but Tonga was not—a substantial fraction of the land in Fiji was owned by whites, whereas all the land in Tonga was owned by Tongans—but from 1874 on (except for a short period in Fiji), no land in either group of islands would be transferred from indigenous people to whites.

How can we explain these events?

CAREFUL ATTENTION TO AGRICULTURE

The early European accounts of Fiji consistently emphasized the skill with which Fijians farmed their land. "Nothing could exceed the beauty of the Country," William Bligh marveled, upon visiting Ngau in 1792. "It was cultivated far up into the Mountains, in a regular and pretty manner." The whalers and bêche-de-mer traders who washed up on the islands in the early nineteenth century provided similar accounts. So did the missionaries who arrived in increasing numbers at midcentury. "They are an industrious people," reported the missionary John Hunt in 1842. "Their houses, gardens, plantations, and canoes, are a proof of this." The Wesleyan minister Joseph Waterhouse declared that the Fijian "by inclination and habit . . . is a cultivator of the soil. . . . He understands the art of planting simultaneously two or three crops of various kinds, to arrive severally at maturity during successive periods." That reputed cannibals could be such accomplished farmers struck some European observers as a paradox. "The union of savage wildness with careful attention to agriculture is remarkable in the character of the Fijians," one missionary exclaimed. On Fiji one could see rows of taro, yams, bananas, and many other plants, "side by side with the wildest savagism." Paradoxical or not, however, Fijian agriculture was widely known among whites.[1]

Early reports of Tonga likewise emphasized the ubiquity of agriculture. Abel Tasman landed on the island of Nomuka in 1643 and found "many enclosures or gardens, with plots elegantly squared, and planted with all sorts of earth-fruit. In several places we saw bananas and other fruit-trees, most of them growing so straight, that they were good to look at." Tasman deduced that although Tongans possessed "inhuman manners and customs," nevertheless they "were by no means destitute of human intelligence." James Cook reached Tonga on his second voyage in 1773. "I thought I was transported into one of the most fertile plains in Europe," he noted. "Here was not an inch of waste ground." Cook's colleagues felt the same way. Johann Forster, the naturalist on Cook's second voyage, reported walking through "a number of rich plantations or gardens" containing "bananas and yams planted in rows on both sides, with as much order and regularity as we employ in our agriculture." Forster's son George was on board, too; he praised "the industry and elegance of the natives, which they displayed in planting every piece of ground to the greatest advantage." George Forster reached an important conclusion. "Doubtless all land here is private property," he reasoned, "for where the soil is cultivated with such extraordinary care that not a spot remains unused hardly anything can be common property."[2]

The existence of farms, and thus property rights, in Tonga was a theme echoed by many of the early English-speaking visitors. George Hamilton, the surgeon on the ship sent to arrest the *Bounty* mutineers in 1790–1791, inspected planted fields divided by ornate fences and concluded that "private property is more exactly ascertained" in Tonga than in other parts of the Pacific. "Their fences are reed, set in a trench, planted close, and fastened to stakes on the inside," observed the ship captain James Wilson, who carried a group of missionaries to Tongatapu in 1797. The fences bordered extensive cultivated fields, each evidently owned by the family living in the house the fields surrounded. "Every hut has its garden and plantation, laid out with taste, carefully inclosed, and from its productiveness shewing the goodness of its culture," remarked John Orlebar, a British naval lieutenant who visited Tongatapu in 1830. "Everywhere we perceived the greatest attention to neatness, cleanliness, and comfort—all so endearing to an Englishman." To whites in the early nineteenth century, Tongan agriculture was, if anything, even more well known than Fijian agriculture. "The verdant shores of Tonga," as an 1819 poem put it, were famous.[3]

Indeed, by 1840, when the United States Exploring Expedition reached Tongatapu, Charles Wilkes had read so many glowing accounts of Tongan cultivation that he was disappointed when he saw the real thing. To be sure, there were well-ordered fields of yams, sweet potatoes, bananas, coconuts, breadfruit, sugar cane, limes, corn, papayas, and watermelon, as well as shaddock (a large citrus fruit, also called pomelo, resembling the grapefruit), and ti and pandanus, two sorts of leaves used in cooking and for making mats. The Tongans were also growing nutmeg and a variety of ornamental shrubs. Wilkes may not have been aware that after decades of European contact many Tongans had died from imported diseases, but he did know that he had arrived in the midst of a war that made farming temporarily perilous on much of the island, so he must have had some appreciation that Tongan farming had seen better days. His expectations had been so high, however, that he reluctantly concluded: "Tongataboo is not the cultivated garden it has been represented to be." But this was an unusual opinion for a white visitor to Tonga in the first half of the nineteenth century. Tongans, like Fijians, were known for their gardens.[4]

The early white arrivals in both Tonga and Fiji were traders and missionaries. They arrived as individuals and small groups, not powerful enough to take land by force. Their weakness, combined with the obvious property rights in land that already existed among the inhabitants of both groups of islands, prompted them to obtain permission before taking control of land. The Wesleyan missionary David Cargill and his wife, for instance, arrived in Lakemba, Fiji, in 1835. After an interview with the local king, Cargill explained, the king "pledged himself to grant the Missionaries a piece of ground to live on; to erect houses for them; to protect them, and their families and property, from molestation; and to listen to instruction." In Tonga, the missionary George Vason reported a similar experience in the late 1790s. Soon after arriving, he met a chief called Moomooe, who "made us a friendly offer of a habitation and land." A few years later, after Vason had married a Tongan woman and given up missionary work, another chief named Mulkaamair granted him a fifteen-acre farm.[5] The early white settlers in both Fiji and Tonga, like those in New Zealand and Hawaii, needed the good opinion of the indigenous residents to survive. If they wanted land, they had to ask for it.

In later years, both Fiji and Tonga attracted whites interested in farming. Both groups of islands were clearly suited for it, as the indigenous residents had themselves demonstrated. The two were close enough to each other to have approximately the same climate and to be, as a practical matter, equally distant from established markets for the commodities like cotton and sugar that Europeans expected to grow there. In terms of their geography, neither had an advantage over the other as a place for a white emigrant to acquire land.

Fiji and Tonga differed, however, in one crucial respect. Fiji was divided politically into many small chiefdoms. The sandalwood trader William Lockerby, marooned on Vanua Levu in 1808, counted "four persons who call themselves Kings" on that island alone, and he only saw a small part of the island. These small political units waged intermittent war against one another all through the first half of the nineteenth century.[6] As in New Zealand, political authority was too fragmented to permit a coordinated Fijian land policy, and the frequency of war encouraged tribes to grant land to whites in order to acquire allies.

The politics of Tonga were very different. By the 1840s the islands were more or less united as a single polity, under the leadership of a Christianized chief who took the name King George Tupou.[7] King George remained the head of state until his death in 1893. Except in the earliest years of contact, therefore, Europeans in Tonga interacted with a relatively stable monarchy capable of developing and enforcing a unified land policy throughout the islands. The absence of significant intertribal warfare meant there was little to gain in attracting white allies, and thus removed what might otherwise have been a major incentive to grant land to whites. As in Hawaii, Europeans encountered a political entity capable of holding its own against weak and scattered settlers.

THE EARTH DOES NOT LIE IN OUR HANDS

By the early 1860s there were approximately two thousand whites in Fiji, most from Britain, but some from the United States, Germany, France, Poland, and Russia. Some were traders and missionaries, but others were planters and ranchers, people who needed large tracts of land.

This number grew in the early 1870s, as depression in Australia and New Zealand prompted much emigration to the islands. By then there was "no question as to the right to settle in Fiji," reasoned Charles St. Julian, Hawaii's consul in the Australian colonies.[8] Whites had been moving to Fiji for decades.

Most of them purchased land.[9] "My host had been in possession of his property for about three years," one English visitor to Fiji reported, "the purchase having been effected for cloth, knives, axes, &c., to the value of about one shilling per acre. The land had formerly belonged to a chief, who, as none of his dependents occupied it, was only too glad to part with it." Similar transactions between white settlers and Fijian chiefs became routine by the 1860s. In the absence of any Fiji-wide government capable of keeping a registry or judging the validity of sales, the British consul filled both roles. The consul in principle investigated the seller's title to the land, made sure that the heads of families living there approved of the purchase, and, if those conditions were satisfied, placed his seal of approval on the deed, which was kept on file at the consulate. "It was my great satisfaction to see these rules gladly adopted by all land-purchasers," declared W. T. Pritchard, the consul who inaugurated this system. "When I left Fiji in 1863, any deed bearing the Consular seal was held *per se* absolutely valid and unquestionable." The botanist Berthold Seemann, who visited Fiji in the early 1860s, found Pritchard's regulation of land purchasing exemplary. "I believe that in most instances a fair price is given," Seemann reported, "remembering that the very best land in America may be had for a dollar and a quarter an acre," while comparable land in Fiji often sold for more. "The whole history of the purchase of land by whites in Fiji teaches that the white man has been imposed upon as thoroughly, and probably as often, as the native has been by the white man," maintained the physician Litton Forbes. "Indeed, considering the difficulty of buying land, the uncertainty of tenure, the unsettled state of the country, and, finally, the price as compared with that of first-rate agricultural land in New Zealand or Australia, it has always seemed marvellous that planters in Fiji cared to pay as much for their plantations as they did."[10]

But not everyone was as satisfied with the way Europeans bought land from Fijians. Some European observers thought that sellers did not have the same understanding of these transactions as buyers. "A common practice was to draw up the deeds in English, to have them translated to the native chief by some one professing to understand the Fijian language, but generally as ignorant of it as the principal who employed him," complained the gentleman explorer Julius Brenchley, who cruised through the Pacific in the mid-1860s. "The transaction was complete when it received the chief's mark, who was induced to sign it by threats or cajolery, but frequently by making him drunk beforehand."[11] Even apart from translation problems, Fijian conceptions of property were different from European conceptions, so, as was true throughout the world, the earliest land transactions between Europeans and non-Europeans were almost certainly understood differently by the two sides.

Other critics pointed out that the ostensible sellers of the tracts purchased by Europeans lacked the authority to sell. Sometimes, charged the Australian journalist Henry Britton, chiefs simply sold land that had never belonged to them. In other instances, chiefs sold land without obtaining the consent of the land's inhabitants, a practice that some Europeans found inconsistent with indigenous Fijian law. "The occupants of lands cannot alienate their holdings without the consent of the ruling Chief," insisted the barrister J. H. de Ricci, "nor can such lands be alienated by the ruling Chief without the consent of the occupants." As a result, he reasoned, "a considerable amount of land is at present held by settlers on very doubtful tenure." By the 1870s, guidebooks for prospective emigrants cautioned that buying land from chiefs could be a tricky business for this reason. "We should not recommend a beginner to purchase direct from the natives," one such book instructed. "Fijian laws and customs with regard to the tenure of land are so intricate, that only after paying for the land he may find out that it never belonged to the chief he bought it of, or only belonged partially to him and partially to those settled upon it; or a lot of natives may be living on it, and dispute possession, or otherwise annoy him." Land purchasing was best left to the old hands, whites who "are *au fait* in the knowledge of Fiji customs."[12]

After two decades of such transactions, much of the good agricultural land in Fiji had been purchased by Europeans. By 1870 the fertile island of Taveuni was mostly European-owned. The Australian journalist David

Blair estimated in the late 1870s that whites had bought 350,000 acres throughout the islands, of which they were already farming 10,000 acres. Arthur Gordon, Fiji's first colonial governor, noted around the same time that "nearly the whole of the sea coast of Fiji is in the hands of private proprietors." Much of this land, however, had been purchased as tracts with nebulous boundaries, from sellers with dubious authority to sell, and at prices that many found unfairly low. "Some of the early purchases were so manifestly irregular, and the imposition upon the natives so glaring, that I caused many of them to be cancelled," recalled the British consul W. T. Pritchard. Many white visitors to Fiji feared for the future as a result. When the Fijians "come to see how very much below its real value they have sold it," one predicted, "I feel sure they will make desperate efforts to recover it, in the same manner as the Maories in New Zealand have done." Henry Britton foresaw "endless disputes about boundaries," between European purchasers with inconsistent claims and between Europeans and Fijians.[13] Land purchasing in Fiji was sowing the seeds of conflict for years to come, just as it had in the early years of white settlement in North America and in New Zealand.

And as in New Zealand and Hawaii, land purchasing paved the way for colonization. The more white settlers there were in Fiji, and the more European money that was invested in Fiji, the greater would be the pressure exerted by settlers for the establishment of a colonial government they considered adequate for the protection of their interests. The first step toward colonization was taken in 1865, with the British-backed formation of a confederation of chiefs, under the leadership of Cakobau, the chief of the island of Bau. This confederation was unsuccessful, as was an attempt a few years later to establish Cakobau as a king governing all of Fiji. These efforts were undertaken primarily for the benefit of white landowners. As one contemporary American magazine said of Cakobau, it was "white settlers, primarily from Great Britain and the United States, who were mainly instrumental in putting him on the throne, and who would, in all probability, take him off again to-morrow, if it should suit their convenience to do so."[14]

The fragmented nature of power in Fiji, however, rendered these attempts at confederation futile, because Cakobau and his government had little practical control over most of the islands. That futility was reflected in the constitution the confederation adopted in 1867. Fijians would probably have been best served by a constitutional provision barring land sales to whites or at least making them more difficult. Settlers would have been best served by creating a standard Fiji-wide process of buying land, which would have made their new titles more secure and facilitated the development of a real estate market. But neither whites nor Fijians got what they wanted in the 1867 constitution. It provided instead that "throughout the confederation, it shall be lawful for any foreigners to buy, or to sell, to transfer, or to hold in fee simple, real estate." Rather than standardizing land transfer practice, the constitution instead acknowledged that "the head of every Chiefdom shall please himself as to the selling of lands."[15] It was impossible for a Fijian government, even one largely created by white settlers, to exercise power over most of the territory it ostensibly governed.

In 1874, after the failure of these efforts, Britain annexed Fiji. Annexation had been discussed for years, but never undertaken—indeed, Cakobau had offered it in the late 1850s, but Britain rejected the offer—because the Colonial Office had perceived little gain from governing Fiji as a colony. It was pressure from the growing and increasingly powerful European community that tipped the balance, a community that existed in large part because of the freewheeling nature of land transactions in the previous two decades.

The 1874 Deed of Cession divided the land in Fiji into three categories. Land "alienated so as to have become bona fide the property of Europeans or other foreigners" was to remain under foreign ownership. Land "now in the actual use or occupation of some Chief or tribe" or "required for the probable future support and maintenance of some Chief or tribe" was to remain owned by Fijians. All other land—all land neither alienated to Europeans, nor possessed in the present by Fijians, nor likely to be needed in the future by Fijians—was declared to be vested in the Crown.[16]

Arthur Hamilton Gordon, the first British governor of Fiji, arrived in 1875.[17] Gordon was an experienced colonial administrator in the middle of his career: he had previously held posts in New Brunswick, Trinidad, and Mauritius, and after leaving Fiji in 1880 he would go on to be governor of

New Zealand, western Pacific high commissioner, and governor of Ceylon. In many of these places Gordon was unpopular with settlers, who believed he sympathized too much with the indigenous people while exhibiting disdain for local whites. Fiji was no exception.

Gordon quickly developed a respect for Fijians that far exceeded his respect for many of his own countrymen in Fiji. "The people are not nomadic," he explained to the Royal Colonial Institute on one of his periodic trips back to Britain. "They live a settled life in towns of good and comfortable houses; they respect and follow agriculture; their social and political organization is complex; they amass property, and have laws for its descent; their land tenures are elaborate; they read, they write and cypher." After a lifetime of encountering people from all over the world, Gordon concluded that the Fijians were closer to the top than the bottom. "No one would dream of placing on one level the acute and cultivated Hindoo or Cingalese and the wandering and naked savage of the Australian bush," he reasoned. "The Fijian resembles neither; but he has more affinity with the former than the latter. He has not, indeed, the literature, the art, the culture, and luxury of eastern civilization, but he has in many ways advanced beyond the ruder stages of savage life, and possesses those receptive powers which fit him for far higher social and intellectual advancement." As he explained to William Gladstone, Fijians "are as superior to the savages of Australia as we are to Fijians—perhaps more so." They reminded him of his own Scotch ancestors from four hundred years before. "Like those Scotch they are eminently improveable," he told Gladstone, "and the problem is if I may so express it, how to get them from the 15th century to the 19th."[18]

Gordon's view of the Europeans in Fiji was considerably darker. "The white population," he noted in 1876, "is of a very heterogenous character. Among the planters are to be found men of the highest character & men of the most abandoned depravity—men of good family & breeding & men of the grossest ignorance & commoners—sober men & drunkards honest men & dishonest kind hearted men & hard cruel men fools & sensible men." Gordon had particular contempt for whites who had emigrated from Australia, where the treatment of indigenous people was the harshest. Ex-Australians "may be divided into two," he explained—"those who simply desire the extermination of the natives and those who desire to utilize them as serfs or slaves." Most of the planters, he concluded, "are professionally convinced that the sole object of a native's existence is to work for white men." Gordon may well have been correct here; certainly whites in Fiji, like whites throughout the empire, left ample record of their disgust for the indigenous people they governed and employed. Many of the settlers, of course, had a different perspective. A New Zealand newspaper snidely summed up Gordon's career, shortly after he left Fiji for New Zealand, by saying, "He is one of those excellent persons who hold that the dark-complexioned races have a first claim upon humanity; who believe that the chief office of philanthropy is to protect the aboriginals in our distant possessions from the sanguinary British colonist; who incline to the theory that Englishmen, as a rule, are not to be trusted with the government of a subject people, but require special watching lest they should oppress and spoil their poor dark-skinned brother."[19] This was perhaps an overstatement, but it captured an important truth in Gordon's approach to his work in Fiji. He viewed himself, apparently sincerely, as a protector of Fijians against mistreatment by whites.

Gordon's attitude was not uncommon among British colonial officials. He was an aristocrat, the youngest son of the Earl of Aberdeen. Like other Britons of his class, he saw native aristocracies as a reflection of the British, and considered himself to have more in common with local chiefs than with the lower-class whites who washed up in the Pacific.[20] Gordon found value in many aspects of what he understood to be traditional Fijian life, including Fijian land ownership, and he accordingly took several steps to preserve it.

Soon after arriving in Fiji, Gordon secured the passage of an ordinance temporarily prohibiting the alienation of land possessed by Fijians. The prohibition was made permanent in 1880. The result was to put an end to the transfer of land from Fijians to Europeans. With one brief exception during the first decade of the twentieth century, that prohibition would remain in place as long as Fiji was a British colony.[21]

The Deed of Cession had guaranteed land to pre-1874 European purchasers but had said nothing about how that guarantee was to be implemented. Gordon, following instructions from the Colonial Office, quickly appointed a Lands Commission, which for the next seven years would adjudicate claims by Europeans to ownership of parts of Fiji. In all, the commission received nearly 1,700 applications covering more than 850,000 acres. For each claimed purchase, the land commissioners were charged with determining whether the ostensible sellers had the right to sell the land, and whether the price was fair. By the time it wrapped up its work in 1882, the commission had granted only about 500 of these claims. In approximately 400 other cases, the commission granted land *ex gratia* (that is, as a matter of grace rather than as of right) to Europeans who were actually occupying purchased tracts that did not satisfy these conditions. All told, even considering the large number of *ex gratia* grants, the commissioners granted less than half of the acreage claimed by European applicants.[22]

Some of the claims the commission rejected were obviously fraudulent, under any standard. In one 1869 purchase, the local chief was tied up and carried on board a vessel lying at anchor, and told that he would be kidnapped if he refused to sign a deed conveying a tract to English purchasers. Commissioner Walter Carew reported that another purchaser's claim was to "a quadrangular block with only three sides!" that belonged, in any event, to a different set of Fijians than those who had purported to sell it. One sale he found to be "a gross fraud," another "a piece of downright deliberate robbery." The process of proving claims before the Lands Commission prompted even more fraud, on the part of purchasers desperately trying to cover up their past efforts to cheat the Fijians. Some of these claims grew so absurd that they moved John Gorrie, a member of the Commission and Fiji's first colonial chief justice, to some satirical poetry:

> The planter came with his land claim,
>   He swore that white was black;
> The pious missionary, too,
>   Swore black was white—alack!
>
> . . . . .

> And when the oaths had all been sworn,
>   The lies in form recorded;
> What could we do but make report,
>   That men were mean and sordid?

Gorrie was a close friend and advisor of Arthur Gordon—he had followed Gordon from Mauritius to Fiji—but he resigned from the Commission soon after, apparently in a fit of exasperation with the sorts of claims that came before him.[23] As in New Zealand, where a scarcely regulated precolonial regime of private purchasing had likewise been replaced by formal colonization, the first task was to weed out the clearly invalid purchases.

But many of the commissioners' decisions were much harder. The Commission was to discern whether the sellers of a given parcel had the right to sell it, not under the law of England but under the law of Fiji in effect at the time of the transactions. Traditional Fijian land tenure—the question of who had the right to do what with respect to land before Europeans arrived—thus assumed considerable importance in colonial Fiji. There soon developed among the British residents of Fiji an earnest and long-lasting debate on the topic, with a particular focus on the sub-issue most relevant to the work of the Lands Commission: Who, exactly, had the right to sell land? Many of the precolonial purchasers had contracts signed by chiefs but had never obtained the consent of the people who actually lived on the land. Were these transactions valid?

Land claimants of course argued that they were. Basil Thomson, who began his varied career as a colonial administrator in Fiji, recalled that "it was the object of every claimant to land to show that the proprietary unit was the chief who had signed the deed upon which he relied." Some claimants accordingly painted a picture of Fijian custom in which chiefs held near-absolute power over ordinary people, a picture similar to the view of Hawaiian land tenure held by many of the pre-Māhele white settlers of Hawaii. Others put forward a weaker version of the argument. John Newmarch, the secretary of the Land Claimants Protection Association of Fiji, was willing to concede that a valid sale required the consent of *some* of the land's inhabitants, but insisted that only a majority vote was necessary.[24]

The missionary and anthropologist Lorimer Fison occupied the opposite end of the spectrum of white opinion. In Fison's view, *no* land sales could have been valid, because under Fijian land tenure no one had the right to alienate land. "The tenure of land in Fiji is tribal," Fison argued. "The title is vested in all the full born members of the tribe, commoners as well as chiefs." Chiefs had no special rights with respect to land: "the chief is their lord," Fison explained, "but he is not their landlord." And even a tribe, acting unanimously, could not convey its land permanently to a nonmember, because the living members of the tribe had a responsibility to preserve the land for future generations. "No man, whether chief or commoner, is the absolute owner of the soil," Fison concluded. "He has no more than a life interest in it. He may dispose of that interest if he please, but he can do no more. Nor is the whole tribe the absolute owner. Each generation does but hold in trust for the next, and the tribe is under obligation to hand down the tribal estate undiminished for ever." This obligation arose from the fact that "land with the Fijian is not a chattel to be bought and sold. 'The earth does not lie in our hands,' he says."[25] This view was alarming to land claimants, because it would have invalidated all transactions with Europeans, past and future.

Most government officials seem to have been somewhere in the middle. One school of thought held that under traditional Fijian tenure a land sale required the consent of the local chief and the heads of all the families living on the land. "Every inch of land in Fiji has an owner," W. T. Pritchard, Britain's first consul, had reasoned in the 1860s. "The proprietorship rests in families, the *heads of families* being the representatives of the title." Chiefs too held land as heads of their own families, but the tribe was like a larger family, and the chief was the head of the tribe, which gave him rights in the tribe's land as a whole. "From this complicated tenure," Pritchard had concluded, "it is clear that the alienation of land, however large or small the tract, can be made valid only by the collective act of the whole tribe, in the persons of the ruling chief and the heads of families."[26] Pritchard's opinion was widely reproduced after colonization, when the subject acquired a new importance. It suggested that some of the precolonial transactions were valid but others, perhaps most, were not.

John Bates Thurston depicted a more complex arrangement. Thurston had been a British official in Fiji since the 1860s. In a memorandum he prepared for the new colonial government in 1874, he explained that he considered Pritchard's account insufficiently sensitive to distinctions Fijians made among chiefs, some of whom had more power than others. Fijian land tenure, Thurston reasoned, was "a feudal system that has existed from time immemorial," in which "the lands belong to the head or ruling chiefs." Subordinate chiefs and commoners held land under these superior chiefs, in exchange for providing military or domestic service. In light of this system, Thurston concluded, "I do not think any subordinate Fijian landholder or occupant can, or should, alienate land without the consent of the ruling chief," because such a transaction would upset the delicate network of reciprocal obligations among commoners, subordinate chiefs, and superior chiefs. For the same reason, Thurston did not "think the ruling chief should alienate land, except with the consent of the occupants, so long as they (the occupants) render the services demanded by their chief."[27]

This was not the most edifying of debates. Every participant's opinion of the true nature of traditional Fijian practice was colored by one ulterior motive or another—whether the self-serving desire for land or the more high-minded goal of seeing the land remain in Fijian hands. None of the men who wrote with such certitude about Fijian custom seems to have known as much about Fiji as he professed. Their views were drawn at least as much from theoretical principles of the emerging discipline of anthropology as from empirical observation. Some of the ostensible experts on the subject, meanwhile, particularly those in government service, had an interest in making Fijian land tenure look forbiddingly arcane, in order to buttress their own status as interpreters of it.[28] All these layers of self-interest would have stood in the way of an accurate account of Fijian land tenure even under the best of circumstances.

What made the debate particularly fruitless, however, was that it addressed a question that on its own terms simply could not be answered. A search for the "traditional" Fijian rules governing the sale of land to non-

Fijians was bound to fail, because there were no such transactions before Europeans arrived. Fijians, the Lands Commission discovered, had often alienated lands among themselves. Land had passed from chiefs to commoners in exchange for services, between families as part of marriage arrangements, and even between larger social units—for instance, as aid during wartime. These transfers sometimes complicated the Commission's search for the "true" Fijian owners of particular parcels.[29] As in much of the rest of the Pacific, however, the arrival of Europeans gave rise to land sales of a type that had not occurred before, and rules governing such sales had to be improvised on the fly. Tradition, in one light, was the apparent precontact practice of not alienating land to outsiders, but in another light, tradition was the undoubted frequency of land sales to Europeans afterward, sometimes with the consent of local inhabitants and sometimes with the consent only of chiefs. To choose which tradition was the relevant one for the purpose of the Lands Commission was not merely or even primarily to make an empirical historical observation of what Fijians did at some point in the past. It was, rather, to make a forward-looking policy judgment as to how much land Europeans should possess in the future.

In the end, Arthur Gordon concluded, following Fison, that under traditional principles of tenure, land in Fiji was inalienable. It is probably not a coincidence that this was his preferred policy outcome as well. The Lands Commission in its public pronouncements agreed. Yet neither Gordon nor the Commission actually applied this principle to the land claims of European purchasers. If land was inalienable, *all* the claims should have been rejected, but the Commission in fact approved nearly a third of them. The Commission, with Gordon's approval, simply disregarded general principles in favor of examining the substantive fairness of each transaction.[30]

In several hundred other cases, the Commission made land grants *ex gratia* to Europeans who could not demonstrate that they had made a legitimate purchase but who were living on land without drawing complaints from Fijians or other European claimants. Samuel Drew, for example, was a Sheffield doctor who held a supposed deed to a tract of land in Fiji that his brother claimed to have purchased before 1874 from a Fijian

10. By the time Britain exercised sovereignty over Fiji in 1874, whites had purchased much of the good agricultural land, including this plantation, where two white men are shown (ca. 1875) overseeing a large Fijian workforce. The British government ratified many of these past transactions but prohibited future sales. PA1-q-330-49-2, Alexander Turnbull Library, Wellington, New Zealand.

tribe. The Lands Commission disallowed Drew's claim. "The owners of the land had been no parties to its alienation," Gordon explained, and "even if they had been, the deeds were too carelessly drawn to permit any accurate identification of the ground said to be alienated. I remember well that the boundaries were described as consisting of a frontage and two parallel lines produced to their point of junction, a point which I need not say their prolongation round the whole of the earth's surface would never have attained!" The Commission nevertheless granted Drew one hundred acres, out of the eight hundred he had claimed, because "it was shown that Mr. Drew had at one time put up a hut on the land, and been allowed to occupy it without molestation for a short, though but a very short, time by the natives."[31] In such cases the Commission departed even more clearly from its ostensible governing principle of the inalienability of Fijian land.

The net effect of this divergence between theory and practice was to ratify hundreds of past transactions but to prohibit all future transactions. Most of the land in Fiji would be retained by Fijians. This result was aided by a final component of Gordon's land policy, his decision to recognize Fijians as owners of virtually all of the unalienated land in Fiji, and to classify only a very small quantity of land as public domain. The Deed of Cession had contemplated a third category of land, that which was neither possessed by Fijians nor purchased by Europeans, land that would be vested in the Crown. In other colonies, a substantial percentage of the land was Crown land (or public land, as it was called in the colonies of the United States). It was generally presumed to be available, either in the present or the future, for sale to white settlers. In Fiji, by contrast, the public domain was tiny. "There are in Fiji no Crown lands in the ordinary sense of that expression," one government-sponsored guidebook for prospective settlers explained. "The lands of the Colony belong to Native or European owners, respectively, as the case may be, and the only lands in the present (or prospective) possession of the Crown are such as have fallen to it for the non-payment of advances made to planters."[32] The decision to have only a very small public domain flowed from Gordon's view of Fiji as a colony that should not attract white settlers in large numbers.

Without the prospect of future English settlement, there was no need for large tracts of Crown land.

These decisions were extremely unpopular with white settlers. Some were upset by the Commission's failure to uphold the legitimacy of their past transactions. "Claims to very large and valuable blocks of honestly bought land have been rejected," one group of English planters complained. In cases before the Commission, "evidence has not been taken in accordance with English law," another group declared in a petition to Queen Victoria. "More weight has been given to oral native testimony than to properly attested Title Deeds and other documentary evidence brought forward by claimants." Longtime settlers were certain that they had done the Fijians no wrong by buying their land. "I say the Pioneers of Fiji (i.e. whites prior to 1868) and the Wesleyan missionaries did all good to the natives," insisted Edwin Turpin, a planter and trader who had arrived in 1866. In Turpin's view it was the British colonial government, not the old-timers, who had turned Fijians into "the greatest slaves on the earth." The settler press, speaking for the large class of disgruntled claimants, was even more adamant. "It is absolutely impossible for the outside world to realise the depth of moral and social degradation, the unutterable horrors of pollution from which the land has been rescued, not by the British Government or Sir Arthur Gordon, but by the white traders, settlers, and missionaries, who are thus so summarily disposed of," one editorialist maintained. "The pioneers of missionary and commercial enterprise found it the foulest blot upon the fair face of creation; a terrestrial pandemonium, and veritable abode of fiends." It was their hard work that "gave a definite value to the lands, which up to that time had been valueless, and they opened a career for the country to which, without them, it never could have aspired."[33] And now the government was turning its back on them.

Within a year after Gordon arrived in Fiji, some of the early settlers were already nostalgic for an era that had only just ended. Anatole von Hügel would become the first curator of Cambridge University's Museum of Archaeology and Anthropology, but in 1875 he was a twenty-one-year-old who traveled around Fiji jotting down what he heard. The common view among settlers, von Hügel reported, was "good old days, gone by, never to return, now that the bloody niggers are by law treated as one's equal."[34] Land policy was not the only factor contributing to this opinion, but it may have been the most important.

Many more whites were critical of the government, not for the outcomes of its cases, but for how slowly it decided them. Until the Lands Commission approved a claim and the governor granted a title, "no capitalist would dream of investing in what might prove so worthless a speculation," the missionary Constance Cumming observed. The planters who had so wanted Fiji to become a colony "actually are worse off than they were before annexation—a sad discovery for men who had looked on that event as a magic spell which would at once disentangle this disordered skein. And now they are more down-hearted than ever." This was a common refrain by the late 1870s: that until outstanding claims were resolved, land titles "cannot be made use of by the settlers to raise money to cultivate their land." Colonization, many noticed, was having the paradoxical effect of deterring investment in land.[35]

Within the colonial government, the delay in resolving land claims looked rather different. "Land claims alone occupied a large portion of my time," recalled William Des Voeux, Gordon's successor as governor of Fiji. "As of the date of the cession there had been some 1,650 of such claims by white men to land alleged to have been sold to them by natives." The problem, from Des Voeux's perspective, was that nearly all of them were in dispute, whether by the purported Fijian sellers or by Europeans with inconsistent claims of their own. Simply figuring out what happened with each parcel was an "incredibly large" task, Des Voeux explained, and the time it took was multiplied by the ability of dissatisfied claimants or opponents of a claim to seek rehearing of cases already decided. Des Voeux left Fiji for a less stressful post in Newfoundland in 1886, thoroughly exasperated by the quantity of work. "To convey in words an adequate idea of it," he declared, "is practically impossible."[36]

Whether or not it was attributable to overwork, the delay in allocating land titles almost certainly reduced the attractiveness to Britons of living in or investing in Fiji. In the late 1870s and early 1880s, it was widely observed that land in Fiji was selling very cheap, at prices well below what its value would have been had titles been more secure. Fiji offered fertile land

and a perfect climate for tropical commodities like sugar and coffee. It was already anglicized to some degree, with English schools and clubs, an English-language settler press, and even grounds for cricket and lawn tennis. But the influx of Britons that had taken place in the decades before 1874 slowed considerably afterward. The colonial government made white emigration doubly difficult, first by proceeding very slowly in confirming Europeans' land titles, and then by prohibiting, with few exceptions, additional transfers of land from Fijians to non-Fijians. Just as Arthur Gordon predicted, Fiji would not become a white man's colony. It would instead become a colony populated largely by laborers imported from India, who would outnumber Europeans nearly four to one by 1891, and nearly seven to one by the end of the century.[37]

NOT ONE INCH OF SOIL

In Tonga, meanwhile, the government of King George Tupou I was nervously watching events in Fiji and the rest of the Pacific. George had worried about being annexed by a European power ever since the 1840s, when France exercised sovereignty over Tahiti. Indeed, for a time he was so fearful of French aggression that he asked to have Tonga become a British colony, a request that Britain had refused.[38] But the fear of colonization never went away.

By the later part of the century, especially after Britain annexed Fiji, Tongans were just as worried about Britain as they were about France. "We all know that Britain is a loving country & right doing," a writer in the Tongan-language newspaper *Koe Taimi O Tonga* noted in 1882, "but the Chiefs working for her Govt. in these parts wish to make to a name for themselves" by adding "another jewel to the Government of Britain." After Fiji in 1874, and Rotuma (which became part of the colony of Fiji) in 1881, perhaps Tonga would be next. Some of the Europeans in Tonga shared this concern. "I certainly should be sorry for the British to get a hold of Tonga so long as Tonga can rule herself," the missionary Frederick Langham explained. "Fiji has not been a grand success so far." A British naval officer who visited Tonga in the late 1870s agreed that although it was "far from perfect, the government under entirely native administration will bear favourable comparison with some of our Colonies."[39] Tonga remained independent, but annexation was in the air.

As the primary component of a strategy to ward off colonization, King George Tupou prohibited the sale of land to foreigners. The first of these laws was part of a code George promulgated in 1850. "I will not verily sell any piece of land in this Tonga," he declared to one of the missionaries, "for it is small; then, what of it can we sell? and what would be left for ourselves?" He knew all too well that land sales in other places had led to annexation. "It is not my mind, nor the mind of my people, that we should be subject to any other people or kingdom in this world," he explained. "But it is our mind to sit down (that is, remain) an independent nation." The ban on sales to foreigners was repeated, with stiff penalties attached, in each subsequent recodification of Tongan law. The 1862 Code, right after delineating the power of the king, turned to land: "It shall in no wise be lawful for a chief or people in this kingdom of Tonga to sell a piece of land to a foreign people—it is verily, verily forbidden for ever and ever; and should any one break this law he shall work as a convict all the days of his life until he die, and his progeny shall be expelled from the land." In Tonga's first constitution, that of 1875, the same prohibition was declared to be "a most solemn covenant binding on the King and Chiefs of this Kingdom, for themselves and their successors forever."[40] The ban remained in force even after Britain assumed control of Tonga's foreign affairs (but not Tongan domestic policy) by treaty in 1900.

The 1875 Constitution was promulgated soon after Britain annexed Fiji. In strengthening the wording of the ban on land sales to foreigners, King George clearly had Fiji in mind. Shortly before the annexation of Fiji, George had delivered a stern lecture to a group of white traders in Tonga that they should not expect to have any influence in the government of the nation. When the traders pointed out the power exercised by white residents of Fiji, George rejected the analogy immediately. "His Majesty wishes to be clearly understood that there is no parallel between the positions of the two Kingdoms," he insisted. "The King of Fiji and his Chiefs have alienated whole tracts of land to British subjects and other foreign subjects consequently the land is theirs but in Tonga not one inch of soil has ever been alienated from His Majesty to any foreigners whatever."[41]

When he introduced the 1875 Constitution in the Tongan Parliament, George specified that the prohibition on selling land to foreigners was intended to keep Tonga from following the path of Fiji. "There is one thing I am very much pleased with," he declared to the Tongan Parliament— "that our course is quite clear yet, and that we are not entangled with any of the great Governments." He emphasized the importance of not selling land to Europeans if Tonga wished to remain independent. "It is quite true that matters of this nature do not as a rule belong to the Constitution of other countries," George explained, "but we are different from all the other countries of the world, for no part of Tonga has been sold, the whole of the land being intact up to the present time; and in the Constitution I have again made sure that this law shall be perpetual, that it is absolutely forbidden to sell any part of Tonga for ever." As George warned his Parliament a few years later, "the day that the chiefs shall be allowed to please themselves concerning their hereditary lands, that day will Tonga most certainly be lost."[42]

The no-sale policy was part of a broader land tenure reform gradually undertaken by George throughout his reign. The other major components of the reform included grants of land to individual Tongans (George at first claimed ownership of all the land in Tonga) and a prohibition of *all* sales, not just sales to foreigners. Because land could not be sold to anyone, it had to be passed along to one's children at death. This system, in its main features, still exists today.[43]

The ban on selling land to foreigners began at midcentury as George's own policy, but by the later part of the century it was largely implemented in practice by his prime minister, the British ex-missionary Shirley Baker. Baker arrived in Tonga in 1860; within a few years he was the king's most important advisor, and he was officially appointed prime minister in 1880. The consensus among Britons with experience in the Pacific was that King George was under the sway of Baker, who made the important decisions in George's name. "The King's relations with Baker are very curious, and reminded me of those between Louis XIII and Richelieu," Arthur

Gordon noted in his journal after a visit to Tonga in 1878. "He writhes under his tyranny, but cannot and will not shake it off." Britons often accused Baker of using his influence for his own enrichment, but at least so far as land policy was concerned this accusation was clearly untrue. Baker, like some of Kamehameha's white officials in Hawaii, seems to have developed a genuine affection for Tonga and a sincere interest in its welfare. "I love Tonga and love the old King," he explained to his former employers, the men who governed the Australasian Wesleyan Church. "I thought the best thing I could do would be to concede to his wishes, and become his responsible advisor for the next 5 or 6 years in order to save the country."[44] By the 1880s, whites attributed the prohibition on land sales as much to Baker as to King George.

Baker shared George's view that the only way to stave off colonization would be to prevent land from shifting into European ownership. "Taking as a mottoe that annexation was not a necessity to missionary effort," Baker resolved, "I determined to make it my life work to make the Tongans a nation, independent and free." He recorded in his private notes that "[King George] is conversant a little with the history of the various nations etc. and especially of the fact that the native races die out before the white men." He noted that the king "has tried to prevent this by adopting several measures," which included sanitary laws and quarantines to avoid European diseases, as well as taxes on liquor. At the head of the list, however, was "not selling land." Britain would banish Baker from Tonga in 1890 for his role in a religious schism that preoccupied the country through the 1880s, but even after he left, he was widely praised (outside of Tonga) for his success in preserving Tongan ownership of Tongan land. Because of Baker, one New Zealand newspaper suggested, "they had no land difficulties, with antagonistic European claimants, such as have arisen in Fiji and Samoa, and have been the curse of these places." A correspondent to another newspaper pointed out that "the land of Tonga has been preserved inviolable for the people of Tonga, and earth-hungry Europeans have been unable to satiate their appetites with Tongan broad acres." Despite his banishment, a third paper observed, "he has at least the satisfaction when leaving the islands, of knowing that they remain intact for the sole benefit and support of the Tongan people. He has neither yielded to the temptation to lay hands upon them for himself, nor has he allowed any foreigner to do so. How many men—early missionaries or traders—who have enjoyed the same opportunities can say as much?"[45] Baker's support for the ban on selling land to foreigners made him extremely unpopular with Tonga's small white community of disappointed would-be land purchasers, but Britons without personal stakes in the issue could recognize a certain nobility in his behavior.

Such eulogies gave Baker perhaps too much credit. He was neither the originator of the no-sale policy nor the sole European to favor it. Alfred Maudslay, the British consul in Tonga in the 1870s, also recognized that selling land would be disastrous. He realized that the pace of land sales in Samoa "makes it almost a certainty that in a short time they [the Samoans] will be ousted from the soil & die out." Maudslay accordingly advised King George to retain the no-sale policy, and to reinforce it by taking care not to assume too much sovereign debt, which would bring the danger of annexation by whichever country most of the government's creditors had come from.[46] Had the British government wished to force the Tongan government to sell land, Baker's opinion would have made little difference, so the sympathetic views of Maudslay and his fellow colonial officials were just as important as Baker's.

Had Tonga not banned land sales, it is almost certain that a large fraction of the land would have wound up in European hands, some directly through sales, and perhaps more indirectly, as a means of collecting on debts. Tonga was (and indeed still is) an intensely religious country. By the late 1870s it became clear that British missionaries had been encouraging Tongans to run up considerable debts in the form of pledges to missionary societies. After preaching, the missionaries would take contributions in the form of promises to pay. They would then sell the promises to the German trading firm of Godeffroy and Sons, for cash. The firm would seize the belongings of the contributors. "In some cases," Maudslay reported, "married men with families have had the whole of their property sold, house, furniture & clothing, to satisfy these debts."[47] Had Tongan land been alienable to Europeans, it would have been available to be foreclosed upon in payment of the same debts.

11. William Hodges, *Afia-too-ca: A burying place in the Isle of Amsterdam,* engraving by William Byrne (1777). Early European accounts of Tonga emphasized the fertility of its soil and the ubiquity of agriculture, shown here in a late eighteenth-century engraving based on a drawing by William Hodges, the artist who accompanied James Cook on his second expedition. Despite the attractions of Tonga as a location for a European colony, the Tongan government successfully prevented the sale of any land. C-051-022, Alexander Turnbull Library, Wellington, New Zealand.

Denied the ability to purchase land, whites in Tonga leased it instead. The 1875 Constitution allowed leases of up to twenty-one or ninety-nine years, depending on the land involved. These leases were typically transferable to other Europeans. For those traders and missionaries who had no interest in moving permanently to Tonga, such a lease was nearly as good as ownership.[48] For prospective farmers, however, who hoped to move to Tonga, invest heavily in land, and then pass the land on to their children decades later, even a ninety-nine-year lease was not long enough. The ban on land sales thus yielded precisely the result intended by King George. It allowed a small community of traders and missionaries to live in Tonga, but it deterred other whites from emigrating.

The white population of Tonga accordingly did not grow as quickly as the white population of Fiji. In 1876, white residents numbered themselves as only about a hundred male adults. A decade later the British government counted only 213 whites in Tonga, women and children included. These were much smaller numbers than in Fiji, where the white population was around 2,000 in 1870, and more than 2,600 by 1881. With only a tiny white population, mostly people with no interest in staying permanently, Tonga never grew a local white constituency for colonization like the ones that developed in much of the rest of the Pacific. Europeans in Tonga were too scarce to be worth sending a military force to protect them from the Tongans, and they were too weak to justify sending a military force to protect the Tongans from them. As William Des Voeux put it, from the British perspective, "Tonga is no doubt an insignificant spot on the earth's surface."[49] With such a trivial white presence, Tonga held no attraction as a potential colony.

The plan King George Tupou I originally implemented in 1850 thus worked perfectly. By not selling land, Tongans prevented their own annexation. George I lived so long that he was succeeded by his great-grandson, who took the name Tupou II. In 1897, while listing all that he was thankful for, Tupou II saved the most important for last. "The best of all," he concluded, "and that which comes first and brings true peace to my heart is that the land is still intact, not one inch is lost." As most of the rest of the world was incorporated into a few empires in the nineteenth and early twentieth centuries, Tonga would remain one of the very few places in the Pacific where no land was alienated to Europeans.[50]

Comparing nineteenth-century Fiji and Tonga highlights the importance of indigenous political organization in determining whether and how land would be sold to Europeans. Tonga was able to avoid land sales because it had a single government. "On one point, I think, there can be no difference of opinion," the colonial official Charles Mitchell once remarked, toward the end of George's reign, "and that is on the absolute loyalty of all the people, without distinction of rank or creed, to King George."[51] Fiji, by contrast, lacked a single indigenous government. Before annexation, Fijians could not prevent their neighbors from selling land to white settlers. The British colonial government was the first institution in Fiji powerful enough to put a stop to sales.

chapter nine

Alaska

Occupancy and Neglect

I N 1898, WHEN A GROUP of Tlingit chiefs met in Juneau with Alaska governor John Green Brady, each explained that his village had been pushed off its land by white settlers. "By and by they began to build canneries and take the creeks away from us, where they make salmon," complained Kah-du-shan, the head of a village near Wrangell. "When we told them these creeks belonged to us, they would not pay any attention to us and said all this country belonged to the President, the big chief in Washington." Meanwhile, the village's former fur-trapping sites had been seized by gold miners. "They take our property, take away ground, and when we complain to them about it, they employ a lawyer and go to court and win the case," Kah-du-shan added. "We are not fish. We like to live like other people live. We make this complaint because we are very poor now. The time will come when we will not have anything left. The money and everything else in this country will be the property of the white man, and we will have nothing." Yash-noosh, from a village near Juneau, told a similar tale. "Our people we have simple patches of ground raising vegetables and places where our people go hunting; creeks where they fish, we want you to give them back to us," he insisted. "The Thlingit are getting poor because their ground is taken away from them."

Koogh-see, a chief from Hoonah, offered an analogy to drive home to

Brady the unfairness of how his village had been treated. "I have been down to Seattle and Tacoma," he began. "I have seen very nice towns. I have seen how white men live, and I like it very much. Now supposing I come back here and tell my people, the leading men such as Kah-du-shan, to go down to Seattle and Tacoma. I have seen white men raising at those towns all kinds of fruit and vegetables. Suppose I tell those people to go with me on certain days to burn certain ground and next day same thing and third day same thing and destroy all these things, don't you suppose the white people would say something to us if we destroyed all these grounds by fire and get on places where white people [have] goats and other animals and commenced to shoot them?" This was exactly how Koogh-see's village had been treated by whites, he suggested, and he hoped the government would provide redress. "That is why I ask you, governor, to return all these things which white men took from us," he concluded. "Creeks, for instance, where we make dry fish, places where we trap. We make our living altogether by trapping and hunting, and I ask you to give all those places back. And if white men should like to take possession of any of those places, we should like to ask you to tell them to not take them for nothing, but to pay for them."

Kah-ea-tchiss, also from Hoonah, provided another analogy grounded in the experience of white Alaskans. "When a man goes into a store and buys different things, he pays for them," Kah-ea-tchiss suggested. "He does not take those things for nothing when he leaves the store. That is why I should like you to tell your people to do the same thing to us. When we tell the white people to pay for this ground, they refuse to make any payment for the ground and say this land belongs to Washington."[1]

Brady could not have been surprised to hear the Tlingits' grievances, but he was unlikely to have been moved by them either. Only a few years before, he himself had provoked similar complaints when he built a lumber mill and a house on a Tlingit burial ground.[2]

NO KNOWLEDGE OF SEEDS

The natives of Alaska, like their counterparts to the south, lacked agriculture before European contact. Alaska is so big that Europeans found very different sorts of people in different areas, but this was one characteristic they had in common. "Their food is fish, sea Animals, Birds, roots and berries and even sea-weed," James Cook noted of the Aleutians in 1778. A year later and two thousand miles to the east, the Spanish explorer Juan Francisco Bodega y Quadra reached the islands of southeast Alaska and reported that the local diet consisted chiefly of fish, deer, bear, and ducks, along with the spontaneously growing plants of the forest. Another Spanish explorer, Estéban José Martínez Fernández y Martínez de la Sierra, encountered the inhabitants of the area around Prince William Sound in 1788. "They have no knowledge of seeds," he reported. Martínez attributed the absence of agriculture to the climate. "The country is very mountainous and covered with snow," he concluded. "From everything we have seen, there is no opportunity for seeding." The early Russian explorers provided similar accounts. "It was deplorable to see how ignorant they were," Grigorii Shelikhov said of the inhabitants of Kodiak Island. In the mid-1780s, when Shelikhov's crew showed them that one could grow crops deliberately by planting seeds, "they evinced nothing but surprise." All over Alaska, Europeans encountered indigenous people who knew no agriculture.[3]

As in nearby British Columbia, the natives of southeast Alaska—the region most visited by Europeans—normally spent the summer in coastal fishing camps and the winter in more permanent villages. The American trader John D'Wolf, who was in southeast Alaska in the summer of 1805, found natives catching fish and drying them in the sun, in preparation for the winter. "One could call the Tlingits (like all peoples on the northwest coast of America), costal or sea nomads," explained the early Finnish ethnographer Heinrich Holmberg, "since they have permanent quarters only in winter, while they spend most of the summer gathering winter provisions."[4]

Some of the early English descriptions of Alaska natives were highly favorable. Cook thought the Aleutians "the most peaceable inoffensive people I ever met with," and he even suggested that "as to honisty they might serve as a pattern to the most civilized nation on earth." Archibald Menzies, the naturalist on the Vancouver expedition of the 1790s, found the Eskimos near present-day Anchorage "good naturd friendly & Peaceable."

They were highly skilled as well: "Most of their implements exhibit a degree of neatness in the execution, that far surpassd all other rude nations
we met with," Menzies explained, "for if we examind their clothing & see
with what care they form & sow them, so as not to admit the least drop of
rain; & their canoes are equally neat having their Seams sowd so tight as
not to admit any water. Their Harpoons darts cordage & little leather
bags shew a degree of art that would do credit even to the most civilized
nations." David Samwell, Cook's surgeon, observed that the Aleutians
even exhibited a system of property rights in land and water. "Whenever
any one has fixed his Habitation nobody else dares to hunt or fish in the
Neighbourhood," Samwell noted, "nor appropriate to himself what the
Sea has cast up unless he has previously engaged with him for a part of the
Produce."[5]

As in other parts of the Pacific, however, the early years of contact produced a wide range of European perceptions of indigenous people. "A
more hideous set of beings, in the form of men and women, I had never
before seen," exclaimed the American trader Richard Cleveland. William
Beresford, the supercargo on the English navigator George Dixon's voyage
to Alaska in 1787, concluded that the experience "served to shew us, in
how wretched a state it is possible for human beings to exist." The American missionary Jonathan Green toured the southeastern islands in 1829
and was similarly unimpressed. "In their persons and habitations they are
intolerably slovenly," Green reported. "They seem for the most part, to
have a mortal aversion to the external application of water. . . . Their habitations are generally wretched hovels, without doors, windows, floor, or
chimney." Even these words were too kind for the English sailor Francis
Simpkinson, who pronounced the natives of Sitka "the most degraded,
worthless, & filthy race of people on the earth."[6] Had Alaska been an English-speaking colony from the onset of European contact, Britain or the
United States might have purchased land from its indigenous occupants
or they might not have—there would have been ample ammunition for
proponents of either course.

But Alaska was a Russian colony first. Some of the early Russian accounts of Alaska natives were as negative as those of Cleveland, Beresford,
or Green. "Their appearance has something repelling in it," Ivan Banner

complained of the Tlingits near the Russian fort at New Archangel. "One could not describe a better monster. It is regrettable that painters do not have the fortune of seeing them; one could hardly paint a better likeness of a devil." Banner was writing when Russian–native relations were at their worst—the Tlingits had destroyed the fort the previous year—and he blamed the colony's troubles on the Tlingits' utter barbarism. "It is impossible to imagine that they can ever be trained to obedience and submission or willing subjugation to the scepter of the Russian State," he despaired. "Human virtues are foreign to them; they have no wishes other than the satisfaction of their lists, and it is difficult to find in them even the slightest resemblance to God in whose image man was created." Kiril Khlebnikov, who spent fifteen years in Alaska in the employ of the Russian-American Company, the trading company that administered the colony from 1799 to 1867, concluded that the Tlingits were "sybarites in their cabins" who "are ready to lie around with their wives all day long," except when they were gambling. Such sneers concealed (and were perhaps compensating for) the fact that the small Russian settlements along the coast depended so heavily upon Alaska natives for food and furs that Alaska could scarcely have been a Russian colony at all without substantial native labor.[7]

More important than such observations, in the development of Russian land policy, was that the Russian population of Alaska never grew large enough for indigenous property rights to be a pressing issue. Alaska was never intended to be a settler colony. The Russian government was interested only in the extraction of resources, not in governing a distant population. By the mid-1850s, after half a century of colonization and with only a decade more to go, the Russian-American Company counted only 658 Russians in Alaska, and only 1,902 "creoles," or children of Russian fathers and native mothers. These Russians and part-Russians occupied some land—they lived in houses, they grew crops, and the company had built an infirmary, some icehouses and fish storage units, a lumber mill, and other buildings.[8] But the total amount of land actually occupied by Russians, even at the peak of Russian colonization, was minuscule relative to the inhabitable portion of Alaska.

The Russian government thus never had any occasion to formulate any explicit land policy. Russia made no written land grants to settlers and entered into no treaties with Alaska natives. Russian colonists simply used whatever land they thought they needed and could take without provoking native opposition. The result in practice, as in the earliest trading-post stages of British Columbia and Oregon, was the treatment of Alaska as terra nullius.

The Russian government's fullest explanation of its land policy came only in late 1867, *after* it had sold Alaska to the United States, when Secretary of State William Seward, recognizing the administrative demands that lay ahead, finally asked what Russian practice had been with respect to the natives and their land. Sergei Kostlivtsev of the Russian finance ministry, the part of the government responsible for overseeing the Russian-American Company's activities in Alaska, responded with a detailed memorandum. In much of the colony, Kostlivtsev explained, there had been no Russian settlement at all, so the government had not interfered with indigenous property systems. The islands off the west coast of Alaska, such as Saint Lawrence and Nunivak, had been sites only of trade, not of settlement, so "neither the imperial government nor the company ever had any influence upon the mode of division of lands between said natives, who, to the present time, use such lands in perfect freedom, without any foreign interference." The same was true of the Aleutian Islands, where Russians had likewise declined to settle because of the harsh climate and barren soil. In other parts of Alaska, however, such as Kodiak Island and the area around the company's headquarters at New Archangel, the company had allowed some of its retired employees to settle, but as to such land "there were no particular regulations, restrictions, or formalities." The chief administrator of the company would assign a plot of land for housekeeping and fishing, taking care only "to avoid contestations between the settlers and the natives." These assignments did not generate any written land titles or other legal documents. Rather, "the first occupation and using of a certain locality, whether by an individual or by a community, notwithstanding the lack of formalities, conferred unquestionable right of possession." No one—neither the Russians nor the Alaska natives—had anything more under Russian law.

On the interior of the mainland, Kostlivtsev continued, "we meet with phenomena very different." There "every symptom not only of social, but even of settled life, disappears, because these natives, having no other occupation but hunting, migrate in the track of game from one part to another." The Russian-American Company had in any event not penetrated much into the interior and had never established any settlements, so "no attempts were ever made, and no necessity ever occurred to introduce any system of land-ownership."[9]

When the United States purchased sovereignty over Alaska in 1867, the American government was thus not constrained, in either direction, by anything the government of Russia had done with respect to native land rights. Russia had not created any indigenous property rights the incoming American government was bound to respect. Nor could the United States benefit from anything Russia had done to extinguish indigenous property rights, as some had argued (in the end unsuccessfully) the Spanish had done in California. As of 1867, with respect to natives and their land, Alaska was a blank slate.

A FRESH FIELD OF OPERATION

The treaty by which the United States purchased Alaska mentioned natives only to exclude them from the rights reserved to Russian settlers. Russians wishing to remain in Alaska were guaranteed their "private individual property." Russians were also "to be admitted to the enjoyment of all the rights, advantages, and immunities of citizens of the United States" and to be "protected in the free enjoyment of their liberty, property, and religion." These benefits, however, were not granted to members of "uncivilized native tribes," who would thenceforth be "subject to such laws and regulations as the United States may, from time to time, adopt in regard to aboriginal tribes of that country."[10] In this respect, the purchase of Alaska differed little from earlier American territorial expansions, in which non-Indian recipients of land grants from earlier sovereigns saw their property rights protected, while questions concerning the property rights of Indians were given little thought, and effectively deferred to a later time, when the pressure of white settlement would bring them to public attention.

There *was* a flurry of writing in the years after 1867 about the exotic peoples newly incorporated into American territory, but virtually none of it took any account of whether they owned their land. To the extent indigenous people figured at all in the debate over the Alaska purchase, it was merely to be cited by opponents as yet another reason the government was wasting its money. Just as the federal government was fighting a series of costly Indian wars, critics charged, it was planning to take on the supervision of even more aboriginals who were even farther away. "Have we not Indians enough on hand now to take care of?" wondered Congressman Hiram Price of Iowa, a future commissioner of Indian affairs; "or do gentlemen think we had better buy a few more thousand of them, and thus furnish a field for still further cash expenditures, a few more Indian agencies, speculations, &c.?" Supporters of the purchase responded by insisting that the Alaska natives could take care of themselves, and that the expensive apparatus of the Indian Office would be unnecessary. "There is something in their nature which does not altogether reject the improvements of civilization," Massachusetts senator Charles Sumner maintained. "Unlike our Indians, they are willing to learn." Major John Tindall, sent to investigate conditions in Alaska, reported that while the natives "are savages, and possess the villainous traits of character usually found in that class," nevertheless "by way of comparison, I do not think they are so bad as the Indians of the plains or of Arizona." But most of the debate over Alaska took little or no account of the new territory's inhabitants. Mark Twain may have captured the tone of public discourse best when he joked that Alaska "was only an iceberg . . . with a population composed of bears, walruses, Indians, and other animals."[11] The status of native property rights was not a topic of much concern.

This inattention must have been attributable, at least in part, to the conviction of many government officials that Alaska was unlikely to see any significant white settlement for the foreseeable future. Alaska was known to be very cold. For years it would be widely considered inhospitable to agriculture. H. H. McIntyre, the United States customs official sent to Alaska, reported that the prospects for farming were nil. "As a financial measure," he concluded, "it might not be the worst policy to abandon the territory for the present." After spending time as U.S. treasury agent on the remote Pribilof Islands (then called the Seal Islands, when seals were plentiful), George Wardman cautioned that "it would seem wicked to suggest emigration from any part of the United States to a land the coast lines of which are characterized by snow, rain, and fog to such an extent as to almost entirely preclude the ripening of any sort of vegetables suitable for man's food." Anywhere in the United States, Wardman concluded, would be a better place to live than Alaska.[12] If the white population of Alaska was unlikely to grow beyond a few hundred permanent residents, officials may well have reasoned, there was no point in worrying about the tenure by which Alaska natives held their land. There would be enough land for everyone.

But inattention to the issue may also have been partly attributable, paradoxically, to the opposite expectation—that white settlers would soon come to Alaska in such great numbers that Alaska natives would die out. Such was the view of William Seward, who engineered the acquisition of Alaska as Andrew Johnson's secretary of state. After retiring from public service in 1869, Seward traveled around the world, including to Alaska, where he visited Sitka, the newly renamed capital, the city the Russians had called New Archangel. There he addressed the tiny white community on the subject of the natives. "They must steadily decline in numbers, and unhappily this decline is accelerated by their borrowing ruinous vices from the white man," Seward predicted. He expressed his regret "that a people so gifted by nature, so vigorous and energetic, and withal so docile and gentle in their intercourse with the white man, can neither be preserved as a distinct social community, nor incorporated into our society." That Alaska natives would wither away was a simple fact of nature, about which nothing could be done. "The Indian tribes will do here as they seem to have done in Washington Territory and British Columbia," Seward concluded; "they will merely serve the turn until civilized white men come."[13] On this view too, indigenous property rights presented a theoretical question only, one unlikely to arise in practice.

The 1868 statute by which Congress extended American law to Alaska accordingly said nothing about the land or its inhabitants. The statute spoke only of law "relating to customs, commerce, and navigation," because in the short run those were the only topics expected to be of any significance. Congress authorized the appointment of a customs collector for Alaska and prohibited the killing of fur-bearing animals without a license from the Treasury Department, but took no steps to establish any kind of territorial government or any procedure for allocating land.[14] Until 1884, when Congress would finally provide a territorial government, Alaska would be a territory without much written law. It was governed, more in principle than in practice, by the military.

The army sent a small group of soldiers to Sitka in 1867, under the command of General Jefferson Columbus Davis, a veteran of the Civil War (for the North) and a future leader of battles against the Modoc Indians along the California-Oregon border. Davis received his instructions from the commander of the army's Pacific division, Henry Halleck, also a Civil War veteran, and, before that, secretary of state of the military government of California and then a resident of California for the next fifteen years, including the period when the Senate rejected the California Indian treaties. "In the absence of any organized civil territorial government," Halleck told Davis, he would have to take charge of relations with the Indians. Davis was instructed to "be careful to cultivate friendly relations with all the inhabitants of your district, whether Russian, creole, or aboriginal."

Halleck was especially insistent on a point that deserves some emphasis, because it would prefigure federal policy with respect to Alaska natives for the next several decades. Rather than modeling the administration of native affairs on the past policy of the United States, Davis was to follow the models offered by Russia and Britain. "The Russians have occupied the territory which constitutes your command for a long period of years," Halleck reminded Davis. "Their number has always been small, and their military forces never equal to those which will be placed under your orders; nevertheless, their officers, agents, and merchants have travelled unmolested through most parts of that vast country." The only conflict between Russians and natives in all those years, Halleck noted, had been "one or two temporary outbreaks near Sitka." The British, meanwhile, controlled vast areas in Canada, a territory even larger than the United States with an even larger Indian population, with a very small contingent of government employees. "And yet we have never heard of hostilities and wars between that government and its native subjects in America," Halleck pointed out, "although trade has been carried on with savage tribes in its remotest extremities." Halleck then drew a pointed comparison with the Indian policy of the United States, the results of which had not been nearly as good, despite the expenditure of much more money. "But our people and the tribal Indians have been for years, and are still, in continual hostilities," he reminded Davis, "and there is scarcely a county or district in our frontier States or Territories which does not demand and expect a military force for its local protection larger than the Russian or British governments have deemed necessary for the control of its vast Indian possessions on this continent."

The lesson Halleck drew was that the entire apparatus of federal Indian policy—land purchases, annual payments, superintendents, and so on—had been a failure, and that Alaska provided the federal government with the opportunity to start anew. Here Halleck was veering a bit off-message, in that the army had no power to depart from the Indian policy established by Congress or to ignore the line of Supreme Court cases recognizing aboriginal land title. But Halleck, evidently warming to his subject in light of his experiences in California in the 1840s and 1850s, urged Davis to look to Russian and British practice as a template for his treatment of Alaska natives. "Neither the Russian nor the British government on this continent has ever made Indian treaties, had an Indian bureau or Indian superintendents or agents, or paid millions of dollars for Indian annuities and Indian goods which were promised to, but never received by, the native Indians," Halleck maintained. He was wrong about Britain if he intended to describe all of British North America, but mostly right if he meant only British Columbia, the closest and most recently colonized part of it. "These facts should receive your careful and serious consideration," he lectured Davis, "in assuming the command of a military district in which there are some fifty thousand natives and a population of only a few thousand whites and creoles."[15]

Halleck's argument—that abandoning the practice of purchasing land from indigenous people would be better for settlers and natives alike, because it would reduce conflict without causing any loss to the natives—was precisely the view that had been implemented a few years earlier by

James Douglas in British Columbia. It was a view that was gaining increasing acceptance in the United States. Four years after Halleck instructed Davis, Congress, motivated in part by a similar disillusionment with Indian treaties, would prohibit the executive branch from entering into any more treaties. Alaska became an American territory at a moment when terra nullius was in the ascendant, and that accident of timing would have a profound influence on federal policy.

As for the Alaska natives themselves, to the extent their views are knowable today, they were unimpressed with any version of colonial land policy. The Treasury agent Charles Bryant, sent to Alaska in 1868 to appraise the territory's natural resources, found the Tlingits around Sitka unhappy with the news of the American purchase. Their dissatisfaction arose "from the fact that it was sold without their consent," Bryant reported. They argued "that their fathers originally owned all the country, but allowed the Russians to occupy it for their mutual benefit, in that the articles desired by them could be obtained from the Russians in exchange for furs." But they had never intended "the right of the Russians to sell the Territory," unless the Russians were to turn over the proceeds of the sale. Davis heard the same complaint. The natives "frequently take occasion to express their dislike at not having been consulted about the transfer of the territory," he explained. "They do not like the idea of the whites settling in their midst without being subjected to their jurisdiction."[16] The American assertion of sovereignty over Alaska was strange and new from the native perspective, but of course from the American perspective it was backed by centuries of tradition. From the sixteenth century onward, indigenous people had never been understood to possess the power to withstand a claim of sovereignty by Europeans or their descendants.

The existence of indigenous *property* rights, by contrast, remained an open question in Alaska for decades. The issue came before Congress repeatedly in the 1870s and 1880s, as Congress considered how to govern Alaska. "Never was a country so much investigated and reported upon," the *New York Times* could remark as early as 1875. "Congress regularly and habitually sends out a special Commissioner with instructions to examine into an infinite variety of subjects," one of which was the question of what to do about the natives.[17] On each occasion, the government's informants argued against purchasing land from Alaska natives, and against any form of recognition of native property rights, on the theory that any land policy would be better than the one the government followed in the contiguous United States.

The painter Henry Wood Elliott, for example, was sent to Alaska in 1872 as a special agent of the Treasury Department to gather information about the territory's natural resources. The best policy with respect to the natives, he concluded after three years of study, was to do nothing. "Any scheme of establishing Indian reservations or agencies in this country, with an idle and mischievous retinue of superintendents, chaplains, and schoolteachers, seems to me entirely uncalled for," Elliott advised. "The people here are keen hunters and quick-witted traders, and need no help or care." He recommended the extension of U.S. mining law to Alaska, but not the American law of indigenous property rights.[18]

James Swan made the point more emphatically. Swan had been one of the earliest white settlers in the area that became Washington Territory. In the 1850s he had been secretary to Isaac Stevens when Stevens, as governor, had entered into several treaties with the Washington tribes, and then again when Stevens, as the territory's delegate to Congress, had secured the Senate's confirmation of the treaties. In 1875 he had visited Alaska as an agent of the federal government charged with procuring northwestern Indian artifacts for display at the Centennial Exposition the following year in Philadelphia. By the late 1870s, after living in the Northwest for twenty-five years, he was a local elder statesman with firm views on Indian land policy. His experience with the Washington treaties had taught him "that it is folly to think of making any more treaties with Indians." It wasn't the treaties that had been the problem in Washington, but rather "it is the non-fulfillment of those treaties which has been the prime cause of all the trouble we have had with the Indians in this Territory." As future treaties were not likely to be carried out any differently, Swan argued, Alaska provided the opportunity to make a clean break with the failed policy of the past. "So far as Alaska is considered," Swan reasoned, "I see no object to be attained by repeating a worn-out farce of treating with a people who are living in a territory which we have acquired the fee-simple of by the purchase the United States made of Russia, in which purchase no mention is made of any reserved rights of Indians or of any other people. The land belongs to the United States, and no treaties are necessary to extinguish Indian titles. We must, therefore, meet this Alaskan question other than by the time-honored custom of making a solemn treaty with a horde of breechless savages in the same formal manner and with more imposing ceremony than we are wont to do with such great nations as Great Britain, France, Germany, and Russia."

Instead of acquiring land by treaty, Swan concluded, "I respectfully suggest that the British Columbia plan, which has proved so eminently successful, be adopted." Settlers and Indians were living peacefully in British Columbia, he declared, with no treaties, no reservations, no Office of Indian Affairs, no annual presents—none of the apparatus of Indian policy in the United States. "That policy has been the ruling one since the days of George Washington," Swan observed. "We have all seen the great error and the little good of that policy, but have been unable to avert or amend it." Alaska, however, provided the chance for a new start, because Alaska natives had not yet learned to expect property rights, or treaties, or annuities. "Alaska is an exception to our Indian population. Separated from the States and Territories by British Columbia, her Indian tribes have no affinity with or knowledge of the working of our treaty system, and they present a fresh field of operation."[19]

Similar advice came in from other Americans in Alaska. Lieutenant Colonel Robert Scott, part of the military garrison sent to Alaska in 1867, suggested that British Columbia's policy of terra nullius offered a better model than anything that could be found at home. In British Columbia "there is no pretended recognition of the Indian's 'title' in fee simple to the lands over which he roams for fish or game," Scott maintained, and yet, despite the absence of British military protection, "white men travel through the length and breadth of the province in almost absolute security." He concluded that the same could be true in Alaska. Longtime Alaska resident Ivan Petroff, a Russian expatriate who became a U.S. citizen after the purchase of Alaska, was in charge of counting the Alaska population for the Census Office. "It must be a source of much satisfaction to the Government of the United States to know that in the acquisition of this extended land," he affirmed in his report, the natives were unlikely "to appeal for food and raiment at the cost of the public Treasury; [and] that it is not at all necessary to send a retinue of Indian agents, with their costly supplies and dubious machinery, into this country." The outdoorsman Charles Hallock praised the lack of recognition of native title in British Columbia and found it "gratifying to know that this view is likely to obtain with us henceforth" in Alaska.[20] Dissatisfaction with U.S. Indian land policy had been growing for decades. British Columbia seemed to offer a better solution, and Alaska was the first U.S. colony in which that solution could be put into practice.

There was another side of the argument, of course, just as in British Columbia. Federal Indian policy was easy to criticize, but a policy of terra nullius posed the possibility of unconstrained white settlement on land once used by Alaska natives, and that promised to be far worse. Vincent Colyer was a member of the Board of Indian Commissioners, the government-appointed group of Protestant philanthropists charged in 1869 with overseeing much of the government's relations with Indians. After a tour of Alaska and interviews with natives Colyer recommended "securing to them, beyond the possibility of failure, . . . all their rights, tribal and individual, to lands or moneys due them," and protecting them on reservations, just as the government professed to be doing in the rest of the United States. The Presbyterian missionary Aaron Lindsley recognized in 1881 that Congress had thus far neglected to protect native property from white settlers. "It ill becomes a brave and magnanimous people," Lindsley declared, "to seize lands and confiscate the scant resources of a depressed and vanishing race." Sheldon Jackson, the leading missionary in Alaska, pointed out that trespassing on the land of the natives would be not just immoral but counterproductive, because it was sure to lead to the same brutal and costly Indian wars that had taken place after similar encroachments in the earlier-settled parts of the country.[21] Terra nullius looked less appealing when examined closely.

As time passed the question became harder to ignore, because settlers in Alaska were persistent in pushing it forward. "You cannot take up land under any legal title," Petroff complained, because Congress had neglected to extend the public land laws to Alaska. "People on Kadiak Island or Cook's Inlet hold land, but they have no title." Sheldon Jackson was certain that the lack of land titles had deterred many potential settlers from moving to Alaska in the first place. "A large number of people have been to see me in regard to emigrating to Alaska," he testified before the Senate subcommittee considering the establishment of a territorial government. "When people have said they wanted to go there, I said to them, 'If you go there and open up a farm, you can get no title to your farm. If you build a store-house and put in a stock of goods, you have got no protection except your musket and your own bearing.' There is no inducement to go there now, but the moment you extend the land laws over that Territory, hundreds of people will go up and open the resources and develop mines there." Jackson had heard from several people who claimed to know where minerals could be found but who were waiting for the opportunity to acquire land titles before they began mining, for fear of being muscled aside by desperados as soon as their mines proved productive. "Consequently," Jackson concluded, "everything is left in abeyance until such time as the government will extend law over that country and give titles to land."[22]

But granting formal property rights to settlers would be impossible without first either purchasing the property rights of Alaska natives or declaring they had none. "The rights of the Indians to the land, or some necessary part of it, have not yet been the subject of negotiation or inquiry," acknowledged the Senate Committee on Territories. "It would be obviously unjust to throw the whole district open to settlement under our land laws until we are advised what just claim the Indians may have upon the land." Preston Plumb of Kansas made the same point when the bill to establish a territorial government was being debated on the Senate floor. "We are passing upon the rights and the duties of a people about whom we know practically nothing and a people who are entirely helpless," Plumb declared. "We can not, in legislating at this long range, be too careful not to substitute some other person's rights for the right of some one now on the soil and to whom we are bound, or ought to be bound, at least by ties of sympathy and by ties of justice."[23] How could settlers be granted land titles before the government either purchased the land from Alaska natives or proclaimed a policy of terra nullius?

Faced with this dilemma, Congress procrastinated. The Alaska Organic

Act, the 1884 statute establishing Alaska's first territorial government, extended to Alaska the federal mining law in force elsewhere in the United States, by which miners were allowed to stake claims. The Organic Act, however, denied to settlers land titles for other purposes, such as homes or farms, by explicitly providing that the general land laws of the United States were not in force in Alaska. The act put off for the future the question of native property rights, by providing that for the time being native Alaskans "shall not be disturbed in the possession of any lands actually in their use or occupation or now claimed by them." The method by which such land could be acquired by settlers was declared to be "reserved for future legislation by Congress." To help prepare for such legislation, the secretary of the interior was instructed to establish "a commission to examine into and report upon the condition of the Indians residing in" Alaska, "what lands, if any, should be reserved for their use," and "what rights by occupation of settlers should be recognized." In the short run the government would recognize only mining claims, and, in theory, only those claims that were not inconsistent with the claims of natives. As Senator (and future president) Benjamin Harrison explained, the idea "was to save from all possible invasion the rights of the Indian residents of Alaska" until those rights could be determined.[24]

The commission contemplated by the Organic Act was organized quickly, under the supervision of Alaska governor John Kinkead. The commission's report, issued in 1885, concluded that "the Natives claim only the land on which their houses are built and some garden patches near their villages; they ask or expect nothing more." The commission also recommended protecting native fisheries against white encroachment. On this view, most of the land in Alaska would be open to white settlement. But this conclusion seems to have been based on only the most cursory research. Within a few months of the report's publication, Kinkead's successor as governor, A. P. Swineford, called for a reexamination of the question. The report "was based wholly on information obtained by individual members of the Commission who do not claim to have visited any of the Indian settlements other than the comparatively few which are located in Southeastern Alaska," Swineford charged. "If Congress desires correct information in this regard, the Commission should be revived and a sufficient appropriation made to cover the expense of a visit of inspection to all the Indian settlements." No such appropriation was ever made. But whether the Kinkead commission's report was accurate or not made little difference, because once it was sent to Washington it disappeared without a trace. The commission "filed a valueless report relating to Indian affairs with the commissioner of the land office and ceased to exist when the paltry appropriation of $2,000 for its expenses was exhausted," the Alaska judge John Bugbee lamented a decade later. "It accomplished nothing and no attention has ever been paid to its report."[25]

Settlers and prospective emigrants, meanwhile, continued to press for additional property rights, beyond mining claims, through the 1880s. "Land and timber laws are an absolute necessity," complained Alexander Badlam, the treasurer of the California-Russian Fur Company. "The land taken up, that is, what is occupied, is held under precarious conditions, the people being able to get no titles to their claims and living in a consequent state of insecurity. The lands are valuable and the people should be secured in their possession of them." As the popular writer Maturin Ballou pointed out, the early accounts of Alaska as a desolate wasteland had been overblown. "It would be foolish to suggest the idea that Alaska promises to become eventually a great agricultural country," Ballou acknowledged, but nevertheless "there are considerable areas of good arable land now under profitable cultivation." Not long after enacting the Organic Act, Congress accordingly began considering whether to grant titles to Alaskan settlers. After all, the House Committee on the Territories reasoned, "there are more white people in Alaska now than there were in Dakota when that Territory was first organized," and the Dakota settlers had not been denied the benefits of property ownership. And parts of Alaska were not much less hospitable than parts of Dakota. "The climate along the coast and in Southeastern Alaska is mild and healthful," but few whites were heading that way, because "our American people are indisposed to go to a country for permanent settlement where they cannot secure to their families a home."[26] In 1891 Congress accordingly permitted U.S. citizens to purchase 160-acre homesteads in Alaska, and allowed timber companies entry for logging, on terms similar to those available in the West.

These expansions of the property rights available to whites in Alaska once again raised the question of whether Alaska natives possessed any prior rights in the same land. In an effort to facilitate white settlement without completely ignoring existing native land uses, Congress settled on a compromise. Rather than committing itself to the purchase of all of Alaska (as was federal policy with respect to the rest of the United States except California), on the one hand, or announcing a blanket policy of terra nullius (as in California), on the other, Congress simply declared that no rights could be granted to settlers in land "to which the natives of Alaska have prior rights by virtue of actual occupation."[27] Natives were not to be kicked off of land they were physically using, that is, but they were not accorded any rights in the land they were not using.

This formulation was repeated in 1900 when Congress reorganized the territorial government. In allocating land to whites, the new statute read, "Indians . . . shall not be disturbed in the possession of any lands now actually in their use or occupation." This would remain official policy for the next several decades. It was a narrower conception of property rights than that which prevailed in the contiguous United States (except California), where the government deemed itself bound to purchase the Indian right of occupancy in *all* the land, not just the land actually being used by Indians. Given the enormity of Alaska and the sparseness of its population, most of the land in Alaska was terra nullius under this definition. But it was a broader conception of indigenous property rights than one could find in Australia, British Columbia, or California. As a formal matter, Alaska natives possessed property rights in their current uses of land. As the federal court of appeals judge Erskine Ross explained, in barring a cannery from intruding in an area customarily used by natives for salmon fishing, Congress, "in first dealing with the then sparsely settled country, was disposed to protect its few inhabitants in the possession of lands, of whatever character, by which they eked out their hard and precarious existence."[28]

By deferring for decades any decision as to the scope of Alaska natives' property rights, the government had backed itself into this position. The 1900 census found thirty-six thousand whites in Alaska. Most, it seems likely, were beneficiaries of a government-derived property right—a

homestead, a mining claim, or a right to cut timber. It was too late to declare Alaska natives the owners of Alaska, or even the possessors of a right
of occupancy to all of Alaska, because to do either would have been to upset the investment-backed expectations of the white population, many of
whom were enjoying rights to resources that would have been inconsistent
with either. Ever since 1884, meanwhile, the government had acknowledged that native Alaskans should not be disturbed in their ongoing uses
of land. It was too late to declare a policy of terra nullius. The only option
left was the one the government adopted, a policy midway between terra
nullius and the right of occupancy as it was known in most of the rest of
the United States.

OVERRUNNING THE LAND

There developed by the turn of the century two distinct ways of understanding the relationship between Alaska natives and their land. The
Interior Department, which was ultimately responsible for formally confirming settlers' land titles in Alaska, took native property rights seriously.
The department and its General Land Office consistently rejected white
claims to resources on land or water that interfered with prior and ongoing native uses of those resources. Among whites in Alaska, by contrast,
the prevailing view seems to have been that natives possessed no prior
rights at all. This tension—between the formal recognition of use-rights
and terra nullius on the ground—lasted well into the twentieth century.

Sometime before 1895, for example, Benjamin Arnold set up a trading
post on Kodiak Island, on land near a native village. The land had not
been previously occupied, or so Arnold claimed, but his request for title to
the seven-acre parcel would have cut the village off from access to a stream
that was the villagers' source of fresh water. Interior Secretary Cornelius
Bliss denied Arnold's request, on the ground that the natives had a right to
the water with which Arnold could not interfere. When the Fort Alexander Fishing Station and the Point Roberts Canning Company tried to
claim tracts that would likewise have prevented native villages from reaching their accustomed sources of fresh water, and when the Alaska Commercial Company tried to claim a trading post sandwiched between a na-

tive village and its harbor, the department rendered similar decisions. Interior Secretary Ethan Hitchcock made the department's view clear in granting the request of ten native petitioners to have their village excluded from the town site of Juneau. Native land use, Hitchcock declared, "was notice to the world of their rights in the premises and was sufficient to prevent any one from becoming a *bona fide* purchaser of said lands."[29] On paper, Alaska natives' property rights seemed secure.

The legal basis for recognizing native use rights was the wording of the 1884 and 1891 statutes, but the ethnographic basis was the growing realization that Alaska natives themselves recognized property rights in the land and water of Alaska. Henry Wood Elliott returned to Alaska in the 1880s, this time on a trip sponsored by the Smithsonian to gather information about seals. On his return he wrote a best-selling travel book in which he emphasized the resemblance between Alaskan and American methods of dividing property. Around Sitka, he explained,

> the coast line, and especially the margins of the rivers and streams, are duly divided up among the different families. These tracts are regarded as strictly private property, just as we would regard them if fenced in as farms and cattle ranches—and they are passed from one generation to the other in the line of savage inheritance; they may be sold, or even rented by one family desiring to fish, to gather berries, to cut timber, or to hunt on the domain of another. So settled and so strict are these ideas of proprietary and vested rights in the soil, that, on some parts of the coast, corner-stones and stakes may be seen to-day set up there to define the limits of such properties between savages, by savages; and furthermore, woe to the disreputable trespassing Siwash who steps over these boundaries and appropriates anything of value, such, for instance, as a stranded whale, shark, seal, or otter—berries, wreckage, or shell-fish.

The New York physiology professor Bushrod James was so moved by his vacation in Alaska that he wrote a book-length poem about the territory, in which he too observed that Alaska natives had ideas about property that would be familiar to Anglo-American readers.

> Yet these soul-warped people ever
> Live to rules firm set and guarded,

> By which tribes and subdivisions
> Know and hold the land assigned them,
> Certain that the bold encroacher
> Pays most sadly for his folly.[30]

Attitudes like these suggested a policy of respecting native property rights, at least to the extent that they were respected by the natives themselves.

Reinforcing this conclusion was the view among some whites that Alaska natives were superior to the Indians of the contiguous United States and deserved to be treated at least as well. "Unlike the Indians of other territories," affirmed the professor Horace Briggs, "these people seek employment, and are to be found in canneries, in mills, and voluntarily engage in service as sailors, as longshoremen, and even as house-servants." Alaska governor A. P. Swineford reported that "they are a very superior race intellectually, as compared with the people generally known as North American Indians," and accordingly recommended that they be made American citizens. "With proper encouragement this tribe will never call on Uncle Sam for support nor for a reservation," declared William Carle, a missionary to the Tlingit at Hoonah. "They will show themselves to be men." Bessie Putnam visited the Sitka mission school and found the Tlingit students "ingenious, imitative, [and] bright." They had learned enough about white Americans' views of indigenous people to object when Putnam called them Indians. "We are Alaskans," they insisted. Within the government, the students' view was widely enough shared to raise doubts, for decades, as to whether Alaska natives were covered by the many federal statutes that by their terms applied only to "Indians."[31]

This sunny opinion was hardly unanimous. Septima Collis, the wife of the Civil War hero Charles Collis, took a cruise through the Inland Passage in 1890 and came away with a view considerably more snide. "For the information of our Darwinian friends," she observed, "I may as well say that I was unable to detect the monkey among any of the ancestral specimens. Since the Indian had come into contact with the pale-face he has adopted those of our traits and customs which he approves, among them being exchanging any thing he has got for money; and another, drinking as much whiskey as he can get." But one did not need to think highly of

Alaska natives to sympathize with them. "When the United States purchased this country from Russia," asked one white Sitka resident, "did we not bring upon ourselves the obligation of caring for a people laboring under great natural disadvantages, and upon whom great harm had already been brought by contact with more civilized races? If the duty of liberating the negro race from slavery was so great a one that it had to be done even at the expense of thousands of lives and millions of dollars' worth of property, is it now a great thing to ask that a few thousand dollars be spent in elevating from worse than slavery and rescuing from annihilation a people more intelligent and as much entitled to our guardianship as the negro?"[32] The Interior Department's efforts to protect indigenous property rights in Alaska were backed by at least some sentiment among whites that such was the right thing to do.

If the rights of Alaska natives seemed strong on paper, however, they were often extremely weak in practice. Alaska governors reported to the Interior Department that whites typically took control of land without paying any attention to whether the land was already used by natives. The accounts of missionaries to Alaska, for example, routinely mentioned the building of houses and schools, without ever indicating that the property rights of the natives being proselytized posed any sort of obstacle to the acquisition of the necessary land. The books of advice written for prospective gold miners—a flourishing genre once gold was discovered in a few different parts of Alaska around the turn of the century—never suggested that the rights of natives might prevent one from staking a claim. Canneries, timber camps, commercial fisheries—all were located on native land. Indeed, the Interior Department's own promotional material encouraging emigration to Alaska did not mention the possibility that native land claims might constrain white settlement. One could travel around much of Alaska without finding anything inconsistent with a policy of terra nullius.[33]

Alaska natives protested these incursions, but there was little they could do about them. When the Chilkat Kinto Cush complained to white fishermen that the trap they were setting up would cut off his village's supply of salmon, "they only laughed at him," he reported, "and said they were the government, and would not desist for anyone." In Wrangell, the

Stikines hired Willoughby Clark, a white lawyer, to tell the government that whites were taking all the salmon from their creeks, but Clark had no more success than Kinto Cush. From Metlakatla, the missionary William Duncan described how the Loring Canning Company, "not being content with by far the largest share of salmon streams which they have exclusively controlled in defiance of the natives," were now "preparing to send their nets to the few little streams" the natives had left. When a settler named Peter Eserd claimed possession of an entire Auk village near Juneau and began barring villagers from cutting their own trees, the land's owners lodged complaints with the territorial governor. But territorial officials did little about such complaints, because they tended to view the new commercial land uses as unambiguous progress over traditional native uses. "It is the intention of the Government to protect the Indian in all his rights," Governor James Sheakley assured the superintendent of the Bald Eagle Mining Company, "but he can not nor must not stand in the way of the development of the country, as no one is more benefited by such development than himself."[34]

By the turn of the century, in the parts of Alaska most attractive to whites, trespassing on native land was so common that terra nullius seems in practice to have been more the rule than the exception. The Baptist missionary Charles Replogle reported in 1904 that "it sometimes happened that a mining claim would be located for no other purpose than to hold the surface rights on which to build a town. If the Indians occupied the land, their rights were ignored and the company would claim all the rights to the surface grounds; have a patent issued, declaring the ground unoccupied, and then maliciously force the Indians to pay rent or tear down their cabins and move elsewhere." Thomas Shepard, a mining lawyer in Nome, admitted that absurdly large claims blanketed the areas attractive to white settlement, to the point where there was "not a foot of the country within miles of Nome or Council, for instance, but has been staked and restaked from three to ten times," by "roving prospectors crossing in every direction." The gold rushes only made matters worse, as Alaska attracted thousands of miners uninterested in any native property rights that might stand in the way of gold.[35]

This view also had an ethnographic basis—the belief among many

12. A group of Chilkat Tlingit women and girls, photographed in the 1890s when the Klondike gold rush brought whites to Alaska in unprecedented numbers. The federal government formally recognized the right of Alaska natives to remain on the small fraction of Alaska's land they were physically occupying, but opened the rest to white exploitation, and even these weak property rights were disregarded by the mining and fishing companies that frequently trespassed on native land. Photograph by Frank LaRoche, X-33919, Western History Collection, Denver Public Library.

whites that Alaska natives were too primitive to be accorded property rights. "In morals the Alaskans are much inferior to most Indian tribes of the plains," insisted one traveler. "Theft, if successful, brings no disgrace." The English mountaineer Heywood Seton-Karr portrayed Alaska natives as simple, animal-like creatures unable to plan for the future, people who would never work "until driven by hunger to do so," who "will only go where the caprice of the moment inclines them." The International Polar Expedition found that the residents of Alaska's north coast were so primitive as to lack any form of social organization. "These people have not yet made the transition from the stone to the iron age," the expedition's report marveled. "They have no form of government, but live in a condition of anarchy." If one conceived of Alaska natives this way, they could seem more like natural features of the land than owners of it, more like wild beasts than like fellow human beings with rights to be respected.[36]

It was not long before accounts of Alaska began to include laments for the way white settlement was "overrunning the land," as the New York journalist John Corbett put it, by arrogating the resources that had once belonged to Alaska natives. The Treasury Department reported as early as 1892 that the indigenous residents of the Seal Islands were nearing starvation, because commercial seal hunting had almost wiped out the population of seals, on which natives depended for food. The Canadian anthropologist Diamond Jenness found such great ecological change on Alaska's north coast, the result of commercial whaling, sealing, and trapping, that the Eskimos were likewise on the brink of perishing. Natives all over Alaska, a House committee recognized in 1906, "have their little homes upon land to which they have no title, nor can they obtain a title under existing laws. It does not signify that because an Alaska Indian has lived for many years in the same hut and reared a family there that he is to continue in peaceable possession of what he has always regarded as his home. Some one who regards that particular spot as a desirable location for a home can file upon it for a homestead, and the Indian or Eskimo, as the case may be, is forced to move and give way to his white brother." Without any enforceable property rights in their land or water, without any treaties or reservations, Alaska natives were even less able to withstand white emigration than were the Indians of the contiguous United States. "To the shame of the white man," John Underwood acknowledged in his travel guide, "his government, while making reservations and conferring many other blessings upon the murderous Sioux and Apaches and dog-eating Iggorotes of warmer climes, has done little for the benefit of these kind-hearted people who became wards of the United States when their territory was purchased from Russia."[37] Had Alaska been a warmer place, it would have attracted many more whites, and the natives might have been entirely obliterated.

The government had not formally adopted a policy of terra nullius, as in British Columbia, but it had adopted one by default, by repeatedly failing to grant Alaska natives any formal recognition of property rights in their land, and by doing little to stem the tide of white settlement or resource extraction. As the advocates of terra nullius had predicted, Alaska natives were spared many of the problems of American Indians to the south: they did not have to live on dismally poor reservations, they were not bullied into signing sham treaties, they were not defrauded by the Office of Indian Affairs or its private contractors, and they were not left waiting for promises never to be fulfilled. Instead, Alaska natives were saddled with the problems of terra nullius, the problems faced by the Indians of British Columbia and, before that, by Aboriginal Australians.

Land policy in Alaska would change only slightly before the late twentieth century. The government did create occasional native reserves, beginning with the Metlakatla reserve in 1891. In 1906 Congress authorized Alaska natives to obtain allotments, or parcels in fee simple, on terms similar to those that had applied to American Indians in the contiguous United States for the past two decades. Few Alaska natives, however, acquired land in this manner. The main lines of U.S. land policy in Alaska would not change until the second half of the twentieth century, when Alaska natives forced them to change by bringing lawsuits and threatening others.[38]

Until then, the property rights of Alaska natives were weaker than those of Indians in the rest of the United States (excluding California). In 1911, at the annual Lake Mohonk conference of Friends of the Indian, the largest gathering of white Americans interested in the welfare of indigenous people, one of the topics on the agenda was the poorly defined property rights of Alaska natives. "Forty-four years have elapsed since we acquired Alaska, and yet the legal status of the Native remains undetermined," lamented the naval lieutenant and early ethnologist George Emmons, who had spent many years there. "He has no reservation of land nor receives any gratuity from the Government" on the one hand, but on the other "he can neither acquire land [nor] locate mineral claims." Emmons urged that "the granting of property rights would not only be an act of justice, but it would be an incentive to discovery, and would open up a field of labor to a body of hardy prospectors well equipped in local knowledge"— the natives, who could contribute to the economic development of Alaska if they were allowed a share of the profits. John Green Brady, the former governor of Alaska, reminded his listeners that the lack of formal property rights left natives open to exploitation from whites. "No inquiry has been made into their rights with a view of treating them justly," Brady complained. "In many places their ancient fishing grounds have been entered and appropriated against their feeble protests."[39] He did not mention that he had been one of the exploiters himself.

Conclusion

What Produced Colonial Land Policy?

BETWEEN 1992 AND JUNE 2006, the government of New Zealand paid NZ$750 million to Maori groups, to settle claims that the government had breached the 1840 Treaty of Waitangi by failing to guarantee Maori property rights. Many more claims remained outstanding. The government expected to continue spending on settlements at approximately the same pace for as long as anyone could see.[1] There have been no such payments in Australia. Aboriginal Australians had their land taken without a treaty.

In the state of Washington, meanwhile, Indian tribes play an important role in commercial fishing and in the way the industry is regulated, largely because of a federal court decision recognizing the Indians as owners of half the salmon in the state. The decision was based on the text of the treaties Isaac Stevens dictated to the tribes in the 1850s, which guaranteed them customary fishing rights.[2] (Had Stevens anticipated that fishing rights would one day become commercially meaningful, he would never have included them in the treaties.) The California tribes have no analogous rights, because they had their land taken without a treaty.

Rights derived from treaties are not the only rights possessed by indigenous people, and of course there is much more to the relationship between governments and indigenous people than issues of property. But the method by which land was acquired during the nineteenth century continues to influence that relationship today. The fact that land was acquired differently in different places is not just a matter of historical interest.

Colonial governments respected the property rights of some indigenous people more than others. Some indigenous people were better able than others to prevent land from slipping away. How can we explain the differences among these stories? Why was colonial land policy with respect to indigenous people so different in places that were otherwise so similar?

One factor that was clearly relevant was the presence or absence of agriculture before European contact. Where indigenous people were farmers—in New Zealand, Hawaii, Fiji, and Tonga—whites formally recognized them as the owners of their land. The strength of this recognition varied considerably in actual practice, but in these places there was never a formal policy of *not* recognizing indigenous property rights in land. Where indigenous people lacked agriculture before European contact—in Australia, California, British Columbia, Oregon/Washington, and Alaska—the colonial acknowledgment of indigenous property rights was weaker or nonexistent.

Farming thus led to the recognition of property rights, but the mechanism by which it did so is less clear. On the one hand, there was a long European intellectual tradition of associating agriculture with the ownership of land. Farmers obviously mixed their labor with the land. They drew boundaries between their parcels. This way of thinking no doubt predisposed English-speakers to think of farmers as landowners, regardless of the farmers' skin color. On the other hand, the indigenous societies that practiced agriculture also tended to be more technologically advanced in other ways than the societies that did not. They tended to form larger political units and to be more formidable military opponents. Those factors would also have made it more likely that colonizers would recognize indigenous property rights simply as a matter of self-defense, even if indigenous people had not also been farmers. It is hard to disentangle the effects of agriculture from the effects of military and technological power.

The importance of indigenous agriculture to the decision whether to recognize indigenous property rights is something that can only be inferred from actual practice, because neither Britain nor the United States ever made such a distinction as a matter of formal policy. Both empires were long accustomed to purchasing land from (and thus recognizing the property rights of) the nonfarming tribes in the interior of North America, and indeed both continued doing so even *after* adopting terra nullius in selected parts of the Pacific. When the Colonial Office approved terra nullius in Australia and British Columbia, and when Congress and the Interior Department effectively implemented terra nullius in California, it thus seems unlikely that anyone involved conceived that either Britain or the United States was laying down a general rule to govern all future colonies. Neither government ever announced such a rule. Rather, Australia, British Columbia, and California were understood as local exceptions to a general practice of acquiring land by treaty.

A second factor contributing to differences in colonial land policy was the degree of indigenous political organization. Again, this was never explicitly declared by either Britain or the United States as formal policy; it can only be inferred from actual practice. In Australia and on the west coast of North America, tribes were too small and too divided to formulate any sort of unified land policy in response to white settlement. The importance of indigenous political organization can be seen most clearly in the four Polynesian agricultural colonies. Two of them, New Zealand and Fiji, were likewise divided into multiple small tribes. In these colonies, indigenous people sold a large amount of land to settlers relatively soon after the onset of significant white settlement. Members of small tribes at war with other small tribes found it useful to have white allies. They found it useful to acquire guns. When areas of land were subject to claims of more than one tribe, each tribe had an incentive to sell it before the other sold it first. There was no supratribal government capable of putting a stop to land sales. The other two agricultural colonies, Hawaii and Tonga, were organized as unitary kingdoms. In these colonies, land was sold either very slowly at first (in Hawaii) or not at all (in Tonga). When indigenous people recognized the dangers posed by selling land, unitary governments were able to promulgate and enforce rules restricting land sales.

A third factor contributing to differences in colonial land policy was the relative speed of white settlement and the establishment of imperial control. Where whites arrived in substantial numbers before the formal exercise of colonial sovereignty, settlers established practices that tended to endure long after the arrival of colonial government. Those practices could be either purchasing or terra nullius. Whites had been purchasing land in New Zealand and Fiji for years before New Zealand and Fiji became British colonies, and the recognition of indigenous people as owners of their land continued afterward. Whites implemented terra nullius in Oregon and California before Oregon and California became parts of the United States, and again that practice continued long afterward, as formal policy in California and as de facto policy in Oregon.

In other places, by contrast, the colonial government arrived before the settlers did, and in these colonies land policy was determined more by the decisions of government officials than by the repeated practices of settlers. British officials were able to declare and implement terra nullius in Australia and British Columbia largely because there were no settlers with prior purchases there to complain. They would have had a much harder time doing so in New Zealand or Fiji, and the U.S. government would have a much harder time doing so in Hawaii, because terra nullius would have disappointed all the settlers who had already purchased land from indigenous people. Colonial land policy was highly path dependent. Early land acquisition practices, sometimes adopted very informally in response to local conditions, tended to harden as formal colonial policy in later years, as the imperial governments of Britain and the United States had little choice but to comply with established local practice.

Many of the differences in land policy among Pacific colonies can be explained by these three factors—the presence of agriculture before contact, the degree of indigenous political organization, and the relative speed of white settlement and the establishment of imperial control. They don't explain everything. We can divide the residual causes of difference into two categories, a long-term trend and several case-specific contingencies.

The trend is that over the course of the nineteenth century, whites in Britain and the United States who considered themselves to be concerned with the welfare of indigenous people grew progressively disenchanted with the tradition of acquiring land by treaty. This was particularly true in the United States, where treaties were abolished in 1871. The shift in thought clearly played a part in the adoption of terra nullius in British Columbia and the development of a watered down form of terra nullius in Alaska. Had either been colonized fifty years earlier, land might well have been acquired by treaty. The disenchantment with treaties also played a role, although perhaps a murkier one, in California and Oregon, where it most likely dampened the political force behind the ratification of the treaties of the early 1850s.

Much also depended on local contingencies. In some places, individual colonial administrators played an important role in formulating land policy. Had the first governor of British Columbia been someone other than James Douglas, or had the first governor of Fiji been someone other than Arthur Gordon, events in these colonies might have gone very differently. In other places, indigenous people made strategic decisions in response to perceived needs specific to the time and place. Had the Hawaiian nobility been unaware of events elsewhere in the Pacific, or had they been more confident in their ability to withstand annexation, they might never have undertaken land tenure reform at midcentury. Had the Maori of the North Island not come together in a concerted effort to put a halt to land sales in the 1850s, the colonial government of New Zealand might never have created the Native Land Court. These sorts of contingencies frustrate any attempt to reduce land policy to the output of a set of general principles.

These differences among colonies matter more today than they did in the nineteenth century. They *did* matter to some extent in the nineteenth century: Hawaiians, Tongans, and Fijians, for example, held on to much more of their land than indigenous people elsewhere in the Pacific, and colonial land policy was partly responsible. But for some indigenous groups in the nineteenth century, the formal recognition of their property rights in land had little practical effect on their lives. By the end of the century, the Maori occupied a social and economic position not much better than that of Aboriginal Australians, despite the dramatic difference in the colonial property law of Australia and New Zealand, and to the extent the Maori were better situated, that was attributable to a variety of causes of which land policy was just one. The Indians of Oregon and

Washington, whose land was formally acquired by treaty, were not much better off than the Indians of California, whose land was taken by force, and again, to the extent they *were* better off, that was due to a range of factors within which land policy may not have been especially prominent. It would be hard to say that the tribes living at the southern tip of Vancouver Island, whose land was acquired by treaty, ended up in better circumstances than the tribes living in the rest of British Columbia, whose land was not. The formal choice of land acquisition method was, in much of the Pacific, peripheral to actual on-the-ground outcomes in the nineteenth century.

A century later, the formal colonial law governing land acquisition has come to matter a great deal. As indigenous people throughout the region gained political power in the second half of the twentieth century, their claims for redress for the misdeeds of the colonial past began to be taken more seriously.[3] Many of those claims were for land wrongfully taken. Some were political, directed at the present-day sympathies of the voting public, but many others were legal, filed in court. The legal claims tended to be evaluated by the law in effect at the time of the actions complained of—not the law of the present, or some abstract standard of justice, but the law that the colonists themselves established and by which they considered themselves governed. Differences between colonies in the colonial law governing indigenous land have thus acquired a new importance in recent decades. And because the realistic possibility of winning a lawsuit is often the best leverage for obtaining an attractive political settlement, differences in colonial law are important today in a political as well as a legal sense.

Decisions made in the nineteenth century about how to separate indigenous people from their land—decisions often made locally, without much thought as to their long-term implications—thus continue to shape our lives today.

Abbreviations

Notes

Index

Abbreviations

AJHR	*Appendix to the Journal of the [New Zealand] House of Representatives*
ANZ	Archives New Zealand, Wellington
ASA	Alaska State Archives, Juneau
ASL	Alaska State Library, Juneau
ATL	Alexander Turnbull Library, Wellington
BCA	British Columbia Archives, Victoria
BL	British Library, London
BPPA	*British Parliamentary Papers: Colonies: Australia* (Shannon: Irish University Press, 1968–)
BPPC	*British Parliamentary Papers: Colonies: Canada* (Shannon: Irish University Press, 1968–71)
BPPNZ	*British Parliamentary Papers: Colonies: New Zealand* (Shannon: Irish University Press, 1968–70)
BRB	Beinecke Rare Book and Manuscript Library, Yale University, New Haven
HHS	Hawaiian Historical Society, Honolulu
HL	Huntington Library, San Marino, California
HSA	Hawaii State Archives, Honolulu
ML	Mitchell Library, Sydney
NZPD	*New Zealand Parliamentary Debates*
OHS	Oregon Historical Society, Portland
PRO	U.K. National Archives (formerly called the Public Record Office), Kew
SRNSW	State Records New South Wales, Sydney
UA	University of Auckland Library
UCB	Bancroft Library, University of California, Berkeley
UCSD	Mandeville Special Collections Library, University of California, San Diego
UO	Knight Library, University of Oregon, Eugene

Notes

Introduction

1. David Igler, "Diseased Goods: Global Exchanges in the Eastern Pacific Basin, 1770–1850," *American Historical Review* 109 (2004): 693–719.

2. The most thorough analysis to date is in chapter 4 of John C. Weaver, *The Great Land Rush and the Making of the Modern World, 1650–1900* (Montreal: McGill-Queen's University Press, 2003), a book that has been extremely helpful to me in thinking of how to structure a comparative history of colonization. Equally helpful for the same reason has been P. G. McHugh, *Aboriginal Societies and the Common Law: A History of Sovereignty, Status, and Self-Determination* (Oxford: Oxford University Press, 2004), although McHugh focuses primarily on indigenous sovereignty rather than property rights.

3. Martti Koskenniemi, *The Gentle Civilizer of Nations: The Rise and Fall of International Law, 1870–1960* (Cambridge: Cambridge University Press, 2002).

4. This section summarizes material discussed in more detail in Stuart Banner, *How the Indians Lost Their Land: Law and Power on the Frontier* (Cambridge, Mass.: Harvard University Press, 2005), chaps. 1 and 2.

5. CO 5/65, p. 43, PRO; *The Papers of Sir William Johnson* (Albany: University of the State of New York, 1921–1965), 3:319.

1. Australia

1. Henry Reynolds, *The Law of the Land* (Ringwood, Victoria: Penguin, 1987).
2. J. C. Beaglehole, ed., *The Journals of Captain Cook on His Voyages of Discovery* (Cambridge: Cambridge University Press, 1955–1974), 1:514.
3. J. M. Bennett and Alex C. Castles, eds., *A Source Book of Australian Legal History* (Sydney: Law Book Company, 1979), 253–254 (emphasis added).
4. Clarence S. Brigham, ed., *British Royal Proclamations Relating to America, 1603–1783* (1911; New York: Burt Franklin, 1964), 212–218; Marete Borch, "Rethinking the Origins of *Terra Nullius*," *Australian Historical Studies* 117 (2001): 222–239.
5. Alan Frost, *Convicts and Empire: A Naval Question, 1776–1811* (Melbourne: Oxford University Press, 1980), 32; Jonathan King, ed., *"In the Beginning . . .": The Story of the Creation of Australia from the Original Writings* (South Melbourne: Macmillan, 1985), 76.
6. Beaglehole, *Journals of Captain James Cook,* 1:312; J. C. Beaglehole, ed., *The* Endeavour *Journal of Joseph Banks, 1768–1771* (Sydney: Angus and Robertson, 1962), 2:122–123; Beaglehole, *Journals of Captain James Cook,* 2:735; King, *"In the Beginning . . . ,"* 115.
7. Walter Raleigh, "A Discourse of the Original and Fundamental Cause of Natural, Arbitrary, Necessary, and Unnatural War," in *The Works of Sir Walter Ralegh, Kt.* (Oxford: Oxford University Press, 1829), 8:255; Emerich de Vattel, *The Law of Nations* (1758), ed. Edward D. Ingraham (Philadelphia: T. and J. W. Johnson, 1853), 36.
8. Beaglehole, *Journals of Captain James Cook,* 1:312, 1:396, 1:393, 2:735.
9. Vattel, *The Law of Nations,* 100.
10. Colin G. Calloway, ed., *Revolution and Confederation* (1994), vol. 18 of Alden T. Vaughan, ed., *Early American Indian Documents: Treaties and Laws, 1607–1789* (Washington, D.C.: University Publications of America, 1979–), 452–453; Beaglehole, *Journals of Captain James Cook,* 1:396; King, *"In the Beginning . . . ,"* 60–61.
11. Beaglehole, *Journals of Captain James Cook,* 1:312, 1:399; King, *"In the Beginning . . . ,"* 55–56.
12. Paul Carter, *The Road to Botany Bay: An Exploration of Landscape and History* (Chicago: University of Chicago Press, 1987); *Historical Records of New South Wales* (Sydney: Charles Potter, 1892–1901), 1(2):1; *A Descrip-*

tion of Botany Bay, on the East Side of New Holland (1787; Sydney: National Library of Australia, 1983), 8.

13. *Historical Records of New South Wales,* 1(2):87; Alan Frost, "New South Wales as *Terra Nullius:* The British Denial of Aboriginal Land Rights," *Historical Studies* 19 (1981): 513–523; Robert J. King, "Terra Australis: Terra Nullius aut Terra Aboriginium?" *Journal of the Royal Australian Historical Society* 72 (1986): 75–91.

14. Karen Ordahl Kupperman, *Indians and English: Facing Off in Early America* (Ithaca, N.Y.: Cornell University Press, 2000); William Dampier, *A New Voyage Round the World* (1697; London: Argonaut Press, 1927), 312; *Historical Records of New South Wales,* 1(2):222, 2:744, 2:748; Beaglehole, *Journals of Captain Cook,* 3:786; *Historical Records of New South Wales,* 2:796, 2:818; William Walker to Richard Watson, 5 Dec. 1821, Bonwick Transcripts, 52:1047, ML; George Caley to Joseph Banks, 16 Feb. 1809, in George Caley, *Reflections on the Colony of New South Wales,* ed. J. E. B. Currey (Melbourne: Landsdowne Press, 1966), 177–178.

15. *Historical Records of New South Wales,* 2:663; Ann Gore to "My dear Mary Ann," 29 Sept. 1837, in Helen Heney, ed., *Dear Fanny: Women's Letters to and from New South Wales, 1788–1857* (Rushcutters Bay, New South Wales: Australian National University Press, 1985), 130; George Worgan to his brother, June 1788, C830, ML; Edward Lucett, *Rovings in the Pacific, from 1837 to 1849* (London: Longman, Brown, Green, and Longmans, 1851), 1:56; John Hunter, *An Historical Journal of the Transactions at Port Jackson and Norfolk Island* (London: John Stockdale, 1793), 58; James Campbell to Dr. Farr, 24 Mar. 1791, Doc. 1174, ML; Robert Mudie, *The Picture of Australia* (London: Whittaker, Treacher, 1829), 228.

16. William Pascoe Crook to Joseph Hardcastle, 8 Nov. 1803, Bonwick Transcripts, 49:215, ML; Nance Irvine, ed., *The Sirius Letters: The Complete Letters of Newton Fowell, Midshipman and Lieutenant Aboard the Sirius* (Sydney: Fairfax Library, 1988), 90; *A Voyage to New South Wales: The Journal of Lieutenant William Bradley RN of HMS* Sirius, *1786–1792* (Sydney: Trustees of the Public Library of New South Wales, 1969), 140; Hunter, *An Historical Journal,* 59–60; *The Voyage of Governor Phillip to Botany Bay* (London: John Stockdale, 1789), 106–107.

17. Watkin Tench, *A Narrative of the Expedition to Botany Bay* (1789), reprinted in Watkin Tench, *Sydney's First Four Years* (Sydney: Angus and Robertson, 1961), 48; J. H. Tuckey, *An Account of a Voyage to Establish a*

Colony at Port Philip in Bass's Strait, on the South Coast of New South Wales (London: Longman, Hurst, Rees, and Orme, 1805), 180.

18. D. Blackburn to R. Knight, 19 Mar. 1791, Ab 163, ML; R. J. B. Knight and Alan Frost, eds., *The Journal of Daniel Paine, 1794–1797* (Sydney: Library of Australian History, 1983), 39; Watkin Tench, *A Complete Account of the Settlement at Port Jackson* (1793), reprinted in Tench, *Sydney's First Four Years,* 281; Thomas M'Combie, *Australian Sketches,* 2nd ed. (Melbourne: Gazette Office, 1847), 244; "Civilization of the Aborigines," *Arden's Sydney Magazine,* Oct. 1843, 66; John Henderson, *Observations on the Colonies of New South Wales and Van Diemen's Land* (Calcutta: Baptist Mission Press, 1832), 152; "A Few Words on the Aborigines of Australia," *New South Wales Magazine* 1 (1843): 58–59; Barron Field, "On the Aborigines of New Holland and Van Diemen's Land," in Barron Field, ed., *Geographical Memoirs on New South Wales* (London: John Murray, 1825), 202–204; Russell to George Gipps, 25 Aug. 1840, BPPA, 8:73.

19. James Holman, *Travels in China, New Zealand, New South Wales, Van Diemen's Land, Cape Horn, etc., etc.,* 2nd ed. (London: George Routledge, 1840), 475; Matthew Flinders, *Observations on the Coasts of Van Diemen's Land, on Bass's Strait and Its Islands, and on Part of the Coasts of New South Wales* (London: John Nicholas, 1801), 20; T. Dove, "Moral and Social Characteristics of the Aborigines of Tasmania," *Tasmanian Journal of Natural Science* 1 (1842): 249; Joseph Orton, *Aborigines of Australia* (London: Thoms, 1836), 3.

20. Robert Scott to his mother, 16 Aug. 1801, Doc. 1109, ML; Peter Cunningham, *Two Years in New South Wales* (London: Henry Colburn, 1827), 2:46; T. Betts, *An Account of the Colony of Van Diemen's Land* (Calcutta: Baptist Mission Press, 1830), 95; Charles James Napier, *Colonization: Particularly in Southern Australia* (London: T. and W. Boone, 1835), 94; James Dredge, *Brief Notices of the Aborigines of New South Wales* (Geelong: James Harrison, 1845), 9–10.

21. Cunningham, *Two Years in New South Wales,* 2:46; James Grant, *The Narrative of a Voyage of Discovery, Performed in His Majesty's Vessel The Lady Nelson* (London: T. Egerton, 1803), 167; David Collins, *An Account of the English Colony in New South Wales* (1798–1802; Christchurch: Whitcombe and Tombs, 1910), 299.

22. Sharon Morgan, *Land Settlement in Early Tasmania: Creating an Antipodean England* (Cambridge: Cambridge University Press, 1992), 143–160;

John C. Weaver, "Beyond the Fatal Shore: Pastoral Squatting and the Occupation of Australia, 1826 to 1852," *American Historical Review* 101 (1996): 981–1007; *Historical Records of New South Wales,* 1(2):346, 2:769; Henry Reynolds, *The Other Side of the Frontier: Aboriginal Resistance to the European Invasion of Australia* (Ringwood, Victoria: Penguin, 1982); BPPA, 3:199.

23. James Scott, *Remarks on a Passage to Botany Bay, 1787–1792* (Sydney: Trustees of the Public Library of New South Wales, 1963), 34; H. W. Breton, *Excursions in New South Wales, Western Australia, and Van Dieman's Land* [sic] (London: Richard Bentley, 1833), 219.

24. *Historical Records of Australia* (Sydney: Library Committee of the Commonwealth Parliament, 1914–), ser. 4, 1:330. There may be earlier formal statements of terra nullius lurking in unpublished court records. Continuous law reporting did not begin in New South Wales until the 1860s.

25. *Historical Records of Australia,* ser. 4, 1:414.

26. Phillip to Nepean, 9 July 1788, *Historical Records of New South Wales,* 1(2):153; William Bradley, manuscript journal, 75 (4 Feb. 1788), A3631, ML; N. G. Butlin, *Economics and the Dreamtime: A Hypothetical History* (Cambridge: Cambridge University Press, 1993), 139.

27. Hunter, *An Historical Journal,* 62; Phillip to Sydney, 13 Feb. 1790, *Historical Records of New South Wales,* 1(2):309; Robert Dawson, *The Present State of Australia,* 2nd ed. (London: Smith, Elder, 1831), 63.

28. Collins, *An Account of the English Colony,* 327; George Fletcher Moore, *Diary of Ten Years Eventful Life of an Early Settler in Western Australia* (London: M. Walbrook, 1884), 259 (diary entry for 26 Mar. 1835); Ian D. Clark, ed., *The Journals of George Augustus Robinson, Chief Protector, Port Phillip Aboriginal Protectorate,* 2nd ed. (Ballarat, Victoria: Heritage Matters, 2000), 2:311 (journal entry for 17 July 1841).

29. King to Hobart, 20 Dec. 1804, *Historical Records of Australia,* ser. 1, 5:166; N. J. B. Plomley, ed., *Friendly Mission: The Tasmania Journals and Papers of George Augustus Robinson, 1829–1834* (Kingsgrove, New South Wales: Tasmanian Historical Research Association, 1966), 88 (journal entry for 23 Nov. 1829).

30. Portland to Hunter, 26 Feb. 1800, *Historical Records of New South Wales,* 4:58.

31. Baudin to King, 23 Dec. 1802, *Historical Records of New South Wales,* 5:830.

32. King to Bligh, n.d., 1807, Philip Gidley King Papers, C189, p. 273, ML.

33. John Ritchie, *Lachlan Macquarie: A Biography* (Carlton, Victoria: Melbourne University Press, 1986), 132; proclamation, 10 Dec. 1814, Supreme Court: Miscellaneous Correspondence Relating to Aborigines, 5/1161, 1:16–17, SRNSW.

34. *Sydney Gazette,* 20 Apr. 1827, 2; *Australia: An Appeal to the World on Behalf of the Younger Branch of the Family of Shem* (Sydney: Spilsbury and M'Eachern, 1839), ix; "New Holland," *South-Asian Register* 2 (1828): 115.

35. Plomley, *Friendly Mission,* 202–203; Lancelot E. Threlkeld, *Report of the Mission to the Aborigines at Lake Macquarie, New South Wales* (Sydney: Herald Office, 1838), 2; *The Report of the Aborigines' Committee of the Meeting for Sufferings, Read at the Yearly Meeting 1840* (London: Harvey and Darton, 1840), 9.

36. *Sydney Herald,* 16 Feb. 1835, 2; *Southern Australian,* 8 May 1839, 3; Paul Edmund de Strzelecki, *Physical Description of New South Wales and Van Diemen's Land* (London: Longman, Brown, Green, and Longmans, 1845), 348 n. *, 340; Dredge, *Brief Notices,* 14; Thomas M'Combie, *Adventures of a Colonist* (London: John and Daniel A. Darling, 1845), 267.

37. Bruce Kercher, "Native Title in the Shadows: The Origins of the Myth of *Terra Nullius* in Early New South Wales Courts," in Gregory Blue et al., eds., *Colonialism and the Modern World: Selected Studies* (Armonk, N.Y.: M. E. Sharpe, 2002), 100–119; Bruce Kercher, "The Recognition of Aboriginal Status and Laws in the Supreme Court of New South Wales under Forbes, CJ, 1824–1836," in A. R. Buck, John McLaren, and Nancy E. Wright, eds., *Land and Freedom: Law, Property Rights and the British Diaspora* (Aldershot: Ashgate, 2001), 83–102; *R. v. Lowe* (1827), in Bruce Kercher, ed., *Decisions of the Superior Courts of New South Wales, 1788–1899,* www.law.mq.edu.au/scnsw.

38. *R. v. Jackey* (1834), *R. v. Lego'me* (1835), *R. v. Murrell* (1836), in Kercher, *Decisions.*

39. Paul Knaplund, *James Stephen and the British Colonial System, 1813–1847* (Madison: University of Wisconsin Press, 1953), 83–84; *British Parliamentary Papers: Anthropology: Aborigines,* 2:4, 5, 82–83.

40. Grey to Torrens, 15 Dec. 1835, CO 13/3, p. 112, PRO; Julie Cassidy, "A Reappraisal of Aboriginal Land Policy in Colonial Australia: Imperial and Colonial Instruments and Legislation Recognising the Special Rights and

Status of the Australian Aboriginals," *Journal of Legal History* 10 (1989): 365–379.

41. Torrens to Grey, Dec. 1835, CO 13/3, p. 161, PRO; "First Annual Report of the Colonization Commissioners for South Australia," 14 June 1836, BPPA, 4:480; "Second Letter of Instructions by the Colonization Commissioners for South Australia to James Hurtle Fisher, Esq., Resident Commissioner in South Australia," 8 Oct. 1836, BPPA, 5:192.

42. Gawler to Russell, 1 Aug. 1840, CO 13/16, p. 56, PRO.

43. James Bonwick, *John Batman: The Founder of Victoria,* 2nd ed. (1868), ed. C. E. Sayers (Melbourne: Wren, 1973), 84–87; enclosure in Mercer to Glenelg, 6 Apr. 1836, *Historical Records of Australia,* ser. 1, 18:389; opinion of the lawyer and MP William Burge, 16 Jan. 1836, reprinted in William Westgarth, *Australia Felix* (Edinburgh: Oliver and Boyd, 1848), 394–397; George Grey to George Mercer, 14 Apr. 1836, *Historical Records of Australia,* ser. 1, 18:390.

44. A. G. L. Shaw, "British Policy towards the Australian Aborigines, 1830–1850," *Australian Historical Studies* 25 (1992): 265–285; J. M. Bennett, ed., *Some Papers of Sir Francis Forbes* (Sydney: Parliament of New South Wales, 1998), 228; *R. v. Steele* (1834), in Kercher, *Decisions;* Normanby to Gipps, 29 June 1839, CO 202/40, p. 127, PRO; *Attorney-General v. Brown,* 1 Legge 312 (1847); A. R. Buck, "'Strangers in Their Own Land': Capitalism, Dispossession and the Law," in Buck, McLaren, and Wright, *Land and Freedom,* 39–56.

45. BPPA, 2:147; Campbell to Burton, 22 June 1838, Supreme Court: Miscellaneous Correspondence Relating to Aborigines, 5/1161, 2:492, SRNSW; Clement Hodgkinson, *Australia, from Port Macquarie to Moreton Bay* (London: T. and W. Boone, 1845), 242; Henry William Haygarth, *Reminiscences of Bush Life in Australia, during a Residence of Eight Years in the Interior* (1848; London: John Murray, 1861), 107.

46. *Sydney Gazette,* 19 Aug. 1824, 4; Richard Windeyer, "On the Rights of the Aborigines of Australia" (ca. 1842), A1400, p. 32, ML; *Southern Australian,* 8 May 1839, 2; "The Aborigines of New Holland," *The Blossom* 1 (1828): 46–47; *Sydney Herald,* 5 Dec. 1838, 2; Richard Howitt, *Impressions of Australia Felix, during Four Years' Residence in That Colony* (London: Longman, Brown, Green, and Longmans, 1845), 277; Samuel Kittle, *A Concise History of the Colony and Natives of New South Wales* (Edinburgh: Oliver and Boyd, 1815), 7.

47. *Report from the Select Committee on the Aborigines and Protectorate* (Sydney: W. W. Davies, 1849), 20; Edward Stone Parker, *The Aborigines of Australia* (Melbourne: Hugh M'Coll, 1854), 30; N. G. Butlin, *Forming a Colonial Economy, Australia, 1810–1850* (Cambridge: Cambridge University Press, 1994), 210–213.

48. William Pridden, *Australia, Its History and Present Condition,* 2nd ed. (London: James Burns, 1845), 72–73; *Graham's Town Journal,* 22 Feb. 1844, CO 386/155, p. 164, PRO; Lachlan Macquarie, *Journals of His Tours in New South Wales and Van Diemen's Land, 1810–1822* (Sydney: Trustees of the Public Library of New South Wales, 1956), 160.

49. R. H. W. Reece, *Aborigines and Colonists: Aborigines and Colonial Society in New South Wales in the 1830s and 1840s* (Sydney: Sydney University Press, 1974), 166–169.

50. Saxe Bannister, *Humane Policy; or Justice to the Aborigines of New Settlements* (London: Thomas and George Underwood, 1830), 51, 87; *Report from the Committee on the Aborigines Question* (Sydney: J. Spilsbury, 1838), 31, 33; Alexander Maconochie, *Thoughts on Convict Management* (Hobart: J. C. MacDougall, 1838), 192; Christopher Pemberton Hodgson, *Reminiscences of Australia, with Hints on the Squatter's Life* (London: W. N. Wright, 1846), 76; *Report from the Select Committee on the Condition of the Aborigines* (Sydney: W. W. Davies, 1845), 10.

51. Grey quoted in Henry Reynolds, *An Indelible Stain? The Question of Genocide in Australia's History* (Ringwood, Victoria: Viking, 2001), 99; William Walker to Richard Watson, 29 Nov. 1821, Bonwick Transcripts, 52:1043–44, ML.

52. BPPA, 2:211, 2:216–217.

53. Heather Goodall, *Invasion to Embassy: Land in Aboriginal Politics in New South Wales, 1770–1992* (St. Leonards, New South Wales: Allen and Unwin, 1996), 44–56; Macquarie to Bathurst, 24 Feb. 1820, BPPA, 4:155; Macquarie to Bathurst, 27 July 1822, BPPA, 3:329; proclamation, June 1838, Supreme Court: Miscellaneous Correspondence Relating to Aborigines, 5/1161, 2:495, SRNSW.

54. Glenelg to Bourke, 13 Apr. 1836, *Historical Records of Australia,* ser. 1, 18:379; Grey to Mercer, 14 Apr. 1836, *Historical Records of Australia,* ser. 1, 18:390; *South Australian Register,* 1 Aug. 1840, 5.

55. CO 1/63, pp. 119, 116, PRO; *The Declaration of the Gentlemen, Merchants, and Inhabitants of Boston* (Boston, 1689), in W. H. Whitmore, ed., *The Andros Tracts* (Boston: Prince Society, 1868–1874), 1:15–16.

2. New Zealand

1. John Savage, *Some Account of New Zealand* (1807; Christchurch: Capper Press, 1973), 3; J. C. Beaglehole, ed., *The Journals of Captain James Cook on His Voyages of Discovery* (Cambridge: Cambridge University Press, 1955–1974), 1:188, 183; J. C. Beaglehole, ed., *The* Endeavour *Journal of Joseph Banks 1768–1771*, 2nd ed. (Sydney: Halstead Press, 1963), 1:417.

2. William Richard Wade, *A Journey in the Northern Island of New Zealand* (1842; Christchurch: Capper Press, 1977), 19; John Rawson Elder, ed., *The Letters and Journals of Samuel Marsden 1765–1838* (Dunedin, NZ: Otago University Council, 1932), 100; John King, Journal, 25–26 May 1819, qMS-1111, ATL; Augustus Earle, *Narrative of a Residence in New Zealand* (1832), ed. E. H. McCormick (Oxford: Clarendon Press, 1966), 62–63.

3. *New Zealand Journal* 4 (1844): 399; William Brown, *New Zealand and Its Aborigines* (London: Smith, Elder, 1845), 163; James Radcliffe, Report on the Aborigines of New Zealand (1842), 3–4, fMS-Papers-4086, ATL.

4. Angela Ballara, "Porangahau: The Formation of an Eighteenth-Century Community in Southern Hawke's Bay," *New Zealand Journal of History* 29 (1995): 7; I. H. Kawharu, *Maori Land Tenure: Studies of a Changing Institution* (Oxford: Oxford University Press, 1977), 58–63; New Zealand Ministry of Maori Affairs, *Customary Maori Land and Sea Tenure: Nga Tikanga Tiaki Taonga O Nehera* (Wellington: Ministry of Maori Affairs, 1991), 14.

5. Richard Taylor, *Te Ika a Maui, or New Zealand and Its Inhabitants* (1855; Wellington: A. H. and A. W. Reed, 1974), 385–386; J. C. Firth to [recipient illegible], 16 Nov. 1865, MS-Papers-5059, ATL.

6. Peter Cleave, "Tribal and State-like Political Formations in New Zealand Maori Society 1750–1900," *Journal of the Polynesian Society* 92 (1983): 53–54; J. M. McEwen, *Rangitane: A Tribal History* (Auckland: Reed Methuen, 1986), 58–59; Raymond Firth, *Economics of the New Zealand Maori* (Wellington: A. R. Shearer, 1972), 374, 378; Pei te Hurinui Jones and Bruce Biggs, *Nga Iwi o Tainui: The Traditional History of the Tainui People* (Auckland: Auckland University Press, 1995), 324–325.

7. Kwen Fee Lian, "Tribe, Class and Colonisation: The Political Organisation of Maori Society in the 19th Century," *Journal of the Polynesian Society* 101 (1992): 392–393; Judith Binney, Judith Bassett, and Erik Olssen, *The People and the Land: Te Tangata me Te Whenua; An Illustrated History*

of New Zealand, 1820–1920 (Wellington: Allen and Unwin, 1990), 144; John White, *The Ancient History of the Maori* (Wellington: George Didsbury, 1888), 5:121; Adolphus James Ross, statement to the Correspondence Committee of the Church Missionary Society, 1 Aug. 1837, last page, translation of undated letter, qMS-1722, ATL.

8. I. H. Kawharu, introduction to *Conflict and Compromise: Essays on the Maori since Colonisation,* ed. I. H. Kawharu (Wellington: A. H. and A. W. Reed, 1975), 9–10; Kawharu, *Maori Land Tenure,* 55–58; Alan Ward, "Alienation Rights in Traditional Maori Society: A Comment," *Journal of the Polynesian Society* 95 (1986): 259–265.

9. W. S. Holdsworth, *A History of English Law* (London: Methuen, 1936–1972), 9:92–94.

10. William Swainson, *A Review of "The Art of Colonization"* (1850; Auckland: Pettifogging Press, 1987), 27, 29; Te Rangi Hiroa (Peter Buck), *The Coming of the Maori* (Wellington: Maori Purposes Fund Board, 1949), 381–382; Douglas Sinclair, "Land: Maori View and European Response," in Michael King, ed., *Te Ao Hurihuri: Aspects of Maoritanga* (Auckland: Reed, 1992), 64; Eddie Durie, "The Law and the Land," in Jock Phillips, ed., *Te Whenua, Te Iwi: The Land and the People* (Wellington: Allen and Unwin, 1987), 78.

11. Nin Tomas, "Land, Sovereignty and Tino Rangatiratanga in Aotearoa," in Emma Greenwood, Klaus Newman and Andrew Sartori, eds., *Work in Flux* (Parkville, Australia: University of Melbourne History Department, 1995), 23; Hong-Key Yoon, *Maori Mind, Maori Land* (Bern: Peter Lang, 1986), 18; Frances Porter, *Born to New Zealand: A Biography of Jane Maria Atkinson* (1989; Wellington: Bridget Williams Books, 1995), 56–58; George Augustus Selwyn and William Martin, *England and the New Zealanders* (Auckland: College Press, 1847), 51.

12. 1876 NZ Stats., no. 47, sec. 41; 1886 NZ Stats., no. 49, sec. 60; 1886 NZ Stats., no. 50, sec. 62; Tom Brooking, *Lands for the People? The Highland Clearances and the Colonisation of New Zealand; A Biography of John McKenzie* (Dunedin, NZ: University of Otago Press, 1996), 79.

13. NZPD, 15:1369; Thomas Hobbes, *De Cive* (1642), in Bernard Gert, ed., *Man and Citizen* (Garden City: Anchor Books, 1972), 116–117; John Locke, *Two Treatises of Government* (1698), ed. Peter Laslett, 2nd ed. (Cambridge: Cambridge University Press, 1970), 312; F. E. Maning, *Old New Zealand: A Tale of the Good Old Times* (1863; Auckland: Golden Press, 1973), 79–80; BPPNZ, 2:71.

14. BPPNZ, 1 Commons 42; W. L. Rees, *Reports of Meetings Held, and Addresses Given, by Mr. W. L. Rees, in Poverty Bay and Tologa Bay, upon the Subject of Native Lands* (Gisborne: Henry Edwin Webb, 1879), 1.

15. Charles Hursthouse, *New Zealand, or Zealandia, the Britain of the South* (London: Edward Stanford, 1857), 177; Arthur S. Thomson, *The Story of New Zealand* (1859; Christchurch: Capper Press, 1974), 1:98; *New Zealand Gazette,* 4 Oct. 1843, 2; undated memo (received 12 May 1871), MA 13/2c, ANZ; Thomas Buddle, *The Aborigines of New Zealand* (Auckland: Williamson and Wilson, 1851), 46.

16. M. P. K. Sorrenson, *Maori Origins and Migrations* (Auckland: Auckland University Press, 1979), 59; BPPNZ, 1 Lords 61, 1 Lords 117, 2:16, 1 Commons 65, 2:178, 2:230, 1 Lords 61; John Ward, ed., *Supplementary Information relative to New-Zealand* (London: John W. Parker, 1840), 20.

17. William Colenso, "On the Maori Race of New Zealand," *Transactions and Proceedings of the New Zealand Institute, 1868,* 2nd ed. (Wellington: George Didsbury, 1875), 363; Edward Shortland, *Maori Religion and Mythology* (1882; New York: AMS Press, 1977), 90–91; William Yate, *An Account of New Zealand,* 2nd ed. (1835; Shannon: Irish University Press, 1970), 103–104; BPPNZ, 2:App. 355–356; Ernst Dieffenbach, *Travels in New Zealand* (1843; Christchurch: Capper Press, 1974), 2:114; BPPNZ, 2:26; William Swainson, *New Zealand and Its Colonization* (London: Smith, Elder, 1859), 151.

18. William Martin, *The Taranaki Question* (1860; Dunedin, NZ: Hocken Library, 1967), 8–9; Rees, *Reports of Meetings Held,* 2; Singleton Rochfort, *The Constitutional Law of England in Its Relation to Colonial Settlements* (Auckland: Southern Cross Office, 1860), 11; Michael Belgrave, "The Waitangi Tribunal: Reviewing the Past; Changing the Future," in *Proceedings of the Symposium on New Zealand and the Pacific: Structural Change and Societal Response* (Hamilton, NZ: Waikato University, 1987), 97.

19. Russell to Hobson, 9 Dec. 1840, CO 209/8, p. 480, PRO; Stephen to Vernon Smith, 28 July 1839, CO 209/4, p. 343–344, PRO.

20. Peter Adams, *Fatal Necessity: British Intervention in New Zealand, 1830–1847* (Auckland: Auckland University Press, 1977), 176–187; Paul Moon, *Te Ara Kī Te Tiriti: The Path to the Treaty of Waitangi* (Auckland: David Ling, 2002).

21. John Beecham, *Colonization: Being Remarks on Colonization in General, with an Examination of the Proposals of the Association Which Has Been*

Formed for Colonizing New Zealand, 3rd ed. (London: Hatchards, 1838), 4; Dandeson Coates, *The New Zealanders and Their Lands* (London: Hatchards, Seeleys, Nisbet, 1844), 25; Michael Belgrave, *The Recognition of Aboriginal Tenure in New Zealand, 1840–1860* (Waitangi Tribunal, WAI 45/G4, n.d.), 4; Edward Gibbon Wakefield, *The British Colonization of New Zealand* (London: John W. Parker, 1837), 53–54.

22. *New Zealand Gazette,* 9 Aug. 1843, 2; BPPNZ, 5:524; Selwyn and Martin, *England and the New Zealanders,* 39.

23. Ian Wards, *The Shadow of the Land: A Study of British Policy and Racial Conflict in New Zealand, 1832–1952* (Wellington: Department of Internal Affairs, 1968), 385–389; C. Partridge, *Calumny Refuted, the Colonists Vindicated, and the Right Horse Saddled: Or a Brief Review of Mis-Government in New Zealand the Cause of the Native Rebellion* (Auckland: Creighton and Scales, 1864), 13.

24. J. S. Polack, *New Zealand: Being a Narrative of Travels and Adventures during a Residence in that Country between the Years 1831 and 1837* (1838; Christchurch: Capper Press, 1974), 2:205–206; BPPNZ, 1 Lords 48.

25. John Dunmore Lang, *New Zealand in 1839* (London: Smith, Elder, 1839), 14; MSO-Papers-3730, ATL; fMS-257, ATL; BPPNZ, 1 Commons 71–74.

26. Patricia Burns, *Fatal Success: A History of the New Zealand Company* (Auckland: Heinemann Reed, 1989), 89; John Miller, *Early Victorian New Zealand: A Study of Racial Tension and Social Attitudes, 1839–1852* (London: Oxford University Press, 1958), 65–67.

27. *New Zealand Spectator,* 22 Feb. 1845, 4; Duncan Moore, Barry Rigby, and Matthew Russell, *Old Land Claims (Rangahaua Whanui National Theme A)* (Wellington: Waitangi Tribunal, 1997), 258, 279.

28. Paul McHugh, *The Maori Magna Carta: New Zealand Law and the Treaty of Waitangi* (Auckland: Oxford University Press, 1991), 102–103; *R. v. Symonds,* NZPCC 387, 388–389 (1847); 1841 NZ Stats., no. 2, sec. 2.

29. AJHR 1891, G-1, 54; qMS-0891, 90–91, ATL; James Belich, *Making Peoples: A History of the New Zealanders* (Auckland: Penguin, 1996), 225; AJHR 1860, E-6A, 3.

30. BPPNZ, 1 Lords 48, 2:108; Robert McNab, ed., *Historical Records of New Zealand* (Wellington: John Mackay, 1908–1914), 1:547; Selwyn and Martin, *England and the New Zealanders,* 53.

31. Stephens to his mother, 15 Jan. 1843, MS-2053, 1:83, ATL; George French Angas, *Savage Life and Scenes in Australia and New Zealand* (1847;

Wellington: A. H. and A. W. Reed, 1967), 2:50; Alfred N. Brown, Journal of a Visit to the Waikato (1834), MS-Papers-4403-2, 23, ATL; BPPNZ, 1 Lords 115; AJHR 1879, G-1, 2.

32. Ann R. Parsonson, "The Expansion of a Competitive Society: A Study in Nineteenth-Century Maori Social History," *New Zealand Journal of History* 14 (1980): 54; Campbell to her mother, 27 June 1843, qMS-0369, ATL.

33. D. M. Stafford, *Te Arawa: A History of the Arawa People* (Auckland: Reed Books, 1967), 195; Angela Ballara, "The Pursuit of *Mana?* A Re-evaluation of the Process of Land Alienation by the Maori, 1840–1890," *Journal of the Polynesian Society* 91 (1982): 519–541; Lian, "Tribe, Class and Colonisation," 390.

34. Ann Parsonson, "The Challenge to Mana Maori," in Geoffrey W. Rice, ed., *The Oxford History of New Zealand,* 2nd ed. (Auckland: Oxford University Press, 1992), 178–179.

35. Laurie Barber, "Maori Societal Response to Pakeha Entry into the Southern Waikato (1828–1870)," in *Proceedings of the Symposium on New Zealand and the Pacific: Structural Change and Societal Response* (Hamilton, NZ: Waikato University, 1987), 25–26; Richard Hodgskin Jr., *A Narrative of Eight Months' Sojourn in New Zealand* (Coleraine: S. Hart, 1841), 10.

36. Joan Metge, *Cross Cultural Communication and Land Transfer in Western Muriwhenua, 1832–1840* (Waitangi Tribunal, WAI 45/F13, 1992).

37. Claudia Orange, *The Treaty of Waitangi* (Wellington: Allen and Unwin, 1987), 115; G. S. Cooper to Sinclair, 28 June 1852, qMS-1810, no. 145, ATL.

38. Charles Terry, *New Zealand, Its Advantages and Prospects, as a British Colony* (London: T. and W. Boone, 1842), 73; Thomas Cholmondeley, *Ultima Thule: Or, Thoughts Suggested by a Residence in New Zealand* (London: John Chapman, 1854), 189; BPPNZ, 3:72; Wakefield, journal, 21 May 1839, qMS-2101, ATL.

39. Philippa Wyatt, "The Old Land Claims and the Concept of a 'Sale': A Case Study" (M.A. thesis, University of Auckland, 1991), 87–91; Harry C. Evison, *Te Wai Pounamu, The Greenstone Island: A History of the Southern Maori during the European Colonization of New Zealand* (Christchurch: Aoraki Press, 1993), 266–268; Patricia Burns, *Te Rauparaha: A New Perspective* (Wellington: A. H. and A. W. Reed, 1980), 203–204.

40. Beecham, *Colonization,* 29; Montague Hawtrey, "Exceptional Laws in

Favour of the Natives of New Zealand," in Wakefield, *British Colonization,* 400.

41. Elder, *Letters and Journals of Samuel Marsden,* 219; MS-2054, 351, 355, ATL; Brown, *New Zealand and Its Aborigines,* 71; Ronaldson, 9 July 1844, MS-Papers-2456-1, ATL; BPPNZ, 2:40.

42. *New Zealand Gazette,* 6 Sept. 1839, 8; BPPNZ, 1 Lords 61; *R. v. Symonds,* NZPCC 387, 391 (1847).

43. R. P. Boast, *Surplus Lands: Policy-Making and Practice in the Nineteenth Century* (Waitangi Tribunal, WAI 45/F16, 1992), 16.

44. AJHR 1860, E-1, 31; C. G. F. Simkin, *Statistics of New Zealand for the Crown Colony Period, 1840–1852* (Auckland: Auckland University College Department of Economics, 1954), 66–67, 72; Barry Rigby, *Empire on the Cheap: Crown Policies and Purchases in Muriwhenua, 1840–1850* (Waitangi Tribunal, WAI 45/F8, 1992).

45. BPPNZ, 10:555.

46. *New Zealand Journal* 4 (1844): 487; NZPD, 1855:480.

47. Dean Cowie, *Hawke's Bay (Rangahaua Whanui Series, District 11B)* (Wellington: Waitangi Tribunal, 1996), 60, 99; Mantell to Labouchere, 5 July 1856, MS-Micro-48, ATL. Mantell's figures may have been a bit off (see G. V. Butterworth and H. R. Young, *Maori Affairs: A Department and the People Who Made It* [Wellington: Iwi Transition Agency, 1990], 25), but they were not far enough to make much difference.

48. Louis Alexis Chamerovzow, *The New Zealand Question and the Rights of Aborigines* (London: T. C. Newby, 1848), 382, 386.

49. McLean, diary, 27 Sept. 1844, MS-Micro-0664, ATL; AJHR 1871, A-2a, 18.

50. Edward Shortland, *Traditions and Superstitions of the New Zealanders,* 2nd ed. (1856; Christchurch: Capper Press, 1980), 284–285; LE 1/1854/106, ANZ; AJHR 1858, C-3, 42–43.

51. Giselle Byrnes, "Surveying—Maori and the Land: An Essay in Historical Representation," *New Zealand Journal of History* 31 (1997): 85–98; White, MS-Papers-4542, 10, ATL; Mantell, 5 Sept. 1848, MS-1543, ATL; *New Zealand Spectator,* 21 July 1847, 3; Keith Sinclair, *The Maori Land League* (Auckland: Auckland University College, 1950), 11; Rogan to McLean, 16 Feb. 1855, MS-1318, 29, ATL.

52. BPPNZ, 10:514; *New Zealand Spectator,* 24 Dec. 1856, 3; Keith Sinclair, *The Origins of the Maori Wars,* 2nd ed. (Auckland: Auckland University

Press and Oxford University Press, 1961), 75; Thomas Buddle, *The Maori King Movement in New Zealand* (1860; New York: AMS Press, 1979), 51; MA 1/2/63/69, ANZ; Judith Binney, *Redemption Songs: A Life of Te Kooti Arikirangi Te Turuki* (Auckland: Auckland University Press, 1995), 36.

53. AJHR 1860, E-6a, 4; AJHR 1861, E-1, 11–12; James Buller, *Forty Years in New Zealand* (London: Hodder and Stoughton, 1878), 407; *New Zealand Spectator,* 23 June 1860, 3; A. G. Bagnall, "No Known Copy? T. S. Grace's Suppressed Circular, W264," *Turnbull Library Record* 15 (1982): 77–92; H. Halse to McLean, 31 Aug. 1857, J. Flight to McLean, 9 Apr. 1857, MS-1319, 166, 97, ATL.

54. M. P. K. Sorrenson, "The Politics of Land," in J. G. A. Pocock, ed., *The Maori and New Zealand Politics* (Auckland: Blackwood and Janet Paul, 1965), 23; M. D. N. Campbell, "The Evolution of Hawke's Bay Landed Society, 1850–1914" (Ph.D. diss., Victoria University, 1972), 38; Michael Belgrave, "Pre-emption, the Treaty of Waitangi, and the Politics of Crown Purchase," *New Zealand Journal of History* 31 (1997): 36–37; Sinclair, *Origins,* 58–59; Renata Tamakihikurangi, *Renata's Speech and Letter to the Superintendent of Hawke's Bay on the Taranaki War Question* (Wellington: Spectator Office, 1861), 11.

55. James Belich, *The New Zealand Wars and the Victorian Interpretation of Racial Conflict* (Auckland: Penguin, 1988); *Daily Southern Cross,* 19 Dec. 1868, 4; AJHR 1891, G-1, 39.

3. New Zealand

1. Aristoboulos, *The Universal Destruction of the Aboriginal Races by Colonizing Nations, and Eventually of the New Zealanders: The Cause of This Evil and Its Sure Preventive* (London: Smith, Elder, 1847), 23–24.

2. Edmund Bohan, *Edward Stafford: New Zealand's First Statesman* (Christchurch: Hazard Press, 1994), 140; AJHR 1860, E-1, 25, 31.

3. Hadfield to C. W. Richmond, 8 Feb. 1858, in Guy H. Scholefield, ed., *The Richmond-Atkinson Papers* (Wellington: R. E. Owen, 1960), 1:347; NZPD, 1861:307; LE 1/1860/227, ANZ.

4. AJHR 1862, E-5, 11; NZPD, 1862:684.

5. *Taranaki Herald,* 26 Feb. 1859, 3; AJHR, 1891, G-1, 14.

6. *New Zealand Gazette,* 22 June 1842, 3; *New Zealand Spectator,* 17 June 1848, 2; *New Zealand Spectator,* 10 Oct. 1846, 2.

7. AJHR 1871, A-1, 5; Morgan to Secretaries of the Church Missionary Society, 29 May 1861, qMS-1392, 712, ATL.

8. NZPD, 1862:690.

9. James Buller, *Forty Years in New Zealand* (London: Hodder and Stoughton, 1878), 405; MA 16/3, clipping pasted to back of page 5, ANZ.

10. MA 1/1/60/82, ANZ.

11. NZPD, 11:35; BPPNZ, 10:512.

12. BPPNZ, 10:560; Locke to McLean, 23 Jan. 1865, MS-1329, 162–163, ATL; BPPNZ, 10:556; AJHR 1867, A-10, 7.

13. LE 1/1854/106, ANZ; AJHR 1860, E-1c, 9–10, 31.

14. A. H. McLintock, *Crown Colony Government in New Zealand* (Wellington: R. E. Owen, 1958), 344–345; Frances Porter, *Born to New Zealand: A Biography of Jane Maria Atkinson* (1989; Wellington: Bridget Williams Books, 1995), 155–156.

15. J. G. A. Pocock, "Tangata Whenua and Enlightenment Anthropology," *New Zealand Journal of History* 26 (1992): 42–43; AJHR 1871, A-2a, 15; Charles Brown, "Memorandum on the Present Condition of the North Island" (1863), 9, MS-0319, ATL.

16. AJHR 1867, A-10, 8; NZPD, 1861:297, 248; AJHR 1862, E-5, 11.

17. AJHR 1860, E-1, 7; AJHR 1880, G-4, 15; NZPD, 1865:624; NZPD, 24:253–254; Flight to McLean, 19 Aug. 1855, MS-1318, 47, ATL; NZPD, 11:35.

18. NZPD, 14:616–617.

19. 1865 NZ Stats., no. 71; David V. Williams, *"Te Kooti Tango Whenua": The Native Land Court, 1864–1909* (Wellington: Huia, 1999).

20. AJHR 1867, A-10, 4; Maning to McLean, 20 Feb. 1867, MS-1333, 41, ATL; AJHR 1867, A-10, 8.

21. AJHR 1873, G-7, 2.

22. 1869 NZ Stats., no. 26, sec. 15; 1873 NZ Stats., no. 56, secs. 59, 62, 38; 1878 NZ Stats., no. 40, sec. 6.

23. AJHR 1880, G-4, 14.

24. John Lincoln Hutton, "'Troublesome Specimens': A Study of the Relationship between the Crown and the Tangata Whenua of Hauraki 1863–1869" (M.A. thesis, University of Auckland, 1995), 109, 143.

25. AJHR 1871, A-2a, 18; AJHR 1868, A-11; AJHR 1869, A-20; AJHR 1873, G-5; AJHR 1874, G-3; AJHR 1875, G-9; AJHR 1876, G-6; AJHR 1877, G-8; AJHR 1881, G-12; Alan Ward, *National Overview (Waitangi Tribunal Rangahaua Whanui Series)* (Wellington: GP Publications, 1997), 2:248.

26. 1870 NZ Stats. no. 75, secs. 4–6; Ward, *National Overview,* 232; 1878 NZ Stats., no. 40, sec. 4; AJHR 1867, A-10, 4.

27. Pease to Haultain, 9 May 1871, MA 13/2f, ANZ; *Otago Daily Times,* 11 Oct. 1870, 3.

28. NZPD, 3:49; AJHR 1871, A-2, 3; AJHR 1891, G-1, 71.

29. AJHR 1871, A-2a, 14; Fenton to McLean, 12 Aug. 1871, MS-Copy-Micro-0535-052, ATL; MA 13/2e, ANZ; AJHR 1891, G-1, 65.

30. Alan Ward, *A Show of Justice: Racial "Amalgamation" in Nineteenth-Century New Zealand* (1974; Auckland: Auckland University Press, 1995), 256; Whitmore to McLean, 24 Nov. 1864, MS-1329, 96–97, ATL; Fenton to McLean, n.d., MS-Copy-Micro-0535-052, ATL; Raewyn Dalziel, *Julius Vogel: Business Politician* (Auckland: Auckland University Press and Oxford University Press, 1986), 205–206; Eruera Stirling as told to Anne Salmond, *Eruera: The Teachings of a Maori Elder* (Auckland: Oxford University Press, 1980), 74; AJHR 1886, G-13.

31. AJHR 1871, A-2a, 41.

32. AJHR 1871, A-2a, 4; AJHR 1872, I-2; AJHR 1891, G-1, vii; 1867 NZ Stats., no. 43, sec. 17; AJHR 1871, A-2a, 41; Bryan D. Gilling, "Engine of Destruction? An Introduction to the History of the Maori Land Court," *Victoria University of Wellington Law Review* 24 (1994): 131 n. 63; AJHR 1871, A-2a, 50; 1873 NZ Stats., no. 56, sec. 47.

33. Maning, 2 Sept. 1871, MA 13/2e, ANZ; NZPD, 24:251.

34. AJHR 1891, G-1, 75; AJHR 1871, A-2a, 29.

35. Edward William Stafford, "Native Lands" (ca. 1870s), 5, MS-2044, ATL; NZPD, 14:604; 1873 NZ Stats., no. 56, sec. 38; MA 13/2e, ANZ; NZPD, 24:251; 1878 NZ Stats., no. 40, sec. 6.

36. AJHR 1871, A-2a, 28.

37. *New Zealand Mail,* 13 Oct. 1877, 10.

38. AJHR 1891, G-1, 130, minutes 76.

39. AJHR 1891, G-1, 73; White, undated memorandum received 29 June 1871, MA 13/2c, ANZ; AJHR 1891, G-1, 43, 79.

40. Maning to von Stürmer, 3 July 1876, qMS-1235, ATL; *How the Native Land Court and Land Purchase Department Behave on the East Coast: A Series of Letters from an "Occasional Correspondent" to "The Otago Daily Times"* (Auckland: William Atkin, 1877), 25–26; AJHR 1891, G-1, 65–66.

41. Fenton to Native Minister, 3 July 1868, LE 1/1868/130, ANZ; NZPD, 24:251.

42. *Te Wananga,* 11 Dec. 1875, 423; AJHR 1891, G-1, xiii; AJHR 1880, G-5, 14, 8, 23.

43. 1869 NZ Stats., no. 26, secs. 12 and 14.

44. Circular, 20 July 1875, MA 6/1, 291, ANZ; 1873 NZ Stats., no. 56, sec. 35; NZPD, 16:937; 1878 NZ Stats., no. 40, sec. 5; NZPD, 36:178; AJHR 1871, A-2a, 36.

45. Maning to J. Webster, 21 Mar. 1869, quoted in M. P. K. Sorrenson, "The Purchase of Maori Lands, 1865–1892" (M.A. thesis, Auckland University College, 1955), 231–232; Maning to von Stürmer, 5 Aug. ca. 1872, qMS-1238; to von Stürmer, 19 May ca. 1872, qMS-1238; to von Stürmer, n.d. ("Saturday"), ca. 1872, qMS-1238; to von Stürmer, 9 Feb. 1873, qMS-1234; to Jonathan Webster, 7 July 1867, MS-Papers-247; to von Stürmer, 10 Jan. 1872, qMS-1234; to von Stürmer, 13 Mar. 1873, qMS-1234; to von Stürmer, 21 July 1873, qMS-1234; to von Stürmer, 2 Dec. 1876, qMS-1235; to von Stürmer, n.d. ("Friday"), ca. 1879, qMS-1235; to von Stürmer, 30 Nov. 1879, qMS-1235; all ATL.

46. Miles Fairburn, *Nearly Out of Heart and Hope: The Puzzle of a Colonial Labourer's Diary* (Auckland: Auckland University Press, 1995), 18.

47. AJHR 1884, G-1, 17; AJHR 1891, G-1, 9.

48. Cuthbert Edgar Peek to his father, 8 Apr. 1883, MS-Papers-3602, ATL; AJHR 1891, G-1, 78; AJHR 1883, G-5, 2.

49. Paul Monin, "The Maori Economy of Hauraki, 1840–1880," *New Zealand Journal of History* 29 (1995): 208; AJHR 1891, G-1, 9, 88; NZPD, 46:124

50. *New Zealand Herald,* 2 Mar. 1883, 4; AJHR 1881, G-8, 4; AJHR 1886, G-1, 16; M. P. K. Sorrenson, "Land Purchase Methods and Their Effect on Maori Population, 1865–1901," *Journal of the Polynesian Society* 65 (1956): 183–199.

51. William Martin, *Notes on the Best Mode of Introducing and Working the Native Lands Act* (Auckland: Mitchell and Seffern, 1865), 8; AJHR 1880, G-4, 15; NZPD, 35:221; Seth-Smith to Mackay, 11 Dec. 1890, Mackay to Seth-Smith, 15 Nov. 1890, MLC 8/2, ANZ; Fenton to McLean, n.d., MS-Copy-Micro-0535-052, ATL.

52. AJHR 1891, G-1, 65; MA 13/2e, ANZ; AJHR 1883, G-5, 1; AJHR 1891, G-1, minutes 91; MA 13/2e, ANZ.

53. *New Zealand Herald,* 2 Mar. 1883, 4.

54. *General Rules of Native Land Court* (Wellington: G. Didsbury, 1880), 12–13; AJHR 1891, G-1, 9, 17, 21; AJHR 1871, A-2a, 30.

55. *General Rules,* 9; AJHR 1867, A-10, 5, 10, 8.

56. Heaphy, 15 Apr. 1871, MA 13/2c, ANZ; AJHR 1871, A-2a, 10.

57. AJHR 1871, A-2a, 28; 1873 NZ Stats., no. 56, sec. 44; 1878 NZ Stats., no. 1, sec. 3; *New Zealand Herald,* 2 Mar. 1883, 4.

58. NZPD, 45:458; AJHR 1891, G-1, 115.

59. Land sale prices were further depressed when the colonial government resumed land purchasing on a significant scale in the 1870s. The government, like private purchasers, had to go through the Native Land Court, but it was able to buy land without competition from private purchasers. As in the pre–Land Court era, the government's effective monopsony power enabled it to pay far less for Maori land than private purchasers paid. In the 1870s and 1880s, for example, the government paid, on average, only 53 percent as much as other purchasers. AJHR 1884, C-2; AJHR 1885, G-6.

60. Te Wheoro to McLean, 8 Apr. 1871, MA 13/2b, ANZ.

61. James Belich, *Making Peoples: A History of the New Zealanders* (Auckland: Penguin, 1996), 259; Miles Fairburn, *The Ideal Society and Its Enemies: The Foundations of Modern New Zealand Society, 1850–1900* (Auckland: Auckland University Press, 1989), 92–93; Donald Denoon, *Settler Capitalism: The Dynamics of Dependent Development in the Southern Hemisphere* (Oxford: Clarendon Press, 1983), 224.

62. NZPD, 46:128; NZPD, 37:519; AJHR 1876, G-7, 4; Buller, *Forty Years,* 406.

63. AJHR 1891, G-1, 168; NZPD, 24:391; 11 Feb. 1883, MS-Papers-3602, ATL; Elsdon Craig, *Destiny Well Sown: A Biography of W. E. Gudgeon* (Whakatane: Whakatane and District Historical Society, 1985), 65.

64. *New Zealand Herald,* 18 Mar. 1882, 6; "Native Lands," editorial in unidentified newspaper, 2 Dec. 1897, MLC 8/13, ANZ.

4. Hawaii

1. Cf. Jonathan Kay Kamakawiwoʻle, *Dismembering Lāhui: A History of the Hawaiian Nation to 1887* (Honolulu: University of Hawaii Press, 2002), 44–56; Linda S. Parker, *Native American Estate: The Struggle over Indian*

and Hawaiian Lands (Honolulu: University of Hawaii Press, 1989), 105–115; Maivan Lam, "The Imposition of Anglo-American Land Tenure Law on Hawaiians," *Journal of Legal Pluralism* 23 (1985): 103–128.

2. J. C. Beaglehole, ed., *The Journals of Captain Cook on His Voyages of Discovery* (Cambridge: Cambridge University Press, 1955–1974), 3:521, 524; Joseph Ingraham, *The Log of the Brig Hope* (written in 1791) (Honolulu: Hawaiian Historical Society, 1918), 4, 33; George Vancouver, *A Voyage of Discovery to the North Pacific Ocean and Round the World, 1791–1795* (1798), ed. W. Kaye Lamb (London: Hakluyt Society, 1984), 860 n. 3.

3. Archibald Campbell, *A Voyage Round the World, from 1806 to 1812* (Roxbury, Mass.: Allen and Watts, 1825), 124–125; William Ellis, *A Journal of a Tour around Hawaii, the Largest of the Sandwich Islands* (Boston: Crocker and Brewster, 1825), 28; *Voyage of H.M.S. Blonde to the Sandwich Islands, in the Years 1824–1825* (London: John Murray, 1826), 107; *With Lord Byron at the Sandwich Islands in 1825: Being Extracts from the MS Diary of James Macrae, Scottish Botanist* (Hilo: Petroglyph Press, 1972), 12; Robert Dampier, *To the Sandwich Islands on H.M.S. Blonde,* ed. Pauline King Joerger (Honolulu: University Press of Hawaii, 1971), 34.

4. Ross H. Cordy, "The Effects of European Contact on Hawaiian Agricultural Systems, 1778–1819," *Ethnohistory* 19 (1972): 393–418; O. A. Bushnell, *The Gifts of Civilization: Germs and Genocide in Hawai'i* (Honolulu: University of Hawaii Press, 1993); David E. Stannard, *Before the Horror: The Population of Hawai'i on the Eve of Western Contact* (Honolulu: University of Hawaii, Social Science Research Institute, 1989); Sumner J. La Croix and James Roumasset, "An Economic Theory of Political Change in Premissionary Hawaii," *Explorations in Economic History* 21 (1984): 162–163; Auguste Duhaut-Cilly, *A Voyage to California, the Sandwich Islands, and Around the World in the Years 1826–1829* (1834–1835), trans. and ed. August Frugé and Neal Harlow (San Francisco: Book Club of California, 1997), 217.

5. *Polynesian,* 23 June 1849, 22:1.

6. Marion Kelly, "Changes in Land Tenure in Hawaii, 1778–1850" (M.A. thesis, University of Hawaii, 1956), 1–49; Davianna Pōmaika'i McGregor, "An Introduction to the *Hoa'āina* and Their Rights," *Hawaiian Journal of History* 30 (1996): 6–8; Jocelyn Linnekin, "The *Hui* Lands of Keanae: Hawaiian Land Tenure and the Great Mahele," *Journal of the Polynesian Society* 92 (1983): 169–171.

7. Samuel Manaiakalani Kamakau, *The Works of the People of Old: Na Hana a ka Po'e Kahiko,* trans. Mary Kawena Pukui, ed. Dorothy B. Barrère (Honolulu: Bishop Museum Press, 1976), 8.

8. Samuel M. Kamakau, *Ruling Chiefs of Hawaii* (Honolulu: Kamehameha Schools Press, 1961), 229; T. Dwight Hunt, *The Past and Present of the Sandwich Islands* (San Francisco: Whitton, Towne, 1853), 15–16.

9. William Ellis, *Narrative of a Tour through Hawaii* (London: H. Fisher and P. Jackson, 1826), 399–400; Lilikalā Kame'eleihiwa, *Native Land and Foreign Desires: Ko Hawai'i Āina a me Nā Koi Pu'umake a ka Po'e Haole* (Honolulu: Bishop Museum Press, 1992), 26–33.

10. Proclamation, 14 Mar. 1833, F.O. & Ex., ser. 402, box 3, file 44, HSA; David Malo, *Hawaiian Antiquities,* trans. Nathaniel B. Emerson (1898; Honolulu: Bishop Museum, 1951), 58, 195–196; David Malo, "On the Decrease of Population on the Hawaiian Islands," trans. L. Andrews, *Hawaiian Spectator* 2 (1839): 127.

11. *Narrative of the Adventures and Sufferings of Samuel Patterson* (Palmer, Mass.: The Press in Palmer, 1817), 67–68; Campbell, *A Voyage Round the World,* 111–112.

12. Richard A. Greer, "Notes on Early Land Titles and Tenure in Hawai'i," *Hawaiian Journal of History* 30 (1996): 29–52; G. P. Judd, memorandum, 7 Sept. 1844, F.O. & Ex., ser. 402, box 11, folder 269, HSA.

13. Harold Whitman Bradley, *The American Frontier in Hawaii: The Pioneers, 1789–1843* (Stanford: Stanford University Press, 1942), 278–282; Gavan Daws, "Government and Land in Honolulu to 1850," in Richard A. Greer, ed., *Hawaiian Historical Review: Selected Readings* (Honolulu: Hawaiian Historical Society, 1969), 246–257; Peter R. Mills, "Neo in Oceania: Foreign Vessels Owned by Hawaiian Chiefs before 1830," *Journal of Pacific History* 38 (2003): 53–67; William French et al. to His Majesty Kaukioli, 7 Apr. 1831, F.O. & Ex., ser. 402, box 3, file 36, HSA.

14. Théodore-Adolphe Barrot, *Unless Haste Is Made: A French Skeptic's Account of the Sandwich Islands in 1836,* trans. Daniel Dole (Kailua: Press Pacifica, 1978), 118; Gorham D. Gilman, "1848: Honolulu As it Is—Notes for Amplification" (1848), eds. Jean S. Sharpless and Richard A. Greer, *Hawaiian Journal of History* 4 (1970): 142.

15. James Jackson Jarves, *History of the Hawaiian or Sandwich Islands* (London: Edward Moxon, 1843), 279–280; Anthony Ten Eyck to James Buchanan, 23 Nov. 1847 and 15 Feb. 1848, National Archives microfilm ser.

T30, roll 2, RG 59; minutes, 15 June 1846 and 13 Aug. 1846, Privy Council Records, ser. 421, 1:149, 189–191, HSA; *Polynesian,* 19 June 1841, 7:1.

16. *Polynesian,* 13 Nov. 1841, 90:4; Henry Augustus Wise, *Los Gringos: or, An Inside View of Mexico and California, with Wanderings in Peru, Chili, and Polynesia* (New York: Baker and Scribner, 1849), 374–375.

17. Kathryn E. Holland Braund, *Deerskins and Duffels: The Creek Indian Trade with Anglo-America, 1685–1815* (Lincoln: University of Nebraska Press, 1993), 150–152.

18. *Correspondence Relative to the Sandwich Islands* (London: n.p., 1844), A10–A11; John Turnbull, *A Voyage Round the World in the Years 1800, 1801, 1802, 1803, and 1804,* 2nd ed. (London: A. Maxwell, 1813), 201.

19. William F. Swindler, ed., *Sources and Documents of United States Constitutions* (Dobbs Ferry, N.Y.: Oceana, 1973–1979), 3:16.

20. Gavan Daws, *Shoal of Time: A History of the Hawaiian Islands* (Honolulu: University of Hawaii Press, 1968), 107–108; G. P. Judd, memorandum, 7 Sept. 1844, F.O. & Ex., ser. 402, box 11, folder 269, HSA; minutes, 24 Aug. 1846, Privy Council Records, ser. 421, 2:20, HSA; Brown to Robert Rantoul Jr., 1 Apr. 1846, George Brown Correspondence Collection, HHS; G. P. Judd to William Miller, 2 Apr. 1844, Foreign Office Letterbooks, ser. 410, vol. 1-T, HSA.

21. Jon J. Chinen, *The Great Mahele: Hawaii's Land Division of 1848* (Honolulu: University of Hawaii Press, 1958); *Statute Laws of His Majesty Kamehameha III* (Honolulu: Charles E. Hitchcock, 1846), 107–110.

22. *Polynesian,* 14 Feb. 1846, 169:2; *Principles Adopted by the Board of Commissioners to Quiet Land Titles* (Honolulu: Charles E. Hitchcock, 1847).

23. Petition, 12 June 1845, F.O. & Ex., ser. 402, box 13, folder 316, HSA; petition, Apr. 1845, reproduced in Kameʻeleihiwa, *Native Land and Foreign Desires,* 333; *The Friend,* 1 Aug. 1845, 119:2.

24. Minutes, 9 July 1850 and 10 July 1850, Journal of the Legislature, 1841–1850, ser. 221, vol. 4, HSA; *Polynesian,* 13 July 1850, 34:2.

25. Maivan Clech Lam, "The Kuleana Act Revisited: The Survival of Traditional Hawaiian Commoner Rights to Land," *Washington Law Review* 64 (1989): 287–288; *Polynesian,* 16 Feb. 1850, 157:5.

26. "Final Report of the Board of Commissioners to Quiet Land Titles," in *Report of the Minister of the Interior* (Honolulu: n.p., 1856), 13–15; Jocelyn Linnekin, "Statistical Analysis of the Great Māhele: Some Preliminary

Findings," *Journal of Pacific History* 22 (1987): 27; Jon J. Chinen, *Original Land Titles in Hawaii* (n.p., 1961), 20–21, 32–33.

27. Jon J. Chinen, *They Cried for Help: The Hawaiian Land Revolution of the 1840s and 1850s* (n.p.: Xlibris, 2002), 75–96.

28. William Lee to Titus Coan et al., 9 Dec. 1847, and Lee to J. S. Emerson, 8 Jan. 1848, Supreme Court Letter Book of Chief Justice William Little Lee, 1847–1854, ser. 240, box 1, HSA.

29. Linnekin, "Statistical Analysis," 30; Robert C. Schmitt, *Historical Statistics of Hawaii* (Honolulu: University Press of Hawaii, 1977), 298.

30. C. S. Stewart, *A Residence in the Sandwich Islands,* 5th ed. (Boston: Weeks, Jordan, 1839), 117–118; Gilbert Farquhar Mathison, *Narrative of a Visit to Brazil, Chile, Peru, and the Sandwich Islands, during the Years 1821 and 1822* (London: Charles Knight, 1825), 449–450; Ephraim Eveleth, *History of the Sandwich Islands: With an Account of the American Mission Established There in 1820,* 3rd ed. (Philadelphia: American Sunday-School Union, 1839), 30; Artemas Bishop, "An Inquiry into the Causes of Decrease in the Population of the Sandwich Islands," *Hawaiian Spectator* 1 (1838): 56–57.

31. *Answers to Questions Proposed by His Excellency, R. C. Wyllie, His Hawaiian Majesty's Minister of Foreign Relations* (Honolulu: n.p., 1848), 7–13; *Polynesian,* 31 May 1845, 6:4.

32. William Lee to J. S. Emerson, 23 Dec. 1847, and Lee to C. B. Andrews, 12 Jan. 1848, Supreme Court Letter Book of Chief Justice William Little Lee, 1847–1854, ser. 240, box 1, HSA; William Lee to Kamehameha III, 14 Dec. 1847, F.O. & Ex., ser. 402, box 21, folder 454, HSA.

33. R. C. Wyllie to Kamehameha III, 1 Dec. 1847, F.O. & Ex., ser. 402, box 21, folder 452, HSA; *Polynesian,* 25 Nov. 1848, 110:3.

34. William Lee to J. L. Green, 19 Jan. 1848, Supreme Court Letter Book of Chief Justice William Little Lee, 1847–1854, ser. 240, box 1, HSA; *Kekiekie v. Dennis,* 1 Haw. 42, 43 (1851); *Polynesian,* 3 Feb. 1849, p. 150, and 16 Sept. 1848, p. 70.

35. David Malo to William Richards, 2 June 1846, F.O. & Ex., ser. 402, box 17, file 386, HSA.

36. *Polynesian,* 14 Nov. 1846, p. 103, 26 Dec. 1846, p. 129, and 26 Jan. 1850, p. 147; *Report of the Minister of the Interior* (Honolulu: Polynesian Press, 1845), 9.

37. G. P. Judd, memorandum, 11 Dec. 1847, F.O. & Ex., ser. 402, box 21, folder 453, HSA.

38. Stephen Reynolds Journal, 8 Aug. 1842, HSA; Pomare quoted in Kame'eleihiwa, *Native Land and Foreign Desires,* 189.

39. Samuel N. Castle, *An Account of the Visit of the French Frigate l'Artemise, to the Sandwich Islands, July, 1839* (Honolulu: n.p., 1839); Charles Wilkes, *Narrative of the United States Exploring Expedition* (Philadelphia: Lea and Blanchard, 1845), 4:8–19.

40. Ralph S. Kuykendall, *The Hawaiian Kingdom* (Honolulu: University of Hawaii Press, 1938–1967), 1:206–226.

41. Daws, *Shoal of Time,* 133–134; minutes, 20 Dec. 1849, Privy Council Records, ser. 421, 3:415, HSA; William Lee to "Marshall," 10 Oct. 1854, Supreme Court Letter Book of Chief Justice William Little Lee and others, 1854–1869, ser. 240, box 1, HSA; Charles de Varigny, *Fourteen Years in the Sandwich Islands, 1855–1868* (1874; Honolulu: University Press of Hawaii, 1981), 149.

42. *Wood v. Stark,* 1 Haw. 9, 10 (1847); *Shillaber v. Waldo,* 1 Haw. 21, 22–23 (1847); *Mitchel v. United States,* 34 U.S. 711, 734 (1835).

43. *Johnson v. M'Intosh,* 21 U.S. 543 (1823).

44. Minutes, 18 Dec. 1847, Privy Council Records, ser. 421, 4:304, HSA. Legal historians of mid-nineteenth-century Hawaii conclude that Hawaiians were quick to adopt Anglo-American legal concepts and to use them to their advantage. Sally Engle Merry, *Colonizing Hawai'i: The Cultural Power of Law* (Princeton: Princeton University Press, 2000), 35–114; Mari J. Matsuda, "Law and Culture in the District Court of Honolulu, 1844–1845: A Case Study of the Rise of Legal Consciousness," *American Journal of Legal History* 32 (1988): 16–41.

45. *Principles Adopted by the Board of Commissioners to Quiet Land Titles,* 7; minutes, 11 and 14 Dec. 1847, Privy Council Records, ser. 421, 4:254 and 4:272, HSA; William Lee to R. C. Wyllie, 14 Dec. 1847, F.O. & Ex., ser. 402, box 21, folder 454, HSA. Two decades later, after reading through the Privy Council records from the 1840s, the justices of the Hawaii Supreme Court concluded: "The records of the discussion in Council show plainly his Majesty's anxious desire to free his lands from the burden of being considered public domain, and as such, subjected to the danger of confiscation in the event of his islands being seized by any foreign

power." *In re Estate of His Majesty Kamehameha IV,* 2 Haw. 715, 722 (1864).

46. Minutes, 6 June 1848, Journal of the Legislature, ser. 221, 4:42, HSA.

47. R. C. Wyllie to Gerrit P. Judd, 19 Mar. 1849, in R. C. Wyllie, *Report of the Secretary at War, to the Legislature of 1855* (Honolulu: n.p., 1855), appendix, 7–8.

48. Jean Hobbs, *Hawaii: A Pageant of the Soil* (Stanford: Stanford University Press, 1935), 128.

49. William L. Lee to Joel Turrill, 29 Dec. 1850 and 1 July 1851, in "The Turrill Collection," *Sixty-Sixth Annual Report of the Hawaiian Historical Society for the Year 1957* (Honolulu: Hawaiian Historical Society, 1958), 35, 43; Ethel M. Damon, *Father Bond of Kohala: A Chronicle of Pioneer Life in Hawaii* (Honolulu: The Friend, 1927), 180; Pauline King, ed., *The Diaries of David Lawrence Gregg: An American Diplomat in Hawaii, 1853–1858* (Honolulu: Hawaiian Historical Society, 1982), 69–70.

50. Mark Twain, *Letters from the Sandwich Islands,* ed. G. Ezra Dane (Stanford: Stanford University Press, 1938), 104; Charles Nordhoff, *Northern California, Oregon, and the Sandwich Islands* (1874; Berkeley: Ten Speed Press, 1974), 90; Hugh Wilkinson, *Sunny Lands and Seas* (London: John Murray, 1883), 243.

51. *In re Estate of His Majesty Kamehameha IV,* 2 Haw. 715 (1864).

52. The statute is reproduced in Hobbs, *Hawaii: A Pageant of the Soil,* 68–69.

53. *Liliuokalani v. United States,* 45 Ct. Cl. 418, 426–427 (1910).

5. California

1. James J. Rawls, *Indians of California: The Changing Image* (Norman: University of Oklahoma Press, 1984), 44–55; Lansford W. Hastings, *The Emigrants' Guide, to Oregon and California* (1845; Princeton: Princeton University Press, 1932), 116–117; David H. Coyner, *The Lost Trappers* (1847), ed. David J. Weber (Albuquerque: University of New Mexico Press, 1970), 137; Edmund Randolph, *Address on the History of California from the Discovery of the Country to the Year 1849* (San Francisco: Alta Vista Job Office, 1860), 21; D. Lancelot, *California* (n.p.: privately printed, 1869), 123.

2. Edwin Bryant, *What I Saw in California,* 5th ed. (New York: D.

Appleton, 1849), 266; "The Californian Indians," *New Monthly Magazine* 100 (1854): 181; Daniel B. Woods, *Sixteen Months at the Gold Diggings* (New York: Harper and Bros., 1851), 49.

3. Pringle Shaw, *Ramblings in California* (Toronto: J. Bain, 1857), 77; George Harwood Phillips, *Indians and Intruders in Central California, 1769–1849* (Norman: University of Oklahoma Press, 1993), 99–100, 122; Florence Connolly Shipek, *Pushed into the Rocks: Southern California Indian Land Tenure, 1769–1986* (Lincoln: University of Nebraska Press, 1988), 11–18; Felix P. Wierzbicki, *California As It Is and As It May Be* (1849; San Francisco: Grabhorn Press, 1933), 18; Franklin Langworthy, *Scenery of the Plains, Mountains and Mines* (1855), ed. Paul C. Phillips (Princeton: Princeton University Press, 1932), 189; Richard Owen, *Key to the Geology of the Globe* (Boston: Gould and Lincoln, 1857), 173; Sim Moak, *The Last of the Mill Creeks, and Early Life in California* (Chico: n.p., 1923), 12; Hinton R. Helper, *The Land of Gold* (Baltimore: Henry Taylor, 1855), 268; David Rohrer Leeper, *The Argonauts of 'Forty-Nine: Some Recollections of the Plains and the Diggings* (South Bend: J. B. Stoll, 1894), 57; Robert F. Heizer and Albert B. Elsasser, *The Natural World of the California Indians* (Berkeley: University of California Press, 1980), 82–113.

4. Horace Bushnell, *California: Its Characteristics and Prospects* (San Francisco: Whitton, Towne, 1858), 28; Theodore T. Johnson, *Sights in the Gold Region, and Scenes by the Way* (New York: Baker and Scribner, 1849), 155; Samuel Augustus Mitchell, *Description of Oregon and California* (Philadelphia: Thomas, Cowperthwait, 1849), 38; Louise Amelia Knapp Smith Clappe, *The Shirley Letters from the California Mines, 1851–1852,* ed. Marlene Smith-Baranzini (Berkeley: Heyday Books, 1998), 124; E. S. Capron, *History of California, from Its Discovery to the Present Time* (Boston: John P. Jewett, 1854), 19; Frank Marryat, *Mountains and Molehills* (1855), ed. Marguerite Eyer Wilbur (Stanford: Stanford University Press, 1952), 83; J. D. Borthwick, *Three Years in California* (Edinburgh: William Blackwood and Sons, 1857), 128; Robert Greenhow, *The Geography of Oregon and California* (Boston: Freeman and Bolles, 1845), 14; Francis P. Farquhar, *Up and Down California in 1860–1864: The Journal of William H. Brewer,* 3rd ed. (Berkeley: University of California Press, 1966), 302.

5. Franklin Tuthill, *The History of California* (San Francisco: H. H.

Bancroft, 1866), 88–89; Mrs. D. B. Bates, *Incidents on Land and Water, or Four Years on the Pacific Coast,* 3rd ed. (Boston: James French, 1857), 150–151; Alice Bradley Haven, *"All's Not Gold That Glitters": or The Young Californian* (1853; New York: D. Appleton, 1863), 131.

6. James H. Carson, *Life in California* (1852; Tarrytown, N.Y.: William Abbatt, 1931), 47; William Kelly, *An Excursion to California* (London: Chapman and Hall, 1851), 1:252–253; George G. Foster, ed., *The Gold Regions of California,* 3rd ed. (New York: Dewitt and Davenport, 1849), 11; William M'Ilvaine Jr., *Sketches of Scenery and Notes of Personal Adventure in California and Mexico* (1850; n.p.: Book Club of California, 1951), 33; Silas Weston, *Life in the Mountains: Or Four Months in the Mines of California* (Providence: E. P. Weston, 1854), 8.

7. James W. Redfield, *Comparative Physiognomy; or, Resemblances between Men and Animals* (New York: Redfield, 1852), 198; Charles Loring Brace, *The New West; or, California in 1867–1868* (New York: G. P. Putnam and Son, 1869), 152.

8. James A. Sandos, *Converting California: Indians and Franciscans in the Missions* (New Haven: Yale University Press, 2004); S. F. Cook, "Conflict between the California Indian and White Civilization," in R. F. Heizer and M. A. Whipple, eds., *The California Indians: A Source Book,* 2nd ed. (Berkeley: University of California Press, 1971), 563–564.

9. John Coulter, *Adventures on the West Coast of South America, and the Interior of California* (London: Longman, Brown, Green, and Longmans, 1847), 1:136.

10. Thomas S. Martin, *With Frémont to California and the Southwest, 1845–1849,* ed. Ferol Egan (Ashland, Ore.: Lewis Osborne, 1975), 7; Henry Augustus Wise, *Los Gringos: Or, An Inside View of Mexico and California, with Wanderings in Peru, Chili, and Polynesia* (New York: Baker and Scribner, 1849), 50–51; Naglee to R. B. Mason, July 1847, in Robert F. Heizer, ed., *The Destruction of California Indians* (Santa Barbara: Peregrine Smith, 1974), 8.

11. Clifford E. Trafzer and Joel R. Hyer, eds., *Exterminate Them! Written Accounts of the Murder, Rape, and Enslavement of Native Americans during the California Gold Rush* (East Lansing: Michigan State University Press, 1999); John M. Letts, *A Pictorial View of California* (New York: Henry Bill, 1853), 111; J. Ely Sherwood, *California: Her Wealth and Resources* (1848; Tarrytown, N.Y.: William Abbatt, 1929), 26, 27, 31; E. Gould

Buffum, *Six Months in the Gold Mines: From a Journal of Three Years' Residence in Upper and Lower California, in 1847–8–9* (London: Richard Bentley, 1850), 51; Albert L. Hurtado, *Indian Survival on the California Frontier* (New Haven: Yale University Press, 1988), 100–124.

12. Richard Henry Dana, *Two Years before the Mast: A Personal Narrative of Life at Sea* (1840), ed. Thomas Philbrick (New York: Penguin Books, 1981), 131; Charles Preuss, *Exploring with Fremont: The Private Diaries of Charles Preuss,* trans. and ed. Erwin G. and Elisabeth K. Gudde (Norman: University of Oklahoma Press, 1958), 134; James Delavan, *Notes on California and the Placers: How to Get There, and What to Do Afterwards* (1850; Oakland: Biobooks, 1956), 54; H. Willis Baxley, *What I Saw on the West Coast of South and North America, and at the Hawaiian Islands* (New York: D. Appleton, 1865), 466.

13. "Album of Joseph W. Revere," 14, mssHM 56913, HL; Joseph Warren Revere, *A Tour of Duty in California* (New York: C. S. Francis, 1849), 128–129; Mary Lee Spence and Donald Jackson, eds., *The Expeditions of John Charles Frémont* (Urbana: University of Illinois Press, 1970–1984), 2:36–37; John Yates, "Sketch of a Journey in the Year 1842 from Sacramento in California, through the Valley" (1872), 17, UCB.

14. H. Rep. Ex. Doc. No. 1, 30th Cong., 2nd Sess. (1848), 407; William Medill to Adam Johnston, 14 Apr. 1849, *Report of the Secretary of the Interior, Communicating . . . Correspondence between the Department of the Interior and the Indian Agents and Commissioners in California,* S. Ex. Doc. No. 4, 33rd Cong., special session (1853), 2 (hereafter *California Correspondence*).

15. Adam Johnston to Orlando Brown, 31 Jan. 1850, *California Correspondence,* 35.

16. Adam Johnston to Orlando Brown, 16 Sept. 1850, S. Ex. Doc. No. 1, 31st Cong., 2nd Sess. (1850), 123.

17. H. Rep. Ex. Doc. No. 59, 31st Cong., 1st Sess. (1850), 8. King's report was also published as a book: Thomas Butler King, *California: The Wonder of the Age* (New York: William Gowans, 1850).

18. William Carey Jones, *Report on the Subject of Land Titles in California* (Washington, D.C.: Gideon, 1850), 36–37.

19. H. Rep. Ex. Doc. No. 17, 31st Cong., 1st Sess. (1850), 128–129.

20. *Johnson v. M'Intosh,* 21 U.S. 543 (1823); *Mitchel v. United States,* 34 U.S. 711 (1835).

21. *Congressional Globe,* 31st Cong., 1st Sess. (1850), 1802–1803, 1816.

22. 9 Stat. 519, 558 (1850).

23. *California Correspondence,* 8–9; Ray Raphael, *Little White Father: Redick McKee on the California Frontier* (Eureka: Humboldt County Historical Society, 1993), 16–18; George Harwood Phillips, *Indians and Indian Agents: The Origins of the Reservation System in California, 1849–1852* (Norman: University of Oklahoma Press, 1997), 13.

24. *California Correspondence,* 59.

25. William Taylor, *California Life Illustrated* (New York: Carlton and Porter, 1858), 73–74.

26. Phillips, *Indians and Indian Agents;* Robert A. Trennert Jr., *Alternative to Extinction: Federal Indian Policy and the Beginnings of the Reservation System, 1846–51* (Philadelphia: Temple University Press, 1975); Alban W. Hoopes, *Indian Affairs and Their Administration with Special Reference to the Far West* (Philadelphia: University of Pennsylvania Press, 1932).

27. *California Correspondence,* 67, 70, 74–75, 79. For an account of the commissioners' work, see George E. Anderson and Robert F. Heizer, "Treaty-Making by the Federal Government in California, 1851–1852," in George E. Anderson, W. H. Ellison, and Robert F. Heizer, *Treaty Making and Treaty Rejection by the Federal Government in California, 1850–1852* (Socorro, N.M.: Ballena Press, 1978), 1–36.

28. "Indian Affairs, 1849–50: Statement of Dr. O. M. Wozencraft" (1877), 4–5, note preceding p. 1, UCB; Charles J. Kappler, comp., *Indian Affairs: Laws and Treaties* (Washington, D.C.: Government Printing Office, 1904), 4:1081–1128; William H. Ellison, "The Federal Indian Policy in California," *Mississippi Valley Historical Review* 9 (1922): 57.

29. Robert F. Heizer, "Treaties," in Robert F. Heizer, ed., *California,* vol. 8 of *Handbook of North American Indians* (Washington, D.C.: Smithsonian Institution, 1978), 702–704.

30. Robert F. Heizer, ed., *George Gibbs [sic] Journal of Redick McKee's Expedition through Northwestern California in 1851* (Berkeley: University of California, Department of Anthropology, Archeological Research Facility, 1972), 18, 21; Stephen Dow Beckham, *George Gibbs, 1815–1873: Historian and Ethnologist* (Ph.D. diss., UCLA, 1969), 95; Alban W. Hoopes, ed., "The Journal of George W. Barbour, May 1, to October 4, 1851," *Southwestern Historical Quarterly* 40 (1936): 145–153, 247–257; *California Correspondence,* 260–261.

31. George Harwood Phillips, *Chiefs and Challengers: Indian Resistance and Cooperation in Southern California* (Berkeley: University of California Press, 1975), 119; Chad L. Hoopes, "Redick McKee and the Humboldt Bay Region, 1851–1852," *California Historical Society Quarterly* 49 (1970): 198.

32. G. W. Barbour to Luke Lea, 5 Jan. 1852, S. Ex. Doc. No. 61, 32nd Cong., 1st Sess. (1852), 3; O. M. Wozencraft to Luke Lea, 14 Oct. 1851, S. Ex. Doc. No. 1, 32nd Cong., 1st Sess. (1851), 507.

33. *California Correspondence,* 187–188, 223.

34. Ibid., 129.

35. Ibid., 212, 248, 296.

36. Ibid., 272, 274.

37. *Journal of the Third Session of the Legislature of the State of California* (San Francisco: G. K. Fitch and V. E. Geiger, 1852), 597–598 (Senate); S. Ex. Doc. No. 104, 32nd Cong., 1st Sess. (1852), 3.

38. *Congressional Globe,* 32nd Cong., 1st Sess. (1852), 888–889.

39. Ibid., 2104, 2106.

40. Ibid., 2109; S. Ex. Doc. No. 1, 32nd Cong., 2nd Sess. (1852), 32. There is no evidence to support the view of Harry Kelsey, in "The California Indian Treaty Myth," *Southern California Quarterly* 55 (1973): 225–238, that the Senate rejected the eighteen California treaties because senators believed that the California Indians lacked any property rights in the land, and that the commissioners had accordingly never been authorized to negotiate treaties with them. Senator William Gwin of California did object in 1850 to the appointment of commissioners on this ground, but, as we have seen, he lost that battle. In 1852 the only senator on record as claiming that the commissioners had been unauthorized to enter into the treaties was Isaac Walker, but he was promptly corrected by John Weller, the leader of the opposition to the treaties, and Walker did not press the point any farther. *Congressional Globe,* 32nd Cong., 1st Sess. (1852), 2103.

41. Sherburne F. Cook, *The Conflict between the California Indian and White Civilization* (Berkeley: University of California Press, 1976), 236; Sylvester Woodbridge Jr., *Sermon, Preached at the Dedication of the First Presbyterian Church, Benicia, California, March 9, 1851* (Benicia, Calif.: St. Clair, Pinkham, 1851), 9–10; Alfred Robinson, *Life in California: During a Residence of Several Years in That Territory* (New York: Wiley and Putnam, 1846), 215; Alonzo Delano, *Life on the Plains and Among the Dig-*

gings (Auburn, N.Y.: Miller, Orton and Mulligan, 1854), 320; John Archbald, *On the Contact of Races: Considered Especially with Relation to the Chinese Question* (San Francisco: Towne and Bacon, 1860), 28; John S. Hittel, *The Resources of California* (San Francisco: A. Roman, 1863), 388; Lucia Norman, *A Youth's History of California* (San Francisco: A. Roman, 1867), 153; "Affairs of the Republic, 1852," *Debow's Review* 14 (1853): 164.

42. Heizer, *Destruction of California Indians,* 36; Burnett quoted in Robert F. Heizer and Alan J. Almquist, *The Other Californians: Prejudice and Discrimination under Spain, Mexico, and the United States to 1920* (Berkeley: University of California Press, 1971), 26.

43. *Congressional Globe,* 32nd Cong., 1st Sess. (1852), 2173, 2174.

44. S. Ex. Doc. No. 57, 32nd Cong., 2nd Sess. (1853), 2.

45. *New York Times,* 14 Nov. 1853, 6 (reprinting an article from the *San Francisco Herald*); Stevenson to Thomas J. Henley, 31 Dec. 1853, in Heizer, *Destruction of California Indians,* 14; John Russell Bartlett, *Personal Narrative of Explorations and Incidents in Texas, New Mexico, California, Sonora, and Chihuahua, Connected with the United States and Mexican Boundary Commission during the Years 1850, '51, '52, and '53* (New York: D. Appleton, 1854), 2:82; Benjamin Ignatius Hayes, *Pioneer Notes from the Diaries of Judge Benjamin Hayes, 1849–1875* (Los Angeles: privately printed, 1929), 115; John Walton Caughey, ed., *The Indians of Southern California in 1852: The B. D. Wilson Report and a Selection of Contemporary Comment* (Lincoln: University of Nebraska Press, 1995), 66; Wilson to Edward F. Beale, 11 Nov. 1852, Papers of Benjamin Davis Wilson, mssWN1–1926, box 2, HL; *New York Times,* 14 Apr. 1853, 4; William B. Secrest, *When the Great Spirit Died: The Destruction of the California Indians, 1850–1860* (Sanger, Calif.: Word Dancer Press, 2003).

46. Gerald Thompson, *Edward F. Beale and the American West* (Albuquerque: University of New Mexico Press, 1983), 52–69; S. Ex. Doc. No. 1, 33rd Cong., 1st Sess. (1853), 476, 470–471; Richard E. Crouter and Andrew F. Rolle, "Edward Fitzgerald Beale and the Indian Peace Commissioners in California, 1851–1854," *Southern California Quarterly* 42 (1960): 123–127; George Harwood Phillips, *"Bringing Them Under Subjection": California's Tejón Indian Reservation and Beyond, 1852–1864* (Lincoln: University of Nebraska Press, 2004), 251–258; S. Ex. Doc. No. 5, 34th Cong., 3rd Sess. (1856), 567.

47. Edward E. Chever, "The Indians of California," *American Naturalist* 4 (1870): 147.

48. S. Ex. Doc. No. 46, 36th Cong., 1st Sess. (1860), 15; Buck to Mary Sewall Bradley, 9 June 1852, Papers of Franklin Augustus Buck, mssHM 60481, HL; Albert L. Hurtado, "'Hardly a Farm House—a Kitchen Without Them': Indian and White Households on the California Borderland Frontier in 1860," *Western Historical Quarterly* 13 (1982): 245–270.

49. "Majority and Minority Reports of the Special Joint Committee on the Mendocino War," 5, *Appendix to the Journals of the Senate, of the Eleventh Session of the Legislature of the State of California* (Sacramento: C. T. Botts, 1860).

50. *Report of Colonel Robert J. Stevens, Special Commissioner to Make an Investigation and Report upon Indian Affairs in California* (Washington, D.C.: Government Printing Office, 1868), 30; J. Ross Browne, *Crusoe's Island: A Ramble in the Footsteps of Alexander Selkirk* (London: Sampson Low, Son, and Marston, 1864), 286; H.R. Ex. Doc. No. 91, 43rd Cong., 1st Sess. (1874), 3; Charles A. Wetmore, *Report of Charles A. Wetmore: Special U.S. Commissioner of Mission Indians of Southern California* (Washington, D.C.: Government Printing Office, 1875), 5; William Vandever, *Mission Indians of California* (Washington, D.C.: Government Printing Office, 1876), 3; H. H., "The Present Condition of the Mission Indians in Southern California," *The Century* 26 (1883): 512; Stephen Powers, *Tribes of California* (1877), ed. Robert F. Heizer (Berkeley: University of California Press, 1976), 400.

51. John R. Wunder, "No More Treaties: The Resolution of 1871 and the Alteration of Indian Rights to Their Homelands," in John R. Wunder, ed., *Working the Range: Essays on the History of Western Land Management and the Environment* (Westport, Conn.: Greenwood Press, 1985), 39–56.

52. Bruce S. Flushman and Joe Barbieri, "Aboriginal Title: The Special Case of California," *Pacific Law Journal* 17 (1986): 409–415.

6. British Columbia

1. *Delgamuukw v. R.,* 3 S.C.R. 1010 (1997). The one later exception to the treatment of British Columbia as terra nullius was Canada's purchase in 1899 of a large area that included the northeastern corner of mainland British Columbia along with parts of Alberta and the Northwest Terri-

tories. Arthur J. Ray, "Treaty 8: A British Columbian Anomaly," *BC Studies* 123 (1999): 5–58.

2. Robin Fisher, *Contact and Conflict: Indian-European Relations in British Columbia, 1774–1890* (Vancouver: UBC Press, 1977), 150–157; Robert E. Cail, *Land, Man, and the Law: The Disposal of Crown Lands in British Columbia, 1871–1913* (Vancouver: UBC Press, 1974), 171–173; Barry M. Gough, *Gunboat Frontier: British Maritime Authority and Northwest Coast Indians, 1846–90* (Vancouver: UBC Press, 1984), 70–72.

3. J. C. Beaglehole, ed., *The Journals of Captain James Cook on His Voyages of Discovery* (Cambridge: Cambridge University Press, 1955–1974), 3:1407 (King), 3:306 (Cook), 3:1326–27 (Clerke).

4. Nellie B. Pipes, ed., *The Memorial of John Mears [sic] to the House of Commons Respecting the Capture of Vessels in Nootka Sound* (1790; Portland: Metropolitan Press, 1933), 2–3. In another version of Meares's story, Maquinna gave him the land as a gift. John Meares, *Voyages Made in the Years 1788 and 1789, from China to the North West Coast of America* (London: Logographic Press, 1790), 114. Both versions of the story were intended to buttress British claims of sovereignty as against Spain, so historians have debated their accuracy ever since. See, for example, Daniel Clayton, *Islands of Truth: The Imperial Refashioning of Vancouver Island* (Vancouver: UBC Press, 2000), 170–188; J. Richard Nokes, *Almost a Hero: The Voyage of John Meares, R.N., to China, Hawaii and the Northwest Coast* (Pullman: Washington State University Press, 1998), 55.

5. Alexander Dalrymple, *The Spanish Pretensions Fairly Discussed* (London: George Bigg, 1790), 7–8; José Mariano Moziño, *Noticias de Nutka: An Account of Nootka Sound in 1792,* trans. and ed. Iris Higbie Wilson (Seattle: University of Washington Press, 1970), 40; Edmund Hayes, ed., *Log of the Union: John Boit's Remarkable Voyage to the Northwest Coast and Around the World, 1794–1796* (Portland: Oregon Historical Society, 1981), 41; William Robert Broughton, *A Voyage of Discovery to the North Pacific Ocean* (London: T. Cadell and W. Davies, 1804), 52.

6. James R. Gibson, *Otter Skins, Boston Ships, and China Goods: The Maritime Fur Trade of the Northwest Coast, 1785–1841* (Seattle: University of Washington Press, 1992); Cole Harris, "Social Power and Cultural Change in Pre-Colonial British Columbia," *BC Studies* 115/116 (1997–1998): 56, 60; John Dunn, *The Oregon Territory, and the British North American Fur Trade* (Philadelphia: G. B. Zieber, 1845), 63–64; Robert

Montgomery Martin, *The Hudson's Bay Territories and Vancouver's Island* (London: T. and W. Boone, 1849), 94–95; Richard Somerset Mackie, *Trading beyond the Mountains: The British Fur Trade on the Pacific, 1793–1843* (Vancouver: UBC Press, 1997), 309; Glyndwr Williams, ed., *London Correspondence Inward from Sir George Simpson, 1841–42* (London: Hudson's Bay Record Society, 1973), 111; Peter Skene Ogden, *Traits of American Indian Life and Character* (1853; San Francisco: Grabhorn Press, 1933), 28.

7. W. Kaye Lamb, ed., *Sixteen Years in the Indian Country: The Journal of Daniel Williams Harmon, 1800–1816* (Toronto: Macmillan, 1957), 250; Arthur J. Ray, "Fur Trade History and the Gitskan-Wet'suwet'en Comprehensive Claim: Men of Property and the Exercise of Title," in Kerry Abel and Jean Friesen, eds., *Aboriginal Land Use in Canada: Historical and Legal Aspects* (Winnipeg: University of Manitoba Press, 1991), 303.

8. John S. Galbraith, *The Hudson's Bay Company as an Imperial Factor, 1821–1869* (Berkeley: University of California Press, 1957), 283–291; "Report on Vancouver Island" (1849), in "Papers Relating to the Colonization of Vancouver Island," *Sessional Papers: Second Session, Thirteenth Parliament of the Province of British Columbia* (Victoria, B.C.: William H. Cullin, 1914), V72.

9. James Edward Fitzgerald, *An Examination of the Charter and Proceedings of the Hudson's Bay Company, with Reference to the Grant of Vancouver's Island* (London: Trelawney Saunders, 1849), 283; "Aborigines of Vancouver's Island," *The Colonial Intelligencer, or, Aborigines' Friend* 2 (1848): 79; "Vancouver's Island," ca. 1852, MS-0310, p. 42, BCA.

10. Elizabeth Vibert, *Traders' Tales: Narratives of Cultural Encounters in the Columbia Plateau, 1807–1846* (Norman: University of Oklahoma Press, 1997); John D'Wolf, *A Voyage to the North Pacific and a Journey through Siberia More Than Half a Century Ago* (1861), ed. Harold M. Turner (Bristol, R.I.: Rulon-Miller Books, 1983), 44; John Schouler, "Observations on the Indigenous Tribes of the N.W. Coast of America" (1841), in Charles Lillard, ed., *The Ghostland People: A Documentary History of the Queen Charlotte Islands, 1859–1906* (Victoria, B.C.: Sono Nis Press, 1989), 78–79.

11. R. C. P. Baylee, "Vancouver and Queen Charlotte's Island," *Colonial Church Chronicle and Missionary Journal* 7 (1854): 414–415; Gilbert Malcolm Sproat, "The West Coast Indians in Vancouver Island," *Transactions of the Ethnological Society of London* 5 (1867): 249.

12. Robin Fisher, *Vancouver's Voyage: Charting the Northwest Coast, 1791–1795* (Seattle: University of Washington Press, 1992), 29; George F. G. Stanley, ed., *Mapping the Frontier: Charles Wilson's Diary of the Survey of the 49th Parallel, 1858–1862, while Secretary of the British Boundary Commission* (Seattle: University of Washington Press, 1970), 56; Roberta L. Bagshaw, ed., *No Better Land: The 1860 Diaries of the Anglican Colonial Bishop George Hills* (Victoria, B.C.: Sono Nis Press, 1996), 270–271; *Cariboo: The Newly Discovered Gold Fields of British Columbia,* 5th ed. (London: Darnton and Hodge, 1862), 48.

13. Alexander C. Anderson, "Notes on the Indian Tribes of British North America, and the Northwest Coast," *Historical Magazine* 7 (1863): 76; John Keast Lord, *The Naturalist in Vancouver Island and British Columbia* (London: Richard Bentley, 1866), 2:226; Robert Boyd, *The Coming of the Spirit of Pestilence: Introduced Infectious Diseases and Population Decline among Northwest Coast Indians, 1774–1874* (Vancouver: UBC Press, 1999); John M'Lean, *Notes of a Twenty-Five Years' Service in the Hudson's Bay Territory* (London, 1849), ed. W. S. Wallace (Toronto: Champlain Society, 1932), 179; Kinahan Cornwallis, *The New El Dorado; or British Columbia,* 2nd ed. (London: Thomas Cautley Newby, 1858), 108; "The Indians of British Columbia," *Church Missionary Intelligencer* 1 (1865): 111; *Victoria Gazette,* 3 Mar. 1859, 1.

14. Wilson Duff, *The Indian History of British Columbia,* vol. 1, *The Impact of the White Man* (Victoria, B.C.: Provincial Museum of Natural History and Anthropology, 1964), 8; Michael E. Harkin, *The Heiltsuks: Dialogues of Culture and History on the Northwest Coast* (Lincoln: University of Nebraska Press, 1997), 7; Keith Thor Carlson et al., eds., *A Stó:lō Coast Salish Historical Atlas* (Vancouver: Douglas and McIntyre, 2001), 62–63; Nathaniel Portlock, *A Voyage Round the World; But More Particularly to the North-West Coast of America: Performed in 1785, 1786, 1787, and 1788* (London: John Stockdale, 1789), 253; Frederick W. Howay, ed., *Voyages of the "Columbia" to the Northwest Coast, 1787–1790 and 1790–1793* (Portland: Oregon Historical Society Press, 1990), 234; Michael Roe, ed., *The Journal and Letters of Captain Charles Bishop on the North-West Coast of America, in the Pacific and in New South Wales, 1794–1799* (Cambridge: Cambridge University Press, 1967), 72, 82.

15. C. F. Newcombe, ed., *Menzies' Journal of Vancouver's Voyage: April to October, 1792* (Victoria, B.C.: Legislative Assembly, 1923), 49; Gabriel

Franchère, *A Voyage to the Northwest Coast of America* (1854), ed. Milo Milton Quaife (Chicago: R. R. Donnelly and Sons, 1954), 203.

16. *Narrative of the Adventures and Sufferings of John R. Jewitt while Held as a Captive of the Nootka Indians of Vancouver Island, 1803 to 1805* (1820), ed. Robert F. Heizer (Ramona, Calif.: Ballena Press, 1975); Paul Kane, *Wanderings of an Artist among the Indians of North America* (1859; Rutland, Vt.: Charles E. Tuttle, 1968), 147; "The Salmon Harvest," *All the Year Round,* 31 Mar. 1866, 270.

17. Henry Drummond Dee, ed., *The Journal of John Work: January to October, 1835* (Victoria, B.C.: Charles F. Banfield, 1945), 40; Wayne Suttles, "The Early Diffusion of the Potato among the Coast Salish," *Southwestern Journal of Anthropology* 7 (1951): 272–288; Duane Thomson, "The Response of Okanagan Indians to European Settlement," *BC Studies* 101 (1994): 99; BPPC, 17:179.

18. Walter N. Sage, *Sir James Douglas and British Columbia* (Toronto: University of Toronto Press, 1930), 17–138; Charles Alfred Bayley, "Early Life on Vancouver Island" (n.d.), 3, E/B/B34.2, BCA; *Instructions to Mr. Blanchard* [*sic*], *Governor of Vancouver Island* (Victoria, B.C.: R. Wolfenden, 1849).

19. Douglas to Archibald Barclay, 3 Sept. 1849, in Hartwell Bowsfield, ed., *Fort Victoria Letters, 1846–1851* (Winnipeg: Hudson's Bay Record Society, 1979), 43. I have silently corrected Douglas's spelling.

20. Robert A. Trennert Jr., *Alternative to Extinction: Federal Indian Policy and the Beginnings of the Reservation System, 1846–51* (Philadelphia: Temple University Press, 1975); George Harwood Phillips, *Indians and Indian Agents: The Origins of the Reservation System in California, 1849–1852* (Norman: University of Oklahoma Press, 1997).

21. Walter Colquhoun Grant, "Report on Vancouver's Island" (1849), A/B/20/G76, BCA.

22. Barclay to Douglas, 17 Dec. 1849, A/C/20.1/Vi7, BCA.

23. Ibid.

24. Wilson Duff, "The Fort Victoria Treaties," *BC Studies* 3 (1969): 3–57; *Papers Connected with the Indian Land Question, 1850–1875* (Victoria, B.C.: Wolfenden, 1875), 5–9; Barclay to Douglas, 10 Aug. 1850, A/C/20.1/Vi7, BCA; Douglas to Barclay, 16 May 1850, in Bowsfield, *Fort Victoria Letters,* 95.

25. Douglas to James Murray Yale, 7 May 1850, MS-0105, BCA; Douglas to Barclay, 16 May 1850, in Bowsfield, *Fort Victoria Letters,* 95.

26. Grant Keddie, *Songhees Pictorial: A History of the Songhees People as Seen by Outsiders, 1790–1912* (Victoria: Royal BC Museum, 2003), 49–50; Saanich tradition quoted in Hamar Foster, "The Saanichton Bay Marina Case: Imperial Law, Colonial History and Competing Theories of Aboriginal Title," *University of British Columbia Law Review* 23 (1989): 632–633.

27. Blanshard to Earl Grey, 12 Feb. 1851, GR-0332, 1:284, BCA; Hawes to J. H. Pelly, 26 June 1851, GR-0332, 1:291, BCA; George Grey to Labouchere, 28 Jan. 1856, MS-0310, p. 12, BCA; Bulwer Lytton to Douglas, 31 July 1858, BPPC, 22:63.

28. Pelly to Douglas, 23 May 1851, A/C/20.1/Vi7, BCA.

29. Newcastle to Douglas, 20 Oct. 1859, enclosure in Douglas to Vancouver Island House of Assembly, 5 May 1860, C/AA/20.2K/1A, BCA; *British Colonist,* 28 June 1860, 4:3; *Papers Connected with the Indian Land Question,* 19; *British Colonist,* 8 Mar. 1861, 2:2; *Papers Connected with the Indian Land Question,* 20; James E. Hendrickson, ed., *Journals of the Colonial Legislatures of the Colonies of Vancouver Island and British Columbia* (Victoria: Provincial Archives of British Columbia, 1980), 1:257.

30. James Douglas, "Report of a Canoe Expedition along the East Coast of Vancouver Island," *Journal of the Royal Geographic Society* 24 (1854): 246 (reprinting an 1852 letter); Daniel P. Marshall, *Those Who Fell from the Sky: A History of the Cowichan Peoples* (Duncan, B.C.: Cultural and Education Centre, Cowichan Tribes, 1999), 116–122. As Marshall suggests, it is not clear whether Douglas declined to make an offer or whether the Cowichan refused an offer as insufficient.

31. Lytton to Douglas, 30 Dec. 1858, CO 398/1 (microfilm reel B0001), pp. 185–187, BCA; Timothy Keegan, *Colonial South Africa and the Origins of the Racial Order* (Charlottesville: University Press of Virginia, 1996), 288.

32. Douglas to Lytton, 14 Mar. 1859, *Papers Connected with the Indian Land Question,* 16–17.

33. This passage comes from an untitled and undated manuscript document authored by Douglas, to which the British Columbia Archives has given the title "Notes on Traditions and Populations of the Indians of the

Northwest Coast." It is in a notebook with journals of trips taken by Douglas between 1827 and 1844, so it was most likely written toward the end of that period. A/B/40/D75.2, p. 124, BCA.

34. Douglas to James Hargrave, 5 Feb. 1843, in G. P. de T. Glazebrook, ed., *The Hargrave Correspondence, 1821–1843* (Toronto: Champlain Society, 1938), 421; Douglas to Stevens, 6 Mar. 1856, C/AA/10.4/1-A, BCA.

35. "British Columbia," *Aborigines' Friend, and the Colonial Intelligencer* 2 (1859): 5; "Beta Mikron" [William Coutts Keppel, the Earl of Albemarle], "British Columbia and Vancouver's Island," *Fraser's Magazine,* Oct. 1858, 500; Robin Fisher, "Indian Warfare and Two Frontiers: A Comparison of British Columbia and Washington Territory during the Early Years of Settlement," *Pacific Historical Review* 50 (1981): 31–51; Barry M. Gough, "The Indian Policies of Great Britain and the United States in the Pacific Northwest in the Mid-Nineteenth Century," *Canadian Journal of Native Studies* 2 (1982): 321–337. For a darker view of Douglas and his Indian land policy, see Sidney L. Harring, *White Man's Law: Native People in Nineteenth-Century Canadian Jurisprudence* (Toronto: University of Toronto Press, 1998), 186–216.

36. John Adams, *Old Square-Toes and His Family: The Life of James and Amelia Douglas* (Victoria, B.C.: Horsdal and Schubart, 2001), 1–8.

37. Douglas to Lytton, 14 Mar. 1859, *Papers Connected with the Indian Land Question,* 17.

38. *Report of the Commissioner of Indian Affairs, Made to the Secretary of the Interior, for the Year 1869* (Washington, D.C.: Government Printing Office, 1870), 50; Henry B. Whipple, "The Indian System," *North American Review* 99 (1864): 450–451; T. S. Williamson, "The Indian Tribes, and the Duty of Government to Them," *American Presbyterian and Theological Review* 2 (1864): 597.

39. David McNab, "Herman Merivale and the Native Question, 1837–1861," *Albion* 9 (1979): 359–384; Frederick E. Hoxie, *A Final Promise: The Campaign to Assimilate the Indians, 1880–1920* (1984; Cambridge: Cambridge University Press, 1989).

40. Douglas to Lytton, 14 Mar. 1859, *Papers Connected with the Indian Land Question,* 17.

41. Carnarvon to Douglas, 20 May 1859, CO 398/1 (reel B0001), pp. 289–290, BCA.

42. Douglas to Newcastle, 18 Feb. 1860, in *Papers Relative to the Affairs of*

British Columbia (London: G. E. Eyre and W. Spottiswoode, 1859–1862), 4:2; Newcastle to Douglas, 25 May 1860, CO 398/1 (reel B0001), pp. 401–402, BCA; Good to Moody, 5 Mar. 1861, *Papers Connected with the Indian Land Question,* 21; Parsons to Turnbull, 1 May 1861, *Papers Connected with the Indian Land Question,* 22; Moody to Douglas, 28 Apr. 1863, *Papers Connected with the Indian Land Question,* 27.

43. Moody to Young, 27 May 1862, and Young to Moody, 18 June 1862, *Papers Connected with the Indian Land Question,* 23–24; Moody to Young, 11 June 1862, GR 1372, reel B01338, file 931, BCA.

44. W. Colquhoun Grant, "Description of Vancouver Island," *Journal of the Royal Geographical Society of London,* 27 (1857): 295; D. G. Forbes MacDonald, *British Columbia and Vancouver's Island,* 3rd ed. (London: Longman, Green, Longman, Roberts, and Green, 1863), 139.

45. "Wild Tribes in Vancouver," *Chambers's Journal,* 27 June 1868, 404–405; Gilbert M. Sproat, "Memorandum," 29 Sept. 1876, MS-0257, file 15, p. 60, BCA.

46. BPPC, 3:291–292; W. C. Grant, "Remarks on Vancouver Island, Principally concerning Townsites and Native Population," *Journal of the Royal Geographical Society of London* 31 (1861): 211.

47. Paul Tennant, *Aboriginal Peoples and Politics: The Indian Land Question in British Columbia, 1849–1989* (Vancouver: UBC Press, 1990), 35–41; Cole Harris, *Making Native Space: Colonialism, Resistance, and Reserves in British Columbia* (Vancouver: UBC Press, 2002), 33–34; Hamar Foster, "Letting Go the Bone: The Idea of Indian Title in British Columbia, 1849–1927," in Hamar Foster and John McLaren, eds., *Essays in the History of Canadian Law,* vol. 6, *British Columbia and the Yukon* (Toronto: University of Toronto Press, 1995), 44.

48. *British Colonist,* 26 Feb. 1859, 2:3; Gilbert Malcolm Sproat, *The Nootka: Scenes and Studies of Savage Life* (1868), ed. Charles Lillard (Victoria, B.C.: Sono Nis Press, 1987), 7–8.

49. *British Columbian,* 2 Dec. 1865, 1:1, 4 Aug. 1866, 1:1; *Cariboo Sentinel,* 11 Jan. 1873, 2:1.

50. Seymour to Cardwell, 4 Oct. 1864, CO 60/19 (reel B1434), p. 298, BCA; Cardwell to Seymour, 1 Dec. 1864, CO 398/2 (reel B0001), p. 272, BCA.

51. Robin Fisher, "Joseph Trutch and Indian Land Policy," *BC Studies* 12 (1971–1972): 3–33; *Papers Connected with the Indian Land Question,* 42.

52. Chesson to Bulwer Lytton, 1858, in BPPC, 22:77; "The Indians of Van-

couver Island," *Colonial Intelligencer,* Dec. 1869, 192; Merivale quoted in
David McNab, "'Vacillation of Purpose': Indian Policies of the Colonial
Office in British North America in the Mid-Nineteenth Century" (unpublished paper presented to the Canadian Historical Association annual
meeting, 1978), MS-0823, p. 22, BCA.

53. *British Colonist,* 17 Dec. 1862, 2:1, 12 May 1863, 2:1, 17 Aug. 1866, 2:2;
   Nanaimo Gazette, 21 Apr. 1866, 1:1; *Mainland Guardian,* 24 Aug. 1878,
   2:1.

54. Lynn A. Blake, "Oblate Missionaries and the 'Indian Land Question,'"
   BC Studies 119 (1998): 27–44; *Papers Connected with the Indian Land
   Question,* 145; Brett Christophers, *Positioning the Missionary: John Booth
   Good and the Confluence of Cultures in Nineteenth-Century British Colum-
   bia* (Vancouver: UBC Press, 1998), 141–152; Peter Murray, *The Devil and
   Mr. Duncan* (Victoria, B.C.: Sono Nis Press, 1985), 170–173.

55. Lucius Samuel Edelblute, "Highlights in the Life of Lucius Samuel
   Edelblute from 1849 to 1873," MS-0484, p. 107, BCA.

56. Douglas to Labouchere, 15 July 1857, BPPC, 21:419; Moody to Douglas, 1
   Apr. 1859, GR 1372, reel B1337, file 915, BCA; John Hayman, ed., *Robert
   Brown and the Vancouver Island Exploring Expedition* (Vancouver: UBC
   Press, 1989), 124; R. C. Lundin Brown, *Klatsassan, and Other Reminis-
   cences of Missionary Life in British Columbia* (London: Society for Pro-
   moting Christian Knowledge, 1873), 9; A. F. Poole, "Two Years amongst
   the Indians of Queen Charlotte's Island," *Mission Life,* 1 Feb. 1868, 104;
   Robert Beaven to I. W. Powell, 16 Apr. 1873, *Papers Connected with the In-
   dian Land Question,* 113; Newton H. Chittenden, *Exploration of the
   Queen Charlotte Islands* (1884; Vancouver: Gordon Soules, 1984), 18;
   Metlakatlah Inquiry, 1884: Report of the Commissioners (Victoria, B.C.:
   Richard Wolfenden, 1885), 133–136; Douglas Harris, "The Nlha7kápmx
   Meeting at Lytton, 1879, and the Rule of Law," *BC Studies* 108 (1995–
   1996): 5–25; Brian C. Hosmer, "'White Men Are Putting Their Hands
   into Our Pockets': Metlakatla and the Struggle for Resource Rights in
   British Columbia, 1862–1887," *Alaska History* 8, no. 2 (1993): 1–19.

57. C. W. de Kiewiet and F. H. Underhill, eds., *Dufferin-Carnarvon Correspondence, 1874–1878* (Toronto: Champlain Society, 1955), 112, 125; Trutch
   to Macdonald, 14 Oct. 1872, quoted in Dennis Madill, *British Columbia
   Indian Treaties in Historical Perspective* (Ottawa: Research Branch, Cor-
   porate Policy, Indian and Northern Affairs Canada, 1981), 37.

58. *Report of the Hon. H. L. Langevin, C.B., Minister of Public Works* (Ottawa: I. B. Taylor, 1872), 26; Alexander Caulfield Anderson, *A Brief Account of British Columbia* (Victoria, B.C.: R. T. Williams, 1883), 14; *Report of the Superintendent of Indian Affairs, for British Columbia, for 1872 and 1873* (Ottawa: I. B. Taylor, 1873), 25.

59. *Papers Relating to the Commission Appointed to Enquire into the Condition of the Indians of the North-West Coast* (Victoria, B.C.: Richard Wolfenden, 1888), 416; *Report of Conferences between the Provincial Government and Indian Delegates from Fort Simpson and Naas River* (Victoria, B.C.: Richard Wolfenden, 1887), 255–256.

60. *British Colonist,* 28 Nov. 1886, 3:5, 4 Nov. 1886, 2:2.

61. Helmcken to Mackay, 30 Nov. 1888, MS-1917, file 15, BCA.

62. Mackay to Helmcken, 3 Dec. 1888, MS-1917, file 27, BCA.

7. Oregon and Washington

1. James P. Ronda, *Astoria and Empire* (Lincoln: University of Nebraska Press, 1990); Ross Cox, *The Columbia River; or, Scenes and Adventures during a Residence of Six Years on the Western Side of the Rocky Mountains among Various Tribes of Indians Hitherto Unknown,* 3rd ed. (London: Henry Colburn and Richard Bentley, 1832), 1:102; David Lavender, ed., *The Oregon Journals of David Douglas* (Ashland: Oregon Book Society, 1972), 39; Daniel Lee and J. H. Frost, *Ten Years in Oregon* (New York: J. Collard, 1844), 104.

2. P. J. Edwards, *Sketch of the Oregon Territory; or, Emigrant's Guide* (Liberty, Mo.: Printed at the "Herald" Office, 1842), 6; A. J. Allen, *Ten Years in Oregon: Travels and Adventures of Doctor E. White and Lady West of the Rocky Mountains* (Ithaca, N.Y.: Mack, Andrus, 1848), 174; John Kirk Townsend, *Narrative of a Journey across the Rocky Mountains, to the Columbia River* (1839; Corvallis: Oregon State University Press, 1999), 106; A. N. Armstrong, *Oregon* (Chicago: Chas. Scott, 1857), 99.

3. S. Doc. 39, 21st Cong., 2nd Sess. (1831), 20; Pierre-Jean de Smet, *Oregon Missions and Travels over the Rocky Mountains, in 1845–46* (New York: Edward Dunigan, 1847), 109; Jeff LaLande, *First Over the Siskiyous: Peter Skene Ogden's 1826–1827 Journey through the Oregon-California Borderlands* (Portland: Oregon Historical Society Press, 1987), 40.

4. David Peterson del Mar, *Oregon's Promise: An Interpretive History*

(Corvallis: Oregon State University Press, 2003), 27–28; Samuel Parker, *Journal of an Exploring Tour beyond the Rocky Mountains, under the Direction of the A.B.C.F.M., Performed in the Years 1835, '36, and '37* (Ithaca, N.Y.: Samuel Parker, 1838), 178; Overton Johnson and William H. Winter, *Route across the Rocky Mountains* (1846; Princeton: Princeton University Press, 1932), 59; George Wilkes, *The History of Oregon* (New York: William H. Colyer, 1845), 44–45; "Rubio" [Thomas Horton James], *Rambles in the United States and Canada during the Year 1845* (London: Samuel Clarke, 1846), 257; Gustavus Hines, *A Voyage Round the World: With a History of the Oregon Mission* (Buffalo: George H. Derby, 1850), 117.

5. Joel Palmer, *Journal of Travels over the Rocky Mountains, to the Mouth of the Columbia River; Made during the Years 1845 and 1846* (1847), ed. Reuben Gold Thwaites (Cleveland: Arthur H. Clark Company, 1906), 111, 114, 116; Thomas J. Farnham, *Travels in the Great Western Prairies, the Anahuac and Rocky Mountains, and in the Oregon Territory* (New York: Greeley and McElrath, 1843), 111; Rufus B. Sage, *Scenes in the Rocky Mountains, and in Oregon, California, New Mexico, Texas, and the Grand Prairies* (Philadelphia: Carey and Hart, 1846), 222.

6. Charles Wilkes, *Western America, including California and Oregon* (Philadelphia: Lea and Blanchard, 1849), 86; John Dunn, *The Oregon Territory, and the British North American Fur Trade* (Philadelphia: G. B. Zieber, 1845), 160; Alexander Ross, *Adventures of the First Settlers on the Oregon or Columbia River* (1849), ed. Milo Milton Quaife (Chicago: R. R. Donnelley and Sons, 1923), 106; Lansford W. Hastings, *The Emigrants' Guide, to Oregon and California* (Cincinnati: George Conclin, 1845), 60; Zachariah Atwell Mudge, *Sketches of Mission Life among the Indians of Oregon* (1854; Fairfield, Wash.: Ye Galleon Press, 1983), 27.

7. Barbara Cloud, "Oregon in the 1820s: The Congressional Perspective," *Western Historical Quarterly* 12 (1981): 145–164.

8. *Niles' Weekly Register*, 28 July 1832, 388; W. J. S., "Oregon Territory," *New-England Magazine* 2 (1832): 130; Hall J. Kelley, *A Geographical Sketch of That Part of North America Called Oregon*, 2nd ed. (1831; Tarrytown, N.Y.: William Abbatt, 1919), 16.

9. J. Quinn Thornton, *Oregon and California in 1848* (New York: Harper and Bros., 1849), 2:29.

10. Eugene O. Smith, "Solomon Smith, Pioneer: Indian–White Relations in

Early Oregon," *Journal of the West* 13, no. 2 (1974): 44–58; "Mr. Parker's Exploring Tour beyond the Rocky Mountains," *Methodist Magazine and Quarterly Review* 10 (1839): 83–84.

11. Peter H. Burnett, "Recollections and Opinions of an Old Pioneer," *Quarterly of the Oregon Historical Society* 5 (1904): 97.

12. "Oregon," *Workingman's Advocate,* 27 Apr. 1844, 1.

13. S. Doc. No. 1, 29th Cong., 1st Sess. (1845), 630.

14. 9 Stat. 323 (1848).

15. S. Misc. Doc. No. 136, 30th Cong., 1st Sess. (1848), 4.

16. S. Ex. Doc. No. 52, 31st Cong., 1st Sess. (1850), 5, 8.

17. "Alas for the Poor Indian!" *The Friend* 21 (1848): 399; *American Quarterly Register and Magazine* 2 (1849): 531.

18. S. Misc. Doc. No. 5, 31st Cong., 2nd Sess. (1851), 1.

19. *Congressional Globe,* 31st Cong., 1st Sess. (1850), 262, 582; 9 Stat. 437 (1850).

20. 9 Stat. 497 (1850).

21. Mrs. W. H. Odell, "Biography of Samuel R. Thurston" (1879), 6, Samuel Royal Thurston Papers, file 3, OHS. The author, Thurston's widow, was quoting one of Thurston's letters, written shortly after he arrived in Washington as Oregon's territorial representative.

22. Richard H. Chused, "The Oregon Donation Act of 1850 and Nineteenth Century Federal Married Women's Property Law," *Law and History Review* 2 (1984): 44–78; "Diary of Samuel Royal Thurston," *Quarterly of the Oregon Historical Society* 15 (1914): 153–205; Samuel Royal Thurston, *To the Electors and People of the Territory of Oregon* (Washington, D.C.: Towers, 1850), 3; Paul W. Gates, *History of Public Land Law Development* (Washington, D.C.: Government Printing Office, 1968), 387–388; James M. Bergquist, "The Oregon Donation Act and the National Land Policy," *Oregon Historical Quarterly* 58 (1957): 29–30; Dart to Lea, 19 July 1851, in *Letters Received by the Office of Indian Affairs, 1824–1850,* National Archives microcopy 234, roll 607, available from the Native American Documents Project, www.csusm.edu/nadp/d10.htm.

23. S. Ex. Doc. No. 1, 31st Cong., 2nd Sess. (1850), 146–147.

24. The commissioners' account of the negotiations is reprinted in Harold Mackey, *The Kalapuyans: A Sourcebook on the Indians of the Willamette Valley* (Salem: Mission Hill Museum Association, 1974), 90–103.

25. Ibid., 103–125.

26. S. Ex. Doc. No. 1, 32nd Cong., 1st Sess. (1851), 467, 469.

27. 9 Stat. 586 (1851). The statute did not affect the commissioners who were then in the midst of negotiating treaties in California, because they had been appointed as regular agents.

28. Francis Paul Prucha, *The Great Father: The United States Government and the American Indians* (Lincoln: University of Nebraska Press, 1984), 1:328–332; Dart to Lea, 7 Nov. 1851, reprinted in C. F. Coan, "The First Stage of the Federal Indian Policy in the Pacific Northwest, 1849–1852," *Quarterly of the Oregon Historical Society* 22 (1921): 66–75.

29. *Congressional Globe,* 32nd Cong., 2nd Sess. (1852), 9; ibid., 1st Sess. (1852), 891–892.

30. S. Ex. Doc. No. 1, 32nd Cong., 2nd Sess. (1852), 463; Arthur A. Denny, *Pioneer Days on Puget Sound* (1888), ed. Alice Harriman (Seattle: Alice Harriman Co., 1908), 33; S. Ex. Doc. No. 1, 33rd Cong., 2nd Sess. (1854), 492; George Gibbs, *Indian Tribes of Washington Territory* (Fairfield, Wash.: Ye Galleon Press, 1967), 28 (reprinting an 1854 report to Congress).

31. Hull to Palmer, 17 Nov. 1853, Joel Palmer Papers, box 1, UO.

32. Nathan Douthit, *Uncertain Encounters: Indians and Whites at Peace and War in Southern Oregon, 1820s–1860s* (Corvallis: Oregon State University Press, 2002); E. A. Schwartz, *The Rogue River Indian War and Its Aftermath, 1850–1980* (Norman: University of Oklahoma Press, 1997); Stephen Dow Beckham, *Requiem for a People: The Rogue Indians and the Frontiersmen* (Norman: University of Oklahoma Press, 1971); John Beeson, "Association for the Protection and Improvement of the Aborigines of This Continent," *Littell's Living Age* 17 (1857): 673; John Beeson, *A Plea for the Indians,* 3rd ed. (New York: John Beeson, 1858), 15; Patricia E. Karlberg and Robert H. Keller, eds., "Oregon Clergy and Indian War in the Northwest: Home Missionary Correspondence, 1855–1857," *Pacific Northwest Quarterly* 79 (1988): 30–31; Anson Dart, "A Striking Illustration of Democratic Economy," *National Era,* 28 July 1859, 118.

33. Robert H. Keller, ed., "A Missionary Tour of Washington Territory: T. Dwight Hunt's 1855 Report," *Pacific Northwest Quarterly* 76 (1985): 151, 150.

34. H.R. Ex. Doc. No. 76, 34th Cong., 3rd Sess. (1857), 13, 9–10; Charles Prosch, *Reminiscences of Washington Territory* (1904; Fairfield, Wash.: Ye Galleon Press, 1969), 48–49.

35. Palmer's notes regarding a letter to the Office of Indian Affairs, 27 Mar. 1854, Joel Palmer Papers, box 1, UO; Palmer to Daniel, 15 May 1854, Joel Palmer Papers, box 1, UO.

36. S. Ex. Doc. No. 34, 33rd Cong., 1st Sess. (1854), 3, 6, 1–2.

37. 10 Stat. 330 (1854).

38. Lee Scott Theisen, "The Oregon Superintendency of Indian Affairs, 1853–1856," *Pacific Historian* 22 (1978): 184–195; David Newsom, *David Newsom: The Western Observer, 1805–1882* (Portland: Oregon Historical Society, 1972), 63; C. F. Coan, "The Adoption of the Reservation Policy in the Pacific Northwest," *Quarterly of the Oregon Historical Society* 23 (1922): 1–38.

39. Robert E. Ficken, *Washington Territory* (Pullman: Washington State University Press, 2002), 44–47; Kent D. Richards, *Isaac Stevens: Young Man in a Hurry* (Provo: Brigham Young University Press, 1979), 197–234.

40. "The Indians," *The Friend* 28 (1855): 373.

41. Terrence O'Donnell, *An Arrow in the Earth: General Joel Palmer and the Indians of Oregon* (Portland: Oregon Historical Society Press, 1991), 167; transcript of unidentified and undated purchasing conference, Joel Palmer Papers, box 1, unnumbered file, OHS; diary entry for 19 Sept. 1853, Joel Palmer Papers, box 1, file 8, OHS.

42. Clifford E. Trafzer and Richard D. Scheuerman, *Renegade Tribe: The Palouse Indians and the Invasion of the Inland Pacific Northwest* (Pullman: Washington State University Press, 1986), 57; Ezra Meeker, *Pioneer Reminiscences of Puget Sound* (Seattle: Lowman and Hanford, 1905), 232–233, 245.

43. Stevens to Gibbs, 30 Aug. 1855, Isaac Ingalls Stevens Papers, box 2, file 7, BRB; Stevens to Davis, 21 Mar. 1856, Isaac Ingalls Stevens Papers, box 2, file 5, BRB.

44. James G. Swan, *The Northwest Coast; or, Three Years' Residence in Washington Territory* (New York: Harper and Bros., 1857), 327–347; Gary C. Collins, "Indian Policy, Government Treaties and the Chehalis River Treaty Council," *Pacific Northwest Forum* 5, no. 2 (1992): 17–36; Charles M. Gates, ed., "The Indian Treaty of Point No Point," *Pacific Northwest Quarterly* 46 (1955): 52–58; Isaac Ingalls Stevens, *A True Copy of the Record of the Official Proceedings at the Council in the Walla Walla Valley, 1855*, ed. Darrell Scott (Fairfield, Wash.: Ye Galleon Press, 1985); Charles M. Gates, ed., *Messages of the Governors of the Territory of Washington to the Legisla-*

tive Assembly, 1854–1889 (Seattle: University of Washington Press, 1940), 24; A. M. Collins to J. S. Collins, Aug. 1856, William Winlock Miller Collection, box 11, folder 121, BRB.

45. "Letters of Governor Isaac I. Stevens," *Pacific Northwest Quarterly* 31 (1940): 427–428; S. Ex. Doc. No. 11, 35th Cong., 1st Sess. (1857), 299; S. Ex. Doc. No. 1, 35th Cong., 2nd Sess. (1858), 355.

46. Alexandra Harmon, *Indians in the Making: Ethnic Relations and Indian Identities around Puget Sound* (Berkeley: University of California Press, 1998), 94–99; H. A. Smith, "Early Reminiscences," William Winlock Miller Collection, box 11, file 121, BRB; Brad Asher, *Beyond the Reservation: Indians, Settlers, and the Law in Washington Territory, 1853–1889* (Norman: University of Oklahoma Press, 1999); William L. Lang, *Confederacy of Ambition: William Winlock Miller and the Making of Washington Territory* (Seattle: University of Washington Press, 1996), 143.

47. *Congressional Globe,* 31st Cong., 3rd Sess. (1871), 764; Andrew H. Fisher, "They Mean to Be Indian Always: The Origins of Columbia River Indian Identity, 1860–1885," *Western Historical Quarterly* 32 (2001): 468–492.

48. "The Public Land System," *American Law Review* 2 (1868): 384–385; Ronald Spores, "Too Small a Place: The Removal of the Willamette Valley Indians, 1850–1856," *American Indian Quarterly* 17 (1993): 171–191.

8. Fiji and Tonga

1. Bligh quoted in G. C. Henderson, *The Discoverers of the Fiji Islands* (London: John Murray, 1933), 163; Samuel Patterson, *Narrative of the Adventures and Sufferings of Samuel Patterson* (Palmer, Mass.: The Press in Palmer, 1817), 88; William S. Cary, *Wrecked on the Feejees* (Fairfield, Wash.: Ye Galleon Press, 1972), 41 (Cary was in Fiji from 1825 to 1830); Peter Bays, *A Narrative of the Wreck of the Minerva* (1831; Fairfield, Wash.: Ye Galleon Press, 1996), 150; William Endicott, *Wrecked among Cannibals in the Fijis* (Salem, Mass.: Marine Research Society, 1923), 42 (Endicott was in Fiji in 1831); Robert Coffin, *The Last of the* Logan*: The True Adventures of Robert Coffin, Mariner, in the Years 1854 to 1859,* ed. Harold W. Thompson (Ithaca, N.Y.: Cornell University Press, 1941), 84–85; Hunt quoted in George Stringer Rowe, *The Life of John Hunt, Missionary to the Cannibals* (London: Hamilton, Adams, 1859), 122; Joseph Waterhouse,

The King and People of Fiji (London: Wesleyan Conference Center, 1866), 304; *The Cannibal Islands; or, Fiji and Its People* (Philadelphia: Presbyterian Publication Committee, 1863), 148; Thomas Williams and James Calvert, *Fiji and the Fijians* (New York: D. Appleton, 1859), 46–47; Berthold Seemann, "Remarks on a Government Mission to the Fiji Islands," *Journal of the Royal Geographical Society* 32 (1862): 52.

2. Edwin N. Ferdon, *Early Tonga: As the Explorers Saw It, 1616–1810* (Tucson: University of Arizona Press, 1987), 205–215; H. G. Cummins, "Tongan Society at the Time of European Contact," in Noel Rutherford, ed., *Friendly Islands: A History of Tonga* (Melbourne: Oxford University Press, 1977), 82–84; G. H. Kenihan, ed., *The Journal of Abel Jansz Tasman* (Adelaide: Australian Heritage Press, n.d.), 57; J. C. Beaglehole, ed., *The Journals of Captain James Cook on His Voyages of Discovery* (Cambridge: Cambridge University Press, 1955–1974), 2:252; George Forster, *A Voyage Round the World* (1777), eds. Nicholas Thomas and Oliver Berghof (Honolulu: University of Hawaii Press, 2000), 240–241, 245, 458.

3. Edward Edwards, *Voyage of H.M.S. "Pandora"* (London: Francis Edwards, 1915), 133; *A Missionary Voyage to the Southern Pacific Ocean, Performed in the Years 1796, 1797, 1798, in the Ship Duff, Commanded by Captain James Wilson* (London: T. Chapman, 1799), 245; John Orlebar, *A Midshipman's Journal, on Board H.M.S. Seringapatam, during the Year, 1830* (London: Whittaker, Treacher, 1833), 50; John Turnbull, *A Voyage Round the World, in the Years 1800, 1801, 1802, 1803, and 1804,* 2nd ed. (London: A. Maxwell, 1813), 388; John Martin, *An Account of the Natives of the Tonga Islands, in the South Pacific Ocean* (Boston: Charles Ewer, 1820), 180; W. Waldegrave, "Extracts from a Private Journal Kept on Board H.M.S. Seringapatam, in the Pacific, 1830," *Journal of the Royal Geographical Society* 3 (1833): 186; Charles Phillips, *The Ocean Cavern: A Tale of the Tonga Isles* (London: William Hone, 1819), 2.

4. Charles Wilkes, *Narrative of the United States Exploring Expedition* (Philadelphia: Lea and Blanchard, 1845–1850), 3:32–33; O. W. Brierly, "Brief Geographical Sketch of the Friendly Islands," *Journal of the Royal Geographical Society of London* 22 (1852): 98; George Selwyn to William Selwyn, 1848, MSS 330, UCSD.

5. Dorothy Shineberg, *They Came for Sandalwood: A Study of the Sandalwood Trade in the South-West Pacific, 1830–1865* (Melbourne: Melbourne University Press, 1967), 7; Niel Gunson, "Missionary Interest in British

Expansion in the South Pacific in the Nineteenth Century," *Journal of Religious History* 3 (1965): 296–313; W. P. Morrell, *Britain in the Pacific Islands* (Oxford: Clarendon Press, 1960), 48–53, 117–128; G. C. Henderson, ed., *The Journal of Thomas Williams, Missionary in Fiji, 1840–1853* (Sydney: Angus and Robertson, 1931); Mary Wallis, *Life in Feejee, or, Five Years among the Cannibals* (Boston: W. Heath, 1851); J. G. Turner, *The Pioneer Missionary: Life of the Rev. Nathaniel Turner, Missionary in New Zealand, Tonga, and Australia* (London: Wesleyan Conference, 1872); David Cargill, *Memoirs of Mrs. Margaret Cargill* (London: John Mason, 1841), 96; George Vason, *An Authentic Narrative of Four Years' Residence at Tongataboo* (London: Longman, Hurst, Rees, and Orme, 1810), 71, 128–129.

6. Everard Im Thurn and Leonard C. Wharton, eds., *The Journal of William Lockerby, Sandalwood Trader in the Fijian Islands during the Years 1808–1809* (London: Hakluyt Society, 1925), 21; J. A. "History of Some Curious Customs Used by the Natives of the Feejee Islands," *Gentleman's Magazine* 90 (1820): 297; David Routledge, *Matanitu: The Struggle for Power in Early Fiji* (Suva: University of the South Pacific, 1985).

7. On the British role in George's consolidation of power, see Jane Samson, *Imperial Benevolence: Making British Authority in the Pacific Islands* (Honolulu: University of Hawaii Press, 1998), 63–72. The most complete account of George's long reign is I. C. Campbell, *Island Kingdom: Tonga Ancient and Modern* (Christchurch: Canterbury University Press, 1992), 51–106.

8. Berthold Seemann, *Viti: An Account of a Government Mission to the Vitian or Fijian Islands in the Years 1860–61* (Cambridge: Macmillan, 1862), 411–412; Litton Forbes, *Two Years in Fiji* (London: Longmans, Green, 1875), 1–3; Charles St. Julian, *The International Status of Fiji* (Sydney: F. Cunninghame, 1872), 12.

9. My account is heavily indebted to Peter France's classic *The Charter of the Land: Custom and Colonization in Fiji* (Melbourne: Oxford University Press, 1969), as well as to J. D. Legge, *Britain in Fiji, 1858–1880* (London: Macmillan, 1958).

10. R. Udal, *Colonization in the Fiji Islands* (London: Edward Stanford, 1871), 11; W. T. Pritchard, *Polynesian Reminiscences; or, Life in the South Pacific Islands* (London: Chapman and Hall, 1866), 243–244; Seemann, *Viti*, 412; Forbes, *Two Years in Fiji*, 196–197.

11. Julius L. Brenchley, *Jottings during the Cruise of H.M.S. Curaçoa among the South Sea Islands in 1865* (London: Longmans, Green, 1873), 185–186.

12. Henry Britton, *Fiji in 1870: Being the Letters of "The Argus" Special Correspondent* (Melbourne: Samuel Mullen, 1870), 19; "R" [J. H. de Ricci], *How About Fiji? Or Annexation versus Non-Annexation* (London: Edward Stanford, 1874), 11–12; W. C. Pechey, *Fijian Cotton Culture, and Planters' Guide to the Islands* (London: Jarrold and Sons, 1870), 65–66.

13. Tim Bayliss-Smith et al., *Islands, Islanders and the World: The Colonial and Post-colonial Experience of Eastern Fiji* (Cambridge: Cambridge University Press, 1988), 51; David Blair, *The History of Australasia* (Glasgow: McGready, Thomson, and Niven, 1878), 706; Stanmore Papers, Add. 49200, p. 176, BL; Udal, *Colonization,* 16; Britton, *Fiji in 1870,* 19.

14. W. W. Crane, "The King of the Cannibal Islands," *Appleton's Journal* 10 (1873): 589.

15. Deryck Scarr, *Fiji: A Short History* (Sydney: Allen and Unwin, 1984), 35–76; *Constitution and Laws of the Tovata e Viti* (Sydney: S. T. Leigh, 1871), 5.

16. The Deed of Cession is reproduced in Legge, *Britain in Fiji,* 284–286.

17. John D. Kelly, "Gordon Was No Amateur: Imperial Legal Strategies in the Colonization of Fiji," in Sally Engle Merry and Donald Brenneis, eds., *Law and Empire in the Pacific: Fiji and Hawaii* (Santa Fe: School of American Research Press, 2003), 61–100.

18. Arthur Gordon, *Paper on the System of Taxation in Force in Fiji* (London: Harrison and Sons, 1879), 12; Arthur Hamilton Gordon, *Fiji: Records of Private and of Public Life* (Edinburgh: R. and R. Clark, 1897–1912), 1:198; Paul Knaplund, ed., *Gladstone-Gordon Correspondence, 1851–1896* (Philadelphia: American Philosophical Society, 1961), 66, 69.

19. Stanmore Papers, Add. 49199, pp. 130–131, BL; Claudia Knapman, *White Women in Fiji, 1835–1930: The Ruin of Empire?* (Sydney: Allen and Unwin, 1986), 119–127; cutting from unidentified New Zealand newspaper, 5 Mar. 1881, "Newspaper Cuttings Concerning Sir Arthur Gordon, 1881–1886," microfilm reel 05–013, UA.

20. David Cannadine, *Ornamentalism: How the British Saw Their Empire* (Oxford: Oxford University Press, 2001), 59.

21. Brij V. Lal, *Broken Waves: A History of the Fiji Islands in the Twentieth Century* (Honolulu: University of Hawaii Press, 1992), 28–33; Timothy J. Macnaught, *The Fijian Colonial Experience: A Study of the Neotraditional*

Order under British Colonial Rule prior to World War II (Canberra: Australian National University, 1982), 28–37.

22. R. Gerard Ward, "Land Use and Land Alienation in Fiji to 1885," *Journal of Pacific History* 4 (1969): 3–25.

23. Gordon, *Fiji,* 2:668–669, 195–196; Bridget Brereton, *Law, Justice and Empire: The Colonial Career of John Gorrie, 1829–1892* (Kingston, Jamaica: Press University of the West Indies, 1997), 122–123.

24. Basil Thomson, *The Fijians: A Study of the Decay of Custom* (London: William Heinemann, 1908), 354; William Fillingham Parr, *Slavery in Fiji* (London: Clarence, 1895), 5; John Newmarch, "Introduction," in T. H. Prichard, *The Land Tenure of Fiji: An Enquiry into the Correct Basis of Native Titles to Land in Fiji* (Levuka: G. L. Griffiths, 1882), 3.

25. Lorimer Fison, "Land Tenure in Fiji," *Journal of the Anthropological Institute of Great Britain and Ireland* 10 (1881): 345, 351.

26. Pritchard, *Polynesian Reminiscences,* 242–243.

27. J. B. Thurston, *Reprint of Memorandum (Dated 6th April 1874) Upon the Native Ownership of Land in Fiji* (Suva: Edward John March, 1886), 4–10.

28. France, *Charter of the Land,* 124–127.

29. Ibid., 120.

30. Ibid., 122.

31. Stanmore Papers, Add. 49200, p. 144, BL.

32. *Handbook to Fiji* (Suva: Government Printing Office, 1892), 40.

33. *Copy of a Despatch to the Right Honorable Earl of Carnarvon, Secretary of State for the Colonies, from the Polynesian Company; Being a Remonstrance Against the Unlawful Withholding of the Company's Lands at Fiji by His Excellency Sir Arthur Gordon* (Melbourne: W. H. Williams, 1877); *Fiji in 1881: Some of the Reasons Why a Royal Commission Should be Sent from England* (Levuka: n.p., 1881), 3; *Petition of the Fiji Agricultural Society* (n.p., ca. 1880), 2; *Fiji Planting and Commercial Directory, 1879* (Levuka: G. L. Griffiths, 1879), 6; "The Diary and Narratives of Edwin J. Turpin, 1870–ca. 1894," 179, microfilm reel 80-2, UA; *Fiji, 1880: The Bane of Sir Arthur Gordon's Disingenuous Utterances and the Antidote of the "Fiji Times" Editorial Comments and Exposure* (Sydney: Gibbs, Shallard, 1883), 12.

34. Jane Roth and Steven Hooper, eds., *The Fiji Journals of Baron Anatole Von Hügel, 1875–1877* (Suva: Fiji Museum, 1990), 227.

35. C. F. Gordon Cumming, *At Home in Fiji,* 2nd ed. (Edinburgh: William

Blackwood and Sons, 1881), 1:97–98; William Fillingham Parr, *Fiji: Remarks on the Address Delivered by Sir Arthur H. Gordon* (Levuka: n.p., 1879), 12; H. Stonehewer Cooper, *Coral Lands* (London: Richard Bentley and Son, 1880), 1:234; E. Vickery, *Fiji at the Sydney International Exhibition 1879* (Sydney: Foster and Fairfax, 1879), 11.

36. G. William Des Voeux, *My Colonial Service* (London: John Murray, 1903), 1:357–359.

37. H. Stonehewer Cooper, *Fiji: Its Resources and Prospects* (London: G. Street, 1879), 10; J. W. Anderson, *Notes of Travel in Fiji and New Caledonia* (London: Ellissen, 1880), 37; John Horne, *A Year in Fiji* (London: George E. Eyre and William Spottiswoode, 1881), 188; H. C. Thurston, ed., *Brett's Guide to Fiji* (Auckland: H. Brett, 1881), 11; John Horne, *Fiji: Remarks on the Agricultural Prospects of Fiji* (Levuka: G. L. Griffiths, 1878), 3, 5; Julian Thomas, *Cannibals and Convicts: Notes of Personal Experiences in the Western Pacific* (London: Cassell, 1886), 7; *Leading Articles Reprinted from the "Ceylon Times"* (n.p., ca. 1878), 8–9; Bruce Knapman, *Fiji's Economic History, 1874–1939: Studies of Capitalist Colonial Development* (Canberra: National Centre for Development Studies, Australian National University, 1987), 127.

38. Walter Lawry, *Friendly and Feejee Islands: A Missionary Visit to Various Stations in the South Seas* (London: Charles Gilpin, 1850), 62; John Elphinstone Erskine, *Journal of a Cruise among the Islands of the Western Pacific* (London: John Murray, 1853), 133–134.

39. H. F. Symonds, English translation of article in *Koe Taimi O Tonga,* 1882, Western Pacific Archives, BCT 1/43, folder 22, UA; Langham to Baker, 6 Nov. 1878, in Shirley W. Baker, *Tongan Papers,* microfilm 05-034, reel 1, SB/27, UA; statement of E. W. Sanders and John Parsons, 4 Apr. 1885, Papers of Rev. J. E. Moulton, correspondence 1885–1886, in Sione Lātūkefu, ed., *Collected Tongan Papers, 1884–1965* (Canberra: Australian National University, Pacific Manuscripts Bureau, 1998), reel 2; *Appendix to Report by Sir C. Mitchell* (London: Harrison and Sons, 1887), 113; *Islands of the Western Pacific: Commodore Wilson to Secretary of Admiralty. No. 128, 5th July 1879* (n.p.: confidential Admiralty printing, 1879), 5.

40. Sione Lātūkefu, *Church and State in Tonga: The Wesleyan Methodist Missionaries and Political Development, 1822–1875* (Honolulu: University of Hawaii Press, 1974), 234; Walter Lawry, *A Second Missionary Visit to the*

Friendly and Feejee Islands (London: John Mason, 1851), 72; Lātūkefu, *Church and State in Tonga*, 238, 278.

41. Cocker to Goring et al., 25 Nov. 1873, *Government of Tonga* (Canberra: Pacific Manuscript Bureau, 1873–1936), reel 1, pp. 51–52.

42. "The King's Speech at the Opening of Parliament, 1875," in *Annexures to Report by the High Commissioner for the Western Pacific on Events in the Tonga Islands in December, 1904, and January, 1905* (Suva: Edward John March, 1905), 53, 55; H. G. Cummins, comp., *Sources of Tongan History* (Nuku'alofa: n.p., 1972), 285.

43. Christine Ward Gailey, *Kinship to Kingship: Gender Hierarchy and State Formation in the Tongan Islands* (Austin: University of Texas Press, 1987), 196–200; Alaric Maude and Feleti Sevele, "Tonga: Equality Overtaking Privilege," in Ron Crocombe, ed., *Land Tenure in the Pacific,* 3rd ed. (Suva: University of the South Pacific, 1987), 114–142.

44. Noel Rutherford, *Shirley Baker and the King of Tonga* (Melbourne: Oxford University Press, 1971); *The Persecutions in Tonga, as Narrated by Onlookers* (London: William Clowes and Sons, 1886), iii; Gordon, *Fiji,* 3:100; Baker to the New South Wales and Queensland Conference of the Australasian Wesleyan Church, 15 Oct. 1880, Western Pacific Archives, WPHC 21, item 13, UA.

45. Undated and unattributed typescript of interview with Baker, in Shirley Waldemar Baker Papers, UA; undated notes, in Baker, *Tongan Papers,* reel 2, SB/206, pp. 9–10; Deryck Scarr, *Fragments of Empire: A History of the Western Pacific High Commission, 1877–1914* (Canberra: Australian National University Press, 1967), 86–107; *New Zealand Herald,* 23 July 1890; *New Zealand Times,* 30 July 1890; *Auckland Star,* 22 July 1890; all in Shirley Waldemar Baker Papers, UA.

46. Maudslay to Secretary of State for Foreign Affairs, 29 Apr. 1879, Western Pacific Archives, BCT 1/13/1, UA; Maudslay's notes, 1879, Western Pacific Archives, BCT 1/43/10, UA.

47. Maudslay to Secretary of the Australasian Wesleyan-Methodist Missionary Society, 5 Sept. 1878, Western Pacific Archives, BCT 1/5, UA.

48. Lātūkefu, *Church and State in Tonga,* 278; John Parsons, "Epitome of a Tongan Lease" (1876), Western Pacific Archives, BCT 1/43/2, UA; Emma H. Adams, *The Tonga Islands and Other Groups* (Oakland, Calif.: Pacific Press, 1890), 35; Cooper, *Coral Lands,* 2:163; "Vagabond," *Holy Tonga* (Melbourne: Melbourne Leader, 1890), 32.

49. Petition of the white residents of Tonga, 16 Feb. 1876, Western Pacific Archives, BCT 1/43/2, UA; *Secret Correspondence Respecting Samoa and Tonga, 1886–87* (London: Foreign Office, 1888), 17; Legge, *Britain in Fiji,* 44–45; Knapman, *Fiji's Economic History,* 127; Des Voeux to Granville, 1 Aug. 1883, Western Pacific Archives, WPHC 21/17, UA.

50. Cummins, *Sources of Tongan History,* 516; Ron Crocombe, *The South Pacific* (Suva: University of the South Pacific, 2001), 306; Kerry James, "Right and Privilege in Tongan Land Tenure," in R. Gerard Ward and Elizabeth Kingdon, eds., *Land, Custom and Practice in the South Pacific* (Cambridge: Cambridge University Press, 1995), 188–192.

51. C. B. H. Mitchell, *Report by Sir C. Mitchell, High Commissioner for the Western Pacific, in Connection with the Recent Disturbances in and the Affairs of Tonga* (Sydney: Samuel E. Lees, 1887), 13.

9. Alaska

1. Ted C. Hinckley, ed., "'The Canoe Rocks—We Do Not Know What Will Become of Us': The Complete Transcript of a Meeting between Governor John Green Brady of Alaska and a Group of Tlingit Chiefs, Juneau, December 14, 1898," *Western Historical Quarterly* 1 (1970): 270–271, 273, 275–276, 277.

2. A. P. Swineford to L. Q. C. Lamar, 19 May 1887, RG 101, box 2619, ASA; *The Alaskan,* 9 Feb. 1895, 2; Ted C. Hinckley, *Alaskan John G. Brady: Missionary, Businessman, Judge, and Governor, 1878–1918* (Columbus: Ohio State University Press, 1982), 139–142.

3. J. C. Beaglehole, ed., *The Journals of Captain James Cook on His Voyages of Discovery* (Cambridge: Cambridge University Press, 1955–1974), 3:460; Wallace M. Olson, ed., *Through Spanish Eyes: The Spanish Voyages to Alaska, 1774–1792* (Auke Bay, Alaska: Heritage Research, 2002), 87, 206, 210; James W. VanStone, ed., *Russian Exploration in Southwest Alaska: The Travel Journals of Petr Korsakovskiy (1818) and Ivan Ya. Vasilev (1829),* trans. David H. Kraus (Fairbanks: University of Alaska Press, 1988), 31; Karl K. Hillsen, "A Voyage of the Sloop 'Blagonamerennyi' to Explore the Asiatic and American Coasts of Bering Strait, 1819 to 1822," ed. Dorothy Jean Ray, trans. Rhea Josephson, in Dorothy Jean Ray, *Ethnohistory in the Arctic: The Bering Strait Eskimo,* ed. R. A. Pierce (Kingston, Ontario: Limestone Press, 1983), 51; Basil Dmytryshyn et al., eds., *Russian*

Penetration of the North Pacific Ocean, 1700–1797: A Documentary Record (Portland: Oregon Historical Society Press, 1988), 304; Dorothy Jean Ray, *The Eskimos of Bering Strait, 1650–1898* (Seattle: University of Washington Press, 1975), 111–120; William E. Simeone, *A History of Alaskan Athapaskans* (Anchorage: Alaska Historical Commission, 1982), 9–16; Wendell H. Oswalt, *Bashful No Longer: An Alaskan Eskimo Ethnohistory, 1778–1988* (Norman: University of Oklahoma Press, 1990), 25–31.

4. Walter R. Goldschmidt and Theodore H. Haas, *Haa Aaní, Our Land: Tlingit and Haida Land Rights and Use* (Seattle: University of Washington Press, 1998), 17–18; R. N. De Armond, ed., *Early Visitors to Southeastern Alaska: Nine Accounts* (Anchorage: Alaska Northwest, 1978), 101–102; Heinrich Johan Holmberg, *Holmberg's Ethnographic Sketches* (1855–1863), ed. Marvin W. Falk, trans. Fritz Jaensch (Fairbanks: University of Alaska Press, 1985), 14.

5. Beaglehole, *Journals of Captain Cook,* 3:459; Wallace M. Olson, ed., *The Alaska Travel Journal of Archibald Menzies, 1793–1794* (Fairbanks: University of Alaska Press, 1993), 109; Beaglehole, *Journals of Captain Cook,* 3:1145.

6. De Armond, *Early Visitors to Southeastern Alaska,* 69, 16; Charles Lillard, ed., *Warriors of the North Pacific: Missionary Accounts of the Northwest Coast, the Skeena and Stikine Rivers and the Klondike, 1829–1900* (Victoria, B.C.: Sono Nis Press, 1984), 35; Richard A. Pierce and John H. Winslow, eds., *H.M.S. Sulphur on the Northwest and California Coasts, 1837 and 1839: The Accounts of Captain Edward Belcher and Midshipman Francis Guillemard Simpkinson* (Kingston, Ontario: Limestone Press, 1979), 94.

7. Ivan Banner, "About the Koliuzh Peoples" (1803), in Richard A. Pierce, ed., *Documents on the History of the Russian-American Company,* trans. Marina Ramsay (Kingston, Ontario: Limestone Press, 1976), 156–159; Kiril Timofeevich Khlebnikov, *Notes on Russian America,* ed. Richard Pierce, trans. Serge LeCompte and Richard Pierce (Kingston, Ontario: Limestone Press, 1994), 1:55; James R. Gibson, "Russian Dependence upon the Natives of Alaska," in S. Frederick Starr, ed., *Russia's American Colony* (Durham: Duke University Press, 1987), 77–104.

8. Lydia T. Black, *Russians in Alaska, 1732–1867* (Fairbanks: University of Alaska Press, 2004), 209; Basil Dmytryshyn et al., eds. and trans., *The Russian American Colonies, 1798–1867: A Documentary Record* (Portland: Oregon Historical Society Press, 1989), 500–503.

9. H. Rep. Ex. Doc. No. 177, 40th Cong., 2nd Sess. (1868), 22–24.

10. 15 Stat. 541–542 (1867).

11. Charles C. Beaman, "Our New Northwest," *Harper's New Monthly Magazine* 35 (1867): 170–185; "An Artist in Alaska," *Harper's New Monthly Magazine* 38 (1869): 589–602; William H. Dall, *Alaska and Its Resources* (Boston: Lee and Shepard, 1870), 147–154; *Congressional Globe,* 40th Cong., 2nd Sess. (1868), 381; *Speech of Hon. Charles Sumner, of Massachusetts, on the Cession of Russian America to the United States* (Washington, D.C.: Congressional Globe, 1867), 25; H. Rep. Ex. Doc. No. 5, 40th Cong., 1st Sess. (1871), 8; Mark Twain, "Memoranda," *The Galaxy* 10 (1870): 726.

12. Frederick Whymper, *Travel and Adventure in the Territory of Alaska* (New York: Harper and Bros., 1869), 98–99; H. Rep. Ex. Doc. No. 36, 41st Cong., 2nd Sess. (1870), 3–4, 10; George Wardman, *A Trip to Alaska* (San Francisco: Samuel Carson, 1884), 235–237.

13. William H. Seward, *Alaska* (Washington: James J. Chapman, 1879), 11.

14. 15 Stat. 240–241 (1868).

15. H.R. Ex. Doc. No. 177, 40th Cong., 2nd Sess. (1868), 102–103.

16. S. Ex. Doc. No. 32, 41st Cong., 2nd Sess. (1870), 14; Davis quoted in Stephen Haycox, *Alaska: An American Colony* (Seattle: University of Washington Press, 2002), 175.

17. *New York Times,* 16 Oct. 1875, 6.

18. Henry W. Elliott, *A Report upon the Condition of Affairs in the Territory of Alaska* (Washington, D.C.: Government Printing Office, 1875), 37–38.

19. S. Ex. Doc. No. 59, 45th Cong., 3rd Sess. (1879), 71–72.

20. Ibid., 69; H. Rep. Ex. Doc. No. 40, 46th Cong., 3rd Sess. (1881), 70; Charles Hallock, *Our New Alaska; or, The Seward Purchase Vindicated* (New York: Forest and Stream, 1886), 93.

21. *Report of the Board of Indian Commissioners* (Washington, D.C.: Government Printing Office, 1870), 108; A. L. Lindsley, *Sketches of an Excursion to Southern Alaska* (Portland: n.p., 1881), 50; Sheldon Jackson, *Alaska, and Missions on the North Pacific Coast* (New York: Dodd, Mead, 1880), 399.

22. S. Rep. No. 457, 47th Cong., 1st Sess. (1882), 23, 15.

23. S. Rep. No. 3, 48th Cong., 1st Sess. (1883), 2; *Congressional Record,* 48th Cong., 1st Sess. (1884), 531.

24. 23 Stat. 26, 27 (1884); *Congressional Record,* 48th Cong., 1st Sess. (1884), 531.

25. Alaska Territorial Secretary, Record Book, 1884 (typescript), 7, ASL; *Report of the Governor of Alaska to the Secretary of the Interior* (Washington, D.C.: Government Printing Office, 1885), 15; John S. Bugbee, "Land Tenures in Alaska," *Alaska Searchlight,* 12 Oct. 1895, 3.

26. Alexander Badlam, *The Wonders of Alaska,* 2nd ed. (San Francisco: Bancroft, 1890), 9; Maturin M. Ballou, *The New Eldorado: A Summer Journey to Alaska* (Boston: Houghton Mifflin, 1891), 310–311; H.R. Rep. No. 3232, 49th Cong., 1st Sess. (1886), 1.

27. 26 Stat. 1095, 1100 (1891).

28. 31 Stat. 321, 330 (1900); *Heckman v. Sutter,* 119 F. 83, 88 (1902).

29. S. V. Proudfit, ed., *Decisions of the Department of the Interior and General Land Office in Cases Relating to the Public Lands* (Washington, D.C.: Government Printing Office, 1897), 24:312–313, 23:335, 26:517, 26:512, 28:431.

30. Henry W. Elliott, *An Arctic Province: Alaska and the Seal Islands* (London: Sampson, Low, Marston, Searle and Rivington, 1886), 54–55 (*Siwash* was a term often used pejoratively by Anglo-Americans for the Indians of the northwest coast); Bushrod W. James, *Alaskana, or Alaska in Descriptive and Legendary Poems* (Philadelphia: Porter and Coates, 1892), 41.

31. Horace Briggs, *Letters from Alaska and the Pacific Coast* (Buffalo: E. H. Hutchinson, 1889), 46; *Report of the Governor of Alaska for the Fiscal Year 1886* (Washington, D.C.: Government Printing Office, 1886), 941; William M. Carle to E. A. Hitchcock, 31 July 1903, "Alaska File: A Selection of Letters and a Report from the U.S. Bureau of Education Teachers in Alaska, 1903–1932," folder 1, ASL; Bessie L. Putnam, "The Thling of Alaska," *Goldthwaite's Geographical Magazine* 6 (1894): 23; H.R. Ex. Doc. No. 197, 42nd Cong., 2nd Sess. (1872), 1–4; *Kie v. United States,* 27 F. 351 (C.C.D. Or. 1886); S. Doc. No. 101, 59th Cong., 1st Sess. (1906), 2–7.

32. Septima M. Collis, *A Woman's Trip to Alaska* (New York: Cassell, 1890), 80–81; *The Alaskan,* 21 Dec. 1889, 1.

33. *Report of the Governor of Alaska for the Fiscal Year 1888* (Washington, D.C.: Government Printing Office, 1889), 8; Eva McClintock, ed., *Life in Alaska: Letters of Mrs. Eugene S. Willard* (Philadelphia: Presbyterian Board of Publication, 1884); J. Taylor Hamilton, *The Beginnings of the Moravian Mission in Alaska* (Bethlehem, Pa.: Comenius Press, 1890); A. C. Harris, *Alaska and the Klondike Gold Fields* (Chicago: J. S. Ziegler,

1897); H. O. S. Heistand, *The Territory of Alaska* (Kansas City: Hudson-Kimberly, 1898); Ted C. Hinckley, *The Canoe Rocks: Alaska's Tlingit and the Euroamerican Frontier, 1800–1912* (Lanham, Md.: University Press of America, 1996), 199; U.S. Department of the Interior, *General Information regarding the Territory of Alaska* (Washington, D.C.: Government Printing Office, 1930). Some writers argued that native property rights *were* impeding white settlement (for example, Bushrod Washington James, *Alaska: Its Neglected Past, Its Brilliant Future* [Philadelphia: Sunshine, 1897], 28; Agnes Rush Burr, *Alaska: Our Beautiful Northland of Opportunity* [Boston: Page, 1919], 407), but these were accounts from tourists who may not have been especially knowledgeable on the subject, and they are in any event contrary to the great weight of contemporary opinion.

34. Hugh Murray to Lyman Knapp, 31 May 1890, RG 101, box 2607, ASA; Willoughby Clark to the President of the United States, 19 Jan. 1890, RG 101, box 2607, ASA; William Duncan to James Sheakley, 20 Apr. 1896, RG 101, box 2607, ASA; A. P. Swineford to M. D. Ball, 20 May 1887, RG 101, box 2619, ASA; James Sheakley to N. S. Trowbridge, 17 May 1897, RG 101, box 2620, ASA.

35. Donald Craig Mitchell, *Sold American: The Story of Alaska Natives and Their Land, 1867–1959* (Hanover, N.H.: University Press of New England, 1997), 154–156; Charles Replogle, *Among the Indians of Alaska* (London: Headley Bros., 1904), 30; Thomas R. Shepard, "Placer Mining Law in Alaska," *Yale Law Journal* 18 (1909): 540; John Scudder McLain, *Alaska and the Klondike* (New York: McClure, Phillips, 1907), 276.

36. C. E. S. Wood, "Among the Thlinkits in Alaska," *Century Illustrated Magazine* 24 (1882): 338; H. W. Seton-Karr, *Shores and Alps of Alaska* (London: Sampson Low, Marston, Searle, and Irvington, 1887), 224; *Report of the International Polar Expedition to Point Barrow, Alaska* (Washington, D.C.: Government Printing Office, 1885), 48, 38; Julia McNair Wright, *Among the Alaskans* (Philadelphia: Presbyterian Board of Publication, 1883), 52; Eliza Ruhamah Scidmore, *Alaska: Its Southern Coast and the Sitkan Archipelago* (Boston: D. Lothrop, 1885), 231.

37. John Corbett, *The Lake Country* (Rochester: Democrat and Chronicle Print, 1898), 159; H.R. Ex. Doc. No. 154, 52nd Cong., 1st Sess. (1892), 2; Diamond Jenness, "The Eskimos of Northern Alaska: A Study in the Ef-

fect of Civilization," *Geographical Review* 5 (1918): 90–91; H.R. Rep. No. 3295, 59th Cong., 1st Sess. (1906), 1; John J. Underwood, *Alaska: An Empire in the Making* (1913), rev. ed. (New York: Dodd, Mead, 1925), 21.

38. David S. Case, *Alaska Natives and American Laws* (Fairbanks: University of Alaska Press, 1984), 83–129; Haycox, *Alaska,* 219; Hinckley, *The Canoe Rocks,* 339–340; Donald Craig Mitchell, *Take My Land, Take My Life: The Story of Congress's Historic Settlement of Alaska Native Land Claims, 1960– 1971* (Fairbanks: University of Alaska Press, 2001).

39. *Report of the Twenty-Ninth Annual Lake Mohonk Conference of Friends of the Indian and Other Dependent Peoples* (Lake Mohonk, N.Y.: Lake Mohonk Conference of Friends of the Indian and Other Dependent Peoples, 1911), 56, 64, 81.

Conclusion

1. Office of Treaty Settlements, *Quarterly Report to 30 June 2006,* nz01.terabyte.co.nz/ots/DocumentLibrary/QuarterlyReport30June2006 .pdf.

2. Fronda Woods, "Who's in Charge of Fishing?" *Oregon Historical Quarterly* 106 (2005): 412–441.

3. P. G. McHugh, *Aboriginal Societies and the Common Law: A History of Sovereignty, Status, and Self-Determination* (Oxford: Oxford University Press, 2004); Christa Scholtz, *Negotiating Claims: The Emergence of Indigenous Land Claim Negotiation Policies in Australia, Canada, New Zealand, and the United States* (New York: Routledge, 2006).

Index